Experiencing
Heaven

Experiencing Heaven

Three True Stories

MARVIN J. BESTEMAN
with LORILEE CRAKER,

CAPT. DALE BLACK
with KEN GIRE,

AND

DON PIPER
with CECIL MURPHEY

Revell

a division of Baker Publishing Group
Grand Rapids, Michigan

© 2014 by Baker Publishing Group

Published by Revell
a division of Baker Publishing Group
P.O. Box 6287, Grand Rapids, MI 49516-6287
www.revellbooks.com

ISBN 978-0-8007-2367-5

Previously published in three separate volumes:
My Journey to Heaven © 2012 by the estate of Marvin J. Besteman
Flight to Heaven © 2010 by Dale Black
90 Minutes in Heaven © 2004 by Don Piper

Printed in the United States of America

In keeping with biblical principles of creation stewardship, Baker Publishing Group advocates the responsible use of our natural resources. As a member of the Green Press Initiative, our company uses recycled paper when possible. The text paper of this book is composed in part of post-consumer waste.

green press INITIATIVE

Contents

Contents

BOOK TWO

Flight to Heaven

by Capt. Dale Black, with Ken Gire

BOOK THREE

90 Minutes in Heaven

by Don Piper, with Cecil Murphey

My Journey
to
Heaven

MARVIN J. BESTEMAN

with LORILEE CRAKER

Dedicated to

Ruth,
my wife of fifty-four adventurous years

Steve Yasick,
my dear son-in-law,
who went to be with his Lord in 2006

Irvin Zylstra,
my friend since childhood,
who went to be with his Lord in July 2011

Acknowledgments

My pastor, Cal Compagner, who helped me with this major project. He and I share a loyalty to the University of Michigan football team.

My dear children, Joe and Julie Wendth, Amy Yasick, Mark and Susan Besteman. My five grandchildren.

My brothers and their wives, Ron and MaryLou and Ken and MaryLou Besteman. My brother-in-law and sister-in-law, Bill and Rose Kalkman.

My co-writer, Lorilee Craker, who inspired me when words failed me.

A special thanks to my friends at "Coffee Break," who encouraged me when I would get discouraged.

The entire staff of Revell—Vicki Crumpton, Twila Bennett, Janelle Mahlman, Barb Barnes—who were instrumental in making this book a reality.

My literary agent, Esther Fedorkevich, who guided me through the maze of the literary world.

Special friends through the years, Ken and Joyce Ball, and our skiing buddies, Ed and Jo Westenbroek.

My special Christian friends who traveled through the education world and far beyond with me. Marlan Arnoys, Roger Boerema, Herb DeJonge, Marv Huizenga, Tom O'Hara, Norm Roobol, Jack Smant, and Irv Zylstra. Their wives have also played a major role in my life.

My thanks to a special group of friends who believed in and encouraged this project from the start.

Introduction

It's been six years since I had a life-changing preview of eternity, visiting heaven's gate for about half an hour, give or take.

In that short round-trip, I was reunited with loved ones; saw babies, children, and angels; peeked at the throne of God and Book of Life; and had a conversation with the apostle Peter, who I must say was a little bit shaggy looking. He always has been my favorite character in the Bible.

At first, I promised myself that no one would ever know what had happened to me. *I* knew that it was true, and that it hadn't been a dream or a hallucination. But I felt others would question my sanity if I told them what I saw and experienced on the other side. And when you get to be my age, you don't need any more excuses for people to question your sanity.

Why would anyone believe me? I asked myself. So by and large, I kept quiet, stewing like a stubborn old goat about why I had to be sent back.

Then one day God gave me a good shove in the pants, basically telling me to open my mouth and start talking. Yes, he spoke to me out loud, and though he didn't add "or else," I didn't want to push my luck. Obviously, God wanted me to tell others about his heaven.

Soon after, I began sharing my story with grief groups, church groups, and individuals young and old.

My spiritual mentors, including my pastor, felt that about 20 percent of the people who heard my story wouldn't believe it—such is human nature and people's tendency to be cynical in the face of anything unverifiable. But in reality, it's been more like 2 percent.

Maybe that's because people can tell I'm not the kind of man to put up with a lot of malarkey. I'm a Dutchman, which means I put up with even less bunk than most. I'm a veteran of the United States Army, having served for four years in the late fifties and early sixties. I was in active duty from 1956 until 1958, and then reserve duty until 1962.

Plus, I'm a banker by trade, someone who likes to deal in concrete numbers and percentages.

So, yes, most folks have believed my story, for which I am most grateful. Oh, a few here and there chalk it up to my being at a ripe old age—"Old Marv slipped a gear or two when he dreamed this one up"—but the truth is, I'm old, but I still have all my marbles (although, don't ask my wife Ruth about that; she might change that to "most of his marbles"!).

I hope you believe me, but even if you don't, I am under orders to tell you what happened to me on the night of April 28, 2006, when God gave this grandpa a bonus, a preview of heaven beyond anything I could have dreamed up in my banker's head.

And he who commanded me to tell my story—well, I believe he thought of you personally reading this book, and how my story would fill you with wonder and give you the comfort and assurance you've been wanting all along.

At Heaven's Gate

In the middle of the night, as I lay in my hospital bed in Ann Arbor, Michigan, visions of celestial beauty were the last thing on my mind. At seventy-one, I had just had surgery at the University of Michigan Medical Center to remove a rare pancreatic tumor called *insulinoma*. It was after visiting hours, and Ruth and my family had left for the day. I was alone and racked with pain and more than a little bit grumpy as I tossed and turned; more than anything, I just wanted to sleep and escape the misery and discomfort for just a little while. I had no idea I was about to get an escape beyond my wildest dreams.

Suddenly, two men I had never seen before in my life walked into my hospital room. Don't ask me how I knew, but immediately I had a sense that these men were angels. I wasn't the least bit anxious, either.

Once they had detached me from my tangle of tubes, the angels gathered me in their arms and we began to ascend, on a quick journey that felt light and smooth through the bluest of blue skies.

I was deposited on solid ground, in front of a monumental gate. And no, I don't remember it as being "pearly."

Standing in a short line of people, I observed the other thirty-five or so heavenly travelers, people of all nationalities. Some were dressed in what I thought were probably the native costumes of their lands. One man carried a baby in his arms.

I saw color-bursts that lit up the sky, way beyond the northern lights I had seen once on a trip to Alaska. Simply glorious.

My geezer body felt young and strong and fantastic. The aches and pains and limitations of age were just gone. I felt like a teenager again, only better.

The music I heard was incomparable to anything I had ever heard before. There was a choir of a million people, thousands of organs, thousands of pianos. It was the most lush and beautiful music I had ever heard. And do you know that every single day since my experience I have heard a few snatches of that music? I am so blessed to remember that heavenly sound.

And then, a greeting: "Hello, Marv. Welcome to heaven. My name is Peter."

Standing before me was one of my best-loved scriptural figures, the hotheaded apostle Peter, the "rock" upon which Christ built his church and alleged gatekeeper of Glory. I think the reason why I've always felt close to Peter is because I find him so relatable. He's hotheaded and I'm hardheaded, just for starters.

We talked a bit, and even argued (guess who won?), and when I play that conversation over and over in my head, I

16

am thrilled to have had such an encounter with one of the bravest and best men who ever walked this earth.

I'll tell you more about that incredible meeting later on, but for now, you should know that Peter leafed through the Book of Life, which was actually multiple books, looking for my name. But of course he couldn't find it; otherwise I would be in heaven now, possibly having another lively debate with Peter. He left his post at heaven's gate briefly to consult with God about what to do with me—keep me or send me home. My vote was definitely to keep me there. Surely it was on purpose, but Peter left the door to heaven open, revealing a translucent gate through which I could see inside.

What I saw beyond the gate is a kind of revelation. I believe God wants me to share it with you, so that you know some of what to expect when this life is over. I can't wait to tell you about how people were dressed in heaven, how magnificently healthy and happy they all looked, and how the countless babies and children I saw were laughing and playing. One of the biggest reasons I decided to share my story was to offer comfort to those who had lost a baby or a child. So many of you have lost a precious son or daughter, and I know exactly how deeply painful that loss is. Fifty-some years later, we still miss our baby boy, William John, who lived for just ten hours before he was taken from our arms.

I didn't get to see my son in heaven, but I know he's there and I will be with him next time I go. Because next time, I'm not coming back!

Wonderfully, I did see six loved ones beyond the gate, and I'll tell you all about how they looked and what they meant to me in chapters 9 and 10.

Several minutes passed before Peter returned with a divine dispatch: "Marv, I talked to God, and God told me to tell you that you have to go back, that he still has work for you to do on earth. He still has things for you to finish there."

But, but, but . . . ! Peter and I tussled a bit over that matter, you can be sure. Trust me when I say that once you visit heaven, you never, *ever* want to come back to earth. It's truly a place that is everything good and beautiful you can imagine, where you will feel more free and loved than you ever dreamed possible. It's really a future to eagerly await, that "home in Glory Land that outshines the sun," as the song goes.

In the end, I really didn't have much to say about whether I was staying or going. Before I could mount a rebuttal to Peter, I was sent back in the blink of an eye. Next thing I knew, I was back in my hospital bed at U of M (the University of Michigan).

Once again, I was lying flat on my back, riddled with pain and attached to a mess of tubes plugged in all over the place. I made a snap decision then and there never to reveal what I had seen and heard that stunning night.

Why would anyone believe one word? That good old salt-of-the-earth Marv Besteman was chosen, out of millions of people, to take a sneak peek at eternal paradise? I could just imagine what they'd be thinking:

"Sure, Marv hitched a ride with a couple of angels to the clouds above—cloud nine is more like it!"

"Isn't it sad? That nice Mr. Besteman was hallucinating that he argued with St. Peter—he even thinks he told Peter he was a 'hardheaded Hollander'! Well, he is hardheaded . . ."

I felt it in my bones—no one would buy it. I especially knew I could never tell anyone about seeing Steve, the son-in-law who had asked me years ago to be his dad, the bonus son I loved like he was my own boy. Steve had died just two months before I went to heaven, of Ehlers-Danlos syndrome, a cruel and despicable illness I wouldn't wish on my worst enemy. How I wanted to tell my daughter how wonderful her husband looked, how vibrant and content! But I felt at the time it would only confuse and hurt her. Her grief was still so raw.

The only problem was my trip to heaven *had* happened—and just the way I remembered it.

I couldn't stop thinking about my angels, and the radiant and peaceful place called heaven I flew to with them.

Images from that journey bombarded me: the colorbursts that lit up the sky, the hundreds and thousands of babies and children I saw, and for one twinkle in time, the glimpse I had of God's throne with two indescribable images upon it.

In my mind's eye, I could picture Peter perfectly, his bushy hair, his ancient robes, and the look in his eyes when he told me that he couldn't find my name in the Book of Life—"for today."

Would I buy a story like that myself if someone else was telling it? No, probably not, although I'll never know for sure.

"You Have Been Truly Blessed"

For a long time, I was angry at God for taking me to that perfect, joyful place and then bringing me back to life on earth, to an old man's aches and pains, in a place full of dirt and crime, disease and tears. I've since done some reading about people who have visited heaven, and by and large they almost all come back feeling depressed and angry. According to some scholars, even Lazarus, whom Jesus raised from the grave, the brother over whom Mary and Martha wept, struggled in his life after resurrection.

It's hard for people to understand, I know. Wouldn't a heavenly traveler be filled to the brim with marvelous news of things to come for all God's children? Yet, I know how much I wrestled with negative emotions when I came back. In the end, everyone who sees heaven even for one second wants to stay forever, no matter how nice their life might be here on earth.

God had plans for me, a mission for this retiree that went way beyond golfing and having coffee at Arnie's Bakery with my buddies. He had begun a work in me that night, and slowly but surely he showed me his purpose and mission in sending me on a round-trip to heaven and back.

Five months after my return, I broke down and told my sweetheart of fifty years everything. As tears poured down my face, the whole account came tumbling out, even the part about seeing our Amy's Steve.

Ruth's response changed everything.

"Marv, you have been truly blessed," she said, shaking her head, her bright blue eyes wide with wonder.

After I broke the ice with Ruth, my resolve to keep all the hard-to-believe details to myself began to melt. We shared the story with our three children, Julie, Amy, and Mark.

That Christmas, Amy gave me a copy of a book I had never heard of—*90 Minutes in Heaven* by Don Piper.

Somehow, this bestseller had completely escaped my attention until that Christmas morning after the heaven trip. It occurred to me that God might want me to write a book too. But I'm a banker, not a writer, and writing a book seemed to me then about as likely as traveling to heaven.

Then, nine months after my surgery, I was experiencing some issues with my stomach, which was swollen and distended. My visit to a doctor, the conversation we had that day in his office, and the crystal clear voice of direction I heard in my spirit sent me deeper down the path of sharing my story. Withholding what I had experienced was no longer an option.

God had made it perfectly plain: if I would faithfully tell his story, he would use it to bring comfort to the grieving, to encourage those who were dying and their loved ones, and to plant a seed of hope in those who had not yet chosen Christ.

That's why you hold my story today. I invite you to be my companion and I yours on a journey to heaven and back. Together, we'll pull back the curtain separating us from the other side, and we'll learn many intriguing and fantastic things about angels, the Book of Life, the apostle Peter, and heaven itself, where God prepares a place for you and me. At last, we will be with the Person we were made for, in a home we were made to be.

One more thing before we start: I have given many talks over the last few years to people eager for information on what heaven is like. At the end of every talk, I tell folks that next time, I won't be coming back. I'll be staying there forever with my Lord and those I love.

"And I'll be waiting for each one of you at the gate," I say as I close my talk. "Will I see you there?"

Will I see *you*? If you don't already know the answer to this question, will you do an old man a favor and chew on it as we travel through these pages together?

Okay then, let's get going . . .

1

A One-in-a-Million Case

I had never heard of insulinoma before I was diagnosed with it. As diseases go, this wasn't one of the famous ones that cause people to cluck their tongues, grimace, or shake their heads in sympathy. When I told people I had insulinoma, they looked at me like they didn't know what I was talking about—which they didn't.

But, have it I did, and that's what led me to the University of Michigan Medical Center in Ann Arbor, Michigan, in April of 2006.

It all started in 2003, three years before my diagnosis with this strange illness. Ruth and I were in Florida for a few months, basking in the sun and trying to beat each other at golf (at the time, I could still beat her, but barely). It was there I had my first "episode."

Apparently (I have no memory of this), one night we were sitting around the condo, and suddenly I just zoned out. According to Ruth, I just stared into space for an hour, not knowing who she was, completely disoriented and confused, and a little bit agitated. One bonus of having a nurse for a wife is that she can often tell what's wrong with me, or at least she knows what to do to help the situation.

She thought it seemed like a case of low blood sugar, and she shoved a bit of chocolate in my mouth to get my blood sugar evened out. Ruth told me I couldn't even shut my own mouth to chew it, that's how out to lunch I was. She shut my mouth for me, something she probably wishes she could have done a long time ago.

Ruth took me to the ER for tests the next day and they couldn't find anything wrong.

For the next three years, I was fine—no more "episodes" to speak of. Since I hadn't even remembered what happened, I didn't think much about it. Ruth, though, being a nurse and my wife both, tucked it away in the back of her mind, wondering if it would ever happen again and why it happened in the first place.

We were vacationing up north in Boyne Mountain, Michigan, with two of our grandchildren, when I had another spell. It was the same kind of thing as in Florida; I woke up sometime in the night, dazed and incoherent, and had no idea who Ruth was or where I was. When Ruth woke up, she saw that I had pulled my legs up in the fetal position, and I was staring at her without really seeing her. I moaned and moaned, but didn't appear to have any pain.

Ruth got me up to go to the bathroom, and she had to hold me up the whole way because I was so shaky.

She made me eat some more chocolate, but somehow kept me quiet. Our granddaughter was sleeping in the same hotel room, and she didn't want to scare her.

The next morning, I felt perfectly fine, once again, and had no memory of anything happening the night before. We took the kids to the water park, went out for lunch, and drove home to Grand Rapids, where it happened again.

I had fallen asleep on the couch, and when I woke up, once more I didn't know where I was or who Ruth was. According to Ruth, I was acting anxious and a bit crazy, my heart racing and my limbs shaking. I was moaning again, and repeatedly beating the couch cushions.

This time, she was freaking out too, on the inside. I began crawling around on the floor, trying to get out of the condo, trying to get away from poor Ruth. She was grabbing me by the belt, attempting to physically slow me down so I couldn't get out. She finally managed to lock the doors and dial 911. Nurse or no nurse, my wife was definitely alarmed, but her training helped her stay calm and take command of the situation.

"What's he doing?" the 911 dispatcher asked her.

"He's crawling around on the floor, and he has no idea who I am."

The ambulance got there about five minutes later, loaded me up, and took me to Spectrum Health hospital in downtown Grand Rapids. I was at Spectrum for ten days, where I was poked and prodded within an inch of my life. Finally, they diagnosed me with insulinoma, a rare tumor of the pancreas that shows itself as being the exact opposite of diabetes. My pancreas was generating so much insulin it was eating all the sugar in my body, hence the strange spells. I had a blood sugar level of 31, which is apparently very bad news.

I had the dubious honor of being the first case of insulinoma they had ever diagnosed at this hospital, one of the top hospitals in the United States. Literally, less than one in one million people are diagnosed with it each year. Around 200 cases are confirmed annually in the whole country. I was one of those lucky people.

The doctors at Spectrum recommended that I see a very specialized surgeon, either at the University of Michigan Medical Center in Ann Arbor or at the Mayo Clinic in Rochester, Minnesota. I had attended U of M for a short time in my college days; I even laced up skates and played hockey for them back in the day. I figured they already had some of my money, so I might as well give them more of it.

I had to lie around and wait for a couple of days for a bed to be free in Ann Arbor. Ruth had left the hospital for the night and returned to our home, just twenty minutes away, so I was alone when abruptly I was told they had a bed ready at U of M. They packed me in an ambulance and off we sped to Ann Arbor, two and a half hours away. Ruth decided to come the next day, in the daylight, so she could find the place more easily.

Once at U of M, I found out just how special I was. There at the hospital, doctors wouldn't come in my room one at a time; it always was three to five at a time. I guess my condition was so rare the doctors were swarming me so they could inspect this extraordinary guy and his exceptional ailment.

They had diagnosed me with insulinoma in Grand Rapids, but those doctors and the new ones in Ann Arbor still didn't know exactly where the tumor was located on my pancreas.

This was crucial, because apparently a surgeon can't just go in and poke around someone's pancreas. Evidently, you can bleed terribly if they go in without knowing the exact spot they are trying to reach. But finding the right spot was turning out to be easier said than done.

A young doctor at the U of M hospital had a brilliant idea: she would pass a pediatric scope through me to find the exact location of my tumor. It worked, thanks be to God. Ruth and I were so relieved that she had found the tumor. We didn't want to face the possibility of excessive bleeding in surgery.

My surgery lasted for five hours. Dear Ruth had already been through such a roller coaster, wondering what was wrong with me, and knowing there was something way off, but not knowing what it could be. My "episodes" were stressful too, and then the drama of my being diagnosed with this extremely rare illness and the worry over whether or not the doctors would find the site of the tumor.

She says God gave her deep comfort throughout those five hours as she waited to find out how things had gone on the operating table. As it turned out, things had gone well, in terms of the doctor's goals for the surgery. They had found the site of the tumor no problem, and my blood glucose went from a low 80 to 180 and quickly to a normal 115 once the tumor was out. The only problem was that I awakened in more pain than I thought was humanly possible.

According to Ruth and our family and friends, plenty of loved ones stopped by to visit me after my surgery. But I didn't know and didn't care who was in that room. Phil Mickelson could've stopped by to get some golf tips from me, and I wouldn't have cared.

A doctor whose sole job was to control people's pain spent three hours in my hospital room, adjusting my pain medications. From about five p.m. to eight p.m. that evening, she tried to get my pain under control. Whatever she was doing wasn't working one little bit, though it wasn't for lack of her trying.

I'm not being a big baby when I tell you it was horrible. I've been told the reason why I hurt so bad is because the pancreas is behind the stomach, so the surgeon had to move my other organs around to get to it. Plus, with a major surgery like this, the nerve endings are apparently severed, and then later they have to reattach and regenerate. At that point, my nerve endings hadn't regenerated yet, to say the least. Oh, and I almost forgot: the epidural stopped working during the surgery and I had to have a new one midway through the procedure. "Ouch" doesn't begin to cover it.

Nurses like to say, "How's your pain on a scale of one to ten?" This was way beyond a ten.

I was in and out, dozing, coming to and from that fiery pain. I remember just jabbing my pain control button over and over but nothing seemed to work. Ruth says that because it was my first night, post-op, the nurses would have been in about every half an hour to check on me. Ruth wasn't familiar with Ann Arbor, and she wanted to get back to her hotel before it got too dark outside. She kissed me on the cheek, told me she loved me, and walked out of the room. She left at about eight o'clock, just after the pain control doc had given up for the night and left my room.

I lay in my bed, miserable and terribly restless with the pain. There was a clock in my room, but I couldn't see it (and I didn't care what time it was, either). That's why I didn't know exactly what time it was on the night of April 27, 2006, or early in the morning of April 28, when two strangers entered my room and I instantly forgot about all the pain.

2

Two Angels

D on't ask me how I knew the two strangers who had just walked into my hospital room were angels; I just knew they were. Beyond any doubt, these were angelic visitors, come to take me home.

I wasn't one bit worried about it, either. A feeling of deep calm washed over me as these two men approached my bed, one on either side of me. They were smiling and quiet. My angels looked like regular guys, except regular guys usually don't wear white robes. Both looked in their mid-forties and stood about 5'8" to 5'10". One had longish brown hair, and the other one had shorter hair.

Everyone has a mental picture of angels, and so did I. When I had thought of angels before I actually met one, I pictured them as younger than the beings I saw. I also thought angels were men and women both, but maybe that's just because of that old TV show, *Touched by an Angel*.

And no, actually, neither one of them had wings. (I know that's what you were wondering, because that's one of the top questions I get about my experience: Did my angels have wings?) A little while later, I did have an encounter with winged creatures, but we'll get to that part in due time.

The angels were as tender as tender could be, peaceable and silent as they unhooked me from my tubes. (I was attached to about five different tubes—IV, gastric tubes, etc.)

Now, just hold on a minute. Why would angels—with superpowers that make Spiderman and Superman look like wimps—bother to detach me from the tubes holding me to my hospital bed and this earth? Couldn't they just beam me up to heaven, like the Starship Enterprise's chief engineer, Scotty, used to propel Captain Kirk back to the ship?

Of course they *could've* beamed me up, blasted me off like a rocket, floated me like a balloon, but they didn't. My angels chose to carefully and gently unhook each and every tube before we took off, and I'm not totally sure why.

Naturally, I have some theories. They knew, because God told them, that I was a Dutchman, a retired banker, and a Midwesterner to boot. I'm a man who likes my t's crossed and my i's dotted, so perhaps they felt it best to unplug me from planet Earth in an orderly fashion.

My gut tells me they were preparing me for what would come next, easing me into transition from this life to the next.

My angels each put their arms around one side of me; then I had a sudden upward-trend feeling, and the three of us began to fly to heaven. My angels were carrying me with their arms around me. I wasn't at all afraid; just the opposite. I felt perfect serenity, yet also a sense of excitement for what was to come. It was smooth and wonderful, I can assure you, not like some commercial airline, bumping along the skies.

I couldn't say how long the trip took—a few seconds to a couple of minutes, at the most. My angels and I flew through a brilliantly blue sky, and I had a profound sense of lightness and calm.

There was just so much peace.

"Ministers of the Divine Bounty"

Before I met the two angels who came to take me to heaven, I hadn't thought too much about the topic. I knew angels were with me when I was born, and that they would be with me when I died. I had believed in angels as long as I could remember. When I met my two angels, though, and flew with them to heaven, it got me thinking later about all the ways in which angels are with us and for us, in between birth and death.

I can count on one hand the number of good, solid sermons I've heard in my lifetime on the topic of angels. When you're Dutch, you're stoic, proud of the dose of skepticism that runs through your "orange" veins (orange, for those who don't know, is the color of the Dutch Royal Family, the House of Oranje-Nassau). I'm not royalty, but I am Dutch and proud of it. What I'm trying to say is that Dutch Calvinists aren't normally too big on angel sightings.

Even John Calvin, who founded reformed theology, was cautious in discussing the topic of angels. Too much talk of angels, he once said, is apart from the Bible, and therefore not verifiable. (Good thing Calvin wasn't around in the mid-1990s, when angels were all the rage and there seemed to be fluffy, chubby heavenly beings floating behind every bush.)

But even Calvin, with his reluctance to fall into the silliness that can occur when people obsess about angels, said they are "ministers and dispensers of the divine bounty towards us."

There's no doubt the way my angels picked me up in my hospital room, with all the respect and kindness in this world and the next, why, that was a kind of "bounty," or gift, to me.

I bet Lazarus felt the same way, when angels carried him to "Abraham's bosom" in the parable of the poor man and the rich man in Luke 16:22: "Now the poor man died and was carried away by the angels to Abraham's bosom; and the rich man also died and was buried" (NASB). Caring for believers at the moment of death is just one of the many jobs angels fill, according to the Bible.

I always knew, since Sunday School days, that angels were workers of Christ, like Christ, watching over what we say and do.

After my time in heaven, I was much more fascinated with angels than ever before, and I decided to study the Bible and find out as much as I could about the two strangers who entered my hospital room and their fellow beings. Plus, after sharing my heaven story with others, folks started telling me their own incredible angel stories, some of which I will pass on to you.

But first, may I share with you some of the fantastic things I learned about angels in the Bible? I think you'll be as intrigued as I am.

Angels 101

- **Angels are referred to 196 times in Scripture,** 103 times in the Old Testament and 93 times in the New

Testament. These references are scattered through-out the Bible in at least 34 books from Genesis to Revelation.

- **Angels are celestial messengers.** The Hebrew word for angel is *mal'ach*, and the Greek word is *angelos*. Both words mean "messenger" and describe one who carries out the goals and commands of the One they serve.
- **Angels were created *before* the earth.** In the book of Job, when God is questioning Job, we are told that angels were already there when the earth was created:

> Where were you when I created the earth?
>   Tell me, since you know so much!
> Who decided on its size? Certainly you'll know
>   that!
>   Who came up with the blueprints and
>   measurements?
> How was its foundation poured,
>   and who set the cornerstone,
> While the morning stars sang in chorus
>   and *all the angels shouted praise*?
>   Job 38:4–7 Message

- **Angels live in heaven but can travel anywhere in the cosmos and creation.** In the book of Mark, Jesus spoke of "the angels in heaven," which strongly suggests that angels have a home or center there for their activities. However, they have many missions to accomplish, and therefore have access to the entire universe, both heaven and earth. In the Bible, angels have served on earth, as in the case of the angel who flew in and brought Daniel an answer to his prayer, and in heaven: four angels described in Revelation stood at the four corners of earth, "standing steady with a firm grip on the four winds so no wind would blow on earth or sea, not even rustle a tree." From the Milky Way to Milwaukee, from the throne of God to the porch swings of earth—angels have access to the whole universe.

- **Angels are superheroes.** But make no mistake, they are not as powerful as God. In fact, the Bible tells us they are limited. Still, compared to us humans, angels are much smarter and wiser and possess astounding powers. For starters, they can fly, with or without wings (remember, my angels were wingless), and they can turn into a human or heavenly being in the twinkling of an eye. But so often, as the stories later in this chapter illustrate, angels can show up at any time, and then vanish into thin air. They are incredibly strong too. The stone covering Jesus's tomb, for example, weighed an estimated 1,000 to 2,000 pounds, the same heft as a midsize car. An angel rolled it away like it was a bowling ball. In Acts, an angel broke into a jail, snapped iron chains with his bare hands, and let the imprisoned apostles go free. The apostle Peter says it all: Angels are our "superiors in every way" (2 Peter 2:11 Message).

- **Angels are on a mission.** Their main job seems to be worshiping and praising God in heaven (I heard their phenomenal voices when I was at the gate). But angels also reveal God's will to his children, like the angel Gabriel revealed to Mary that she would be with child. They guide and instruct us, giving instructions to Joseph, the women at the tomb, Philip, Cornelius, and many others in the Bible. God used angels to provide physical needs such as food and water for Hagar, Elijah, and Christ after his temptation. They protect us, keeping us out of physical danger—like they protected Daniel in the lions' den—and deliver us from danger once we're in it. Last but not least, one of the angelic duties is to strengthen and encourage us, such as the way an angel encouraged Paul in Acts 27 by telling him that he and everyone else on the ship would survive the impending shipwreck.

- **Angels are spoken of as men in the Bible.** Now, I know in Christ there is no "male or female." Both men and women are made in his image and he loves them equally. My angels were men, and so are the vast majority of angels mentioned in the Bible, at least the ones that took on the appearance of humans. Of course, it's possible that since angels are spirit beings, they can take on the appearance of women, as well as men (see Gordy's story below). There is one exception in the Bible, in the book of Zechariah, that contains a clue that there might be female angels: "Then lifted I up mine eyes, and looked, and, behold, there came out two women, and the wind was in their wings; for they had wings like the wings of a stork" (Zech. 5:9 KJV). A stork, huh? Now that hit a nerve for me, for reasons I'll get to in just a bit. Anyway, it's possible this verse lends some credibility to the existence of female angels. Some theologians think the winged women here are indeed celestial beings, but not necessarily angels. I'll let them work out the fine tuning on that particular point.
- **Angels are invisible, unless God opens our eyes to them or they take on the appearance of real men.** Since they

are spirit beings, we usually can't see the angels that are here with us, taking care of us, ministering to us, and fighting on our behalf. But sometimes God gives us the ability to see them, like I was lucky enough to do. Balaam, the donkey man, could not see the angel standing in his way until the Lord opened his eyes (Num. 22:31), and Elisha's servant was blind to the crowd of angels surrounding him until Elisha prayed for his eyes to be opened (2 Kings 6:17). Over and over again in Scripture, angels were mistaken for men because so often they looked exactly like men! Abraham thought the three angels who approached his tent in the desert were regular visitors, and he offered them food and drink. His nephew Lot thought the same thing when, soon after his uncle's angelic encounter, two angels showed up at his house in Sodom. He invited the angels to wash their feet and stay the night. I don't think he would have thought of clean feet if they didn't look like regular men.

My angels looked like men I might see on the golf course, or at a hockey game, except of course they were wearing long-sleeved robes. Their clothes were white and gauzy, almost filmy, but not quite see-through, and they hung about two or three inches from the floor. Both angels wore ropes or long rags belted around their waists.

Angels are sometimes described in the Bible as having faces like "lightning" and wearing blazing white, dazzling "raiment," which is a ten-dollar word for clothing. At the sight of those angels, people fell on their faces in fear and wonder.

Angels Unaware

After my trip to heaven, I marveled at how many times in my life I must have been surrounded by angels and hadn't known it. How often had I been teeing off on the same golf green as an angel, or sitting next to an angel at a hockey game, strangers who look and act as normal as can be?

So many people have asked me about what my angels were like, and some have even told me their own stories of encountering angels here on earth. I picked several of these stories to share with you, hoping and praying you'll be as captivated, inspired, and encouraged as I was by them.

Janet's Angel

Janet was the kind of lady people didn't even see. Awkwardly lacking in social graces, Janet seemed to be about as unimportant a person as you could possibly imagine.

A worker on the assembly line of a cookie factory, Janet went home each night to a cramped and dingy apartment, where she would call her elderly mother, Millie, to chat, or else turn on the TV and heat up a frozen meal of some kind. Her life was about as dull as you could imagine.

But God, her heavenly Father, loved her so much that he would send an angel to her funeral to deliver a message so powerful that the handful of attendees would never forget it.

One day, when Janet was just in her late forties, she died suddenly of a massive heart attack. With few friends and even fewer family members, it fell to the members of her mother's church small group to plan the funeral of a woman they barely knew.

For Millie's sake, the small group members tried to make Janet's funeral nice and meaningful. They ordered purple flowers for the service, because Millie told them it was Janet's favorite color. Her best-loved songs were sung by a sparse crowd of about thirty people who dribbled into the five-hundred-seat sanctuary. The apples of Janet's eye—her two little grand-nieces—cuddled up to their mother and great-grandmother in the front pew, nearly empty except for the four of them.

It was a risk, but Millie had responded favorably when asked if she thought there should be time given for people to share their memories of Janet. Their worst fears—that no one would walk up to the microphone with a memory—almost came true as an awkward silence fell over the small crowd.

Just as the pastor began to clear his throat to bring the dismal sharing time to a close, a young African-American man seated in a side pew, several rows from everyone else, stood up.

"I have a message," he said in a clear, strong voice that rang out like a bell. The young man was wearing a green T-shirt with three crosses on it. With deep conviction, he began to read from Hebrews 12, starting in verse 22:

> But you have come to Mount Zion, to the heavenly Jerusalem, the city of the living God. You have come to thousands upon thousands of angels in joyful assembly, to the church of the firstborn, whose names are written in heaven. You have come to God, the judge of all men, to the spirits of righteous men made perfect. (vv. 22–23 NIV'84)

The man with the crosses on his shirt continued to read the passage, with perfect clarity and a resounding, authoritative tone. Janet's family stared at him; they had never laid eyes on him before and they were fairly sure Janet hadn't either. The pastor and head elder began to trade glances with each other. With over thirty years in ministry together, they could just about read each other's minds. *Who is this guy? Let's check him out when the service is over.* They nodded at each other in understanding as the man's voice got even more booming and decisive as he got to the last verses in the chapter:

> Therefore, since we are receiving a kingdom that cannot be shaken, let us be thankful, and so worship God accept-ably with reverence and awe, for our *"God is a consuming fire."* (vv. 28–29 NIV'84)

The young man was almost shouting as he delivered the last words of the passage, "Our God is a consuming fire." He closed his Bible and quietly took his seat as the stunned members of the congregation gawked at him. Was he a friend of Janet's? If so, he wasn't sitting with the handful of co-workers and other acquaintances. Several curious attendees made a mental note to meet the mysterious man after the service was done, and they turned their attention to the front and the pastor's sermon.

But when the service ended, and Millie and her tiny family trooped down the aisle to the church foyer, with the other attendees following suit, the young man was nowhere to be seen. Had he slipped out sometime during the pastor's sermon? The head elder, seated up on the stage at the front of the church, had been keeping a close eye on the man. He never saw him leave. In fact, no one remembered seeing the man leave, even though at least a dozen people had a clear view of him from across the church.

It was strange, but then again, Madison Square Church is situated in the inner city, and they have had their share of odd visitors come in off the street over the years. Besides, there was Janet's family to comfort, and a funeral lunch to partake of. Most people forgot about it for the time being, but not the pastor or the head elder.

Both of them knew very well that this stranger was unlike any they had ever received in all their years of ministry. He was clearly sober, tidy (if oddly dressed for a funeral), and completely in command of his speech and delivery. It was as if he had a message to deliver, a message on behalf of someone else.

"Our God is a consuming fire."

. How bold and commanding his voice had been as he read those words from Hebrews 12! The pastor stole away to a quiet room and opened his Bible to Hebrews 12, rereading the passage the visitor had delivered so compellingly. What an unlikely message to be delivered at a funeral, especially for a funeral of one as meek and mild as Janet. Yet somehow, the pastor and everyone gathered there felt the fiery missive was oddly fitting. The takeaway seemed to be that Janet may have lived a quiet life, nearly unnoticeable to all but a few loved ones, yet she believed in the God of "consuming fire," and was with him now in heaven. Her choice, to believe in this God, had been brash and daring—everything she seemed not to be—and it meant that Janet had now joined "thousands upon thousands of angels in joyful assembly."

Speaking of angels, the pastor's suspicion was growing. How had their eagle-eyed head elder, who never missed a single thing, missed the young man's leaving the sanctuary? For that matter, how had *everyone* missed his leaving?

The pastor read every word of the Hebrews passage carefully, praying for wisdom to receive the message in the way God had intended. He came to where the young man had stopped, and instead of ending there, he decided to keep reading, hoping to gain some context for the passage.

A chill ran up his spine as the pastor took in the very next passage following the stranger's reading: "Keep on loving each other as brothers. *Do not forget to entertain strangers, for by so doing some people have entertained angels without knowing it*" (Heb. 13:1–2 NIV'84).

Though there was no proof this stranger was an angel (there never is, by the way), the pastor felt a wave of gratitude wash over him. He felt sure that he and the small crowd of mourners at the funeral had entertained an angel without knowing it. They had been reminded by this heavenly messenger in no uncertain terms of God's overwhelming, all-consuming holiness.

And no one who attended the humble funeral of lonely, unimportant Janet ever thought about her in the same way again, nor did they forget that they had been visited by an angel in a green T-shirt.

"My Name Is Otis"

Janet's angel was on a mission to deliver a message from God, but some of the angel stories people have told me revolve around other purposes. Just as God used angels to supply water for Hagar's thirsty little boy, a cake baked on coals for a hungry Elijah as he hid in the wilderness, and sustenance for Jesus after his temptation, angels are all around us, helping us in often very practical ways. Jamie's story features a hands-on angel called Otis, who couldn't be more down-to-earth.

Jamie is a bubbly young mother from Texas, and she shared three stories of how she believes God had sent angels to watch over and rescue her and her loved ones.

When I was little, I was traveling with my grandparents on a camping trip, when we had some car trouble. My granddad pulled the camper over and looked under the hood of the truck to see what was going on. A man stopped his car and offered to help. He and Granddad looked under the hood together and worked on the engine for quite a while, chatting as they worked. When Granddad followed the man to get something out of the trunk of the man's car, Granddad noticed some fishing gear in there and asked him about it. The man said he and his brothers were fishermen. It seemed odd, because we were nowhere near a body of water big enough to fish commercially.

My grandmother is Southern, and Southern ladies write thank-you notes for all occasions. She tried to get him to write down his address for her so she could send him a thank-you note. The man politely refused. Grandma and Granddad offered to pay him, but he wouldn't accept a thing or give them any information. "At least let us take you out to eat," Grandpa begged him, but the stranger just smiled and said that wasn't necessary, that he was glad to help them. "My name is Otis," he said, when my grandparents asked for his name (Grandma was probably hoping for a last name so she could look him up and send that darn thank-you card anyway!). But he didn't give a last name and they didn't want to push him. Otis followed us in his car, a good bit out of his way, to a dealership where he knew we could get fixed up. He waved to us as he drove on by, and we never saw him again.

Agents of Rescue

Like the mysterious "fourth man" who rescued Shadrach, Meshach, and Abednego from the blazing furnace in Daniel 3, angels are sent out to liberate us from grave danger. King Nebuchadnezzar and his astonished entourage actually saw the rescuing angel, who looked like "a son of the gods" (v. 25), standing in the fire, cool as can be, with the trio of men the king had supposed he had sent to their deaths. But so often, we don't see anyone at all, as the angels who save us from harm are invisible, or maybe just manifested as a flash of light. This was true in Jamie's other stories, the first of which happened to a friend of hers, and the second hit her very close to home.

Missy's Story

"A friend's dad always specifically prayed for his children's protection every time they left the house. On this occasion, he prayed for Missy to be safe on the road before a particular trip. She was driving behind an 18-wheeler, and she saw a flash of light. Her car suddenly died, stopping right in the middle of the road and she watched as the semitruck pulled away from her, swerving wildly as it had had a tire blowout! She knew if her car had not stopped right there at that specific spot on the road, there would have been no way she could have avoided colliding with the semi. There was nothing wrong with the car, before or after it died, and it started right up again as if nothing had happened. She believes her dad's prayers were answered and an angel protected her that day."

Zackary's Story

"Last summer we were at a benefit golf tournament and our one-year-old son, Zackary, was run over by a 700-pound golf cart, driven by an 8-year-old with no adult supervising him. I didn't see it happen as I had turned my back for just a few seconds and was talking to someone. I heard screaming and turned around to see my baby boy under the golf cart. My heart stopped, of course. I have never been more terrified in my life. Someone called 911 and a bunch of men tried to pull him from underneath the cart. When they finally pulled him out, I frantically checked him out, and to my profound relief Zackary only had a few light abrasions on his neck and cheek, and a small scrape on his head. Later, the medics and doctors couldn't believe he had not been seriously injured or killed. One of them said to me that there was just no explanation for it other than an angel had put himself between my baby and the golf cart and saved him."

Just for good measure, and because I want you to go away from this chapter with your eyes wide open to the possibility of angels working in our midst, I want to share two more tales, passed on to me by others full of wonder at what they had experienced.

Sharon's Story

"My girlfriend and I were at a work-related conference in Philadelphia and we went into the city one night for dinner. We didn't realize how late it was getting, and when we finally paid our bill and went out to our rental car, the parking lot was deserted except for one other car across the lot.

"Two guys were standing over by the car, watching us intently, and it seemed to me, in a predatory way. I had a creepy feeling about them and the whole situation. I felt so vulnerable at that moment. Suddenly, the two guys were joined by about eight other men, wearing white robes, who surrounded the two men and their car. My friend and I jumped in our car and locked the doors, watching in amazement as the two men abruptly drove off the lot. We blinked and the men in robes had vanished."

Gordy's Story

"I work as a custodian at an inner-city Christian school, a job I have been blessed to have for years. The children and their joy and laughter make it all worthwhile; they even have a 'Mr. Gordy Day' every year where everyone wears a funny T-shirt like the ones I like to wear.

"I live not too far from the school, and my neighbors also know they can count on me for help with fixing things. One day, I was up in the branches of a neighbor's tree, trying to help him trim a huge dead limb before it fell off and hurt someone. The crotch of the tree was about twenty feet off the ground, and the branch was about twenty-five feet off the ground.

"There was a rope between my neighbor and me (he was standing on the ground). I told him to pull west, but he pulled north, which made me lose my footing and I began to fall.

"As I was falling, I saw a post down below and I knew I had to avoid it or else be impaled by it. I twisted to avoid the post, and landed on a cement riser between the sidewalk and the grass. My pelvis made full contact with the riser, and I knew it was busted. I got up and hobbled two steps before I collapsed.

"As I lay on the ground, in horrible pain, my primary thought was sadness, because I knew I wouldn't be able to work for a while and I love being around those kids. Then I saw an African-American woman around forty years of age cross the street and come toward me. 'I'm going to pray for you,' she said, kneeling beside me and laying her hands on me. She prayed a very simple, short prayer for peace and healing in my body, and then she was gone. I had never seen her before, and I knew almost everyone in the neighborhood.

"Later on, after rehabilitation in the hospital and at home, I asked around the community and no one knew who this woman might be. I wanted to thank her so badly. What really convinced me she was an angel was the way my older body healed. My doctor kept asking me if I had lingering pain, and I kept telling him no, not really. He finally told me that almost everyone who had this type of pelvic ring injury experienced chronic pain afterward, and he couldn't believe I was fine. I truly believe that this woman was one of God's angels, ministering to me as I lay broken in pieces on the sidewalk. This experience taught me you have to be open to God's work, because it's all around us."

A Brush of Angels' Wings

Janet's angel delivered a message from God. "Otis" and the African-American woman cared for God's children in their moments of need. And angels on rescue missions delivered Missy and Zackary from terrible harm or even death.

My two angels cared for me at a most critical hour, comforting me with their gentleness and strength.

This bears repeating: they didn't have wings, even though they flew me to heaven. Still, winged beings do play a part in this story, as I'll explain in a little bit.

In the Bible, some angels, especially the cherubim and seraphim, are represented as winged in several passages, including Exodus 25:20: "The cherubim shall stretch forth their wings on high, covering the mercy seat with their wings, and their faces shall look one to another; toward the mercy seat shall the faces of the cherubim be" (KJV).

These verses in Isaiah talk about both the throne I saw in heaven and the winged angels:

> In the year that King Uzziah died, I saw the Lord seated on a throne, high and exalted, and the train of his robe filled the temple. Above him were seraphs, each with six wings: With two wings they covered their faces, with two they covered their feet, and with two they were flying. (Isa. 6:1–2 NASB)

Cherubim, I learned, not only have four faces (one of each: a man, an ox, a lion, and a griffin), they also have four conjoined wings covered with eyes. After the fall, they guarded the way back to the Garden of Eden and the Tree of Life. They also attend the throne of God. St. Thomas Aquinas had a theory that Satan was a fallen cherub.

Seraphim also serve as caretakers to God's throne as they continuously shout praises to him. I find it fascinating that their name, *seraphim*, means "the burning ones."

Was it the cherubim or seraphim whose wings brushed against my arms and face and head as I stood at the gate of heaven? I couldn't see the creatures that brushed against me, but they felt like the flutter of wings against my skin. To be more specific, the feathers felt soft yet sturdy, like that of a large bird, a Canada goose, a swan, or yes, a stork. The feeling wasn't that of a fluffy, downy baby chick at all.

Peggy's angel story was also told to me after my heaven trip, and when I heard it, I was instantly reminded of how those angels' wings had felt brushing against me.

The Touch of Angels' Wings

Peggy, a Canadian mother of five children, was the kind of mom who always prayed for her kids before they walked out the door to school each morning. One day, Peggy was praying for her two little girls as they were about to leave for school. Immediately after she finished praying for them and opened the door to let them out, she felt a rush of wings graze her head gently. It felt as if a large bird had flown past her, out the door behind the girls. But as Peggy spun around to see what it was, she saw nothing behind her. Still, whatever it was had flown *out* of the house and not into the house. She looked out to the sidewalk where her daughters were walking toward school and saw nothing. No large birds were anywhere to be seen. Suddenly, she knew in her heart of hearts that what she had felt was an angel, following her children and watching them every step of their way.

Isn't that a wonderful, heartening story of God's watch-care for his little ones?

Angelos

I am leaning toward my two heavenly visitors being the most "ordinary" order of angels, simply *angelos*, or messengers. They are the angels most concerned with the affairs of people on earth, and fulfill lots of jobs and undertake all kinds of missions, including flying me to heaven on that incredible night.

As I said, my flight was as smooth as could be, a gliding sensation I'll never forget, because it was like no other flight I ever took on earth. We flew upward at first, for a few seconds or maybe a full minute. Then, I noticed two things: my angels all at once changed course slightly, veering to the right a little bit, before beginning our descent.

Yes, it was a descent, definitely a distinct drop and no longer a climb.

I'm absolutely sure of it. We were gliding downward on an angle when I realized something else. I looked down and saw that my dangling legs had pants on, and that somewhere midair, between this world and the next, my clothes had changed. When my angels picked me up, I had been wearing my blue hospital gown. In the air, I saw that I was now wearing a light brown golf shirt, tan pants, and shoes, the kind of thing I might wear to take my wife out for dinner.

Later, when I would get a glimpse of my precious mother, grandparents, son-in-law, and friends, I would notice that they too were dressed very similarly to what they wore as they lived their lives on this earth.

There's something else I want to tell you about the way I was set down in heaven. Ruth and I are fortunate enough to live in a condo with a bunch of older folks like us as neighbors. I like to relax from time to time in a deck chair by the man-made lake right below our sliding doors, watching the migratory birds that flock to the banks of the lake.

If I've watched one, I've watched a thousand Canada geese come in for a landing by the lake, their brownish-gray wings alight as they coast smoothly toward solid ground.

When I "came ashore" to heaven's gate, I felt like one of those Canada geese, gently gliding toward the ground. As soon as my feet touched down, my two angels disappeared and I never saw them again.

I had landed in another realm, in the very kingdom of heaven, where I was to see and hear and feel things beyond my wildest imagination. Already, in those sacred seconds in the cloudless sky, I was enjoying myself very much.

3

Lights, Colors,
and a Love Story

The colors and lights in heaven were simply sublime. Of course they were. Would you expect anything less?

They were the deepest, richest, most gloriously lush colors I had ever seen, and some I had never seen before. Heaven is a dream-come-true for those who love all things colorful, and our home there is lit by the Father of Lights, who dropped the sun and moon into the sky. Like the apostle John said in his Revelation of heaven: "The city does not need the sun or the moon to shine on it, for *the glory of God gives it light, and the Lamb is its lamp*" (Rev. 21:23).

The lights I saw were far beyond descriptions such as "radiant" and "luminous," soft and delicate shimmers that were somehow robust, and bold and vigorous beams that were somehow gentle to my eyes.

I simply don't think those colors and lights exist on earth. *Now Marvin*, you may be thinking, *that doesn't help me out in the least. Can you be a little more descriptive?*

Well, I'll give it my best shot. I know "indescribable" is a frustrating word, but I promise you, it fits the situation. But I will try to relate to you the colors I saw in heaven.

I did not see streets of gold. Mind you, I didn't get very far, only to the gate and then a brief peek inside the gate. I like to tell people it's as if you were from Nepal or Congo or someplace, and you were dropped via helicopter into Estes Park, Colorado, and picked up by the same helicopter twenty minutes later. Your impression would be that America was one big mountain range with jagged, snowy peaks because that's what you happened to see during your limited time there.

Other heavenly travelers have seen different sights than I had, and credible witnesses to heaven *have* seen golden streets and people with wings (not angels). Colton Burpo, the precious little boy whose story is told in *Heaven Is for Real*, even saw a magnificent rainbow horse. They are not making up their journeys any more than I am making up mine; we simply were given our own short previews based on what God wanted us each to see.

I did see some phenomenal things, though. The colors and lights were just two of those sights.

The Greenest Green and Bluest Blue

I saw babies and children and grown-ups of all ages playing and talking and laughing on grass that was the greenest green I've ever seen. I'm a golf nut, and I love to settle in each year and watch the crème de la crème golf event, the Masters Tournament, held in Augusta, Georgia. I've only been able to see the grass on which the world's greatest golfers play on high definition TV, but that flawless, emerald-colored carpet is the greenest surface I have ever seen in my lifetime. An acquaintance was privileged enough to attend the Masters Tournament, and his wife teased him because he came home with all these snapshots of the grass. "Check out this turf," he had told her, all excited as she rolled her eyes just a little bit. "See how perfect it is, how incredibly green." Picture the verdant, luscious grass at the Masters and then try to imagine grass far greener and more deluxe. That's how green the grass is in heaven.

The sky in which I flew to heaven, and the firmament surrounding the heavens, were a wilder and bluer yonder than you would ever believe. The atmosphere was soaked in color and light, and the blue was again outside of any tint we can brag about down here.

The closest shade I can associate this otherworldly blue with is the surreal tones of the water in the Caribbean or off the coast of Hawaii at sunset. It's a blue to marvel at, to appreciate and admire wholeheartedly. Imagine the ocean or a tropical bay at its bluest, and then think about the fact that a blue far from that color is waiting for you and me on the other side. And if blue is your favorite color, you're in luck. From what I saw, blue is the second-most prevalent shade in heaven. (Can you take a stab at what the first was? Stay tuned.)

The thing about the colors in heaven is that they are all shot through with a brightness, a luster that seems to incorporate the sun's rays, the moon's beams, a fire's flicker, and a star's glitter, stirred together by a master lighting director and splashed out over the canopy we will spend eternity watching.

How this Master loves to add glow and warmth to our dim paths with previews of the brightness to come!

59

The Light of My Life

It was 1956, a leap year, the year I took a leap of faith and love that would improve my life beyond measure since that blessed day in June when I laid eyes on Ruth, the light of my life.

Elvis Presley had just hit it big on the radio with "Hound Dog," Rodgers and Hammerstein came out with *The King and I* at the movies, and General Electric introduced a nifty new gadget called "The Snooz-Alarm," the first alarm clock that allowed you to whack it over and over again before you finally came to.

I was twenty-one years old, just out of Calvin College in Grand Rapids, where I had graduated with a degree in economics and business. It was a summer of endless possibilities, as I was courting the girls, sometimes properly and sometimes with all the charm of a nervous wreck. Girls confused me and confounded me; being the oldest of three boys, I really couldn't begin to fathom their mysterious ways.

That summer day, when I was set up on a blind date with a nursing student named Ruth, I wasn't expecting my world to flip on end. I just thought we would enjoy some gooey pizza at Fricano's pizzeria, and maybe I would get the chance to flirt a little with a pretty girl.

I thought she was beautiful. (I still do.) I can't remember how the pizza was that night, but I will never forget those shining blue eyes and her quiet maturity. She was, I thought, one of the most interesting women I had ever talked to. I still think so, after all these years.

However, the draft board was sending me ominous notices. Ruth says I took a month to call her, and I think it was more like two months. It wasn't that I lacked interest, but I was immature and didn't know where my life was headed. Still, a month or two later, I called her, and that was that. There was no one else for me but Ruth from that day on.

So, off I went to basic training with her loving words. In my mind, I knew it was the first time a woman had offered me words like that so sincerely.

We wrote letters back and forth, and those letters lit up my days in basic training. She was a young nurse, just getting started, and her job entailed so much serious business, matters of life and death. Ruth poured out her heart to me in those letters, and I tried to do the same with mine. Once you put it on paper, you can't take it back. I'm so glad we committed to paper our feelings for one another, and got to know each other so thoroughly as the mail flew back and forth from Grand Rapids to Colorado Springs, where I was stationed.

When I came home on leave, we spent every spare minute together. Ruth moved in with my parents to save money, and one day soon after I returned to Colorado, my dad took Ruth to the jewelry store to pick out her engagement ring.

On her next visit to Colorado, she was faced with a miserable sight: her strapping Army beau, feebly lying in a hospital bed, with red, puffy eyes and a hacking cough. At least I was clutching a diamond ring—I had that much going for me.

I was so sick with pneumonia I couldn't even get out of bed to get down on one knee to pop the question. It popped in spite of this, and she took pity on me and said yes. She said yes! At that moment, sick as I was, I felt my soul fill up with brightness.

Dance of the Spirits

Heaven exhilarated me with its greens and blues, but the number one color there seemed to be white. White! I'm not talking about the famous tunnel with the white light. I never saw a tunnel like that, although others have seen it, so I'm keeping an open mind.

White is one of my favorite colors—white and red. We've never owned a vehicle that wasn't white or red.

The white in heaven was—forgive me!—like none other I can compare. From a brilliant white to an opal stone to a milk glass moon color, the white shades clustered in the sky like a huge bridal bouquet, white on white on white, yet all distinct tinges and tones, including some whites God is saving for us to see in Glory. The multitude of whites included brighter whites and lighter whites—they were all gorgeous.

There are three reference points on earth to which I can compare the variations of color and shades in heaven. The most down-to-earth example is the sugary swirl of cotton candy you might enjoy at the circus or the state fair. As cotton candy has lots of different colors spun into it, the colors in heaven would meld from whites into blues and reds and purples and greens. The multiple colors would change and shift and move constantly, twirling and twisting and floating.

The many lustrous varieties of white were, like every heavenly color, infused with glowing light. Now we "see through a glass darkly," and we screw a lightbulb into the wall so we can see to read newsprint and iron our clothes and pay the bills. The lights in heaven are not bolted to any wall. They are constantly moving and shape-shifting in a way that fixated and enthralled me. The closest I can come to describing what that light show was like is probably the aurora borealis, or the northern lights.

About ten years ago, Ruth and I flew to Anchorage, where we rented a motor home and rambled around the great state of Alaska for a couple of weeks. More than once, our Midwestern mouths hung open as we gawked at the spectacle and pageantry of the northern lights.

The Cree Indians call these lights the "Dance of the Spirits," as they two-step around the polar skies, leaping and twirling in patterns of reds, greens, purples, blues, and pinks. And what place is more filled with spirits—real spirits—than heaven?

There the lit-up colors come together, pull apart, do-si-do . . . they jump and spin and twist and spiral and pulsate, kind of like a dance, sort of like the northern lights.

Then again, if I compare the light show in Alaska to the light show in heaven . . . it's not even close.

The Answer Is No

Ruth said yes to the first question and no to the second.

We were weeks away from getting married when I got orders to ship to Germany for two years. Well, that threw a wrench into things. A fellow finds the perfect girl to marry and then the Army comes along and everything gets stalled. I knew Ruth wouldn't be happy about this piece of news. The date was set, Ruth had sewn her dress, and the cake was ordered. She and my mother had already stuffed a couple hundred engraved invitations, licked the envelopes shut, and crammed them in the mailbox. I didn't know much about women, but I did know this news was going to go over about as well as the Hindenburg. Still, what are two years when a man and a woman are in love?

Nervously, I dialed Ruth's phone number on a payphone at the base in Colorado. "Will you wait for me for two years," I gave my halting delivery, "until I get back from Germany?"

"No," she responded curtly. I literally dropped the phone, I was so shocked.

No? Well, that wasn't the answer I was hoping for. As it turned out, though, Ruth was saying no to the two-year-wait, not to me. The Army, in a flash of kindness, permitted me to return home to be married just before being shipped to Germany. I had recently been promoted to company clerk after fifteen weeks of infantryman training.

We telephoned every single person invited to the wedding and told them it had been moved up. On July 9, 1957, Ruth became my wife and has been with me every step of the way, through thick and thin, richer and poorer, in sickness and in health—and literally, through heaven and earth.

The honeymoon was brief and fumbling, the blunders concealed behind a façade of hopeful yearning.

Then, quicker than you can say "gesundheit," we were packed and off to Germany. We were young and full of promise for what was to come. I was married to someone in whom I saw mountains to climb, valleys to explore, and new wonders beckoning off in the distance.

And together, over half a century, we have climbed mountains, more than I can count, but first we had to stumble over a couple of molehills. I am almost embarrassed to tell

Marv and Ruth, family dinner, 1998

you what sent me into tantrums regarding Ruth's behavior within the first month. You see, I suddenly discovered to my horror that this beautiful creature to whom I was married had a horrendous habit: she squeezed the toothpaste tube in the middle rather than carefully rolling it from the bottom!

She also had a new mother-in-law who spoiled her three boys beyond belief. So it was news to me when I found out Ruth wasn't about to iron my undershirts and undershorts like my mother always had. "I'm sorry," she said, in a tone which indicated she wasn't very sorry at all. "But I just don't do that." Well then, that was that. It was either iron my own shorts or wear them wrinkled.

We settled into our new lives in Heidelberg and found some new friends at a little church on the base. Soon after we arrived, I was promoted to chief clerk for the US Army in Europe, which meant I was in charge of 30,000 soldiers' whereabouts. One of these soldiers, by the way, was one Pvt. Elvis Aaron Presley, who was also stationed in Germany during my time there. Were these men and women on field or off? On sick leave? Our biggest concern at the time was Russia dropping the A-bomb, and I took my responsibilities very seriously.

Obviously, I took myself way too seriously as well, if I was going to roll up my guns and shoot over the matter of improper toothpaste squeezing (and ironing undershorts).

Our biggest newlywed fight was about picnicking on the Sabbath. Now, these days I will picnic with the best of them on a Sunday, but back then, coming fresh from the house of the very Dutch and very staunchly Reformed Marjorie Besteman, I had some issues with it. My bride simply could not understand what was wrong with laying a blanket on some green grass and partaking of deviled eggs and lemonade on the Lord's Day. Didn't the Lord himself make green grass and deviled eggs and lemonade for our pleasure? Actually, what she said was, "That's the stupidest thing I ever heard."

After some "negotiating," I came around to her way of thinking on matters of Sabbath observance, and I realized that if anyone was going to iron my undershorts, it would have to be me. And toothpaste? I just gave up and started squeezing the tube in the middle, right along with my beloved.

So as you can see, it was a big job Ruth took on when she walked down the aisle to take my hand and hear the preacher say, "Dearly beloved, we are assembled here to join this man and this woman in holy wedlock." It wasn't long after that she discovered she had a lot of work to do.

Ah, but I do love the fire in her eyes when she's about to vent the air about something. Life is partly for fun, and part of the fun is working out the problems, handling the differences, and struggling for a meeting of the minds. Sparks can really fly when a red-blooded American man and woman in love face off over something that matters to them. You could even call these sparks fireworks—flashy, bold, and colorful, with lots of zing and tang.

Fireworks in the Firmament

One of my favorite holidays is the Fourth of July, when the burgers are sizzling on the grill, the red, white, and blue flags are waving six deep at the Byron Center (Michigan) parade, and the fireworks are exploding in the black sky.

I've already told you the lights in heaven were most like the aurora borealis, but fireworks are another reference point I can use.

Pyrotechnics boomed and crackled (except they didn't make you want to plug your ears like they do down here), decorating heaven in shapes like cakes, spiders, peonies, and of course shapes and formations not of this world.

Every color you can think of—purples, reds, blues, silvers, greens, whites—interwove with each other in shining sequences. I was rooted to the spot in line at the gate, but if I would turn my eyes for a second, I would look up and see another arrangement.

Anyone who thinks they are going to be bored in heaven, plopped down on a marshmallow cloud in a pastel world of harps and floating babies, is dead wrong, if you'll pardon the pun.

Even just the light show was utterly transfixing.

At times, a gigantic color-ball, in constant yet steady motion, with shades slowly weaving in and out, burst above me, kind of like fireworks, sort of like the Fourth of July.

Then again, if I compare the fireworks in Michigan to the fireworks in heaven . . . it's not even close.

A Jar of Fireflies for the Journey

Ruth and I eventually figured out how to sort what really mattered from what didn't matter at all, such as toothpaste tubes and who irons what.

Fatherhood came quickly for me, and my children and grandchildren became lights of my life.

While we were still in Heidelberg, Ruth became pregnant with our first child, Julie. Our German hosts cried their eyes out when we told them we had to return to the US. They had become as attached to us as we to them, despite the language barrier. We loved our time there, but in those days a tour of duty was two years, and our tour happened to be up. We packed our bags again and headed back for the USA.

The first time I held my baby girl, Julie, in my arms, I was busting my buttons with love and pride. She seemed light enough to float away. Somehow, I managed not to drop her. God blessed us with another daughter, Amy, five years later, and then a son, Mark, five years after that.

I've enjoyed every moment I've spent with my children, watching as they grew and watching their minds and bodies expand. I remember hours spent with them when they were small. I remember the sweaty taste of their cheeks when I kissed them. First days at school, their earliest artworks, the way they played the flute and the trumpet and the cornett—all these many episodes brightened my eyes and my life. All of the years I have spent loving my children, I would not alter in the slightest. The joys all of them have provided will never fade. They lifted my spirits during some dark and trying days.

One of the darkest times in my life was when our baby son, William John, died after just ten hours of life. I will tell you more about William and all the babies I saw in heaven later on in my story. For now, I'll just say that anyone who has lost a child knows that our hearts were broken in a million pieces when William died.

Ruth and I learned to handle adversity the same way anyone learns: by going through it. We both determined that the hard things would be used as sealers rather than dividers of our union. Why life is so dark sometimes we do not know, but we do know this: what happens is not as important as what we do with what happens.

As a husband and a father, I've had a lot to learn about marriage, parenthood, love, and what matters most. So much time and distance has come between that moment and this one. We've had times of great joy and deep sadness, but always Ruth has been my beacon, illuminating the passages both dark and bright with her love and wisdom.

In Ruth, God the Father handed me a jar of fireflies for the camping trip of my life. "Here you go, son," I picture him saying, passing me the beaming jar. "It's going to get dark and scary at times. I will be here always, lighting your path, but here's a little extra light for you, just because I love you."

Today after fifty-five years of marriage, I am more sensitive to the thrill of her presence than I have ever been. When I come on her unexpectedly in a crowd, it is like a glad little song rising up somewhere inside me. When I catch her eye in public, it is as though she is hanging out a sign with the exact words of inspiration I need right then. When I drive home in the evening, I must consciously guard the foot pedal, lest I step on the gas too fast approaching the house where she waits for me. I still count the day's biggest thrill when she comes hurrying from wherever she is to greet me at the door with a kiss. Are these the musings of a sappy old man? you might ask. Guilty as charged.

As I look down the road ahead, I see an elderly man and woman going into the sunset hand in hand. I know in my heart the end will be better by far than the beginning.

Basking Forever

After my trip to heaven, Ruth asked me if I had ever thought about her during my time there. Had I ever once thought of our children, our grandchildren? Just like Ruth, she didn't pose the question defensively or with insecurity. She asked out of pure curiosity.

And the answer is, no, I didn't think of my beloveds, as much as I adore them. In fact, had Peter, via God, given me the choice to go back to Ruth, Julie, Amy, and Mark, on earth, or stay in heaven, there's no doubt I would have chosen to stay in heaven.

I would have chosen to stay in that wondrous place of dancing lights and color-bursting fireworks, enjoying every shimmer and beam and texture and tone.

Of course, it's not just the lights and colors that are worth staying for.

It's HIM. He's the sun, the moon, the stars—everything. One day the Son will return and we will be better, finer people. Nothing shall separate us from each other and him.

Together, Ruth and I and those we love will bask in his glorious light forever.

4

At Heaven's Gate

I had been dropped off by angels at heaven's gate. If you picture yourself in my shoes, being nervous or being afraid, don't worry! Your experience will be the exact opposite. I felt fearless and full of wonder. I experienced no nervousness, even though I had been dropped, literally, into another kingdom. If anything, I was totally serene and calm, more peaceful and at ease than I had ever been on my most relaxed day on earth.

Immediately, I saw an enormous door, several stories tall, attached to the gate, and a wall that wrapped around the kingdom in either direction, with no end in sight. It was the biggest door I had ever seen, not to mention the biggest wall and the biggest gate, and so forth.

The wood grain of the doorway was darker than an oak or an ash. If I could compare it to any wood on earth, I would say it was most like a rich mahogany. A plain design was carved on it, nothing fancy, but beautiful just the same, the way simply carved wood can be. Brilliant lights bounced and danced all over the length and width of the doorway. Would I consider it to be pearly? If I had a dollar for every time someone asked me that, I'd buy myself a new golf club.

Well, no, actually, the gate wasn't pearly, but save that thought and we'll explore it later.

There was no top to the door, at least none that I could see. It seemed to ascend twenty or thirty feet upward into a cloud of mist and then vanish.

How did I know it was a door and not a wall? Another good question. For one thing, I found that many times I just knew things in heaven without being told, and I'm sure everyone else who has ever gone to that place feels the same way. There was no tour guide, pointing out the highlights and hot spots or offering trivia about the sights and sounds. There was no angel parked in the front, with a big "Ask Me" button pinned to his robes like we were at some kind of banker's convention in the sky. You just know what you know when you're there, and I knew this was a doorway.

Besides, a section of this massive doorway had a handle, an old wooden handle like something you'd find on a covered wagon. It was sturdy looking, about two and a half feet long and six inches wide.

Heavenly Travelers

There were probably thirty-five people ahead of me in one big line (it wasn't as if there were angels or heavenly gatekeepers, calling, "I'm open on line five!"—the gate wasn't some version of the DMV). I knew without being told that I was in heaven, and so did everyone else. You just knew where you were. No one was asking their neighbor, "Where am I? Am I lost?"

You could tell by the looks on their faces they knew where they were. Everyone was smiling. No one looked shocked or even awed. They all had a look of deep, thorough contentment. Maybe that's why no one said anything to anyone else. We were all in a reverie of peace, joy, and perfect happiness.

The smiles on everyone's faces seemed to say, "We made it! We finally, finally made it!" We were home at last, and we all knew it.

Now, Byron Center, Michigan, is as about as homogenous as any town can be, unfortunately. I say unfortunately because I enjoy the richness of a diverse culture. I love to travel and learn about other countries, peoples, and their foods and traditions. In Byron Center, everyone is the same shade of pale. I am one of countless Dutch men of a certain age and maturity. To be honest, you can't throw a golf ball around here without hitting a Dutch senior citizen in the head.

Heaven was so different. Even the short line of about three dozen folks was a melting pot of colors, cultures, and costumes. I was wearing my normal "uniform," a golf shirt and khaki pants, the exact kind of outfit I would wear in my everyday life. The smiling people who stood in that line were from all over the world and wore all kinds of different clothing. I saw many different nationalities represented, including Scandinavian, Asian, African, and Middle Eastern. How did I know those people were Scandinavian? (I knew you'd ask.) They looked purely Northern European to me, with classic Scandinavian cheekbones and jawlines. But to be honest, that was one of those things I just knew.

A couple of the people I saw appeared to hail from primitive African tribes; they were wearing loose, flowing tribal gowns and toga-like garb with sandals on their feet.

The man in front of me in line was Middle Eastern look-ing. Several years later, on a trip to Turkey, my feeling that my fellow traveler to heaven's gate was from that area of the world was confirmed. This man was in his early sixties or maybe his late fifties. He wore a baggy, brown-colored caftan that looked like he had been sleeping in the dirt. Maybe he was a shepherd, or a subsistence farmer of some kind; he was definitely dressed like an ancient peasant, not a modern Middle Eastern person on the streets of Istanbul. His pants were slouchy and loose too, and he wore some kind of a headpiece or hat on his head.

Most of the people in line were around my age or older, which is the way things should be. Believe it or not, some were even much older than me. Most of the men in line were between fifty and seventy years of age, and most of the women were between seventy and ninety years of age.

There were three children in line, each of them around four or five years of age. These little ones were not standing still, but moving around, wiggling in their spots in line, like children do. They all had big smiles on their faces.

It's terribly sad, I know, to think about children dying, and of course these precious kids had died or they wouldn't have been in that line. Their loved ones were experiencing the heartrending loss of a child—perhaps the worst and deepest loss anyone can ever experience. I wish I didn't know how awful that is, but I do. So what I'm about to tell you is said from a heart that has felt the wretched loss of a child. I don't share this piece lightly. But I promise you, dear one, those children were delighted to be in that place. Their eyes were shining with life and pleasure, just like everyone else waiting for their turn through the huge doorway.

The Mystery of the Indian Baby

Very soon I would see many, many babies in heaven, just beyond the gate, but while I was in line I noticed just one baby. He was of Indian heritage, and was as tiny as a baby would be on his first day of life.

This baby, or rather the people surrounding him, was and continues to be somewhat of a mystery to me. You see, a man who appeared to be around fifty years old was holding the baby, but I got the impression he wasn't the baby's father. Actually, I felt a strong intuition that he was carrying the tiny boy for another person in line, a young woman standing in front of him. All three of them were Indian, but besides that, they seemed to know one another. The young woman, a beautiful girl of about twenty-five or so, was standing very close to the man and the baby, and every time I glanced at her, she was turned around, standing backward in line, and holding intense eye contact with the baby, as if she didn't want to tear her eyes away from him for one second.

The mystery is twofold. As I said, I didn't get the feeling at all that the man was the baby's father. He didn't look fatherly at all; in fact, he didn't appear to be comfortable holding the baby. In some cultures, men rarely hold babies, even their own, but beyond that, I just felt instinctively he wasn't related to the baby, or at least he wasn't the baby's father.

For one thing, the man was holding the little one gingerly instead of tenderly, as if he was afraid to drop it. So who was this man in relation to the baby and the young woman, who I felt sure was his mother? It seemed that the three of them had died together, but I suppose it's possible they died separately. Others who have heard my story have had theories, that maybe the man was the girl's father and the baby's grandfather. Or maybe the man was their cab driver, and they had all died in the same accident. I just don't know. But I did feel as if the girl had just given birth to the baby.

The second part of the mystery was why this young lady had needed someone else to hold her baby for her. One's frailties, illnesses, and vulnerabilities end the split second one's feet touch down on the holy ground of heaven, so even if she was recovering from a difficult labor, she would have been strong and healthy the moment she died. Yet I felt in my spirit that she had just given birth and was unable for whatever reason to hold her baby.

I know for sure I had a renewed body there. I felt so good. I was in terrible pain when I lay in my hospital bed in Ann Arbor: I was as weak and uncomfortable as I ever want to be. In line at the gate, I felt no weakness. Actually, I felt like a teenager again, vital, very awake and alert, strong and as healthy as a horse. Marv Besteman was restored, completely. I was better than ever, truth be told, better than when I was a strong, young buck, playing hockey for a short time for the University of Michigan.

Seriously, it was incredible, how fantastic I felt! When God tells us he's going to renew and revive our bodies, he means it. Even later on, when I saw so many people worshiping God beyond the gate, I didn't see anybody there with crutches, damaged bodies, missing arms or legs. I didn't see anyone who had Down syndrome, or any kind of special needs whatsoever. When you get there, you're going to feel like a million bucks!

This truth makes the fact of the young lady needing someone else to hold her baby hard to understand. Still, God knows exactly what was going on in that line and the circumstances of each beloved child of his, waiting for their turn through that immense doorway. He knows, and he'll let me know when I go back next time.

At any rate, I was pretty preoccupied by my surroundings as I stood in line. Besides the music being sung and played (which was the most purely lovely sound I had ever heard in my life), there was the greatest laser light show I had ever seen in my life going on in the great bowl of blue above me.

The magnitude of the sky and my surroundings! I couldn't take it all in. The colors were sumptuous and profoundly beautiful, and the lights? They were like 10,000 silent fireworks, all going off at the same time. There was so much movement and variety to the lights—I was in a state of wonder, from the time I set foot in heaven to the time I entered the doorway with Peter.

As you can imagine, I wasn't paying close attention to the people in line. Most of the time, I was looking around, trying to take in the marvelous sights of this amazing place.

When I checked back in to look at the people ahead of me, I realized the young Indian woman who had been staring so intently at the baby was at the front of the line, waiting her turn to go in. The three of them had been about four or five people ahead of me. The man who had been holding her baby stood behind her, and I noticed with surprise then that the baby was gone. He had evidently gone in first. How did he get in? I don't know—I wasn't looking! Logically, I would suppose the older man handed the baby to Peter, but I don't really know what happened.

81

And then again, I had a feeling, confirmed later on when I saw so many babies beyond the gate, that no one had to hold the baby; he could have floated in all by himself. Yes, really. What was it Dorothy said to her dog in *The Wizard of Oz*? "Toto, I've a feeling we're not in Kansas anymore." I and the other thirty-five people in line were in a different world, and the rules of gravity and what people were supposed to be able to do at a certain age just flew out the window, right around the time we lost traction with God's green earth. The baby's mother was next to go in the doorway, followed by the older man.

The line moved quickly. But even if it hadn't, people weren't rolling their eyes and tapping their watches impatiently, saying, "Let's get a move on. My tee time's in twenty minutes." Like me, the others were captivated with every detail of their new world, totally engaged, fascinated, and at ease.

The durations of time between when the giant door opened and closed varied, but the people ahead of me didn't take long. It took thirty seconds to one minute between when one person went in the door and it opened again to receive another newcomer. (I took the most time with the gatekeeper, by far, because I was a special case. But I'll tell you more about that conversation a bit later.) As I made my way through the line, the gate got closer and closer. Soon, I would be first in line to enter heaven.

The Pearly Gates?

The gates of heaven have captivated people's imaginations since the early church, when believers read about John's vision on scrolls, ancient to us but new to them. Through the centuries, the gates have served as the subject of countless discussions, and later on, books, movies, songs, and even jokes. Again, it amazes me how many folks, even believers, wonder whether they'll get past the "pearly gates" and gain admission into heaven. What do the gates look like? Who is the gatekeeper? Is it Peter? And who is allowed through those majestic doors?

I can only report on what I saw, and whom I saw while I was there. As always, the best place to find the answers is in the Bible.

John wrote about the gates after experiencing a vision of heaven while he was imprisoned on Patmos, a Greek island. Bible scholars tell us he had this vision around AD 96, over half a century after his best friend and Savior was crucified and rose from the dead. The written record of his supernatural tour, along with fifteen other visions, makes up the thrilling book of Revelation. Isn't it interesting that this last book of Scripture leaves us with a preview of our future home? We were made for heaven, and John's vision, or "revelation," gives us all a mental picture on which to hang our hopes.

The first details we have of the gates of heaven are spoken in John's own words, and are found near the end of the book at Revelation 21:10–14:

> He took me away in the Spirit to an enormous, high mountain and showed me Holy Jerusalem descending out of Heaven from God, resplendent in the bright glory of God.
>
> The City shimmered like a precious gem, light-filled, pulsing light. She had a wall majestic and high with twelve

gates. At each gate stood an Angel, and on the gates were inscribed the names of the Twelve Tribes of the sons of Israel: three gates on the east, three gates on the north, three gates on the south, three gates on the west. (Message)

I believe I was at one of these gates, one of three in one wall of a four-sided, cube-shaped fortification surrounding that beaming city called the heavenly Jerusalem.

John saw four walls and twelve gates, but I have no idea which one I was at, or which direction we were facing. If "my" gate was inscribed with the name of Dan, Reuben, Levi, or one of the other tribes, I didn't recognize the markings as such.

Plus, this passage says each gate will be attended by an angel, and I saw Peter, not an angel.

And the gates I saw were not pearly. That's right—not pearly!

Now, where does that belief come from, that heaven's gate is "pearly"? Is it just some kind of folktale or story, passed down through the ages? Actually, the Bible offers real evidence for that concept, found in Revelation 21:21, in which the gates are actual huge pearls that cover the twelve entrances to the city: "And the twelve gates were twelve pearls; each one of the gates was a single pearl" (NASB).

As I tell you my story, there will be a few times where I just can't explain what I saw. This is one of those times. Other heavenly travelers have seen pieces of the gate that they have described as pearly; I believe them. I also believe I was given a different vision, an image of heaven that included a gate made of heavy, dark wood and covered in twinkling lights. I'm at peace with that, and I hope you will

84

be too. Rather than try to be as smart as God, we should just quit while we're ahead.

A final note on this matter: my trusted spiritual advisors have prayed with me and for me as I've come to terms with my time in heaven, and they have suggested that perhaps the gates will indeed be enormous pearls when the New Heaven and the New Earth come to be, in God's timing and plan. After all, I was given a hint of the Intermediate Heaven, the place believers go now when they die. It's a different place from the New Heaven and New Earth we will inhabit after Christ's return. That's a very important distinction to make, so please take note.

My spiritual advisors could be right, or maybe it's another answer altogether. Pearly or not, I'm so grateful I had the chance to stand in the shadow of that marvelous gate!

Was Anyone Turned Away?

When I share my heaven experience with people, I always get the same question: "Did you see anyone turned away at the gate? Did anyone ever come back out the same way they went in?" And the answer is no. No one ever came back once they were inside the doorway.

Why is this question such a burning issue for people? I think many folks, even believers, struggle with feeling 100 percent secure in where they will spend the afterlife. They suffer from uncertainty, and secretly wonder, *Is it possible that I might be turned away?* They wonder too about their loved ones who have gone before them. Maybe those loved ones were not vocal in their faith or were not living their lives according to God's will for them before they died.

People I have spoken to wonder if maybe they can work harder to get into heaven. I always say, accept Christ first, that's the key. Folks always seem to want to put the cart before the horse.

You would be amazed at the questions I have been asked, and the fears people harbor, deep in their hearts.

In my mind, every person there was meant to be there. By the time I got to the door, there were fifty or sixty people behind me. We were, all of us, God's children, followers of his Son, destined for the kingdom of heaven. Everyone in front of me was quickly admitted to the presence of God, his Son, the angels, their loved ones, and all of the saints gathered there together.

I was at the top of the line, next to go inside that door of doors. And then abruptly the door swung open, and I was face-to-face with my best-loved person from the Bible, apart from Jesus, the apostle Peter.

5

Hello, Marv,
My Name Is Peter

When the man opened the door, he stuck out his hand, eyes lit up in friendly welcome. "Hello, Marv, my name is Peter. Welcome to heaven."

The man who stood before me, holding the door of heaven open, was the apostle Peter himself, the "rock" on which Christ built his church, and Jesus's dear friend.

I must admit—I gaped at him. How could I not? He had always been someone I admired and related to in the Bible, and here he was thrusting out a hand for me to shake.

Maybe I was too distracted by all the sights and sounds while I was in line at the gate, but I didn't put together who he was before he introduced himself.

That's when the lightning bolt hit me. *Peter!* I thought, *Oh my goodness! It just doesn't get any better than this.* (Actually, it did get better, because that's heaven. Just when you think you've never been happier, somehow you have another experience that tops the one before.)

Peter had a strong, confident handshake, and the look in his eyes was warm and open. Even though he was one of Jesus's twelve disciples, and one of history's most famous and admired men, Peter was as humble and down-to-earth as the guy who mows your lawn, cuts your hair, or catches your fish. He really did seem just like a fisherman, with a scrubby beard, shaggy hair, and clothes that looked like he had been wearing them for 1,000 years of hauling in nets and gutting fish.

He wore a fabric belt knotted around his waist, and his robes were dark and grayish, made of a heavier material than the gauzy white fabric the angels' robes were made from. Not one bit fancy or "heavenly."

It was fascinating to me how Peter's clothes seemed to be real work clothes, genuine fishing garb, durable and warm, made for the cool winds on the sea. It's always colder on the water, and his robes seemed designed for that.

He wore sandals.

Peter stood about five feet ten inches tall, solid and husky, with broad shoulders and narrow hips. He was built like a wrestler, or maybe a bodybuilder who doesn't take lifting weights too seriously but nonetheless is quite bulked up. I got the feeling if you were to find yourself in a conflict with him, Peter would stand there like a rock and fight you head-on. He had the manner of one determined; I knew that this guy, as a fisherman, would fish his heart out even if the waves were ten feet high.

He had a rounder face, and his dark hair was straight, not curly or wavy, mostly gray, and hung down to his neck, but it wasn't too long (spoken like a clean-cut banker). *Here's another typical older guy who needs a haircut*, I thought.

Peter seemed to me to be about fifty-five years old, give or take a few years. His eyes were grayish with a blue tint—that surprised me a bit, since most Jewish men have brown eyes—and his nose fit his face, which is to say it was a pretty good-sized, strong, normal nose. Peter had a really nice smile, and thankfully, he was smiling at me.

Peter seemed pleased and happy to see me, and his manner was warm, personable, confident, and friendly, all the traits I looked for when I used to hire people—or not hire them, as the case could sometimes be.

When I ran a bank, I would interview people for the top positions, and I would look for people I could trust right off the bat. Peter spoke in a way that made you believe what he was saying was true.

When conducting interviews, I could talk to someone for five minutes, and there would be something off about the tone of their voice or the fidgety look in their eyes, their shifty mannerisms, and I wouldn't hire them, even if they paid me.

Over countless interviews, I was always looking for people who were confident and decisive, but not too aggressive, kind but not a pushover. We had all kinds of customers at the bank, including those who never smiled a day in their lives and would make your day miserable if they could. My job was often to find employees who could serve those kinds of customers. Peter would have been one of those guys I would have hired. I kept a lot of secrets over the years as a banker, and I could tell Peter would have made a trustworthy secret-keeper.

Wow—the one and only Peter, standing in front of me! Peter, the Rock, a friend, disciple, apostle, sinner, and saint. He was more than an inspiring figure in Scripture; to me, he was like a friend I knew well. Maybe a role model or mentor would be an even better description. Peter was just like me in some good ways and not-so-good ways. And now it seemed like we two determined, decisive men (not to mention two stubborn mules) could actually be real, face-to-face friends.

He stood a couple of feet away, a comfortable distance to have a conversation with someone. We made a little bit of small talk—don't ask me about what. Maybe I was too excited about meeting my Bible hero, but I honestly can't recall what we chatted about those first few moments. I am pretty sure it wasn't about the weather.

"I've got to tell you, Peter. You were always one of my favorites in the Bible," I said.

"Why is that?" he asked, curious and smiling slightly.

"Because you messed up about as many times as I did in my life," I answered.

Peter got a big, wide smile on his face and nodded his head, as if to say, *Uh huh, I know that's true!* The apostle and I understood one another perfectly.

Peter did blow it a bunch of times. He was a hothead, and he sometimes got his priorities messed up. At times, his judgment was flawed, just like the rest of us.

But he was a good, strong follower of Christ, someone who dropped his fishing nets to take up a life of risk and danger for his Master's sake.

This shaggy guy standing before me, wearing fishing clothes and nodding with an understanding gleam in his eyes—Peter helped change the world!

Who Was Peter?

I had always been intrigued by Peter's life as I knew it from the Bible, but after meeting him face-to-face, my interest in him got a lot stronger. Who was this gatekeeper to the kingdom of heaven? What was his life like?

The scruffy fisherman met Jesus through his brother Andrew. The two brothers came from the fishing village of Bethsaida, which means "place of nets" or "fishery." (That would be like me coming from a town called "Lots of Banks.") Day in and day out, they lugged their nets into old boats and tossed them out, hoping for a good haul of tilapia, the money catch of the Sea of Galilee. Today, tilapia is even nicknamed "St. Peter's Fish."

The brothers, who came, not surprisingly, from a fishing family, were living in Capernaum, a lakeside town at the northern end of Galilee, when Jesus called them to let their fishing nets fall and become his disciples, fishers of men.

The first thing Andrew did after meeting Jesus was run to find his brother, so Peter could meet this Messiah too.

And the first thing his Savior did was give Simon a new name: "Jesus looked at him and said, 'You are Simon son of John. You will be called Cephas' (which, when translated, is Peter)" (John 1:40–42).

Peter, of course, means "rock."

After they met and Jesus gave him his new name, Peter rarely left his Messiah's side, traveling with him in his ministry and quickly becoming the leader and spokesman of the twelve disciples (of whom seven were fishermen).

Obviously, Peter was a grown man when Jesus chose him to be one of his closest disciples, which means he was probably born around the end of the first century BC.

He was also a married man, according to Mark 1:30, the account of Jesus healing Peter's mother-in-law.

I wonder . . . before Jesus healed Peter's mother-in-law later on, what did Peter's wife think about her husband suddenly quitting his job, and the only means of income they likely had known, and following some renegade prophet? I wish I had been a fly on the wall the day Peter came home and made that announcement!

We know he lacked any formal education, as did John, also one of the "inner three" group closest to Jesus. Acts 4:13 says this: "When they saw the courage of Peter and John and realized that they were *unschooled, ordinary men*, they were astonished and they took note that these men had been with Jesus."

Peter was a blue-collar guy in a blue-collar place: Palestine, the area considered by educated Jewish folks to belong to *Am harez*, or "the people of the land." This term is not as nice as it sounds. In their day, the term was used in a belittling way to describe those who were ignorant of the niceties and deeper values of Judaism and the Jewish way of life.

When Peter became a man, his home turf was very poor and terribly tense because it was occupied by the Romans. Can you imagine our country being occupied by anyone? It's hard to even wrap my mind around it. I bet you anything the people in Palestine were fed up with Rome, and they were looking for a way out from under that heavy oppression.

And then came Jesus, who saved Peter in a way he never expected and didn't always understand. He watched Jesus turn water into wine, transform a few fishes and loaves into a meal for a huge crowd, and even walk on water. He witnessed Jesus raising Jairus's daughter and Lazarus from the dead, and was even given a glimpse of his Master in his truest glory, in the transfiguration on Mount Tabor. There Peter saw his dear friend talk to Moses, Israel's greatest teacher, and Elijah, its greatest prophet, though they had been dead for a thousand years or more. There Peter saw Jesus shine as only God can shine:

> Jesus took Peter, James, and John and led them up a high mountain. His appearance changed from the inside out, right before their eyes. His clothes shimmered, glistening white, whiter than any bleach could make them. Elijah, along with Moses, came into view, in deep conversation with Jesus.
>
> Peter interrupted, "Rabbi, this is a great moment! Let's build three memorials—one for you, one for Moses, one for Elijah." He blurted this out without thinking, stunned as they all were by what they were seeing.
>
> Just then a light-radiant cloud enveloped them, and from deep in the cloud, a voice: "This is my Son, marked by my love. Listen to him."
>
> The next minute the disciples were looking around, rubbing their eyes, seeing nothing but Jesus, only Jesus. (Mark 9:2–8 Message)

During my time in heaven, I received a small peek at how God shines, and I know I will never be the same.

Yet, Peter, who witnessed his dear friend's transfiguration, still kind of blew it, interrupting the holiest of moments by blurting out his idea of a memorial! And he managed to make his gravest mistakes *after* seeing all of these wondrous things with his own eyes. The Rock became a stumbling block, more in his own way than anyone else's, an example for the ages of how darn human we all are.

I cringe at the story of how Peter betrayed Jesus, just when he needed him most—it's so hard to read—but I also see my own flawed heart in it:

> All this time, Peter was sitting out in the courtyard. One servant girl came up to him and said, "You were with Jesus the Galilean."
>
> In front of everybody there, he denied it. "I don't know what you're talking about."
>
> As he moved over toward the gate, someone else said to the people there, "This man was with Jesus the Nazarene."
>
> Again he denied it, salting his denial with an oath: "I swear, I never laid eyes on the man."
>
> Shortly after that, some bystanders approached Peter. "You've got to be one of them. Your accent gives you away."
>
> Then he got really nervous and swore. "I don't know the man!"
>
> Just then a rooster crowed. Peter remembered what Jesus had said: "Before the rooster crows, you will deny me three times." He went out and cried and cried and cried. (Matt. 26:69–75 Message)

But Jesus always saw in him the man of rock he would become after this experience of messing up so badly. Kind of like how Jesus saw in me the decent and loving husband and father he knew I could be, even though I wasn't always decent and loving.

In my younger days, I drank too much and didn't take my faith seriously even though I knew better. Peter thought he could do everything, just like I used to think. We all realize at some point we are not as good as we think we are. We disobey. We fail those we love.

I made a lot of mistakes in college, when I really didn't apply myself the way I should have, not to my studies or my growth as a believer. It wasn't until I was married and in the Army that I realized God's way was the right way and my way was the wrong way. And then I began to build my life, step by step, on the rock of my salvation.

Jesus knew Peter felt horrible remorse over disowning him in that courtyard, so after his resurrection, he appeared to him first, before any of the other disciples. Peter, who had failed so badly, became the leader of the newborn church, as Jesus had predicted, and the very first to preach the Gospel. Jesus gave Peter a wonderful gift, entrusting his first followers under Peter's care.

The fisherman spent the rest of his life, after Jesus died and rose again, telling others the Good News. After a lifetime of serving his Lord as a missionary, teacher, and evangelist, brave, stubborn Peter died a cruel death for his faith. Tradition tells us that Peter was crucified upside down in Rome during Emperor Nero's terrible persecution, which began in AD 64, the same persecution Peter warned the early believers about in his first letter. They needed that letter so badly. According to historians, many Christians died heinous deaths, being torn to pieces by dogs, burned alive, or nailed to crosses like Peter.

Peter's message to them was one of comfort and hope, full of encouragement to stand firm in Christ, like he did, to the end. Jesus's faith in him was not misplaced—after all, Peter really proved to be a rock.

A couple of years after my heaven experience, Ruth and I journeyed to some of the Bible lands, including Rome, the place from which Peter wrote his letter of warning and comfort to the first Christians, and the city in which he likely died.

As I stood quietly at St. Peter's tomb, under St. Peter's Basilica in Vatican City, I wondered to myself about the man who greeted me so warmly in heaven. Was that earthy fisherman with the firm handshake really buried here, under this shrine of marble and gold? Many pieces of archaeological evidence suggested he was.

But I knew better. I knew where Peter really was. He was in that beautiful, beautiful place where I met him all too briefly, in the service of his Lord and King, perfectly fulfilled and content forever.

And I bet that whenever Peter got the chance, he hopped in a boat and sailed on the shiny waters of the sea I saw, just beyond the gate.

Wait a minute, old man . . . what sea are you talking about? This is the first we've heard of it.

Hang on there, friend. We'll get to heaven's sea in a minute. But first, let's talk about keys, specifically, who holds the keys to the kingdom of heaven?

Peter, Demystified

Who had the man really been who greeted me at heaven's door, beyond a well-known Bible character, canonized saint, and, oddly enough, the setup to countless jokes? ("A rabbi and a priest die and show up at the pearly gates, where they are met by St. Peter . . .") You know what I'm talking about. We've all heard these jokes and maybe even told them.

Here's a good one, for the sake of example, plus it's funny:

As a young man, Norton was an exceptional golfer. At the age of twenty-six, however, he decided to become a priest, and joined a rather peculiar order. He took the usual vows of poverty and chastity, but his order also required that he quit golf and never play again. This was particularly difficult for Norton, but he agreed and was finally ordained a priest.

One Sunday morning, the Reverend Father Norton woke up and realizing it was an exceptionally beautiful and sunny early spring day, decided he just had to play golf.

So . . . he told the associate pastor that he was feeling sick and convinced him to say Mass for him that day.

As soon as the associate pastor left the room, Father Norton headed out of town to a golf course about forty miles away. This way he knew he wouldn't accidentally meet anyone he knew from his parish.

Setting up on the first tee, he was alone. After all, it was Sunday morning and everyone else was in church!

At about this time, Saint Peter leaned over to the Lord while looking down from the heavens and exclaimed, "You're not going to let him get away with this, are you?"

The Lord sighed, and said, "No, I guess not."

Just then Father Norton hit the ball and it shot straight towards the pin, dropping just short of it, rolled up and fell into the hole. It was a 420-yard hole in one!

St. Peter was astonished. He looked at the Lord and asked, "Why did you let him do that?"

The Lord smiled and replied, "Who is he going to tell?"

Now, there's a joke that hits a nerve with me, a golfer from a faith tradition that can sometimes make a big deal out of what its people do on Sunday!

But seriously, Peter's legacy goes miles beyond the punch lines. How, for example, did he become a fixture in those pearly gate jokes in the first place?

We know that, over the years, a version of "St. Peter" has become a standard character in jokes, cartoons, comedies, dramas, and plays—all kinds of storytelling. This "character" almost always plays upon Peter's role as the "keeper of the keys" of heaven, as told in Matthew 16:13–19:

> When Jesus arrived in the villages of Caesarea Philippi, he asked his disciples, "What are people saying about who the Son of Man is?"
>
> They replied, "Some think he is John the Baptizer, some say Elijah, some Jeremiah or one of the other prophets."
>
> He pressed them, "And how about you? Who do you say I am?"
>
> Simon Peter said, "You're the Christ, the Messiah, the Son of the living God."
>
> Jesus came back, "God bless you, Simon, son of Jonah! You didn't get that answer out of books or from teachers. My Father in heaven, God himself, let you in on this secret of who I really am. And now I'm going to tell you who you are, really are. You are Peter, a rock. This is the rock on which I will put together my church, a church so expansive with energy that not even the gates of hell will be able to keep it out.
>
> "And that's not all. You will have complete and free access to God's kingdom, keys to open any and every door: no more barriers between heaven and earth, earth and heaven." (Message)

That's it—the verse on which all of the stories and folklore about Peter at the gate is based. That's why Peter has come to be depicted as an old, bearded guy who sits at the pearly gates, acting as a sort of hotel front-desk clerk who personally interviews entrants into heaven.

This view of Peter has been perpetuated through history, from Medieval artwork, where Peter is painted as a bald man with a long beard (usually there are keys in the paintings too, dangling from Peter's hands or attached to his belt), to the 2004 movie *Millions*, where St. Peter appears to the main character, a young boy, and refers to himself as the "patron saint of keys, locks, and general security."

I definitely didn't see any keys on Peter, and he sure wasn't bald like I am. He had all his share of hair and then some. He wasn't sitting behind a desk and he didn't toss off a one-liner, although he did seem like a man with a sense of humor.

Some people who have heard my story have been surprised to hear that Peter greeted me, because most Bible scholars agree that Jesus wasn't actually referring to Peter as the gatekeeper of heaven. Rather, he was beginning to prepare his beloved disciples for the suffering that would soon come, and reaffirming their authority as his disciples. What Jesus meant, theologians suggest, was that anything done by Peter, or any of the disciples, in accordance with his will would have permanent power and validity, now and forever.

All I can tell you is what I saw and what I experienced, which was encountering Peter himself at the gates of heaven. In some ways, my encounter actually lines up with the theory that Peter acts as the front door man for heaven, or at least for the gate I went to. However, he seemed to me to be more of the designated greeter for that gate and

101

for that day. He certainly wasn't sitting at a desk with a sign on it: "Saint Peter: Admissions Desk. Ring the bell if no one is here."

For sure, it's not up to Peter who gets in and who doesn't, no matter how many jokes and stories suggest it is. I've said it before and I'll say it again: If you make it that far, you're going to make it all the way into heaven. God and only God decides who and where, if and when.

Peter's purpose was to greet me and make me feel welcome, and to check in the Book of Life to see if my name was in there *for that day*. Maybe God chose Peter for this mission—helping me figure out what was going on during my time in heaven—because he knew how much I had always liked him. It's also likely that God knew we were evenly matched in the obstinate department, and Peter could handle this dogged Dutchman, especially when it came time to deliver bad news. Because when he opened the Book of Life for April 27 or 28, 2006, the name Marv Besteman was nowhere to be found.

6

The Book of Life

W hen I got inside the massive doorway into heaven, there was an area I can best describe as an inner gate. It was like the ones we read about in Scripture, like the ancient gates that still exist in some parts of the world that have been inhabited for many centuries.

As my eyes swept from the left to the right, I saw a long stone shelf that extended about ten to twelve feet in either direction before sort of fading away in a kind of haze or mist. Piled on top of this shelf or table made of stones were books upon books upon books, stacked up three to four books high, all along the surface both left and right.

The stones were rugged and simple. They weren't fancy in any way; rather, they were roughly cut and completely unpolished. It was almost like they fell off the side of a hill and someone said, "Leave them there." I'm quite sure this bench of rocks was, well, rock solid, immovable, able to bear tons of weight. Yet it had a look of loose stones piled one on top of the other, natural and of-the-earth.

In fact, when Ruth and I took a cruise to Turkey, Greece,

and Italy, the kind of gray ash stone we saw all over the Bible lands reminded me of the stones in heaven.

If you've ever been to that beautiful area of the world, you know exactly what I mean. When we traveled there in 2009, I was struck by how rocky and uneven the paths are. When you walk, you have to watch every step—it's so bumpy. On a day trip to Ephesus, the place where Paul sent the book of Ephesians, I stumbled once and fell flat on my face. I thought I had broken my nose.

Not that I'm complaining, because as earthly trips go, this one was wonderful (though we did almost lose Ruth in the Vatican, but that's a story for another day).

On the trip, I kept thinking about the letters delivered to the Romans, the Thessalonians, the Ephesians, etc.—letters written by the apostle Paul, transported by faithful servants, and then read in those very places in which I was walking. Were the letters read aloud to lots of people in coliseums? Or passed from believer to believer? Being in the Bible lands was so inspiring, in more ways than one.

I must confess, I couldn't help but notice Greece had the most beautiful women I had ever seen. Ruth had to hold me back a little bit. I may have been seventy-five, bald, and falling on my face, but I wasn't blind!

Back to heaven and the shelf in that inner sanctum, made of those coarse, jagged stones I saw all over the place in the Bible lands. The shelf was about three feet high, about up to my waist. The books stacked on top of it were about as thick as the Grand Rapids phone book, about two and a half inches. They were bound in what appeared to be ancient black cowhide, worn and antiqued, yet not falling apart at the seams. Like the stones, the books had the patina of ancient days, yet I knew somehow they were stronger and longer-wearing than any books on earth.

It never clicked that these books were the Book of Life, or as I discovered, really, the *Books* of Life, until Peter turned away from me and looked in a specific volume, searching for my name. Then I realized what these books must be, and what their glorious contents were all about.

Peter didn't look through more than one book, nor did he riffle through the pages of the book he opened. He seemed to open it up at the right spot. He knew exactly where to look for my name.

When he opened up the Book, it was as long and wide as an atlas, about ten inches wide by twelve inches long. When Peter turned to look in the Book, he was about three feet away from me. I can't tell you what language the book was written in, whether it was English, Aramaic, or some celestial language only written and read in heaven. I didn't notice that, or the texture of the pages, or how fine the print was, or how small the font.

Why didn't I notice these things? Well, I was a little distracted, let's put it that way. The sights of heaven could hold your attention more than, say, a stunning hockey goal shot from the blue line, or an accident on the highway, or even the lovely ladies of Greece. I had a hard time focusing on the incredible thing happening three feet in front of me—one of Jesus's disciples was looking me up in the Book of Life!—because just beyond that great man and those superb books was a whole new world, the world of heaven itself.

The Greatest and Biggest Roll Call of All Time

Before I saw it with my own two eyes, I thought the Book of Life was like a giant, small-print encyclopedia, like the ones I used to page through as a kid, looking up stuff about constellations and tree frogs and Burma. In my mind, the Book of Life was filled with names, millions and millions of names recorded with care, identifying those who are saved by grace.

I had always been a student of Scripture, studying God's Word for my own spiritual nourishment as well as in my roles over the years as an elder at the churches we attended. But after going to heaven, and seeing some of the things God talks about in his Holy Writ, I wanted to take a closer look at what the Bible says about what I saw, including the Book of Life.

The Book of Life: A Deeper Look

The Book of Life is sacred to Christians as the great registry of those who will be joining the Father, his Son, and his Holy Spirit forever and ever in that perfect place. Christians are not the only ones who consider this book to be holy; it's also a revered teaching in Judaism. In the Jewish faith, the Book of Life is called *Sefer HaChaim* in Hebrew, and is considered to be the book in which God records the name of every person who is destined for heaven.

The New Testament mentions the "book of life" eight times, and seven of those occur in the book of Revelation, in John's vision of heaven. The other reference appears in Philippians 4:1–3, Paul's closing call for faithfulness, loyalty, and unity among the church members in Philippi:

> Therefore, my brothers and sisters, you whom I love and long for, my joy and crown, stand firm in the Lord in this

way, dear friends! I plead with Euodia and I plead with Syntyche to be of the same mind in the Lord. Yes, and I ask you, my true companion, help these women since they have contended at my side in the cause of the gospel, along with Clement and the rest of my co-workers, *whose names are in the book of life.*

Apparently, two women in the church, Euodia and Syntyche, were not getting along very well, as happens with everyone from time to time. But Paul refers to them anyway as co-workers in the cause of the gospel, as those who labored alongside him in his ministry, and servants whose names are written in the Book of Life. To me, this classifies the Book of Life as a record of the names of those who have eternal salvation.

Revelation

The other New Testament references to the Book of Life appear in Revelation, specifically in the apostle John's vision of heaven. The first of the seven mentioned appears in a passage about the great white throne judgment:

> Then I saw a great white throne and him who was seated on it. The earth and the heavens fled from his presence, and there was no place for them. And I saw the dead, great and small, standing before the throne, and *books were opened. Another book was opened, which is the book of life.* The dead were judged according to what they had done as recorded in the books. (20:11–12)

Theologians tell us that the great white throne judgment described here is a judgment for unbelievers. Many Bible teachers believe that no one at that specific judgment has his or her name written in the Book of Life. What that means for sure, I don't know. I wish I did.

Only the one who wrote those names in those books really knows. I do know that Scripture is clear that no true believer should doubt his eternal security in Christ.

I love what Jesus says about this in John's Gospel:

> My sheep recognize my voice. I know them, and they follow me. I give them real and eternal life. They are protected from the Destroyer for good. No one can steal them from out of my hand. The Father who put them under my care is so much greater than the Destroyer and Thief. No one could ever get them away from him. I and the Father are one heart and mind. (John 10:28–30 Message)

"No one can steal them from my hand. . . . No one could ever get them away from him." That comforts me deeply, and I hope it comforts you as well. Many believers spend way too much time worrying that they won't go to heaven when they die, that their names are not written in those ageless books I saw.

I wish everyone could have the same kind of preview of heaven I had, that each person saved by grace would feel safe and sure that their names are written in the Books. To me, the Bible is very straightforward on this matter, but not everyone interprets certain verses the same way. Some people point to Revelation 3:5 and their definition of "victorious" as "proof" that a person can lose his or her salvation:

> The one who is victorious will, like them, be dressed in white. I will never blot out the name of that person from

the book of life, but will acknowledge that name before my Father and his angels.

To me, the promise of Revelation 3:5 is obviously that the Lord will never erase a name: "I will never blot out the name of that person." A "victorious" person is not someone who wins every battle against sin; if that were so, the Book of Life would be filled with blank pages. Rather, I firmly believe that this person referred to here is God's precious child, who, through Christ, is ultimately triumphant over the temptations, trials, and evils of this world—in other words, one who is redeemed, safe, written in God's roll call and destined to spend forever with him there.

I like the way *The Message* paraphrases this verse: "Conquerors will march in the victory parade, their names *indelible in the Book of Life*. I'll lead them up and present them by name to my Father and his Angels."

If you love him and have chosen him, you will be one of those conquerors, dressed in white, marching in the victory parade. You will be led by Jesus, his face lit up with a parent's pride and joy, introduced by name to God the Father and his angels. Why? Because your name is indelible in the Book of Life! Yes, indelible—in other words, impossible to remove, etched, permanent, enduring forever.

God keeps good records. He knows his own, and he has set the names of his children for all time in his book.

God's Muster Roll

The Book of Life has been referred to as "God's Muster Roll" by people trying to wrap their minds around this divine volume, framing it in a way that's understandable to our earthly brains. For those of you who don't know what a "muster roll" is, it has a military connotation as an inventory, a roster, or a register of the officers and men and women in a military unit or ship's company. Those searching for their ancestors who fought in the Civil War will be familiar with this idea; they would have to pour over hundreds and hundreds of dusty, brittle pages to find their relative's precious name.

How much more prized is your name and mine, written in the Book of Life! In the Old Testament, this book is also referred to as the roster in which all the people who are considered righteous before God are recorded for eternity.

The prophet Isaiah talks about God's holy remnant, his "branch," a reference to all believers, being logged or classified as holy children of God: "In that day the Branch of the LORD will be beautiful and glorious, and the fruit of the land will be the pride and glory of the survivors in Israel. Those who are left in Zion, who remain in Jerusalem, will be called holy, *all who are recorded* among the living in Jerusalem" (4:2–3).

The prophets Daniel and Malachi also prophesied in the Bible concerning the Book of Life. Daniel 12:1 promises that, in the endtimes, "your people—everyone whose name is found written in the book—will be delivered."

Malachi had a different name for the Book of Life; he called it "the scroll of remembrance." Writing about the remnant again, he wrote, "Then those who feared the LORD talked with each other, and the LORD listened and heard. A scroll of remembrance was written in his presence concerning those who feared the LORD and honored

112

his name" (3:16). Different translations call this the "book of remembrance."

This passage is significant for a reason other than the beautiful imagery of a "scroll of remembrance." It suggests that the Book of Life contains not only the names of those who will spend forever enjoying God's presence in heaven, but also the good things we have done in his name.

Peter didn't mention any of my good deeds, or bad ones, for that matter, when he searched for my name. He also didn't say anything about the tears I had shed in my lifetime, which the Bible says are also recorded in the Book of Life. "You've kept track of my every toss and turn through the sleepless nights," the psalmist writes in Psalm 56:8, "each tear entered in your ledger, each ache written in your book" (Message).

When the Roll Is Called Up Yonder

That day Peter was on a mission to look and see if my name was in the Book of Life, not for a week from then, or a year, or ten years, but for that day. Unlike the musty muster rolls of old-time military operations and wars, these record books weren't yellowed and easily torn. They have lasted eons and will last eons more. From the dawn of time, one of those durable books has had the name Marvin Besteman inscribed in it, for a certain day and time known only to the Record Keeper. For God's reasons, my name wasn't in the Book of Life for that day.

Remember the old hymn "When the Roll Is Called Up Yonder"? It's not sung so much anymore, though it probably should be. The lyrics express my heart so well: "When the saved of the earth shall gather over on the other shore, and the roll is called up yonder, I'll be there."

I took a peek at the "other shore," but it wasn't my time to have my name called. Next time I go, when that grand roll call is announced "up yonder," I'll be there. I'll definitely be there.

7

Inside the Inner Gate of Heaven

Peter looked in the Book of Life for no more than half a minute to forty seconds at the most. Naturally, it didn't take him long to discover that my name wasn't in that Book, for that day.

As I waited, I had the chance to look around me, in the place I think of as the inner gate, an open-air location between the outer gate and the crystalline passageway that led into heaven.

I stood on green, deluxe grass, the shade of which no earthbound person has ever seen. The space was open and almost empty. Other than the stone shelf I described, the one holding the Book of Life, there was no other furniture, not even a chair for Peter to sit in. Although, when you think about it, Peter probably didn't need a chair. He didn't need to rest even for one minute.

When I looked up, there was no ceiling to the inner gate. In front of me, just a few feet from where Peter was looking at the Book, a glasslike gate rose upward and disappeared into a mist, like the stone shelf did. Behind me, the dark wood gate also vanished in a swirl of filmy vapor.

Peter and the stone shelf were no more than two or three feet away from what I knew instinctively was the gate of heaven. Within moments I would be given a chance to see inside that gate and witness incredible things, but at the moment I was preoccupied with where I stood then and what I saw from there—a shining blue sea.

Lake Heaven

As I said, Peter was wearing the clothes of his day, loose robes tied with a fabric belt of some kind. In my mind, those were fishing clothes, and when I saw the lake or sea ahead, and the fishing boats, I had a sense that Peter could and would enjoy the water whenever he wanted to, though I didn't see a soul out there at the time.

About sixty yards away, in the middle left of the panorama before me, were some old fishing boats pulled up on the shore of a huge, rippling lake. The boats looked worn and aged, not sleek and razzy dazzy like the boats we see zooming around on Lake Michigan. If I saw a boat like the ones I saw in heaven here on earth, I'd think, "There's an old lugger."

There were just a few boats—I didn't count how many—and they lay on a sandy, rocky seashore. The blue of the lake was a darker, less brilliant blue than the shade of heaven's sky, and the surface had a few gentle waves. Like an ocean or one of the Great Lakes, I couldn't see the other side.

I only looked at the lake briefly, because soon Peter was back from checking the Book of Life.

A Hardheaded Hollander

I was in for quite a shock when Peter returned and broke my reverie.

"Marv," he said, looking slightly puzzled. "I can't find your name for today."

"For today." . . . What in the world did that mean? I'm sure my mouth dropped open.

I was instantly disappointed. *What's happening? I thought that once you made it this far, you were in, no turning back?* I was confused, but yet I never once thought that maybe I wasn't really saved.

I knew I was saved. There wasn't the tiniest doubt in my mind.

And Peter had emphasized the words "for today," which meant that I wasn't supposed to go all the way into heaven *that day*. There is, I know, another date God has in mind, known only to him.

Still, I hadn't processed any of this at that point. All I knew was that I did not want to go back in any way, shape, or form. *Nobody who has ever set foot in heaven would want to go back to earth, not even for a second.*

"I don't want to go back," I said. "Can you look again?" Peter obliged, returning to the volume of the Book of Life he had been looking at before. Once again, he couldn't find my name.

The bulldog in me came out as I began to argue with the founder of the worldwide church and one of the New Testament's dominant figures. I might have remembered that Peter did cut off a man's ear one time when he got mad. What can I say? It seemed like a good idea at the time. And I had nothing to lose.

"It's taken me all these years, a long time, to get this far, to heaven, and I'm not going back now," I said. "I'm a hardheaded Hollander. It takes me awhile to figure things out. I'm not going back. What can we do?"

Peter didn't say much, but he seemed to know I wasn't going to go back voluntarily—nobody ever would. "I think you're going to have to go back," he said.

He appeared to be thinking the situation through, and finally he spoke: "Okay, the only thing I can do is go talk to God."

I didn't argue with him this time. I actually felt relieved. If my strange circumstance was going to the top, to God himself, then the matter would surely be settled my way, right?

Later, when I was able to do lots of thinking about my heaven experience, I realized something. There are no mistakes in heaven, none whatsoever. Despite all the jokes out there about St. Peter and the gate, no one has ever been accidentally let in and then turned away due to a clerical error! So why couldn't Peter find my name?

I believe now it was all part of God's plan. God certainly wasn't puzzled or surprised by Peter's news that there was a man waiting at the gate whose name wasn't "on the list" for the day. He wanted me to see exactly what I saw, no more and no less. God put Peter in place strategically to be a welcomer and a guide. And there was no mistake whatsoever in what happened next, no slip-up on God's part in what he allowed me to see and experience after Peter left to go talk to him.

Peter turned and walked through the invisible gateway to heaven, and then vanished.

I got as close as I could to the gate, though I couldn't get through. No, I didn't get zapped, but there was some kind of invisible barrier preventing me from pushing through. There were so many things to take in just beyond where I was standing.

While Peter left to go talk to God, I stepped as close as I could to heaven's entranceway. The gate was as clear as glass, though it was a different texture and feel altogether than the glass of, say, sliding patio doors or windows in a home.

I estimate the height of the gate to be about seven feet tall. I'm 6'2", and shrinking fast; the gate was above my head but not so much taller that I couldn't reach my arms up to try to pull on the steel beams. Yes, steel beams, or at least some heavenly version of steel. These beams seemed to be embedded like a huge ribbon in the glassy surface of the gate, fixed within in a giant X shape.

The shape was nearly invisible too, but it had sort of a faint multicolored outline, with red being the most noticeable color. I pressed in close and stared, my eyes popping out of my head. As I looked out into this surreal and beautiful realm, I saw things I will never forget. I saw children and grown-ups of all ages, each one vibrantly healthy, whole, and contented as can be. I saw a multitude of babies, from the tiniest fetus as small as my little finger to bigger babies, toddlers who could jump and play. Was my son William, with his head of dark, thick hair, in this place? I knew he was, and with every fiber of my being I wanted to find him. And then I saw someone I recognized—two people, actually—a couple I had loved on earth and had lost many years before. I pushed and pulled on the gate, but it wouldn't budge.

The touch and feel of the surface was like no surface I had ever touched in my life. I raised my arms and pulled down on the ribbon of "steel." People have asked me if it felt like an iron bar, rounded, like a subway turnstile or a monkey bar. I have to say it didn't feel like that at all; rather, the surface of the ribbon was flat yet elevated, like a raised beam. I pulled down, and nothing happened. I put the full weight of both my arms on the crux of the X and pushed down. Nothing happened.

At some point, I gave up, knowing I couldn't get in. What I saw still brings tears to my eyes, at least once a day. Beyond the gate into heaven were marvelous sights, a vision of the other side, meant to bring wonder and comfort to me, and to you too.

The first marvels God wanted me to witness and tell you about were the multitude of precious babies.

8

Heaven's Cradle Roll

The first thing I saw when I looked out into the huge kingdom before my eyes were all the babies. The doorway had been left open in that middle space, the "inner gate," and I could see through it as if it were glass. You already know I couldn't go through that door, no matter how much I wanted to.

Believe me when I tell you there were millions of babies, from the tiniest unborn baby, about the size of my pinkie finger, to babies who were preterm to babies who were born full term, and every age on up from there.

I felt a physical jolt of shock at the sheer numbers of babies, babies upon babies upon babies, each one cherished and loved. They seemed to be grouped by age, from the earliest stages of development on up. The unborn little ones were all together, and then there was another group of babies who were newborns and very small infants.

Years ago, in many church nurseries, they had what was called a "Cradle Roll." There would be photos of babies born to church members, posted along the wall with the dates these babies were born. It was like a gallery of pride for these new lives growing in the church family. Seeing these babies, grouped by age, it seemed to me like heaven's version of a Cradle Roll.

On earth, there would be no way for the unborn babies to live outside their mothers' bodies, but yet here they were, alive and thriving. I knew these babes would grow and bloom here, perfectly safe, entirely happy, and wholly loved. The second their lives ended, by whatever sad circumstance, on this side, the babies arrived in a world more wonderful than any dreams their parents might have had for them. And if they were unwanted on earth, for any reason, those babies were wanted in heaven, highly valued and beloved.

Somehow, I knew all these things to be true without being told.

Seeing those babies in heaven later reminded me of an unusual museum exhibit we visited once, many years ago. Ruth and I had taken a trip to Toronto with my daughter Julie and her husband, Joe. Julie was pregnant with her first child, our first grandchild, and so we were all riveted by the exhibit about unborn babies being held at a local museum. The exhibit showed how babies develop, stage by stage, week by week.

Julie was completely enthralled, looking carefully until she found the one that would be the same size, in terms of fetal development, as hers was. Her son was being knit together, "fearfully and wonderfully," even at that moment! We all stared in total fascination. No blockbuster movie or playoff game could have held our attention more. We didn't know then if the baby was a boy or a girl. We didn't know then how much joy this child would bring us, or that he would grow up to be a fine young man, handsome, kind, and good, a skilled fighter pilot for the US Navy.

But we knew this: that at three weeks, before Julie knew she was pregnant, Andrew's heart had begun to beat with his own blood, and that at that time his backbone and spinal column had begun to form. At four weeks, he was already ten thousand times larger than the fertilized egg, and at five weeks, his eyes, legs, and hands were taking shape. I saw babies this small in heaven, and their arms and legs were moving. I knew beyond a shadow of a doubt that they were as happy and contented as could be.

Later, it made me think of all the pre-born lives that end on earth, lives that begin again in heaven. No matter how those lives ended, I knew without being told there was breath, hope, and life abundant there, even in the tiniest fetus.

When I thought about heaven's babies afterward, I thought of our other children, our four babies—one lost just after he was born and three others lost to miscarriage. Where were they? What did those babies look like now? If only I could get through the invisible doorway, I knew I could find each one of our lost dear ones.

I say "lost," because of course we lost them. They were gone, to another world beyond our reach. Time after time, when Ruth miscarried, we felt a loss that we would never forget.

Maybe that's why I understand how important it is to share with you how I saw those babies in heaven. I know if you've lost a baby, you can't ever forget that tiny boy or girl.

There was one baby who dominated my heart and thoughts, even in heaven. I never held him in my arms, but I loved him dearly, this small boy with my father's head of thick, dark hair.

Every year on Memorial Day, Ruth and I visit his miniature grave in a section of the cemetery called "Babyland."
When I think of that sweet bundle now, and the short-but-
cherished life he had, I am brought to tears despite the
many years it's been since I laid eyes on him.

As I stood there at the gate of heaven, taking in the sight
of millions of dear babies, I wanted so intensely to get beyond that impassable partition to the other side. I knew if I
could, I could hold my son in my arms for the very first time.

Baby Questions

When I speak to groups about my heaven experience, pretty
much every single time the dominant questions are about
the babies:

- What did the babies look like?
- Who was holding them?
- Who was taking care of them?
- Were the babies happy?

And on and on, people want to know every little detail
of what I saw in regard to those babies. So many people
I've met after my talks are thinking about their own little
ones, babies who were miscarried or maybe even aborted.

People tend to open up to an old man with a soft heart;
I've heard so many sad stories. It's been my honor to comfort wounded mothers and fathers like me, who also never
got to see their babies grow up.

I try to answer their questions as best I can, and leave
the rest of their healing up to God. Seeing those babies in

heaven feels like a sacred trust to me, one of the most holy and wondrous pieces of my experience.

The babies I saw in heaven were about thirty yards from me, but I could see them clearly and with quite a bit of detail. If you're wondering how I could see them so well, again, it's because I was in a different world, where the limitations of our sight on earth just don't exist.

I've had glasses for years, before and since my trip to heaven. I can't see a thing without them. But once I landed on the other side, my vision improved immeasurably. My eyesight was way beyond what it had been on earth at the peak of my youth and health. But then again, why should that be a surprise? My eyes, my ears, my brain, my body—everything was performing far above par. It's like I went from a broken down old jalopy to a sleek racecar with a high performance engine, and so did everyone else I saw there. By the way, I never spotted one person in heaven wearing glasses or hearing aids. Hallelujah—I didn't need my hearing aid up there, either!

The Baby Who Caught My Eye

The babies were thirty yards ahead of me, yet it was if I was holding them in my arms and gazing at them—that's how plainly I could see them.

Those precious ones were in all stages of development, from a minuscule fetus several weeks after conception to babies twenty to thirty weeks along in their development.

There were little ones with newly shaped eyelids, noses, and toes. Scientists and doctors tell us that even a seven-week-old fetus can kick and swim, and some of these small

129

ones were kicking their legs. We are told that by weeks eleven and twelve, most babies can grab for something with their hands, or even suck their thumbs. I saw babies that small waving their arms and hands, like babies do.

The smallest ones were grouped together. One baby caught my eye, and I knew that he had been aborted—it was one of those times in heaven that I was given a deeper knowledge beyond intuition and impression. This sweet, tiny person was about as big as my finger, and moving slightly. He looked a bit different somehow from the other babies; he was very small yet defined. I can't tell you exactly how old he was, but I would guess between seven and nine weeks. We are told that fetuses that age have every one of their organs in place by then, with miniature bones replacing cartilage, and fingerprints beginning to form. By the eighth week, the baby can begin to hear, and by the ninth week he can hiccup. "Fearfully and wonderfully made," indeed!

I don't know this baby's story, but I knew he was as happy and adored as all the other children in heaven.

Cherished and Nurtured Forever

There seemed to be a continuing graduation of ages and stages. Older babies, those who could walk and talk, were in another group. These older babies had their own special place in heaven, just beyond the littlest ones.

I got the sense the babies were very happy and contented. They seemed completely peaceful and satisfied, lacking in nothing, like a baby who has just had his bottle. I remember feeding my own children and grandchildren, and how they'd be fussy and unsettled before I gave them their bottle. After draining the good stuff to the last drop, they'd just lie there, well fed, cared for, relaxed, without a worry in the world. That's how these babies were in heaven.

One of the top questions folks ask me about the babies is, who was holding them? The answer is, nobody was holding them, because babies in heaven simply don't need to be held. *Well, that doesn't sound very nice,* you may be thinking to yourself. *Those babies were just lying there on the hard ground?*

I might have thought the same thing myself, had I not seen these comfortable tiny ones in heaven with my own eyes. And they really were as comfortable, happy, and fulfilled as any baby I have ever seen on this earth.

None of them wore diapers, although the older babies had some kind of simple clothing on, nothing elaborate. They just didn't have to be fed, burped, changed, or bathed like babies here do.

That's not to say that babies in heaven are never held. I bet they are held and often, because all things are wonderful and pleasing in that place, and what's more wonderful and pleasing than holding a baby?

I imagine the grass they were lying close to was softer than any blanket that ever swaddled a baby down here. I say lying "close to" because there was a layer of space between the babies and that green grass. You could almost say they were resting on air pillows—that's the best way I can describe the surface in which those babies were cradled. They were also cradled in the perfect love of God, wholly joyful and basking in the warmth of his light and presence. Even though there were so many babies, I sensed that the numbers didn't matter. Each one was cherished and nurtured, because there is no more nurturing place we can imagine than God's home. In heaven, there's more than enough love to go around.

William John Besteman

When we lost our little boy in 1960, some people said all the wrong things. They told us it was God's will that he died, or else that there was something wrong with the baby, so that losing him was really for the best.

If you've lost a child, you know these sugarcoated offerings of condolence are about as helpful as a kick in the head. Ruth and I were not comforted by these words. They are the last things we would ever say to someone reeling from the grief of losing a baby.

Right after we had Julie, we lost two babies in a row, within months of each other. Both of them were miscarried very early on, at the six-week mark. Still, they were significant losses.

Ruth had had a totally normal pregnancy with Julie, a textbook-perfect nine months of growing the life inside her. So we were quite unnerved and then overwhelmed by the string of miscarriages and tragedy that followed. When she got pregnant for the third time after Julie, she began spotting almost right away. But we weren't terribly worried, even when the doctor put Ruth on bed rest for the remainder of her pregnancy.

I was working at the bank by then, making peanuts, but that was okay. Back then we were happy to live on love and peanuts (or peanut butter and jelly sandwiches, which was the case). I was at work all day, which left Ruth trapped in her bed, trying to watch a lively toddler and keep her from demolishing the house.

We learned that bed rest doesn't really jive with a busy eighteen-month-old, who loved nothing more than to climb up the cupboards and drink salt—that kind of thing. Soon, relief workers were called in to help, and Julie spent most days with Ruth's mother or mine.

At the thirty-week mark of her pregnancy, Ruth suffered what is called a "placental abruption," a serious complication of later pregnancy; apparently the lining of her placenta had separated from her uterus. She was pale, bleeding, and in lots of pain. Lying in our bed and keeping still was no longer an option, and Ruth needed to be hospitalized immediately. In 1960, this condition also threatened the life of the mother as well as the baby, so we were all worried to pieces. Would I lose Ruth as well as this baby?

Ruth was admitted to the hospital, and she spent the next four weeks on her back, barely moving, a brave warrior mother fighting to save her baby. Still, Ruth is nothing if not resourceful; while lying as flat as a pancake, she managed to knit a sweater for the baby, holding her arms as motionless as possible just above her chest. Later, when she was discharged, a young doctor who had been attending her was surprised to see her walking around. "Ruth, I had no idea you were that tall," he said. The doc had only ever seen her lying there, horizontal. "And I had no idea you were that short," she shot back. Ruth has always been gifted with the one-liner, even in her darkest days.

At thirty-four weeks, Ruth began bleeding heavily, despite her every effort to keep still and the staff's every effort to keep that baby inside of her longer. The doctors had no choice but to perform a C-section and take the baby early. We were told Ruth would have died had they not taken the baby immediately.

Our wonderful doctor, Dr. Grey, had been so good to us throughout the ordeal. (I remember how we paid him $5 a week for a long time, and even that was a hardship. It's funny, the things you keep in your memory, years after a sad event.)

Knowing Ruth was a nurse, Dr. Grey explained the situation to her in medical terms. He was very kind, yet he would not give her any false hope. He told us there was a 10 percent chance the baby would live. Ruth knew this meant the odds were almost impossible. We had very little hope, but the thing about hope is that you grab on to whatever shred of it you possibly can while it still exists.

Our son William John Besteman was born on that day. He weighed two pounds five ounces and had a full head of dark, curly hair. We named him William for Ruth's father and John for my grandfather. (Years later when we had our fourth child, a boy, the last thing we wanted was to name him after me. I am a Marvin Junior, and we had so many mix-ups with people calling our house looking for my dad, and so forth. Our son Mark has thanked us many times that he's not Marvin the Third.)

As Dr. Grey had feared, William had a condition called "hyaline membrane disease," which meant his little lungs were too sticky to expand properly and take in air. Today, they call this infant respiratory distress syndrome, or RDS. In a nutshell, it's a set of symptoms in premature babies caused by lack of a protein that helps keep their airways dry.

This, combined with immature lungs, is what affected our baby. (In 1963, Patrick Bouvier Kennedy, son of President John F. Kennedy and First Lady Jacqueline Kennedy, died of RDS two days after his premature birth at thirty-four weeks, the same number of weeks at which we lost William.)

Today, this disease affects only 1 percent of newborns, yet it's the leading cause of death in preterm babies. Still, had William been born today, undoubtedly the doctors could have saved him, even though he was born six weeks early. Because of the developmental stage at which he was born, and the fact that it was 1960, nothing short of a miracle could have saved our baby.

Ruth never saw her firstborn son. Neither one of us held him in our arms. Back in those days, that was just the way things were done, even though by today's standards it seems cruel. Ruth had lost so much blood she was totally out of it for hours after she had given birth via C-section. She woke up from the surgery a few hours after William was born, but the staff must have felt she was too frail to be wheeled over to the preemie nursery. It was a different time and place back then; the rules were different. As soon as they pulled him out, William was whisked away and placed in an incubator.

I was twenty-six years old; Ruth was twenty-five. I was young and strong and capable, but I felt as beaten down and defeated as a crippled old man that day. I walked down the cold corridor of the hospital in a daze, looking for the preemie nursery where they had taken my son. When I found the right room, I stood rooted to the floor until my feet went numb, and still I kept standing there. A glass window stood between me and my son. Little did I know that many years later another clear divide would separate me and my son, this time in heaven.

Of the ten hours William lived, I must have stood there for six of them, gazing at his tiny little body, swaddled in blankets and lying so still in a glass box. I couldn't hold him, or even touch his arm, smaller than my thumb. I was unable to tell him I loved him, or offer any kind of comfort or reassurance. I was powerless to even stand by his side and tell him, "Daddy's here. Daddy's here." I wasn't allowed any nearer to him than I was, separated by the glass. I felt powerless, and for a father who would do anything for his children, this was a terrible, terrible feeling.

So I did the one thing I could do for him: I stood there and watched over him, staring at him with a mixture of love and agony. Most of the time, I felt numb, because I knew there was little chance he would make it. Tears would roll down my cheeks at different intervals as well; we were losing this baby—it was just a matter of time.

In this miserable fog, I noted that William had his grandfather's full head of dark hair. Our other babies were bald or blonde, but this kid had the Besteman hair in abundance. He lay almost completely still, but every once in a while he would move an arm or a leg. Every time the baby moved at all, it was a big deal.

And then finally he didn't move anymore. When they moved the incubator away from my line of vision, I knew he had passed away.

It didn't take long for me to turn around and make my way to Ruth's room. She had been awake for just a few hours and was still in rough shape from the surgery and losing all the blood. When I walked into her room to tell her our son had died, I didn't have to say a word. She could tell by the look on my face that he was gone.

When I See William Again

People told us afterward, "You can have more children," which is really a knuckleheaded thing to say, if you think about it. Oh, I know, they were trying to be comforting, trying to cheer us up, as if there was a bright side after all. Folks so often don't know what to say when someone loses a loved one, never mind a child. They either say nothing, pretending your loved one never existed, or they blather on with these candy-coated nuggets of "sympathy."

My suggestion in times like these? Say very little, only "I'm so sorry. I love you. I am praying for you." Say little, but show much. Convey your sympathy through hugs, cards, meals, and any practical thing you can do to help.

Because, if you've lost a child, you know that, at that moment, you don't want "more children."

You want the one who has left you, now and always. Oh, you move on, eventually, because that's the way life is. We look at people who lose their first child, and we wonder how they keep going. Our "bright side" was indeed Julie, our busy little girl. We had to keep moving for her sake. But what people don't understand is that your heart never forgets the one you lost, no matter how many more come before or after.

It's a good thing God doesn't put all these things in front of us, for us to know about before they happen.

The worst thing was picking out William's little casket, all by myself. Ruth was in the hospital for at least ten days after the baby died. When I went down to the funeral home, they had these little boxes, all lined up. Oh, it was so very difficult.

The funeral was very small, just me and my parents at the funeral home. Ruth was not allowed to leave the hospital for William's little service.

He has a little headstone, and once a year on Memorial Day we visit the grave and think about what could have been.

We have a nephew, Scott, who would be close to William's age, about fifty-one now. As we've watched Scott grow and as he has reached his various milestones in life, we've thought of William, and what he would have been doing. Would he have played hockey, like me and Mark, or chosen a different hobby? Who would he have married? How many children would he have had?

And then of course we have thought about what he's doing in heaven. What did he look like now? What kind of man did he grow up to be in that perfect place? Or did he grow up? In my mind, he's still my dark-haired baby boy. Others who have shared with me their stories of losing babies long to hold their babies in their arms once they get to heaven. Yet many people believe that babies grow up in heaven. Truly, it's impossible to know on this earth. This is yet another matter best left to God's sovereignty. The most important thing to remember is that all God's children, no matter the age they died, are with him, safe and loved. When the curtain is parted and we can see them again, all will be revealed, perfectly!

Naturally, we didn't have a chance to have William baptized. Now, some people might worry about that, and think that maybe a baby who hasn't been baptized wouldn't make the cut into heaven.

That never bothered me. I never did buy the teaching that you have to be baptized to go to heaven. I knew William was there from the moment the nurses pushed that incubator out of the preemie nursery, and I knew he was in heaven years later, when I was there too.

But once again, I wasn't allowed past the glassy screen to see William.

It was a big disappointment to me that I couldn't get past that gate to find William, but apparently it wasn't the right time for me to find him. Next time I go, God only knows when, I will have a one-way ticket only. That's when all the years of separation will fall away. That's when I'll meet my son, and walk with him and talk with him and be with him until the end of time.

9

The Six People I Saw in Heaven

I grew up on the southwest side of Grand Rapids, Michigan, on Cleveland Street, the oldest of three boys born to hearty Dutch parents who loved us and raised us to love God.

It was all a long, long time ago, but when I think about my childhood and those who raised me up to be the man I am, I feel blessed. Mine wasn't a perfect upbringing, but by and large it was nurturing and secure.

Memories come now in snapshots: we lived close to a pond, and after school on winter afternoons, I would lace up my skates and play hockey with my friends. I'd forget supper. I'd forget homework. I'd forget everything to play hockey. That became my love.

As a family, we would head to Silver Lake on Memorial Day weekend and open up our cottage. What I remember most is my brothers and me shivering in the cold water, trying to get the dock and boat ready. Meanwhile, my dad stood on the dock, giving orders, warm and toasty in his hip waders. Sometimes we'd be in that chilly water for hours. I think my dad thought it would build character.

I was short then. I grew into a tall man, but I was the

143

smallest kid in my class until the summer between ninth and tenth grade. I must have grown five inches during that summer.

So many years have passed between then and now. I had no idea then of the lasting influence my parents and other family members would have in my life. I had no idea how much I would miss them when they died. We don't know until someone is gone what they mean to us.

Beloved Faces

Beyond the impenetrable gate of heaven was a world I had never imagined, of luscious, green grass and a sky of periwinkle, woven with aqua, knit with cobalt, and laced with sapphire. I know bankers don't usually talk like that, but most bankers haven't seen what I've seen. I've also been told I have a poetic streak.

I had already been captivated by the color and light show as I waited outside heaven's gate. But now, I was actually getting the chance to peek inside. I saw the babies first and watched them for a while.

And then, much to my delight and surprise, I started to see people whom I immediately recognized, just a few of those who had meant the world to me before they died and joined God to dwell in that place he has prepared for us.

There were six of them whose beloved faces I knew. Some of them had been living there for many years, and some had left this earth more recently. One dearly loved family member had died just two months before I saw him. I could hardly believe my eyes when I saw how he appeared, how drastic and complete had been his physical transformation. Oh, how wonderful he looked!

I want you to know what these six people meant to me. I want to tell you how they were significant in my life. But most of all, I want you to think about those *you* love, who live in heaven too. I know how dearly you miss their faces, voices, and touch, because I miss my own heavenly residents the same way. When I tell you about the six people I saw in heaven, and how drastically altered, yet utterly familiar, each one was, I hope you find deep comfort in the telling. I know you want them back with you—it's only human to want that. But I promise you, they are healthy and whole beyond your wildest dreams.

What would you do for the chance to lay eyes for just a few more moments on someone you've loved and lost? What would it mean to you to share eye contact and trade smiles and wave at them and have them wave back at you? You'd probably give anything, especially if you knew that your loved ones have never looked better. No matter what manner of death they faced when they left this earth, I'm telling you—those you lost have never looked more alive!

Some of my loved ones died in old age, frail and diminished, yet having lived many good years. Other lives ended much too young, falling to horrible, debilitating diseases. The way they looked when they died broke the hearts of all who treasured them. But how they appeared when I saw them in heaven? Each one was a miracle.

Grandma and Grandpa Besteman

The first people I saw in heaven were my grandparents, Grace and Adrian Besteman.

They were about twenty yards away from me, inside the gate. I could have thrown a football easily and Grandma or Grandpa could have caught it. I tried again to push my way in so I could run over and say hello and hug them, but the unseen "force field" wouldn't shift one iota.

My grandparents were separated by about ten feet; each walked separately but both of them saw me right away. Grandma smiled and waved, and I waved back, hardly believing my eyes. She had been gone for so many years. Grandpa, my old fishing buddy, grinned at me and motioned for me to come inside. He had been gone even longer than Grandma.

My Besteman grandparents had arrived in America as young people, immigrants from the Netherlands. They met in Grand Rapids and raised their family there. Grandpa was in the produce business, like so many of the Dutch immigrants. He dealt with all kinds of fruits and vegetables, buying them from the markets in Chicago and having them transported to Grand Rapids. I remember there were always cut-up carrots and celery with something to dip them in on their table when I'd come to visit as a boy. Grandma, a petite lady with a knack in the kitchen, had a way with banana bread. I never smell a loaf of banana bread baking without thinking of her.

Grandpa had the patience of Job. When I remember him, it's usually a memory involving the two of us sitting for hours in a boat on Baptist Lake, waiting for a fish to nibble. We'd troll for pike or maybe throw in some lures for bass, but it seemed we always sat and sat, he the uncomplaining grandfather, and I the seven-year-old with ants in my pants.

Four generations
of Bestemans:
Marv, his father,
grandfather, and
great-grandfather

Marv (right) and
his brother, Ron

Grandpa and his
son, my dad, both died
with a full head of curly,
black hair. And here I sit,
bald, without a hope in the
world of getting any of it back.

But baldness was the last thing on my mind as I stared
at Grandma and Grandpa. They had both died in their
old age, bedridden and withered versions of who they had
once been.

Yet, here they stood before me, just sixty feet away,
flourishing and vibrant, with rosy cheeks and a spring in

147

their steps. Both of them were wearing clothing similar to what they wore on earth, and they appeared to be the age they were when they died. Still, Grandma and Grandpa looked like no other eighty-five-year-olds I have ever seen walking around here. I kid you not. Had I thrown a pass at them, both of them gave the impression they could've easily jumped up and snatched it, thrown it back to me, and started a rousing game of tackle football. Grandma and Grandpa! I was totally amazed.

Mom

Then I saw my mother, Marjorie Sweers Besteman, the mom who had poured her heart and soul into her three boys. My heart jumped when I saw her—I had dearly missed her—but again I was held back from entering heaven beyond the gate.

She was the best mom a boy could ask for. My parents' place was a favorite spot for my friends to hang out. We lived next door to an empty lot with a basketball hoop, for one. But the main draw was my mother, who fed me and my friends almost continuously. She would take out a batch of cookies and start the next batch before that one had cooled down.

My mother never put away the vacuum cleaner. When she wasn't baking, she was vacuuming. And even though she was a big, strapping Dutch woman, Mom always, always wore a dress. I'm fairly sure she wore some kind of dress/bathing suit hybrid to the beach too.

She was thoroughly dedicated to her three boys, attending all of our ball games in good weather and bad. In some ways, she was a single mom, as my dad worked sixty hours a week or more, six days a week, running the produce distribution company. He bought and sold vegetables and fruits through the J. A. Besteman Company, just like his dad before him.

When I was a teenager, I had a curfew of 11:00 p.m. If I was out too late with the car, I could never get away with it. Dad would leave for work at 1:00 a.m. most nights, and he would feel the hood of the car when he left home to see if it was cool or warm. If it was warm, no car for me for a week. He took the keys away and gave them to my mother for safekeeping. Little did he know Mom would always feel sorry for me and relent after about two days. This is what I mean by us boys being spoiled rotten by the woman.

My mother had a very open mind in some ways, and she had an earthy side to her. She had a saying, "If you put your bottom in this chair, your legs will follow." But she didn't use the word "bottom." Actually, there are a few sayings my mom had that I can't repeat in this book! Ask me sometime and I'll tell you all about it.

Yes, Mom was open-minded, unless one of her boys was being naughty, and that was that. She kept a ruler on a peg over the door to each of our rooms. If we stepped too far out of line, that ruler would come down and she would start whaling on us. Have I mentioned she was a strapping lady? Ouch! But yet, in many ways she let us get away with murder.

Other than us stepping over the line, there was one area in which Marjorie Besteman did not have an open mind: she was a stickler for observing the Sabbath, and that's putting it mildly. In her mind, Sundays were a day for devoted reverence to God, a day set apart for attending church morning and evening, and showing deep piety in the hours in between. At least we had to *show* piety to whoever might be watching us. We boys could dangle our feet in the water off the dock at Silver Lake, but we couldn't immerse our whole bodies in it, no matter how hot it was. We could play ball behind the house where no one could see us, but not out front. And we could ride our bikes in the basement but not outside, where the neighbors might see us and allegedly stumble in their walk with the Lord. If it sounds legalistic to you, imagine how hemmed-in a trio of rambunctious boys felt. But despite this one ironclad rule, Mom was usually a softie to her boys and we loved her dearly.

She adored us boys, but her biggest disappointment in life was that she didn't have a girl. Later in her golden years, she had six granddaughters in a row and she was in her glory.

Mom lived a long, happy life, eventually dying at the age of ninety from heart failure. In her last days, she had lost so much weight she hardly looked like herself. I remember one of the last things she said to me: "I never wanted to be the first one to go. Take care of your dad, Marv. He won't last more than six months after I am gone." Dad actually lived six more years and hadn't yet died when I had my heaven experience. He must have been heartier than Mom thought he was! Incidentally, when my dad died in his nineties, his eyes were terribly clouded, nearly blinded, with macular degeneration. The second before he closed his eyes for the last time, his eyes cleared up completely. God had restored his sight, just in time to see heaven's sights.

The last time I saw Mom, she was fragile and weak, her chubby cheeks sunken and gray. One by one, her organs were shutting down. I wasn't there at the moment her life actually passed on, but when she did, it was such a blow to me. She was old enough to die—even I was old by that time. But you only have one mother.

As I stood there at heaven's gate, feet rooted to holy ground, I was given the gift of seeing this beloved person one more time before I go back for good. She was a little closer than my grandparents, and I could see clearly how she looked and what she wore. Mom looked like she had gained back that fifty pounds she had lost during her illness. She looked robust, with pink, round cheeks and a bounce in her step—just like my old mom, whose whole world was her boys. Other than the fact that there are no vacuum cleaners in heaven, everything was the same. And she was wearing a dress, just like the ones she used to wear around our house on Cleveland Avenue, when she'd bake cookies and vacuum her floors and chase her boys with a ruler or a hug. Mom smiled her beautiful smile at me, her firstborn son. She waved to me and I waved to her. Like my grandparents, she gestured for me, as if to say, "Come here! Come here!" But still, I couldn't get through, no matter how badly I wanted to.

Paul and Norm

At that moment, I caught sight of a good friend of mine, Paul, off in the distance to the left, about a half a mile away. In life, he and I had played many games of tennis together, and he had been a spiritual giant in my life. He was in his middle sixties when he died of acute leukemia. In a bitter twist of irony, Paul died in the same hospital I was a patient in while I was there for my insulinoma. We

151

both went to heaven, but I came back. He's still there. Lucky Paul!

Paul was one of those guys who was just excellent with details. He and I served on many church councils and committees together, and I looked up to him for his tremendous faith. Paul had more trust in God than anyone I knew. He would step out in faith, sometimes without a job, and God would always come through for him.

The last time I saw Paul, he and I both decided to have our cars serviced on the same day at the Cadillac dealership. We sat and talked a long time as we waited for our cars to be worked on. He told me he had had some tests run, as he wasn't feeling real well. Even then, Paul had a suspicion that something was wrong.

He was right. After that chance meeting, Ruth and I drove to Florida for the winter and I never saw him alive again. (Of course, when I saw him in heaven, he was more alive than ever.) Friends reported to us long distance how much he suffered back home in Michigan. Acute onset leukemia is just like it sounds: dire, and sets in fast. Everyone told me that Paul looked terrible before he died. In his prime, Paul was around 6'3", 230–40 pounds, with the kind of belly that sent a clear message: this guy does not like to miss a meal. But if he weighed 140 pounds when he died, he was lucky. He was skinny to the point of being emaciated, like so many cancer patients are in their last days. Once he was admitted to the hospital, he never left. Paul went downhill fast, sleeping all the time and floating in and out of consciousness. I was sad to hear that my old friend had died such a difficult death.

I don't think my eyes could have gotten any wider the entire time I was in heaven, and seeing Paul was just one of many unbelievable sights. He too was hale and hearty—my big, brawny friend was back to his old self, roughly 230 pounds. Those who knew him had one question when they heard I had seen him on the other side: Did Paul still have that Santa Claus belly?

And you know what? He did!

Just seconds after I absorbed the fact that I was seeing Paul with my own two eyes, I spotted another friend, Norm, about six feet away from Paul. (Paul and Norm were friends, yet it didn't seem like they were walking together, at least not at that particular moment.) Norm was also a fine Christian man and devoted church leader. He was also a businessman, like Paul, and I very much appreciated Norm's and Paul's understanding of what it's like being a Christian in the business world.

Norm had been a dedicated golfer and a man who loved to fish. Nothing made Norm smile more than a boat ride on Lake Michigan, casting his fishing rod and reeling in the salmon, one by one.

Both of my friends were prayer warriors, and we had spent many hours praying together. I'm not sure if this is why God chose these two guys for me to see—they were significant to me and my spiritual life.

Everyone I saw had been influential in shaping my life in some way.

Sad to say, Norm had also fallen victim to cancer, and he too died a painful and agonizing death, his weight falling drastically. Those once burly arms that could hoist the biggest salmon out of the lake shriveled down to wasted and bony twigs. He died two months before my trip to heaven.

Now, as I gawked at him and Paul, I could only shake my head in awe. Norm was his same sturdy, strong self. Both of those guys looked as if they had never been sick a day in their lives. Each of them had their full heads of hair back, and they were wearing leisure clothes, the kind of clothes they might have worn on the golf course or out for dinner with their wives.

Both of my friends saw me, and their eyes lit up with recognition, their faces split into grins as they too waved for me to come inside the gate. ("What do you think the people at the gate thought when you didn't come in?" Ruth has asked me from time to time. And the answer is, I don't know. But nobody seemed sad or upset about it, that's for sure. They also didn't seem to realize that I couldn't come in, no matter how much I wanted to. Why? Again, I don't know. Perhaps folks on the other side are blissfully oblivious to everything on our side of heaven. As I knew certain things without being told, I am certain my loved ones also had far wider and deeper knowledge than we have on earth. Yet they didn't appear to know that I couldn't get in, as they all heartily motioned for me to come on in. It's just one more puzzle piece of my experience, to be solved when I go back for good.)

If only I *could've* gotten inside—I so dearly wanted to get closer to my grandparents, my mother, and now Paul and Norm. And I knew if I could get past the gate, I could find William John.

I pushed against the intangible entranceway once again, but it didn't give even an inch.

Why Did I See Those People?

When I talk about who I saw in heaven, people who know me and who have lost loved ones (especially those I knew on earth) are eager to know if I also saw their wife, husband, son, daughter, parents, or friends.

The truth is, there were hundreds of people I *could've* seen—I knew them to be in heaven—whom I just didn't see. This doesn't mean for one second that those I didn't see weren't there. They are there!

This is something I have pondered time and time again— why did I see the six precious faces I did see, and not so many others?

Since my experience, of course, I've read just about everything I can get my hands on written by those who have glimpsed heaven. And one thing seems to be true of them all: they see those who had been influential in their lives. Don Piper, author of *90 Minutes in Heaven*, saw his grandfather, a childhood friend who had died when Don was in his teens and who had been key in leading him to Christ. He saw two teachers, who had also played major roles in his life, and his Native American great-grandmother.

It's never come to me exactly why I saw those particular people and no one else. Oh, I've prayed about it, asked God many times. I've thought about it so many times, and I don't know the answers. Why did I see my Besteman grandparents and not my Sweers grandparents? Why did I see Norm and Paul and not so many other friends who

155

have died? The best answer I've received is simply that God chose them for his reasons, and that's got to be good enough for me. My spiritual advisors have suggested that those people were important to me spiritually, and it's true—they all were in one way or another.

It's endlessly intriguing for me to think about why those six were there to greet me. Who will be there to hail me next time I go (for the second and last time)? Will it be the same six, or others? Think about it a minute. Who do you think will be there to greet you?

At this point, you may be wondering why I called this chapter "The Six People I Saw in Heaven," when any monkey could count the people I've mentioned and arrive at the number five. I haven't told you yet about the best reunion of all. Moments after I spotted Norm and Paul, I saw the one person I longed for the most, the one whose death had cracked this old man's heart in two: I saw Steve.

10

Losing and Finding
My Best Friend

M y eyes went as far left as they could see, over that great gathering of saints. And then, about fifteen yards away, about the length of your average driveway, I saw a really close friend, my unlikely best friend—my forty-two-year-old son-in-law, Steve.

I pressed hard on the invisible gateway again, harder than I had before, but it just didn't move. All over again, my heart hopped with joy, and my eyes and smile got as big as they would stretch. Steve! He was supremely alive in the midst of this wonder and beauty.

The first time I saw Steve, he was a skinny college boy, a fellow student of my daughter Amy's at Central Michigan University. They were dating, and Amy had brought him home to meet Ruth and me. He didn't seem especially nervous, and I remember thinking that he was as polite a fellow as you'd ever want to meet. Never in a million years did I think this smiley kid would one day become, after Ruth, my closest friend and confidante.

When I got to know Steve, I knew I could trust him with my daughter. He was the type of guy who would be a loyal

Marv and son-in-law Steve (right)

husband and faithful provider, working hard to support his family. When he came to me and asked for Amy's hand in marriage, I said the same thing to him that I had said to Joe, Julie's husband: "Are you sure you can support this young lady in the manner to which she is accustomed?" I was joking (well, half joking). "Can you afford to maintain her?" A man with a daughter is probably only going to get the chance to have his prospective son-in-law over the barrel a couple of times in his whole life, if he's lucky. I figured I should make the most of it and have a little fun with the situation. But of course I said yes. And I've never regretted it for a second.

He Called Me "Dad"

Steve was a great guy. With his servant's heart, he was always so willing to help other people. If you happened to be stuck on the side of the road with a flat tire, Steve would be the guy who would stop and help you fix it. He'd come over on a Saturday and say, "Dad, do you need anything done around here?" And we'd go to the hardware store, get what we needed, and get the job done together. He was a terrifically loyal person, someone you wanted for a friend, because if he was your friend now, he'd be your friend forever.

Steve prized fishing the way Ruth and I prize golfing. He'd go pan fishing all the time and come back with walleye and pike. Luckily, he was generous with his catch; our freezer was full of fish.

One time he gave us a huge hunk of all different kinds of fish just frozen together in a massive block. I thought we'd have to host a fish fry for twenty people to get rid of it all!

Good thing Steve loved to eat. He was the first one at the table and the last one to leave, and he never lost a chance to tell Ruth that she was the best cook in the world (she loved that). We marveled at how much food a skinny guy like that could put away. After he finally finished piling all that food in, he would help clear the table and wash the dishes. Seriously, Steve was as perfect a son-in-law as any man could ask for.

Yet, I was taken aback when he came to me with a question not too long after he and Amy got married. Two or three months after their wedding, Steve's dad had died, far too young.

Members of the Besteman family

He came to me about six months later with the question: "I don't have a dad anymore, and I need one. Will you be my dad?"

I said I would pray about it, and that yes, I would try to be his dad. But he didn't want me to tell anyone, not even Ruth. It was our secret, and that change in our relationship was what bonded us so strongly.

In the years to come, Steve would come to me often and ask me for advice about everything. He had lots of questions about raising their two children—how to mete out punishment and praise, parenting techniques, problem solving, and so forth. I felt I had made mistakes many times while I was raising our kids and had learned from

162

those mistakes, so I gave him the answers I had gathered from trial and error. Steve asked me about spiritual matters, marriage, emotions, relationships of all kinds, and quite a bit about financial issues. He didn't always follow my advice, but he asked and I tried to answer as best I could. We talked and talked and talked. And gradually, over years of heartfelt conversation, we became as close as any father and son could be.

The Prime of His Life

By the time Steve was diagnosed with Ehlers-Danlos syndrome, in 2005, I couldn't imagine life without my bonus son.

I had never heard of Ehlers-Danlos syndrome (also known as EDS), but I sure didn't like the sounds of it. Research statistics show that EDS occurs in one in 5,000 people, and it is known to affect both men and women of all racial and ethnic backgrounds.

I'm no doctor, but Ruth is a nurse and a darn good one. She and I became very familiar fast with this rare condition that had stricken our Steve. Ehlers-Danlos syndrome is a group of connective tissue disorders, characterized by extreme joint mobility, skin that pulls easily off the bone (doctors call this "extensibility"), and delicate, fragile skin tissue. The syndrome is named after two doctors, Edvard Ehlers of Denmark, and Henri-Alexandre Danlos of France, who identified it at the turn of the twentieth century.

Apparently, Steve and all those who suffer from EDS have a flaw in their connective tissue, the tissue that provides support to many body parts such as the skin, muscles, and ligaments. The easily breakable skin and unstable joints found in EDS are the result of faulty collagen. (Collagen is a protein that acts as a "glue" in the body, adding strength and elasticity to connective tissue.) EDS patients don't have this glue, and so they are prone to dislocate bones. Steve was always having sports injuries. He would dislocate a knee, and then a shoulder, and then a finger. We just thought he was very unlucky and susceptible to injuries. No one suspected anything more serious than that.

His veins were just dissolving, we learned. One doctor told Steve and Amy that during an operation, trying to suture a vein affected by EDS was like "sewing spaghetti." Another image we were given was comparing his veins to a tire being blown out. His vessels would just burst, causing internal bleeding.

Super-flexible joints are also a key feature of the disease. People with EDS can often bend their fingers all the way back, or grab a section of their skin and pull it up, creating a bizarre-looking tent, as if that person had lost 100 pounds and now their skin was too loose.

Depending on what kind of EDS you have or how it mutates in your body, the severity of the disease can vary from mild to life-threatening.

A biopsy in February of 2005 confirmed that Steve had the syndrome, and that his case was severe, although we didn't begin to grasp how severe until months afterward. There is no cure, and treatment only helps slow down and manage the symptoms. Steve's doctors monitored his condition closely, telling him to use extra caution when engaging in the slightest activity, or even playing with his kids. Any kind of accidental blow, especially to his mid-section, could make his symptoms so much worse (Steve was having aneurisms in his midsection). He couldn't run and jump around and wrestle with the kids like he used to, especially not when a basketball to the belly would have been the worst thing in the world.

He began to tire very easily. Even mowing the grass was so hard on him that he had to come in to lie down for quite a while to recuperate. It took so much out of him.

At one point, around December of 2005, the possibility of surgery to correct the problem was brought up. Spaghetti or not, there was a chance the doctors could operate and possibly fix the blood vessels so they wouldn't be so delicate. People in his life advised him to have the surgery soon. But Steve was firm: "I'm not ruining my kids' Christmas."

Losing Steve

Never once did we think Steve would die from this, although in hindsight I can see that I just did not want to go there in my mind. Amy never asked the doctors if Steve would die; rather, her question was, "What's his life going to be like?"

"Compromised," was their answer, which I took to mean that he would have to sleep a lot more and take extra precautions in his everyday activities. Overall, the doctors had given Steve and Amy quite a bit of confidence that he would live a semi-normal life.

We felt good enough about Steve's prognosis that we left for Arizona for the winter months, as usual. I had no idea when I said goodbye to Steve that I was saying goodbye until our meeting in heaven.

When we got to Sun City, we were in frequent touch with Steve and Amy over phone and email. His surgery was scheduled for the beginning of February, and Ruth flew back to Grand Rapids to take care of the kids while Steve and Amy drove to the Cleveland Clinic in Ohio.

They packed their van and drove the six hours, taking down the seats in the back and making a bed with pillows and a mattress, because the doctor said he would have to lie down the whole trip home. They expected him to come home. I expected the same thing.

Did he know he might die? I think he had a feeling deep down he might. So many people had prayed for him at his church, and when Ruth said goodbye, he was stoic. "Just give me a kiss and we'll be off," he said to her, in a breezy way. I think he was tired of people carrying on like he was on his deathbed already, and wanted the goodbye to be businesslike, not dramatic or drawn out.

His pastor had written him an email in which he asked him if he was ready to die. Steve's answer was yes. But he didn't want to dwell on it, that's for sure.

After his initial surgery at the Cleveland Clinic, Steve suffered a cardiac arrest. Sadly, he never got on top of it again after that cardiac arrest. Three more surgeries followed in the next nine days, and after the second operation, they didn't even bother to close him up again. Things were as grim as they could possibly be.

When I realized that Steve could die, I threw everything in the car and drove from Arizona to Michigan by myself. It's a long trip, and I had many hours to think about what was happening. I prayed and cried and prayed some more.

Back at the hospital, Julie and Mark and Steve's mother and brothers had joined Amy at her husband's bedside, where he hovered between life and death. Steve was on so many pain medications, and he was hallucinating a lot and not making much sense. But he didn't suffer—for that I'm so thankful.

After the fourth surgery, the doctors couldn't stop the internal hemorrhaging, and Steve basically bled to death. That cheerful, skinny kid with the heart of gold was gone—it was impossible to take in.

In the middle of the night, when the phone rang at Amy and Steve's house, Ruth knew it was bad news. Mark was calling to tell her Steve had died. Then I got the dreaded phone call, from Ruth, and . . . well, I'm choked up just remembering it all. I can't even express how I felt. It was the hardest thing I have ever gone through. My daughter had lost her husband and my grandchildren had lost their dad. How those kids would miss their dad! How Amy would miss her husband!

Steve was so talented, and so young—far too young to die. I would have gladly taken his place so he could live into his seventies like I had. His family adored him, and the kids loved him at the school where he taught. I remembered that he was so excited about heading up the robotics club at school and now there would be no one to head it up. You think of the strangest things when someone dies, don't you?

I went over to Amy's house, and together Ruth and I told our grandchildren they had lost their father. There are no words to describe their shock and grief. I myself cried like a baby. I had lost my son-in-law, and I had lost my best friend.

Walking, and Leaping, and Praising God

Two months later, I was to see Steve far sooner than I had ever expected. After my trip to heaven, it took me awhile to tell my family what had happened. At first, I didn't want to tell anyone, not even Ruth. (I'll explain further on in the book why it was so difficult for me to share my experience. But this piece of the story relates to Steve.) When I finally broke down and told Ruth, though, the ice was broken, and not too long afterward I told my three children.

You want to talk about an emotional night? Tell your daughter where her husband is and that he's waiting for her. I'll never forget that evening, the intensity and sorrow of it mixed with joy and awe.

Amy was in deep grief over losing Steve, and she was grappling with a jumble of emotions, like anyone who has grieved a dear one's death. She was very angry and felt so alone. And now her dad was telling her he had seen Steve with his own two eyes in heaven? It was confusing for everyone to know how to feel, especially Amy. She probably wanted to feel as if Steve was one way or another still in tune with her, aware of her struggles on earth. When she heard that Steve was joyful and radiant, blissfully unaware, it seemed, of her mourning and her loneliness, it was not completely great news. In some ways, it made her feel even more detached from him and even more alone.

I tried to be as sensitive as I could. It didn't help matters that I told my kids that all I wanted to do was go back to heaven. "Don't be in such a hurry, Dad," they said, look-ing worried. From their perspective, it was astonishing news, yes, but also hurtful. Didn't I love them and want to be with them?

Oh yes. Those kids and grandkids are my heartbeat, and I'd move mountains for them if need be. But had they seen and heard what I did in that glorious world, they would understand that no one who sets foot in heaven would ever want to come back.

Steve did not want to come back, of that I'm sure. When I saw him beyond the gate, just fifteen yards away, so close and yet still unreachable, I was thrilled. We made eye con-tact, and both of us had huge smiles on our faces. He looked as cheerful as could be, as if he had just caught a world-record bass and was on his way to weighing the thing. The sickliness that had settled around him like a gray blanket those last months was gone, and Steve appeared as strong and vigorous as any man would ever want to be. He was jumping up and down, waving to me enthusiastically. Jumping up and down! The guy who had been living half a life that last year, cautious and constrained, not up for so many of the activities and pleasures he had taken part in when he was healthy, was now bouncing like an exuberant child. The chains of this earth—sickness, weakness, and worry—were gone.

What a sight for sore eyes. My dearest friend, valued son-in-law, cherished gift from above, was free. Steve was free!

11

After I Woke Up

I t felt like forever while Peter went to check with God to see if I could stay or had to return. In reality it was probably only a matter of minutes, maybe five to ten, although it's hard to judge exactly. I wasn't wearing a watch, nor would I have checked it had I been wearing one.

I saw such magnificent sights in those minutes—perfect, contented babies, a divinely beautiful lake, sublime colors, the smiling faces of six loved ones, and so much more. Just to state the obvious, these were the most awesome (in the true sense of the word) moments of my entire life.

As far as I was concerned, the most important thing to me was getting through the gate to join my dear ones and meet the God I loved, whose love I could feel so strongly in that place, warming my soul like a fire.

Peter came back at last, slipping through the imperceptible gate with a slight smile on his face. He had a look in his eyes like he might have a secret for me.

"Marv," he said firmly, looking at me with those intense eyes, "I talked to God, and God told me to tell you that you had to go back, that he still had work for you to do on earth. He still has work for you to finish there."

I was about to start arguing again, but it was too late. The decision had been made, and I had no choice in the matter. The next thing I knew, I was back in my hospital bed at the University of Michigan Medical Center, hooked up to a web of tubes.

"I Want to Go Home"

Back in my hospital room, it was like an attack of lights coming on—harsh, glaring lights assaulting me like a bucket of ice water on a hot day. It was infinitely brighter in heaven; after all, it's lit by God himself, yet there my eyes had no trouble adjusting to the brilliance.

I was attached once more to all of those tubes—and the pain! I hadn't realized how blessedly free of pain I had been in heaven. Now the throbbing and the hurting was back, full throttle.

Two nurses came rushing in to check on me. Ruth told me that it wasn't standard procedure for two nurses to come in. Usually, she said, a nurse will be assigned to a patient and check that patient all by himself or herself. As for why they were rushing in like that, I just don't know. Something on my monitor must have alerted them that I was in trouble.

I think I was crying even before they came hurrying in, checking my blood pressure and oxygen levels and the tubes and IV.

Once they realized I didn't need medical attention (at least, not in the way they were worried about), they noticed I was bawling like a baby.

"Why are you crying?" one of the nurses asked me. I

can't remember if she was nice about it or not. Nothing or nobody seemed particularly nice to me at that moment.

"I want to go home!" I wailed.

"You have to go back. He has more for you to do. . . ."

If I could have, I would have stomped my feet like a ticked-off four-year-old. I didn't care one bit if there was in fact "more for me to do." I wanted to be back in that perfect, gorgeous, painless place, not lying there in misery, covered in tubes.

The nurse's answer was kind and well meaning. "It will be awhile before you get to go home, Marv," she said, peering down at me. The lady had no idea I was talking about heaven, and not Byron Center, Michigan.

How could I even begin to explain this to my nurses? Were they believers? I had no idea. I didn't want to take the chance that they weren't. Obviously, the one nurse already thought I was acting like a dotty old man, confused enough to think I could walk out of there a few hours after major surgery. If I told them which home I was really referring to, they would have thought I had totally cracked up. I could just imagine the snickers at the nursing station!

I really don't remember the next day very well. I was still in horrendous pain no matter how often the nurses upped my pain medications, and Ruth says I was shaking all over.

Apparently, I had some visitors, friends from Grand Rapids. I knew for sure these friends were believers, yet something stopped me from telling them too. Who would believe a story like mine? I didn't want my friends to think I had slipped a cog mentally.

And a spark of resentment had begun to burn inside of me. Why did God pick me to have that experience, and

175

then make it so fantastic and incredible I couldn't even tell anyone? Was he trying to play a joke on me, to transport me to that place of endless wonders—and then send me back?

Why me—Marvin Besteman, retired banker? Why not pick someone flashier and more eloquent? I've wondered that a thousand times. (Later, my spiritual advisors said, "Why not you?" And they had a point.)

He has more for you to do. . . .

Probably a thousand times or more, I thought, *I wonder what he has for me to do?* For months after my experience, I wondered over it like a dog worrying a bone.

After spending five days in the hospital, I went home to Byron Center.

When I had entered the hospital to have my surgery, it had been winter. But when we left, it was the very beginning of springtime; the air had warmed, with blue skies and budding trees.

We were eager to be out of the hospital and outside again. Yet there was no comparison to the beauty and comfort of heaven. As we drove west toward our home, I knew beyond any doubt life as I knew it could never be the same.

Letdown

After settling in at home, first on the couch and then slowly up and about in my normal, everyday life, the thought that I would never tell anyone, not even Ruth, kept getting stronger.

I hoped maybe that the experience would somehow pass away, like a glorious dream, and I wouldn't have to tell anyone. I had no desire to discuss it with one single soul.

But the opposite happened. It didn't fade away at all. I couldn't stop thinking about what I had seen in heaven and the people I had seen there. My time there started to become a kind of obsession.

I became quite depressed, struggling daily with the letdown of coming back from heaven to this dark world. Wrestling constantly with what had happened and why it happened made my depression worse. I was lethargic and apathetic about life, and Ruth began to worry about my mental health.

Then one day, without warning, the dam burst. Five months after my trip to heaven, in the last week of September, I finally broke down and told Ruth. I don't know what made me tell her, at long last, but suddenly the story just poured out of me.

She's a terrific listener, my Ruth, and never have I appreciated that quality of hers more than when I was recounting my time in heaven.

I cried. She cried. We would dampen our hankies, and start boo-hoo-ing all over again. It took hours to tell her everything, and then all at once I was done.

"Marv," she said decisively, when she could finally get a word in. "You have been truly blessed."

We decided together the best course of action would be to tell our children and swear them to secrecy. And that would be it. (Can you believe I still thought I could get away without telling people about heaven?)

We told the kids shortly after I had spilled the beans to Ruth. They weren't jumping for joy, and they weren't

177

calling me a liar, either. I would say their reaction was somewhere in the middle.

Like kids do, even middle-aged ones, they said, "So, now what?" They were naturally shocked and maybe in some disbelief at first. They knew I would never make something like this up, but perhaps they thought I had been dreaming or hallucinating. It would take everyone awhile to process this unbelievable news.

With that load off my chest, I went back to thinking I could sit on this episode for the rest of my life until those two angels came back for me and carted me off to heaven, this time for keeps.

The only problem was, this was really a terrible plan; God knew it and deep down, I knew it too. The Lord decided I needed a shove in the right direction, so he gave me a hernia, of all things, and sent me on my way to the doctor. And not just any doctor would do. No, God handpicked the physician who would be more than a healer to my body, he would be a healer to my troubled, stubborn soul.

Two One-in-a-Million Cases

It's almost impossible to pull one over on Ruth when it comes to my health and well-being. So, as much as I might have liked to hide the mysterious bulge in my stomach that appeared one day, she was having none of it.

The bulge was an abdominal hernia, she announced, in her crisp nurse voice. She made an appointment with a gastroenterologist that day and also shared her view that it was quite possible that in light of this hernia we were not going to go to Arizona for the winter after all. That's what

I was afraid of. After forty-plus years with a woman, you can read her mind, and unfortunately, she can read yours.

So I had no option but to go to the gastroenterologist to have my hernia checked out. I chatted with the doctor about this and that—the weather looked like it was going to storm, they were calling for the coldest winter on record, and so on and so forth.

He examined me and agreed with Ruth on two counts: I did have a hernia, and golfing amid palm trees was probably out of the question in my condition.

Oh, I was going to Arizona, alright. "Just try and stop me," I said, stubbornly.

"Oh no, you're not," he replied, cheerfully.

We bantered back and forth, or was it bickering? Have I mentioned I'm hardheaded?

I was sitting on the examining table, dangling my legs while the doctor sat in his swivel chair, pondering my case.

He wanted to know what happened to me in Ann Arbor; apparently he thought maybe there was a connection between my surgery there and the hernia now. I told him I had been operated on to remove a rare pancreatic tumor called an insulinoma. Had he ever heard of it?

The doctor paused a little too long. "I've never had a patient with insulinoma," he said slowly. "But I know someone who had it."

"Well, who could that be?" I said lightly.

"My brother."

Now it was my turn to pause. I was totally amazed. After all, insulinomas are less than one in a million, and here my doctor's brother had also been stricken with one. I was very curious about his brother's case, and started

179

to ask questions when I noticed he had tears welling up in his eyes.

He told me that when they had opened up his brother to perform the surgery, they found advanced cancer, and the doctor's brother had died three months later.

I began tearing up too, out of compassion for my grieving doctor, and also because I had become so emotional after my heaven experience.

Looking back, I can see now that the incredible "coincidence" of me having experienced the same rare illness as his brother had formed an instant bond between me and my doctor. Suddenly, the boundaries of patient and doctor fell away and we were talking intently about personal things, as though we had known each other for many years.

"Are you a Christian?" he asked me, out of the blue.

When I answered in the affirmative (although somehow I think he already knew the answer), he and I delved into a really meaty conversation in regard to Christianity, the church, theology—you name it.

"Two things I'm concerned about most are heaven and hell," he said after a while. "What do you know about hell?"

"Well, I don't know much about hell," I said, "only what the Bible says about it, which isn't too much. I think it's a terrible place, and basically it's life in the absence of Christ."

By now, the doctor had stopped watching the clock entirely. My appointment had by then taken far longer than a normal visit to the doctor ever should take. I wonder what those poor nurses and receptionists told the doctor's other patients, waiting way too long in the reception area.

His next question, though, blew the lid off everything, and practically guaranteed that anyone waiting to see this doctor might have to wait all day: "Tell me, then, what you know about heaven."

Uh-oh. I was in big trouble. What did I know about heaven? I didn't have a clue where to start. I wasn't planning to tell anyone except for my close family members, and here my doctor and new friend had asked me about it, point-blank. What could I possibly say in reply?

Then God made it perfectly plain, obvious enough for even a hardheaded Hollander to understand. "Marv, this is one of the reasons I sent you back," he said to me in an audible voice. Yes, I heard God's voice, out loud. And he wasn't messing around.

His words were spoken like an order, a direct command from him to me.

Well then, there was no turning back from God's voice. I told my doctor everything, start to finish, ending my story about an hour later.

I believe the Holy Spirit had prepared his heart to receive my story—he was so receptive to every word. Some other physicians we've told my story to have brushed it off, but this doc was completely ready to hear about my heavenly trip.

The doctor and I finally emerged from his office, and we walked over to the nurse's desk to schedule my hernia surgery. We both had red eyes, and we had been in his office for an hour and a half. The look in the nurse's eyes seemed to say, "What in the world just happened in there?"

So much had happened, for both of us. I had been searching since April 28 for the reason I was sent back from heaven.

Unexpectedly, through the course of an appointment with my gastroenterologist, I had the answer I was looking for. That conversation, and God's instruction to me, was an important part of why I sit here today, telling you my story.

Sometimes—and Ruth will gladly attest to this—you have to explain something to me once or twice before I get it. God in his graciousness had revealed to me what he wanted me to do: Tell as many people as possible about my time in heaven.

The next time I visited this doctor for a follow-up appointment, he introduced me to one of his nurses. "This is the man who saved my life," he said, not elaborating one little bit.

I smiled at the poor bewildered nurse. "And this is the man who saved my life."

We were both telling the truth. The doctor never really explained what he meant by it, but if I were to guess, I'd say that hearing my story of heaven gave a man who was unsure about the afterlife all the belief and security he was craving.

As for me, the doctor had played a large part in helping me understand why God had sent me back. It was to give people like that dear man a message of hope, to brighten the darkness in their hearts, to help them not fear death so much and instead truly look forward to their future in heaven.

It was like the reset button was pressed on my life on earth, which became more meaningful with each person I told.

After that first doctor's appointment, it was like the dominoes began to fall, and I started telling folks more and more often. Our dearest friends Jack and Ruth heard the story when we got to Arizona that winter. (I got to go after all. See, I told you I was stubborn!) I told them they'd have to get their hankies out, and so of course they thought I was going to die of some incurable disease. As I told them my news, they were relieved, then shocked, and finally dampening those hankies, just like I predicted they would.

I told one brother, and then the other one. It took me three sessions, but I finally got the whole story choked out to my patient pastor in Michigan. At first, it was so hard to talk about, especially the part about seeing Steve in heaven. I still can't talk about that part without having a lump in my throat.

But now I understand Peter's words. Offering folks some peace, security, and comfort, and reminding them that their inner sense of the eternal—"eternity in their hearts"—is true, that this world is not all there is, that's why God sent me back to earth.

I don't know how long I have, I really don't. None of us do. But while I am still here, I want to tell as many people as possible about heaven, and about God and his Son, whom I saw seated on the brilliant white throne, gleaming in the distance.

12

Until We Meet Again

I didn't see the throne right away when Peter went to talk to God about whether I could stay or go.

I saw so many marvelous things through that crystal clear gateway, but yet they were just a hint of "the things God has prepared for those who love him" (2 Cor. 2:9).

As my eyes eagerly swept over that panoramic view of heaven, soaking in the sight of endless wonders, eventually I beheld the throne, where our God and his Son are seated and will reign forever.

The throne was about three quarters of a mile away, and dazzlingly bright, lit with brilliant, white lights. It's hard to imagine as I sit here in this dark earth, remembering, but in heaven my eyes could see much clearer and much farther away than they ever could down here.

I saw huge white pillars surrounding the throne, and an enormous crowd of people, men and women, boys and girls, dancing and singing along in a mass choir of praise to the two Beings seated on it. Yes, I did say the men were dancing, and their arms were raised, too, in worship!

Some of my Dutch, Christian Reformed friends are going to have a hard time imagining themselves dancing in worship, or even raising their hands. All they have ever known in a worship setting is stand up, sit down, turn to page 54 in the hymnal (I mean, the "blue book," which is really a hymnal but for some reason that's not what it's called anymore). No matter how devoutly we love our God, raising one's hands in praise is unthinkable, even for me. One of these days I am going to give everyone at church fits and just raise my hands high—let 'em think what they want to think.

Probably, what they would think is this: "Good old Marv went to heaven—he can't help himself."

Well, nobody is going to be able to help themselves at the foot of God's throne, worshiping the two Beings I saw from a distance, exalting the Holy Ones with a purity and joy we have never known.

Yes, I saw two Beings, indescribable images really, but they appeared to be two people sitting there. I've always assumed those two people were God and his Son, Jesus.

How I would have loved to be closer! To see my heavenly Father and his Son who died for me, face to face—even I can hardly believe what's ahead for us in heaven.

We'll experience life as we were always meant to live it, before the Fall, without stress, pressure, negativity, fear, anxiety, sickness, and death. We'll never worry again about what people think of us, which means we'll do things there we never thought ourselves capable of here. Sorry, guys, you're going to have to dance. And the strange thing is, you won't mind one bit.

Heaven is like that—in God's sinless home you are finally free to truly live and happily serve your Lord in whatever work he has prepared for you.

Before I had my round-trip, I never would have thought myself capable, either, of being a firsthand witness to the mysteries and majesty of heaven. And by no means could I have imagined the mission he had for me, to become his messenger of hope and comfort to others.

Did I Really Die?

After I started telling people about my heaven experience, the question was often brought up if I thought I had actually died or "just" been given a preview. Soon after I told Ruth about everything, we wrote the University of Michigan Medical Center and tried to find out what had really happened that night in 2006. Many people I spoke with about my experience wanted some kind of proof or verification. Ruth and I also wanted some kind of substantiation, she even more than me on account of her being a nurse. ("That's just the way we nurses are," she told me.) So, we sent away for lab reports, X-ray reports, surgical reports—everything that was printed, they sent to us. We weren't too terribly surprised when all of these documents revealed nothing.

The one thing we didn't get from the hospital that we would have liked to have was the nurses' handwritten notes. That might have told us more about what happened, and especially why those two nurses had come rushing into my room as if I was on fire. Yet the next day when Ruth asked about how my first night post-op had been, no one told her anything had been out of the ordinary.

But what happened to me was way out of the ordinary— it was extra, extra-ordinary, and it doesn't bother me that we don't have some kind of piece of paper with the hospital's stamp on it to prove it.

While I don't know exactly what happened to me that night, for reasons known to God alone, I was given a preview of the life ahead. Somewhere between life and death, here and there, I received a peek of what is to come.

I know that God wants me to tell you what I saw and trust him with the details. I won't know until next time I go to heaven whose lives were touched by my experience, but God has let me pick some of that fruit here on earth.

After the dam broke and I started telling my story to anyone who would listen, I began speaking in front of small groups of people at churches, in homes, in hospice centers. Folks often stay behind afterward to tell me things, often stories they've never told anyone before. I've heard confessions of people's own brushes with angels and heaven, and of babies loved and lost, long ago or recently. Sometimes, I even hear about how my story has comforted someone or led them on a different path.

I once spoke in a home setting to about twenty people, all related to one another via the hostess. She invited a bunch of family members, but she only had one person in mind: her nephew, who had drifted away from the church and his faith.

After my talk, the nephew came up to me and told me something remarkable. "I'm going to make sure I see you at the gate someday," he said with tears in his eyes. "I know now I need to get back to a church that tells the truth about Christ."

Once, in a large church, a twelve-year-old girl came up to me after my talk and grabbed my hand and would not let go. She was crying her eyes out. "I need to tell you, I've made a decision to be baptized and join the church," she said. "I want to make sure you are watching for me and waiting for me at the gate."

Children usually have fantastic questions. They are very direct with what they ask, which I appreciate.

"How did the ground in heaven feel under your feet?"

"Did the angels have wings?"

"Who was taking care of the babies?"

So many people want to know about the babies, and so many have stories of babies they are longing to see someday. A woman came up to Ruth and me after one of my talks and told us about her son who had died of SIDS. A parent never forgets, no matter how old they get. Our friend found deep relief in hearing about the healthy and contented babies I saw in heaven. "It's such a comfort to know he's in a happy place," she said.

At the Departure Gate

I do feel an urgency to tell people about my experience, because who knows how long I've got until I go back? That's why I wrote this book, even though I'd rather be golfing. Ruth has to handle the requests to have me come and give my talk; otherwise I'd say yes to everything. She says God has impressed upon her that she shouldn't let me overdo it, so we are listening to him and praying for wisdom at every turn of this unexpected adventure.

Since going to heaven, I can't say I've become Holy Marv, with a halo around my bald head, floating above the ground. If I tried to walk on the water of the man-made lake outside my condo door, I would surely get my legs wet and muddy, and I'd look like an idiot to boot. I'm still the same old seventy-something sinner, believe me!

But God does feel so much nearer to both of us, probably because we seek him out for everything, the smallest thing, now. Things that we may have considered too insignificant to pray about in the past, we now pray about. One thing I do talk to God about is giving me the chance to tell my story to whomever he might send my way.

A perfect example: Just yesterday Ruth went golfing all day and left me home to do my thing. Our thermostat started to go haywire, and the air-conditioning started failing. I called the heating and cooling company, and they sent over a young man to fix it. After he had made his repairs, the young man spied a book on my table, written by my coauthor. We chatted about that book, and I said she was also writing a book with me about my trip to heaven. He was totally taken aback, as so many people are. I don't know what he expected, but it wasn't that! We talked about ten or fifteen minutes and he told me he had been raised Catholic but hadn't been to church in years. He and his wife had just had a baby, and they were both talking about returning to church for the baby's sake. The young man seemed to take my story as confirmation that he should turn around and get going down the right path again. He ended up leaving our condo with a smile on his face and a DVD of me telling my story tucked under his arm.

One of the most meaningful parts of my mission—and also the hardest part—is becoming a tour guide of sorts for those who will soon be leaving this earth. "Some glad morning, when this life is o'er, I'll fly away," the old song goes. These dear ones I am guiding are at the departure gate, waiting for their own smooth and peaceful flight in the bluest of skies.

My good buddy Irv just died, which broke my heart in pieces. I wish you could have known Irv. Once he was stuck to you, you couldn't get rid of him; good thing you didn't want to. He had a way of attracting people to him and was the most loyal friend a man could have. So many people visited him in his last days it became a joke at the hospice where he eventually died of cancer: "Too bad Irv doesn't have more friends." Everyone loved Irv, including me.

It makes me feel really good to know where he is right now, and that I was able to prepare him somewhat for the journey ahead of him. Before he died, I spent hours at his bedside, telling him every detail I could remember about heaven. Irv even got to read some of this book before he died.

We have a contract: the first one to go to heaven will meet the other one at the gate. Irv and I talked about this pact many times.

When Ruth and I walked in the door of Irv's church for his funeral, we spotted his wife, who is also our dear friend. When we greeted her, the first words out of her mouth were these: "He's waiting for you."

A Choir of Angels and Saints

Every day since I got back from heaven, I have heard some of that divinely beautiful music I heard in God's home. Mostly, I hear from one minute to six minutes of this music in the middle of the night, but sometimes I have heard pieces of it in broad daylight, while I'm golfing, driving, or reading.

From the second I touched down on the holy ground by the gate, I was surrounded by the most gorgeous music I had ever heard. A million stellar voices (there are no cuts in this choir!), a thousand organs, a thousand pianos—it enveloped me like pure grace.

In John's revelation of heaven, he heard the same glory-filled sounds: "Then I looked and heard the voice of many angels, numbering thousands upon thousands, and ten thousand times ten thousand. They encircled the throne and the living creatures and the elders" (Rev. 5:11).

Most of us don't sing too well on this side of life, but in heaven, there are no off-key or tone-deaf singers. If you've always wanted to sing like an angel, but you can't carry a tune in a pail, just wait and see how fantastic your vocals will be over there!

Every note of this music praised and glorified God; I heard so many "alleluias" from the singers.

The songs I heard were mostly familiar to me, songs that had inhabited my praises on earth for so long.

"Jesus, Jesus, there's something about that name . . ."

"The King is coming, oh, the King is coming . . ."

"Praise the Name of Jesus."

"Holy, Holy, Holy."

"What a Friend We Have in Jesus."

A pastor once asked me a great question in regard to the music. "What about someone from a primitive tribe in, say, Africa, who has never heard choir music?" he said. "Would he hear something different, something more familiar and beautiful to him?"

That's a great question, isn't it? I always hate to speculate, though people always want me to, but in this case, I will offer a guess. I happen to think it's very possible that you will hear the music you enjoy. If heaven is going to be pure bliss, why not assume the God who created music in all its forms will offer something for everyone?

It's also possible the music could have changed the second I left heaven, just as Peter could have spoken another language to the next person he met in line at the gate.

Whatever our musical styles, I have no doubt we will all love the music in heaven.

When I hear heaven's music down here, it's always my very favorite songs from what I heard there; there's never anything "played" that I don't absolutely adore. This is music I could listen to forever and ever—and someday, I can!

I'll Wait for You

Listen, Jesus tells us, "I am the way and the truth and the life" (John 14:6). Everyone who believes that is welcome in heaven.

I want you to know about the reality of Christ and the realness of heaven. I want you to know that total peace and joy await you. Are you getting excited?

If you have felt unloved in your life, and we all have from time to time, please know that you will feel so utterly, wholly loved in heaven. Why, there was nothing unloving there! There was love everyplace. I felt the love from the people in line with me, and I loved them too. I sensed the love from God and his Son.

Heaven is just love, plain and pure, something for us to enjoy forever and ever and ever.

Do you remember what I asked you to consider at the outset of this book? Do you have an answer? Will I see you at the gate?

I'll wait for you there. I can hardly wait to go back.

So, until we meet again, I leave you with the words of Christ, ending my own humble revelation with the parting words of his:

"Look, I am coming soon! My reward is with me, and I will give to each person according to what they have done. I am the Alpha and the Omega, the First and the Last, the Beginning and the End. . . .

"I, Jesus, have sent my angel to give you this testimony for the churches. I am the Root and the Offspring of David, and the bright Morning Star."

The Spirit and the bride say, "Come!" And let the one who hears say, "Come!" Let the one who is thirsty come; and let the one who wishes take the free gift of the water of life. . . .

He who testifies to these things says, "Yes, I am coming soon."

Amen. Come, Lord Jesus.

The grace of the Lord Jesus be with God's people. Amen. (Rev. 22:12–21)

Postscript

On December 19, 2011, Marv and I took his co-writer, Lorilee, out for lunch. We wanted to treat her, as well as see her one more time before we left for Arizona, where we had spent the last few winters.

She had one more piece of business for Marv: the dedication and acknowledgments for this book. She walked us through the process of writing those final details, assuring us this was the last book-related task for Marv to do until it was published.

Over chicken salad sandwiches, we dispatched with the business at hand and spent the remaining time together chitchatting, as we always did. Marv and I hugged Lorilee goodbye, and we all promised to keep in touch via email. Marv loved working on the book with Lorilee, but it was also a very difficult project as well. Talking about his heaven experience was emotional and draining for Marv, and working on the chapters about losing our baby son, William, and later, our son-in-law Steve were particularly wrenching.

I knew Marv was relieved to be done. He had faithfully completed the work which God sent him back from heaven to do. Now we could relax in Arizona, golfing and visiting with our friends.

Except God had other plans. Marv had returned to earth almost six years beforehand, and had dearly longed to go back every minute of those years. We didn't know it that day at Russ' Restaurant, but God knew: Marv's time on earth was almost up.

The next day, Marv was hospitalized for pneumonia, and we spent the week of Christmas in the hospital. He was released briefly, only to be readmitted within a couple of days. This time he had pneumonia in the other lung. Marv was very weak, and it was so difficult for me to watch him in such a state, but I fully expected him to spend no more than two or three days in the hospital. During that time, I received more than one hundred emails from friends and family, concerned about Marv. He was so loved on this earth, but so much more loved in heaven.

On January 9, I noticed that Marv was experiencing marked weakness on his left side and had difficulty speaking and gripping the doctors' hands. A "stat" CT scan revealed a blood clot in the right side of the brain. He was transferred to ICU.

Here's an excerpt from my email to family and friends on January 13:

Marv has come through some very difficult days. He was able to pull out the feeding tube on Wednesday night. That had to be reinserted today. Swallowing remains a major problem. The feeding tube is necessary to give him many meds and maintain nutrition. He knows me but remains very tired. The doctors have a major dilemma. They reintroduce the anticoagulants and worry about bleeding around the clot in the brain. Or they stop the anticoagulants and worry about another blood clot. He remains very ill and truly in God's hands.

Marv continued to get worse, and on January 18, I had to make the hardest decision of my life—to have Marv's feeding tube removed. Another email:

After many tears, prayers and questions, we decided to stop all medication, food and keep him comfortable with pain meds. . . . This has been such a difficult decision but I know Marv would not want to live this way. Those of you who have heard him speak about his trip to Heaven know how much he wants to go back. This time it will be a one-way trip.

So many friends and family visited Marv for the next three days, including his co-writer, Lorilee. With tears rolling down her face, she held his hands and told him those two angels were coming for him, again. "Will you wait for me at the gate?" she asked him. Marv was barely coherent or lucid, but we could both tell he said "yes."

Our children and grandchildren were able to express their deep love for Marv, one more time.

On January 21, 2012, at 6:15 in the evening, Marv flew back to heaven. I had sat by his bedside that day, doing all

I could to make him comfortable, and whispering words of devotion. I loved him with all my heart. I knew he was at the departure gate, waiting for the angels.

A friend had brought me the devotional *Jesus Calling*. That day's reading gave me profound comfort. I also read it to Marv in those final hours:

> I want you to be all mine. I am weaning you from all other dependencies, Your security rests in Me alone—not in other people, not in circumstances. Depending only on Me may feel like walking on a tight rope, but there is a safety net underneath: *the everlasting arms*. So don't be afraid of falling. Instead look ahead to Me. I am always before you, beckoning you on—one step at a time. *Neither height nor depth nor anything else in all creation can separate you from My loving Presence.**

That day, God beckoned his child Marv straight into his everlasting arms. My dear one was at rest, back where he so longed to go.

Did those same two angels pick him up this time?

Was Peter there to greet him this time, and if so, what words passed between them?

I don't know the answers to those questions. But I know he has been reunited joyfully with our son William John and with our beloved son-in-law Steve.

I know that no intangible doorway separates him this time from those he cherished: his parents, his grandparents, and many friends.

Marv was sent back to us because God told him, "I have more work for you to do."

* Sarah Young, *Jesus Calling* (Nashville: Thomas Nelson, 2004), 22.

I believe that work was, in large part, this book you hold in your hands, a book completed one day before my husband's health began to fail, and filled with love from Marv to you, the reader. Of course, it is filled, much more than we can imagine, with love from the God who sent his stubborn servant back to write it.

Marv's dearest hope was that many others would glimpse the peace and glory he experienced in heaven. "Heaven is just love, plain and pure, something for us to enjoy forever and ever and ever," he wrote in these pages. Marv is basking in that incomparable love today!

—Ruth Besteman,
Byron Center, Michigan,
May 9, 2012

Coauthor's Acknowledgments

To the following people, my abiding gratitude:
To my precious Guild: Ann Byle, Alison Hodgson, Angela Blyker, Cynthia Beach, Shelly Beach, Sharron Carrns, and Tracy Groot, for unending support and love. Jana Olberg for sharing your beloved Dagny with me. Tracey Bianchi, Pastor David Beelen, Jamie Young, Gordy Van Haitsma. My agent, Esther Fedorkevitch, who never gave up on this project, and who was so good to Marv and Ruth. My old and new friends at Baker Publishing: Dwight Baker, the sales, marketing, editorial, and publicity teams, and especially to the smart and skilled Vicki Crumpton, who chose this project over so many others.

To my family, my love and thanks: Linda Reimer; Ken and Linda Craker; my husband, Doyle, and children,

Jonah, Ezra, and Phoebe—it was my joy to share Marv's slice of heaven with the people I love most.

To Ruth Besteman: Thank you for your huge help in every aspect of this book. Marv and I couldn't have written it without your support, encouragement, savvy insight, medical knowledge, and great memory. I came to love you and Marv dearly.

And to Marv: Thanks so much for trusting me with your story. It is one of the great honors of my life to write this book with you. Thank you for embracing me like a family member, and for being so sweet and funny and open-minded through this whole process. I miss you, but I know you are shining like the sun right now, with your God and those you love. When I die, I know you will be there at the gate, waiting, with a big smile on your face, and probably a crack about the Red Wings beating the Jets. We'll have to wait and see. Until we meet again, my thanks and love.

—Lorilee Craker

Marv Besteman (1934–2012) was a graduate of Calvin College, a veteran of the US Army, and a retired bank president. He spoke frequently during his last few years of life about his experience of heaven. He and his wife, Ruth, are the parents of three children and the grandparents of four. Marv passed away in January of 2012, joyfully anticipating his return to heaven.

Lorilee Craker is the author of twelve books, including *Money Secrets of the Amish*, nominated for a 2012 Audie Award; *A Is for Atticus: Baby Names from Great Books*; and the *New York Times* bestseller *Through the Storm* with Lynne Spears. A native of Winnipeg, Manitoba, she lives with her family in Grand Rapids, Michigan, where she also moonlights as an entertainment reporter for the *Grand Rapids Press*.

Share Marv's amazing story with
your *church*, your *friends*, your
family, or your *small group*.

Visit
www.MyJourneytoHeaven.com
to purchase the inspiring DVD of
Marv telling his story live
and to download the free small group study guide.

FLIGHT TO HEAVEN

CAPT. DALE BLACK

WRITTEN IN COLLABORATION WITH KEN GIRE

This book is dedicated to my wife, Paula,
whom I love and adore, cherish, and respect.
Without her gentle and loving prodding,
you would not be reading about my journey to heaven
or be holding this book in your hands.

IN LOVING MEMORY OF
my grandfather Russell L. Price,
a man who learned to walk by faith and not by sight.

ACKNOWLEDGMENTS

After spending four years writing this book and another two years getting the help needed to bring it to fruition, the credit for the final product is broad based.

The largest thanks goes to the most important person in making this book become reality, my best friend and wife of almost forty years, Paula Black. My love and appreciation also go to my children, Eric and Kara, for enriching my life in so many ways.

I wish to thank author Beverly Swerling Martin, my writing coach, for her invaluable guidance and editing of this project. Much thanks to Lela Gilbert for helping write an earlier manuscript and to Greg Johnson, my literary agent, who believed in this project from the outset and quickly arranged the details for publication. Thank you to Kyle Duncan for being such an instrumental and effective liaison for this project with Bethany House Publishers and embracing it with his heart. Thanks go to Jeff Braun for his strategic suggestions, editing, and invaluable help in bringing this book to completion. A huge thank-you mixed with awe goes to Ken Gire, a writer with amazing skill and talent, who contributed his abilities to enhance the story in major ways.

A big thank-you for her tireless and encouraging work as my personal editor goes to Sandi Gregston. Also thanks to Ray Gregston, Dana McCue, and Nicole Elliott for their suggestions and editing of the earlier manuscript.

Thanks also to Harold Morby, a veteran of sixty years of professional photography, for taking and providing the aerial photos of the crash site.

Thanks to my sweet mother, Joyce Black, for her contagious upbeat attitude, her unending love, and for blessing her family with songs of praise throughout a lifetime.

Lastly, I wish to thank and recognize a loyal and loving friend, Kara Joy Black, the best daughter any father ever had. Kara has developed wisdom well beyond her years and I found myself seeking her counsel regularly in preparing this book.

PROLOGUE

My life was forever changed after a plane crash.

I was the only survivor.

For days I remained in an intensive care unit, but not before taking an uncharted trip . . . to heaven. What I experienced there, words cannot do justice. Even the best words pale before the indescribable. For many months following the crash, due to serious amnesia, I remembered nothing. Nothing of the crash, the first three days in the hospital, or my visit to heaven. At least, my *mind* did not remember. My heart? Well, that's a different story.

I was assigned to Dr. Homer Graham, best known as Evel Knievel's surgeon. My injuries were massive, but when I awoke in the ICU, I was a changed man. Yet I had no memory as to why. It seemed as if I had been given new eyes. I felt as though I were looking into another dimension. That was forty years ago.

What you're about to read is how my life was turned upside down by an airplane crash and why every major decision I've made since then has been a direct result of my journey to heaven. Those who know me may now understand why I've seemed like a bit of a misfit and why my life has often followed an offbeat path.

You'll learn why I've been emboldened and compelled to share the love of God with others. Why I volunteered on almost a thousand flights to more than fifty countries, building churches, orphanages, and medical clinics. And why I've trained lay ministers and medical personnel to help the needy worldwide, usually at my own expense.

Since that fateful day, I have shared my story about the crash and the amazing recovery many times. But I have never shared publicly about my journey to heaven, until now.

How could I keep this life-changing event a secret? There are several reasons.

Right after the crash my memory was like a jigsaw puzzle with only a few recognizable pieces. It would take eight months to start getting my memory back. And even longer for my injured mind and my transformed heart to get in sync.

As soon as my memory returned, I told my grandfather everything that had happened, but he cautioned me about telling others. "Dale," he said, "you can speak about your experience, or you can treat it as sacred and let your life be a reflection of your experience. By that I mean, if you really did see the other side, then live out whatever you believe you saw. Live what you believe you heard. Just live what you learned. Your life's actions will speak louder than your voice."

So I made a solemn promise to myself and to God not to share my experience with anyone until He made it clear to do so. At the time I figured God might want me to keep the secret for only a year or two.

Soon after the crash I attended a church service where a man claimed to have died, visited heaven, and come back to life. To me, the service was more self-serving than sacred. The very essence of heaven is God, yet the people were more interested in the sensation rather than the One who created it all and Whom heaven is all about. I was grieved by the event and my decision not to discuss my journey with anyone was further solidified.

It also wasn't hard to keep my secret because at times in my life, I have been truly disappointed in myself. Why couldn't I have lived an even better life? Since I had clearly seen heaven and was so changed by the experience, why did I fail again and again to be the man I truly wanted to be? Why did I fail often to be a reflection of what I had seen and heard and learned?

I guess seeing heaven didn't change the fact that I'm human. Not only human—but also very flawed.

So why share my experience now? Personally, I was perfectly content to keep my silence longer still. But the Lord orchestrated a series of events that convinced me it is now His time to share about my journey to heaven and back. For four decades I *did live* my experience. Now I am compelled to tell how.

In some ways this story is about me. But it is not about me ultimately, nor should it be. It is about God. And it is about you. The two of you together, entwined in a story that, to me, is still breathtakingly sacred. My hope is that you will read not just with your mind but with an open heart. If you do, you may receive more than you bargained for.

My story begins as I pilot a jet on a volunteer missionary flight in the dark of night over Zambia, Africa . . . at 41,000 feet. So please, fasten your seat belt, put your tray table in its upright and locked position, and hold on. It's quite a ride.

For the first time in forty years, here is my story.

—Capt. Dale Black

① FLIGHT INTO ETERNITY

All passengers and crew will be dead in twenty-seven minutes if something drastic doesn't change.

And I will be responsible.

With very little fuel remaining in our tanks, I'm out of options and out of time. And a lot of things just don't make sense.

The copilot's hand trembles as he brings the microphone close to his ashen face. "Lusaka Approach, Lusaka Tower, Zambia Center. Anyone? Learjet Four-Alpha-Echo. Mayday, Mayday, Mayday."

Still no response.

Thirty-eight-year-old veteran copilot Steve Holmes peers through the jet's windshield from the right seat and demands an answer.

"Where is the city? What is going on here?" He shakes his head slowly in stunned disbelief, for he too has weighed our options, and they are dwindling fast.

Our gleaming luxury jet is equipped with the latest modern avionics package, including dual global navigation systems, but both became INOP (inoperative) over an hour ago. We have no idea why. No one is responding to our radio transmissions either, and in my sixteen years of professional flying, nothing has prepared me for what is happening now.

Nothing could have. I feel my chest constricting as I reach behind me and lock the cockpit door.

Transmitting on one-two-one-point-five, the emergency frequency that all controllers monitor, we try again.

"Mayday, Mayday, Mayday. Learjet November-Four-Two-Four-Alpha-Echo. Can anyone read? Over."

Again nothing. Only the hiss of static.

Trying to slow my breathing and focus my thoughts, I lean forward, looking out the jet's multilayered Plexiglas windshield.

"I've seen campfires from forty thousand feet before, Steve. I don't want to start our descent until we can see the lights of the city. Something should be visible. Keep looking."

Guilt gnaws at my stomach. My heart pounds wildly.

How could I have allowed this to happen? How can so many things go wrong—all at the same time?

As an airline pilot on temporary furlough from Trans World Airlines (TWA), I started a jet pilot training and jet sales corporation in Southern California. I donated airplanes, pilots, and maintenance services to help train and transport individuals to supply Bibles, gospel tracts, medical personnel, and supplies to those in need.

This two-week-long volunteer flight is one of hundreds I've conducted over the last several years, feeling compelled to share God's overwhelming love with others in a hurting world.

This month takes us throughout Europe, the Middle East, and Africa.

So far God has provided the means and the protection to accomplish our mission, but on this flight everything is starting to fall apart. Events are beginning to spiral out of control.

Along with a professional flight planning service, both Steve and I have prepared meticulously for this flight. Three full-time professionals, for three full days, conducted intense flight planning. We accessed the latest international flight data resources and arranged for every foreseeable contingency. We dotted every i and crossed every t—or so we thought.

The latest weather forecast indicated visibility would be unlimited for hundreds of miles around the capital of Zambia, our planned fuel stop. This flight should have been routine even with the extended holding delay required earlier by Sudanese Air Traffic Control.

I pray silently.

Steve rips off his headset and flings it across the cockpit pedestal.

Trying to breathe, trying to steel myself, I speak slowly but firmly. "Steve, we need to work together. Let's believe that God will help us get this aircraft on the ground safely, during our first and only approach. Can you do that?"

Steve shoots me a hard look. "Sure." Then he slams the thick checklist into the Learjet's side pocket. "*Approach Descent Checklist* complete." As a self-proclaimed agnostic, Steve doesn't appreciate my reliance on God. At least not yet.

"I'll land on any runway I can see, Steve. We may be in thin clouds or above a layer of low stratus. The lights of the entire city, the whole country for that matter, may be out for some reason. Now, I've never seen this before, and I've got to admit I've never heard of it either. I know that doesn't explain why we can't see lights from a car, a truck, a campfire, or something. But, Steve, we'll get this aircraft on the ground in just a few minutes, I assure you."

"Flaps 10 degrees," I command.

I hear the familiar whine of flap actuators responding.

Both NAV needles move steadily toward the center of my HSI (horizontal situation indicator), verifying that we are on course. But to where? *Lusaka, right?*

Yes, Lusaka, our planned destination. It must be Lusaka, I tell myself.

"*Glide slope* alive," I continue. "Give me gear down, flaps 20, and the *Before Landing Checklist.*"

"Roger, gear coming down, flaps 20, and the Before Landing Checklist."

Seconds later.

"Flaps 40, please."

I hear the tremor in Steve's voice. "Flaps 40 selected, 40 indicated, the Before Landing Checklist is complete."

The sleek jet is all set for landing. No switches need to be moved again until safely on the ground—if we can find a runway. Making minor adjustments on the power levers and flight controls, I keep the speed at precisely 127 knots while adjusting heading and pitch to stay on course and on glide slope. I fly using reference to the instruments only, while Steve peers into the blackness, straining for any sign of an airport and cross-checking my every move.

The muscles in Steve's face visibly tighten as he speaks.

"One thousand feet above *minimums*." *Minimums* means two hundred feet above the runway and the lowest altitude we can safely fly on instruments. Unless we can see a visible runway, we cannot descend below minimums ... period.

With a feather-like touch on the power levers, I reduce speed a tad while turning right just one degree to stay on course, on speed, and on glide slope.

We will find this runway, on our first approach, I assure myself.

"Five hundred feet above minimums."

"Do you have visual?" I feel my stomach tighten.

"Negative. No visual. No ground contact. One hundred feet above minimums."

Steve shakes his head slowly.

"Keep looking outside, Steve, but call minimums."

A few seconds pass, then Steve winces and barks, "Minimums, minimums. No contact."

For a split second I tear my eyes away from the cockpit instruments to look outside just above the aircraft's long slender nose. Directly ahead there should be a visible runway—only utter blackness stares back. That's when my heart stops.

On the outside I appear calm and cool, but it's only an act.

Forcing my mind to stay in control, I advance the throttles to *go around* thrust for the *missed approach* and pitch the aircraft up to a 15-degree nose-high attitude. My stomach cringes, knowing that the jet's two engines are now guzzling our limited fuel reserves with the force of two fire hoses. At this altitude and with the high drag, we're burning fuel four times faster than at cruise speed. Fuel, our aircraft's life blood, is being sucked dry.

Fighting to keep my thoughts from running wild, Steve and I review our in-flight scenario. There are no clouds, no fog or weather of any kind, verified by the crescent-moon light reflecting off our jet's shiny wings—all the way down to two hundred feet. With a population of over a million people, the city of Lusaka seems to have disappeared. Not a car or truck light is seen. There are no street lights or campfires. We are about down to fumes remaining in the fuel tanks, and at two hundred feet we see no runway—no airport—not even any trace of the *ground.*

It's not just fear that silently strangles me. It's total disbelief. And I can barely breathe.

The radios continue their silence.

In my sixteen years of flying jets and training pilots, I have never heard of this before. *Are we way off course? If so, how far? Are we flying over water? Are we above some invisible layer of fog? Are the altimeters grossly in error?* Nothing makes sense. My once-starched white-collared shirt is now damp and wilted, and my heart is racing.

In a voice just above a whisper I pray out loud, "Lord, what should I do? You always answer prayer; so God, what should I do now?"

While flying a worthless holding pattern twelve-thousand feet somewhere over Zambia, trying to sort out our in-flight midnight emergency, with only minutes of fuel remaining in the Learjet's tanks, my mind flashes back to another flight . . . the life-changing airplane crash in which I was just a passenger—yet the only survivor.

The flight that changed how I see things.
The flight that changed me forever.
The single flight that has defined my very existence.

FRIDAY, JULY 18, 1969

I was nineteen.

It was before daybreak in my hometown of Los Alamitos, about half past four, and the sky was a dove gray with only a light feathering of low clouds. The morning paper had yet to arrive, but the day before, the *LA Times* announced: "Astronauts Prepare Landing Craft as Apollo Nears Moon." The Apollo 11 flight had dominated the news that week. All eyes and ears were on the heavens, tracking the spacecraft's every move, listening to its every transmission. The world was mesmerized. At the moment, though, most of my part of the world, Southern California, was asleep—oblivious to Apollo 11 speeding through space and oblivious to my MGB speeding through its streets on the way to Burbank Airport.[1] A lightweight dark green roadster, it could do 0 to 60 in just over eleven seconds.

What can I say? I was nineteen, with testosterone racing through my veins.

I was an athlete, playing shortstop for Pasadena College, and an aviator on my way to flying jets. I was a driven person, particularly at that time in my life. I went to school full time, played baseball, and worked at my family's business, which manufactured redwood shavings, hauling truckloads off to various places in California for use in landscaping everything from freeways to golf courses. Since childhood I worked in the trucking division, loading and unloading trucks, and performing routine maintenance on the big rigs. Several times a week I came to the plant after hours, looking for some additional work. I often spent my evenings catching up on truck maintenance. Sometimes I would run the packaging machine or baler all

---

[1] Hollywood-Burbank Airport (BUR), mentioned repeatedly in this book, changed its name in 2003 to Bob Hope Airport.

night to fill an order for the next day. But most of the time I would drive an 18-wheeler all night long, filled with bulk redwood shavings, and usually returned just in time to make my morning classes. After paying my way through college, any time and money I had left I spent taking flying lessons at Brackett Air Service in La Verne.

Looking back, I don't know how I did it. The "why" was easy. I wanted everything life had to offer. That meant logging a lot of hours in the class-room, on the playing field, and in the air. All of which took money. I wasn't a trust-fund kid. I didn't get an allowance. I didn't get any help with school, let alone my extracurricular activities. Flying was expensive. Cars were expensive. School was expensive. And though my parents didn't help financially, they did give me the opportunity to work as many hours as I wanted so I could earn the money to pay for those things.

One of those things was the British-made convertible I was driving into the sunrise of a beautiful Southern California morning. Two days of Santa Ana winds had cleared the haze from the San Fernando Valley. The only color in the sky was a streak of orange. The only sound the rpms in my four-cylinder engine, whining for me to shift.

Did I mention I was nineteen?

And did I also mention that a month earlier the college had expelled me? It wasn't a slap-on-the-wrist suspension. It was permanent.

But it didn't matter. With my hand on the gearshift and my pilot's license in my hip pocket, I was living my dream, the star of my own movie.

My life was an action-adventure film waiting for the opening credits to finish so the story could get started and the adrenaline kick in. I was so close to getting that story started. For me, the opening credits were courses taken in school and hours logged in flight.

I shaved a curb with the tires screeching.

Even with Vietnam breathing down my neck, I didn't give a thought to losing my student deferment. After all, I was nineteen, and I was invincible. There were other colleges. And I reasoned that if I didn't get a baseball scholarship to one of them, I'd get one playing football. Other than flying, nothing made me feel more alive than a hard-hitting game of tackle.

But none of that mattered. Not now.

All that mattered was my date with a sleek twin-engine Piper Navajo. Soon I would be in the air, soaring above the snarl of L.A. traffic. All my cares would be behind me, including college with its classwork and course schedules and the thankless, never-ending work of driving a truck.

Once at the airport, I downshifted, careful not to ruffle anyone's feathers. Careful to show proper respect. For this was sacred ground to me, this place where my dreams were on the tarmac, waiting for me to climb into the cockpit and strap on the seat belt.

Ever since I was fourteen, I wanted to become a commercial pilot—to travel, see the world, wear the uniform, live the adventure.

I wanted it all.

And I wanted it bad.

To get there, I needed a mentor. I was meeting with him that morning. His name was Chuck Burns, a twenty-seven-year-old commercial pilot. He had the license, the uniform, the skill, everything. And he was willing to take me under his wing.

I would show up two or three times a week to help him with his work, flying throughout the state to deliver bank checks. Even though I got paid nothing for my efforts, I got to log a lot of flight time. As a young pilot, that was compensation enough, plus it was a golden opportunity to fly in a quality aircraft and learn from an awesome instructor.

I still have the logbook of those early flights. My first flight with Chuck was May 29, 1969, in a Piper Aztec. We had become fast friends. More than friends. He had become like an older brother to me.

I was first to arrive on the tarmac where the red-and-white Piper Navajo was parked. The Navajo was a family of twin-engine planes designed in the mid-'60s by Piper Aircraft and targeted for small-scale cargo operations and the corporate market. The Turbo Navajo could hold up to seven passengers, plus crew, and came with powerful Lycoming engines rated at 310 horsepower each. The propellers were controllable pitch, fully feathering Hartzells. Empty, the plane weighed a little under four thousand pounds with a maximum takeoff weight of almost seven thousand. The maximum speed was 261 mph with a cruising speed of 238.

Chuck and I had taken the Navajo out on the town just the night before. He and I had double-dated, impressing the girls with the lights that were spread over Southern California like a glittering array of jewels on a black velvet background. It had been a beautiful evening—no wind, no clouds, and just a little haze. Chuck had taken off and landed, letting me do the flying in between. We had veered the plane over Van Nuys, then over Los Angeles. Back then, there was limited air traffic control. The air space above three thousand feet was more or less free to roam. And roam we did. Hollywood. Santa Monica. Arcadia. Pasadena. We had seen it all. And, more important, we had impressed our dates. We had gotten home fairly late, so it was an early morning for both of us.

The airplane had flown effortlessly, not giving a bit of trouble or raising any concerns. Even though it had been less than eight hours since our evening flight, I couldn't wait to get back into the air.

It was a thrill to be alone with such an aircraft, its sturdy workhorse function bred with a sleek racehorse form, as beautiful as it was powerful. I checked out the aircraft's structure, examining everything from the wheels to the windshield. I felt like a jockey checking out the Thoroughbred he was about to race, examining the legs, the saddle, the reins.

Everything checked out. That's when I climbed into the cockpit. Sat there a minute, just taking it all in. The dials, the switches. The smell of leather and metal. The feel of my hands gripping the controls. The feel of my dreams ready to take flight.

I made a few checks, then started the engines. They coughed to life but quickly evened out to a strum. The propellers burst into a whirl, then a blur.

The sensation of that much power in your hands, it was exhilarating.

223

I cut the engines, and all that power died at the touch of a hand. *My* hand.

It was more than exhilarating; it was intoxicating.

I got out of the plane and waited near the aircraft's tail, looking over at the giant commercial jets lined up at their respective gates; over at others taxiing on the tarmac, waiting their turn to take off. My blood stirred as the roar of their massive engines launched them into the air.

Though I grew up in the '60s, I was never a child of the '60s. The whole drug scene passed me by without giving me a second look. I did love a lot of the music, though. Many of the lyrics spoke of drug use. "Eight Miles High" by the Byrds, for example: "Eight miles high, and when I touch down . . ."

These jets could fly eight miles high, literally. I had flown pretty high myself in smaller planes. I was sure that no drug could come close to the feeling of flying that high, especially in that powerful of a plane.

Which made you feel powerful yourself.

You can't imagine the feeling of taking off in one of those things, flying in one, landing one—the final approach . . . the stripes on the runway coming at you at over 100 mph . . . the yelp of rubber as you touch down . . . the roar of the engines catching up to you.

What a rush!

My parents didn't share my enthusiasm for flying. They weren't any different from other parents raising kids in the '60s. There were plenty of things to worry about on the ground—drugs, sex, the British invasion and the music they brought with them, Vietnam. What parent would want to add to the list by putting their kid in an oblong box of metal and letting him take it to forty thousand feet?

And besides, they had hopes that I would stay in the family business. Grandpa, who started it, was there. My dad, who started his own company within Grandpa's business, was there. My two uncles. Mom. Grandma. My brothers and several cousins. It was just kind of expected that I would follow suit.

I think they thought I would get flying out of my system someday and come down to earth, get my feet on the ground, and put my nameplate on a desk in the company office. But they saw how passionate I was about flying—how driven—and they indulged me.

Another jet took off, its surging engines causing something to resonate within me that I can't explain. It was like hearing the most stirring music being played, everything within you reverberating to the music, and in one swelling crescendo speaking to your soul, saying, "This is what you were made for."

My daydreams were interrupted by a pleasant man in his thirties who approached me, offering his hand.

"I'm Gene Bain. I'll be flying with you today."

His handshake was firm and confident.

Gene was a Fresno police officer and a friend of the company's chief pilot. He also had his commercial license and on occasion had flown the route by himself. He also had a good reputation as a pilot, which was important. After all, I was putting my life in his hands.

"Have you gone through a pre-flight and engine run-up yet?"

"Well, not really," I said.

Actually I had, and everything checked out, but I didn't want him to know. I felt too inexperienced to shoulder that much responsibility.

"I did warm up the engines," I confessed, "and conducted the pre-flight on the exterior, but you had better go ahead and check it out yourself."

We'll be twice as safe today, I thought.

A few minutes later Chuck joined Gene and me, and the three of us walked briskly to the plane that was to take us northward to Santa Maria, Coalinga, Fresno, Visalia, Bakersfield, and several other stops in the state.

We climbed aboard and settled into our flight positions. Gene took the pilot's seat. I took the seat next to him, the copilot's seat. And Chuck, the most experienced of us, sat on a temporary third seat behind us so that he could monitor our every move.

The weather was calm. The sky clear. And I felt relaxed as Gene started the engines. The propellers kicked in. So did my heart. Revving in anticipation of taking flight.

As Gene taxied the aircraft toward the runway, though, the calm was broken. He seemed overly abrupt and aggressive on the flight controls. I wondered what his problem was.

Chuck wondered too, though he didn't say anything. He just tapped me on the shoulder and motioned for me to change places with him.

As Chuck fastened his seat belt, we approached Runway 15. We would be making an "intersection departure," our usual procedure. This simply meant that instead of taxiing to the far end of the runway, we would leave from the terminal parking lot where the plane was, and we would take off from the place that intersected with the runway. This meant we would not use the twelve hundred feet of runway that was behind us. By doing that, we saved a little time and a little fuel.

We paused for the necessary engine run-ups and to go through the Before Takeoff Checklist. Gene flipped the switches, checked the gauges. I watched him go through every procedure, procedures that by now I could do with my eyes closed.

All primary and secondary systems checked out.

Chuck watched it all, monitored it all. If he was feeling uneasy, he didn't show it.

At last we were cleared for takeoff. Gene throttled the engines and steered the plane toward the southeast horizon.

Through the window I caught a glimpse of a PSA Boeing 727 taxiing a few hundred feet away. Don't get me wrong, the Navajo was a great plane. But it was dwarfed by the 727. *I will be flying one of those someday,* I thought, which was less of a thought and more of a vow.

Words crackled from the control tower.

"Navajo Five-Zero-Yankee, this is Burbank Tower. You're cleared for takeoff, Runway one-five. After takeoff, turn right, heading two-four-zero, climb and maintain three thousand. Departure control will be on one-two-four-point-six-five."

Chuck spoke into the microphone. "Roger. Navajo Five-Zero-Yankee cleared to go. Runway one-five, right heading two-four-zero, climb and maintain three thousand and twenty-four-sixty-five."

All systems were go. Gene throttled to maximum takeoff power, and the plane accelerated down the runway, causing it to bounce slightly. But that usually happened.

What didn't usually happen was that we were suddenly airborne at an abnormally slow speed. I scanned the dials as questions raced through my mind. *Why were we airborne so soon? Why would Gene take off at less than normal airspeed with the plane fully loaded with fuel and cargo?*

I said nothing. After all, he was a good pilot, I was told, and twice my age.

The engines strained under the weight and the lack of lift. They seemed out of sync with each other. Disturbingly so. Instead of the familiar harmony between the two engines, their rpms gave a dissonant whine.

Something was terribly wrong. I knew it. Chuck knew it. Gene knew it.

Chuck barked the bone-chilling words that confirmed my worst fears. "Let's land in that clear area over there." He pointed toward a cemetery a few hundred yards away.

I held my breath as the sight of pine trees filled the front windshield. *We're not climbing,* I said to myself. *We're not going to clear those trees.*

Every muscle in my body froze.

My God, we're going to crash!

Chuck lunged for the flight controls.

I braced myself for impact.

I was nineteen.

②
PORTAL OF THE FOLDED WINGS

Because of that crash, a part of me would forever be nineteen.

And no part of me would ever be the same.

The last thing I remembered was the sight of Chuck's hands on the controls, violently wrenching the flight controls fully left and fully back.

I remembered nothing of the plane clipping the treetops at eighty feet. I remembered nothing of the plane careening head-on into a seventy-five-foot structure with a mosaic dome. Nothing of the sound of metal slamming into concrete or the plane shattering to pieces. I remembered nothing of the impact with the ground, nothing of the excruciating pain, nothing of the eerie silence that undoubtedly followed and the suffocating smell of airplane fuel that would have hung in the air like a toxic cloud.

What I do remember came back to me in the most fragmentary of ways. A piece at a time. My memory was like a jigsaw puzzle with only a few recognizable pieces and no overall picture to serve as a reference. Besides the pieces that were missing, the pieces I did have were turned over in my mind, without color or clue as to where they fit.

Although I remembered nothing of the fall, for example, for years after the crash I would be jolted awake from a sound sleep by my arms flailing in circles, trying to balance myself as I fell helplessly through the air. That is how things came back to me. A frightful image from a dream. A sudden flash of memory. A newspaper article piecing together the events. An eyewitness handing me some missing piece to the puzzle.

228

Not only was the plane shattered, pieces of the wreckage lying everywhere, my mind was shattered, twisted pieces of memory scattered over the landscape of the year that stretched before me. Some of what follows was told to me by ambulance personnel, doctors, and friends who visited the crash sight.

Gene and Chuck were thrown from the plane. Gene was not moving. Chuck was lying on the ground, moaning. Apparently I was still in what remained of the cockpit, lying like a rag doll, limp and motionless. The three of us hit the ground within five feet of each other.

I'm not sure how long I lay there. I was later told that the Burbank Tower had summoned an ambulance that arrived eleven minutes after the crash. When paramedics arrived, they found me staggering through the rubble in a state of shock. I was drenched in fuel, both hands clutching my blood-streaked face with parts of the airplane sticking out of my head and legs. They ran to me and gingerly laid me on the ground.

Chuck and I were put into the same ambulance that sped through the streets, siren blaring. When the ambulance arrived at nearby St. Joseph Hospital, a trauma team was scrubbed and ready for us.

At this point, I didn't know where I was or how I got there.

That is what blunt-force trauma does. The brain goes into autopilot mode. It runs the way it was programmed to run without interference from the conscious mind. It takes control, marshaling the body's resources to deal with the trauma the body is experiencing.

As we burst through the doors of the ER, something inexplicable happened, sending me into uncharted territory.

Suddenly I found myself suspended in midair, hovering over the wreckage of my body. My gray pants and short-sleeve shirt were torn to shreds and soaked in blood and fuel.

I had a bird's-eye view of the entire ER and watched the flurry of activity like a bystander. They wheeled the blue gurney I was on into a room about thirty-five-feet square.

They undid the red straps that held me and moved me onto a metal table. I hovered above the end of the table, near my feet, and just below the acoustical tile ceiling.

A thick-boned, gray-headed doctor approached my body, standing near my left shoulder, and began inspecting me. He gently turned my head to the left, focusing on the damage to my face. He went about his work professionally and unemotionally.

What happened to me? I wondered. *Where am I?*

Three nurses were in the room, the shortest of which stood to the doctor's left. The other two were on the opposite side of the table, cutting off what remained of my clothes, working furiously.

It was then I noticed that my hearing was impaired. I was only a few feet away, but I could barely hear any sounds, barely make out any words, though I could see everything clearly and distinctly.

As the trauma team worked feverishly, I felt surprisingly detached. I recognized myself on the table, but felt no anxiety, no sense of urgency, no pain, no sadness, nothing.

It was a schizophrenic feeling, being two places at once, your body on the table below, another very real part of you floating near the ceiling above. *That may be my body,* I thought, *but I'm up here. I can't be dead because I feel so alive.* Amazingly, I wasn't shocked by all this, just curious, still wondering what had happened.

I looked around the room, surveying the surroundings. The floor was covered in white tiles. Within each were tiny bits of black running in one direction. My eyes followed the tiles from the floor, up the wall, where they stopped about shoulder high.

I noticed the medical equipment, the trays with instruments spread out, the medical staff in gowns. It was all cold and sterile.

All the while, I couldn't stop wondering, *This must be a hospital, but why am I here? What happened?*

Then I experienced the first emotions in my suspended state. A commotion was going on to my left in a room partitioned off by gray curtains. I strained to see what was happening, but I couldn't see through the curtains

230

and I wasn't high enough to look over them. The sounds were garbled, and I couldn't make out what was being said, though I sensed urgency.

I was keenly aware of the atmosphere. Intense, filled with anxiety. Suddenly a wave of sadness washed over me. Medical personnel scurried in and out the room. The sense of loss and grief was heavy beyond belief. The worst feeling I've had in my entire life. The ache was so deep and so intense I couldn't think about anything else.

Then suddenly, without warning, a clear and powerful memory flashed into my mind. I was in the fifth grade. I was a tenderhearted kid who had just received Jesus Christ as his personal Lord and Savior. I remember how truly I believed the Bible's teaching about Jesus being God's only Son and that He loved me. I recall how genuinely sorry I was for my sins and how I prayed that night at church camp for Jesus to be my Savior and friend. I was so full of love for Him, full of zeal. Even at that young age I was filled with purpose and peace.

On the heels of that flashback came a new realization. I was no longer that tenderhearted kid. I was selfish and arrogant. A person who loved a lot of things but not the things God loved. A person who had zeal for a lot of things but not for the things the Lord had zeal for.

It was about me. It was all about me. *My* life. *My* career. *My* hopes. *My* dreams.

My rush.

I felt shame, sadness, grief.

The feelings were palpable. They had weight. And I felt like the weight of those feelings was pulling me down.

Then in a heartbeat the heaviness left. I felt light again. Like I was a hot-air balloon that had been untethered from its moorings and was drifting skyward.

I began moving higher, slowly but steadily. I noticed details in the light fixtures as I approached them. I saw into the air-conditioning ducts in the ceiling. I was moving away from my body, slowly . . . out of the room . . . down the hallway.

I began picking up speed. The movement was effortless, and I had no sensation of self-movement. I didn't know where I was going, but I was distinctly aware that some irresistible force was drawing me there.

The speed of my movement increased. I couldn't stop it, couldn't steer it.

I moved faster, faster, and faster still.

Then suddenly . . .

I was gone.

3

AT THE EDGE OF DEATH

The phone rang at my parents' home in Los Alamitos, interrupting my mother's quiet morning routine.

"Mrs. Black?" said the voice on the other end of the phone.

"Yes."

"This is St. Joseph Hospital in Burbank. I'm sorry to tell you this, but ... there's been a plane crash. One man was killed. At this time there are two survivors. Both are in critical condition. One of them is your son."

My mother listened in stunned silence, said she would be right there, and hung up. She dialed my father's office, and the secretary pulled him out of a meeting to tell him the news and that his wife was on the way to pick him up.

Somehow Mom made the drive to Long Beach Shavings Company, where my dad was co-owner. Along the way her thoughts hounded her. *This can't be happening. I should have asked more questions. Why didn't I ask more questions?*

It was as if she had stepped into a nightmare she couldn't wake up from, and her thoughts were terrifying creatures that just kept coming and coming and coming. She couldn't run from them, and she couldn't hide.

She fumbled with the knob on the car radio, hoping to find a newsbreak that might give her more information. Information she desperately wanted to hear and at the same time didn't.

He's alive, she said to herself. *Thank God, he's still alive.* She gripped the steering wheel tighter, more determined, and stomped on the accelerator, not a minute to lose.

Screeching into the company parking lot, Mom ran toward the door where Dad was pacing. She collapsed in his arms, releasing the tears she could no longer hold back.

But this was no time for tears. They had to hurry. Dad rushed her to the car, took the wheel, and raced north on the Long Beach Freeway. They were weaving in and out of traffic, ignoring the blare of horns. Once again Mom turned on the radio, and once again came the news. Both strained to hear over the noise of the traffic.

"A second fatality has been reported in this morning's airplane crash just outside of Hollywood-Burbank Airport. Names are being withheld pending notification of next of kin."

One was still alive! Which one? The rest of the way neither of them spoke, fearing the worst but praying for the best. The trip seemed like an eternity. Finally they slammed on the brakes in the hospital parking lot. They shot out of the car, raced toward the emergency room, and burst through the doors, their faces wringing with emotion.

"*My son.* He was in a plane crash. Is he alive?" my dad asked breathlessly.

Everything in the ER stopped, all eyes riveted on them. The nurse at the desk froze.

"Well, is he alive or not?" my father demanded.

"It depends on what your last name is," she said.

"Black. My son's name is *Dale* Black."

"Yes, sir, your son is alive." Mom almost collapsed. "But let me warn you," the nurse said, "his injuries are massive. He's suffered a tremendous trauma and is in critical condition."

"Can we see him?"

The nurse shook her head. "He's in surgery. You can go to the waiting room and check in. Someone will come out and let you know how he is doing."

Hours passed, painfully uncertain moments at a time. My parents made a few phone calls, and soon the waiting room was full of friends and family, all in a state of shock, some crying, most of them praying. Talking amongst themselves to bolster their courage. Preparing themselves each time someone in hospital scrubs came to update them on my condition.

I was in the operating room for ten hours. Nurses sponged my body of blood and aviation fuel. They hooked me up to various monitors and IVs, put a tube down my throat, and went to work. A tag team of surgeons, nurses, and anesthesiologists labored to keep me alive.

The free fall undoubtedly caused major trauma to my internal organs. There was concern that they had burst, shut down, or suffered severe lacerations. Another concern was for whatever fractures my skeletal structure had sustained. The primary area of focus, though, was the neurological system. Was there brain damage? Spinal cord injury?

A husky-looking doctor came into the waiting room. "The Black family?" he called. Every conversation stopped. Mom and Dad made themselves known.

"We're his parents."

"Dr. Graham."

Dr. Homer Graham was one of the best orthopedic surgeons in the country. I was in the best care possible. But my parents didn't know this at the time. All they knew was what they'd gotten from the radio on the way to the hospital and then what they heard from the nurse at the front desk.

"He's alive."

"Oh, thank God," they said, breathing a sigh of relief.

"We're still working on him. Should be a long day. Things are touch and go. But we've got a good team in place, and we'll give him our best."

It was indeed a long day, both for the people in the operating room and for the ones in the waiting room. At the end of the day, Dr. Graham came out again, his gown drenched with sweat.

"How is he?" my dad asked.

"Both ankles and knees were broken. Both legs fractured. His back was broken in three places."

My mother gasped. "Is he—"

"Paralyzed?" the doctor said. "Too early to tell."

The doctor paused, seeing these were painful words for my parents. Then he continued.

"His left arm and shoulder were severely dâmaged. The ball-and-socket in his left shoulder exploded on impact. His right arm was fractured. His left ankle was crushed beyond repair."

My mother bit back the tears, wondering about the ramifications of "beyond repair."

"Debris from the aircraft penetrated both legs. His face was brutally lacerated with a gash through the middle of his forehead, eyebrow, and into his right eye," the doctor said, indicating on his own face where the gash occurred. "The right side of his head was virtually shaved off. We'll do the best plastic surgery we can . . ." He paused, searching for the right words. "Regardless, he won't look the way he used to."

The avalanche of bad news buried my parents. All they could do was stand there, frozen and numb.

At last my father spoke. "What's the prognosis, long term?"

"If he survives, he won't regain use of his left arm and leg. All the doctors concur. Paralysis is a threat; we'll be watching closely for that. He'll be blind or nearly blind in his right eye. And—" he paused— "there's a strong possibility of brain damage. He survived a strong blow to the head; it's reasonable to assume he didn't survive it without some permanent damage. The next twenty-four to forty-eight hours are critical."

The words *if he survives* resounded in my parents' thoughts over the days ahead, echoing in the empty moments when they were alone. Walking the hallways of every waking hour. Haunting the stillness at night. Staring at them in the morning.

If he survives . . .

(4)
NEW EYES FOR A NEW DIMENSION

For three days I was in a coma. I was watched around the clock, nurses shuffling in and out at all times of the day and night to check my vitals, change my bandages, see if the stitches were holding, if the swelling was under control.

My parents were at the hospital much of the time. My grandparents came, my brothers, my aunts and uncles. Friends from school. Co-workers at the company. They prayed, they cried, they worried, and they wondered. *Would I survive? Would I be paralyzed? Would I be brain damaged? Would I walk again? Talk again? Play sports again?*

After three very difficult days, of which I had no memory, I regained consciousness. It was early morning of the fourth day, Monday, July 21.

I awoke slowly, groggily, with a strange sensation in my head. It was the sound of glorious music dying away, as if I had just heard the last note of a crescendo that was resonating in the air after it had been played. Now other sounds pushed themselves into the foreground—the sound of rubber-soled shoes scurrying dutifully about in the hallway, of people's voices muffled outside my door, of wheels rolling over linoleum.

I tried to remember where I was. I had a dim memory that it was a hospital, but no memory of what had put me there. Pain smoldered throughout my body, although the drugs kept it from flaring up and raging out of control. It also kept me from thinking straight. *What happened? How did I get here?*

237

A nurse in a pair of those rubber-soled shoes, with one of those muffled voices, quietly stepped onto the linoleum that led to my bed, careful not to disturb me. She smiled while she checked the IVs. I tried to speak, but my voice was garbled. And when I did speak, I felt this tearing sensation as if my face were being ripped open.

The nurse looked at me, studying the reactions in my good eye. "Hello, Dale," she said. "How do you feel? Can you hear me?"

This is hard to explain, but I felt an immediate and overwhelming love for this woman. It wasn't romantic. Nothing like that. It was deeper than that, purer. I wanted to talk with her, to thank her for helping me, but I couldn't. Most of all, I wanted to encourage her by telling her just how much God loved her.

Much of my face and all of my head were covered in bandages. I had stitches in my right eye, and the lid itself had been stitched shut. I could see clearly out of my left eye, but something was different.

The first words I remember saying were "What happened to my eyes?" I wasn't referring to the stitches or the bandages. Even though only one eye was working, it seemed as if I was looking out of both of them. I was seeing with what seemed to be two perfectly healthy eyes. But they were not only healthy, they were strengthened somehow. Nothing looked the same.

It felt as if I were seeing a new dimension, like 4-D, another level of reality. It was as if I had seen the world through a filter all my life, like a film had been over my eyes all these years and now that film was removed. In a very real sense, I was seeing with new and strengthened eyes.

That's how I was seeing this nurse. I had never met her, didn't even know her name. It was not a human love, I was sure of that. It was God's love. I felt as if I were a vessel through which His love was flowing. *Does she know Jesus?* was the first thought that came to my mind. I had met a lot of women in college, and I wondered a lot of things about them. I thought the same things any nineteen-year-old boy would think. Thoughts about appearance. Thoughts about personality. Thoughts about sense of humor.

But thoughts about Jesus Christ, the Son of God, and whether they knew Him? It wasn't even on my radar screen.

The next thoughts were *What if she has an accident and dies? What then? Will she go to heaven?*

I couldn't remember ever having thoughts like this about people. It was strange. Again, it was like seeing in a new dimension. Like watching a 3-D movie with unaided eyes, then suddenly putting on the 3-D glasses. Something indeed had happened to my eyes. And it was infinitely deeper than the gash. If anything, the gash I experienced was severing the veil that separated the physical dimension from the spiritual.

When she left the room, I reflected on the encounter. *What is happening to me? Why am I . . .* But before I could think anything else, the drugs lulled me back to sleep.

I woke to a doctor standing beside my bed. "Good morning, Dale. I'm Dr. Graham. How are you doing today?"

The same feeling came over me. I felt enormous love for this stranger standing beside me. *Why?* I wondered. I had never met him before. Didn't know anything about him, except what he just told me.

"You've been in an accident, Dale," the doctor explained. "A plane crash. You just rest. We'll take good care of you. You've had some serious injuries, but you're going to be OK. You may have trouble remembering things . . . you've had a severe head injury . . . just rest now."

I felt as if I knew this man. *But how? How could that be?* And yet . . . his demeanor . . . his hair . . . his hands . . . his voice. I had seen him before, heard him before. I didn't know how I knew him, but I did. I felt it deeply and with great conviction.

I watched the doctor scribble notes on my chart. As he did, I felt such tenderness toward him. It seemed as if our roles had been reversed. I was looking at him with feelings a doctor would normally have for his patient. It was weird, something I had never experienced before. How do you explain love for someone you've never met? Not sympathy. Not only compassion. But love. A deep and inexplicable love.

It was beyond me, I knew that.

It was beyond human, I knew that too.

I couldn't remember the crash Dr. Graham had mentioned. I couldn't remember anything. It was as if my mind had been taken away and a heart put in its place. A new heart. A real heart. A working heart. The way hearts were meant to work.

I no longer saw the uniform a person wore, let alone desired the uniform for myself, the position for myself, the prestige for myself, the pay for myself. Somehow—don't ask me how—I saw the person's heart and felt enormous love and compassion. I wanted to know each person who crossed my path, from the doctors to the orderlies. I wanted to know their stories, their heartaches. I felt compassion for complete strangers, which was so unlike the person I was before.

It was strange. No, it was supernatural. I don't know what happened during those three days in a coma, but something happened that I couldn't explain. A new way of seeing. Which was leading me to a new way of thinking and feeling. And ultimately to a new way of living.

Is it the morphine? I wondered. *Is it the trauma of the crash that is working its way mysteriously through my psyche?*

I didn't know. I feared it might go away as my body healed. Only time would tell if the change was real . . . and if it was permanent.

As the morphine wore off and I began to be weaned from stronger to weaker painkillers, my new sight remained intact, and my new love for people only increased.

There had been a Copernican shift in my thinking. Before the crash, I was the center of my solar system. Everything orbited around me and for me. Now I was a lesser planet that orbited around something bigger than myself. And that something bigger was the one true God.

Somehow I had been given *His* heart for people. *Any* people. *All* people. Friends. Family. Co-workers. Complete strangers.

Maybe the shift wasn't so much in my thinking as it was in my feeling. Not so much in my head as in my heart. Because it wasn't an intellectual discussion I was having with myself. Or a theological one. It was personal. Deeply, profoundly, and unalterably personal.

No, it wasn't the morphine.

The feelings were real, and they were permanent.

With the decrease in drugs, there was an increase in pain. I felt like a burnt marshmallow, all puffy and hot. The chemicals in the fuel had burned my skin, and it was reddening, swelling, and peeling off.

I tried moving, but it was terribly uncomfortable and painful. I was in so many casts and bandages I felt like a mummy. Hooked up to so many tubes and wires, I felt tied to my bed. It was claustrophobic. I had no idea what I looked like. If I looked anything like I felt, I was in deep trouble. The staff was very professional. The doctors never flinched when they examined me. The nurses didn't wail like peasant women at the funeral of a child when they changed my bandages. And none of the orderlies gawked as if I were a sideshow at a circus.

Then my brother Darrell came to visit.

He took one look at me, rushed to the bathroom, and threw up. The retching. The heaving. The flushing. I'll never forget it.

And I'll never forget thinking, *Do I look* that *bad?*

Dr. Graham checked on me several times a day and he never threw up. He did, however, wonder how I had made it this far, looking at me as I lay there—a miracle of modern medicine and at the same time a mess.

He tested my sight by putting a pen in front of my unbandaged eye and having me track it. He touched a bare patch of skin to see if I had feeling, asking what I may have remembered.

Next to nothing.

I did, however, remember my parents. I especially remember the day they came to the hospital dressed in their Sunday clothes. My dad brought me the Bible they had given me when I graduated from high school. I had hardly opened it since then. Now I couldn't wait to read it. It surprised me how eager I was. I held it in my hand like a newfound treasure. After thumbing through it for a while, I put it down, eager to talk about something else that was on my heart.

"How's Chuck?" I asked.

Neither said a word.

"What about Chuck?"

My dad walked to the window, looked outside, and pointed. "He's buried out there. We just got back from the funeral."

"They were both killed," my mom said.

I kept that knowledge outside me, letting only a little in. It was too much. I couldn't bear it. And I couldn't bear breaking down in front of my parents. They told me Chuck had died in the ambulance. I was so stunned I couldn't speak.

"And if you could have seen the remains of the plane, you'd understand what a wonder it is you are alive." Dad's eyes welled up as he spoke. "God clearly spared your life."

How can it be? I thought. *Why did I survive? The kid who just got his pilot's license the month before. The kid with all the visitors, the cards, the gifts, the flowers. The kid basking in all the attention.*

I was the wonder kid, written about in the morning papers, marveled at on the nightly news, creating a stir at the hospital and sympathy in my friends. Chuck and Gene? They were dead.

I don't remember anything my parents said after that. I didn't want to face the pain of it all, the guilt. I didn't want to talk about it, but I knew that was all people wanted to talk about. The crash. And what a miracle it was that I survived.

To me, it felt nothing like a miracle. It felt like a mistake.

I had survived. Not Gene, the pilot that was better than me. Not Chuck, the pilot that was better than both of us.

My remorse for Chuck was more than I could handle. For the first time since I met him, I worried about his eternal destiny. All the time I had spent with him, and I never told him about God's only Son, Jesus. All the destinations we talked about traveling to someday, and I never talked to him about the one destination that mattered. The pain of that was unbearable. The drugs, the visitors, and the distraction of having my bandages changed gave me a brief reprieve But when I was alone, those thoughts came rushing back. And it was everything I could do to keep my head above those incriminating waters.

Why was I having those feelings about Chuck? About the doctor. And the nurse.

What was happening to me?

5

UNDER HIS WINGS

When Dr. Graham came to visit again, I was more lucid. And more curious.

"What happened to Chuck?"

Dr. Graham was like a machine. He showed no emotion, no reaction at all. "He died in the OR. We tried for twenty minutes to resuscitate him."

"What was the cause of death?"

"Blunt trauma," Dr. Graham said matter-of-factly.

"Was he the one in the emergency room . . . behind the curtains?"

Dr. Graham nodded.

So he hadn't died in the ambulance as my parents thought.

"The other man was pronounced dead at the scene. He died on impact."

I closed my eye. I felt the breath leave my lungs, the very life in me escaping. That was the end of his visit, the end of my day, a dark and lonely end.

On another visit, on another day, my parents were with the doctor. He was going to give me my prognosis and wanted them there for support.

"When are you going to let me out of here, Doc?"

He looked at my parents, then back to me. "Dale, it looks to us at this time that you'll be hospitalized for at least eight months. You have some pretty severe injuries. You're going to require extensive specialized rehabilitation. And we want to keep a close eye on you for head and other internal injuries."

Whether it was faith, youthful enthusiasm, or some genetically ingrained stubbornness, I can't say, but I felt emboldened and blurted out: "I'll be flying over that monument as pilot in command one year from the day of the crash!"

No one smiled. No one encouraged me. They just stared at me in silence. And then, saying their polite good-byes, they left.

Later, a copy of the *LA Times* from the day after the crash found its way onto my bed. The front-page headlines read: "PLANE CRASHES INTO AIR MEMORIAL. TWO MEN DIE, ONE CRITICAL."

I scanned it with my good eye: "Seconds after taking off from Hollywood-Burbank Airport, a twin-engine plane crashed into a cemetery's memorial to aviators Friday morning, killing two men and critically injuring a third. Dead were the pilot, Charles Burns, 27, of Lakewood, and copilot, Eugene Bain, 38, of Fresno. A passenger, Dale Black, 19, of Los Alamitos was taken to St. Joseph Hospital in Burbank in critical condition."

Beside the article was a photograph of the monument we had hit. The ornate cubical structure with the dome on top was built as a memorial to fallen pioneers of aviation history. And there, at the base of that memorial, was what was left of our plane. Our Piper's mangled wings were lying on the ground, folded one over the other.

Other newspapers found their way into my room, describing the monument and giving details of the crash. The cement and marble memorial was seventy-five feet high and fifty feet by fifty wide. The plane impacted the dome just below the top, at the seventy-foot mark. Judging by the gouge left and the damage to the aircraft, the FAA estimated the speed at impact to be 135 mph. The word used in one of the articles to describe the condition of the aircraft after the crash was *disintegrated.*

On the wall above the wings of our plane was the inscription and name of the monument: PORTAL OF THE FOLDED WINGS.

245

Aerial photograph taken within hours of the crash. Just visible are shorn-off trees and the impact site on the Portal of the Folded Wings' dome. Photo taken and used with permission by Harold Morby.

A closer view of the crash site, showing a fire truck, emergency personnel, and the Piper Navajo debris. Photo taken and used with permission by Harold Morby.

The plane that had been so vibrant with power, humming life, promise of adventure, was now on the ground like a featherless baby bird fallen from its nest. Frail. Broken. Irretrievably broken.

As I was sifting through the emotional wreckage, picking up the pieces, trying to make some sense of it all, trying to find some peace, two visitors came and tossed what I had gathered to the ground.

The men were pilots, employees of the company that owned the Navajo. They came, ostensibly, to check on me, to see how I was doing. I had trouble remembering them, but they clearly knew me. The conversation quickly turned to a small newspaper that had apparently blamed me for the crash. The reporter, they told me, said that since I was in the temporary seat behind the other two pilots, I was sitting next to the fuel selector valves. And since the plane had lost power after takeoff, they told me my feet probably moved against the valves, closing them, and causing the engines to lose power. The logical blame pointed to me, they said.

I was so taken aback by the accusation that I couldn't respond. I pretended not to understand, pretended to be drowsy from the medication, and they left without my making a rebuttal. In my mind, none of it seemed logical. But my mind wasn't working all that well. What if it was true? What if I *had* been to blame?

No one could have said anything more devastating. I could live without playing sports. I could live without walking. I could live without flying. But *this*? I couldn't live with this.

At the time, I was living with a tremendous amount of physical pain. I could feel the gash across my eyes, feel the stitches in my eyelid, feel the pull of stitches with the slightest movement in my face. My head felt as if it were going to explode. My whole body ached. My back hurt with every breath. My left shoulder throbbed. My left ankle shot skewers of pain up my leg. And I would be that way for the next eight months? The worst was the thought that I was somehow responsible.

If God spared me, was it for this reason? To be summoned before a jury of my peers? Brought before them not to be celebrated but shamed?

A bystander took this photo of his son next to the mangled cockpit. Two years later Dale met the boy and was given the photo.

However severe the physical pain, the emotional pain was worse. Overwhelmed by both, I lay motionless, staring at the ceiling, my mind wandering in a daze amid the wreckage not only of shattered dreams but a shattered faith.

My father's words came back to haunt me: *God clearly spared you.*
From what? Death with dignity?

A war raged between my mind and heart. Had God spared me or sentenced me? Was I sentenced to life without parole, imprisoned by guilt, shame, humiliation, and accusation?

No. A merciful God had not spared me.
A merciful God would have let me die. Wouldn't He?

✈

The visit of those two pilots put me in a bad place. But it was only a place I visited; I didn't dare stay there. In my heart, the deepest part of me, I knew that a loving God had truly spared my life.

Another part of the reason I didn't stay there was the wonderfully cheerful hospital staff. I had become something of a celebrity and they seemed to enjoy it. They seemed to enjoy me too, which made a huge difference in my mood, which went up and down on an almost hourly basis, tracking with my pain and whatever news happened to find its way into my room.

The days that followed brought with them a revolving door of visitors. "You're *worse* than a celebrity, Dale," one of the nurses quipped. "Who *are* all these people, anyway?"

People I knew from high school showed up to see the miracle that survived the unsurvivable. People I knew from the college I had been kicked out of came by to see what had become of me. Lots and lots of people came. It was all a blur.

It seemed that in every conversation I would eventually hear the same words: "You're so lucky to be alive, Dale." I recoiled from the words. It was amazing to have survived what the FAA called a non-survivable airplane crash. But was it really luck? It couldn't be. There was something more to this than luck. God had chosen to spare my life. I knew it was an absolute miracle. Beyond that, I didn't know.

Through the many friends and acquaintances that stopped by, I had a virtual mirror held up to me, reflecting just how bad things were inside my brain.

One day a group from my high school came by, reminiscing about old times. They talked about one of the teachers we'd had. Everyone in the room laughed, bantering back and forth. Everyone but me, that is. I stared at them, bewildered. *Who are they talking about? And who are all the other people they speak of so casually, like I should know them?*

I couldn't even remember most of the people who were visiting. I not only forgot their names, I forgot *them*. I didn't know who they were. They were complete strangers.

And yet to hear them laugh and carry on, you'd think we were best friends. *Are we? Could it be that I have forgotten who my friends are?*

Later, others from college dropped by, and the same thing happened. After everyone left, I stared at the walls, wondering who I was. My eyes drifted to the IV tethered to my arm. The steady drip made me feel like it was happening to my brain. All the memories, all the people I knew, my friends, even my close friends, were steadily dripping out of my mind. *Will I continue to forget? Am I losing my mind?*

I was aware of my surroundings. I wasn't crazy. I was coherent. I could think. I could follow people's conversations, engage in conversation. I just had these gaping holes in my memory.

And by *gaping*, I mean so big you could drive an 18-wheeler through it.

Visitors continued to come by. I had survived. Their prayers had been answered. And now they were there to cheer me on to recovery. I tried to concentrate. I tried to remember their faces, their names, what they meant to me. Then I stopped trying to make sense of all the remember-when stories, all the good-natured kidding, all the comments they thought would lead to conversation. But that led nowhere. I did a lot of smiling and nodding, as if I understood. A lot of grimacing too, hoping they would see the pain I was in, politely excuse themselves, and leave.

My parents sensed my frustration. "Don't worry, Dale, you've had some slight head injuries. It's probably just temporary," they said, trying to console me. But I knew my parents always looked on the bright side.

I *knew* what was going on. I knew I wasn't just suffering from *slight* head injuries. And I was afraid it wasn't temporary.

Even though my injuries were serious, no one told me *how* serious. Their initial assessment was that I had broken a few bones.

Well, I might have only one good eye, but I could see that it was more than just a few broken bones. *What* isn't *broken?* I wondered. *Why isn't anyone telling me the truth?*

251

I could take the truth. What I couldn't take was the fear of not knowing how bad it was.

My room overlooked the Ventura Freeway, and with my one good eye I watched the cars speed by. I watched and then I wept. I wept for the people inside the cars.

I couldn't understand it, but those people mattered to me. Each and every one of them mattered. Even though I didn't know their names. The type of car they drove didn't matter. My head wasn't turned if it was a Porsche. And it wasn't turned away if it was a Rambler. None of that mattered anymore. It was the person behind the wheel that mattered. Their final destination mattered. Their spiritual destination. And it mattered like nothing else I had ever experienced.

These people need to know about God, I remember thinking. *Not some vague, warm and fuzzy, feel-good concept of God. They need to know the one true God. Those people may think they know where they are going today, but the truth is that most of them are lost. They need to know Jesus Christ, need to know how much He loves them, what He did for them to pave the way to eternity. They can't get there by any road, no matter how smooth it is or how attractive the scenery is along the way. He is the way, the only way. They need Him.*

My thoughts surprised me.

My feelings surprised me even more.

I wept for these people, these people I didn't know who were on their way to somewhere else and in such a hurry to get there.

I stared at the ceiling, dumbfounded. *What has happened to me? I've never thought these thoughts before, never felt these feelings before.* I wasn't the same person I was before the crash. Somehow the answer had to be related to those three days in a coma.

It had to be.

If I could only remember . . . something . . . anything . . .

6
SHRINE TO AVIATION

Because of all the painkillers in my bloodstream, sleep came and went during all hours of the day and night. One day seemed to blend into the next without my being aware of the passage of time.

At some point I began to think about who I was. I didn't focus on all that had happened, things I couldn't remember; I focused on all that *was* happening. To me. Everything about me seemed different. Physically, mentally, emotionally, spiritually.

I felt like the six-million-dollar man. Remember the TV show? He had been in some kind of tragic accident, and the military completely rebuilt him. That's *exactly* what I felt like. Parts of me were definitely me. But parts of me definitely weren't. Who was this new Dale Black?

I thought it was time to take a look.

There was a mirror inside the tray next to my bed. I hadn't bothered to use it before; now I felt compelled to. I pulled the cord to call the nurse. She moved the tray over my bed and lifted the mirror for me.

The startled expressions on some of the faces of visitors seeing me for the first time somewhat prepared me. But nothing could have prepared me for the monster in the mirror.

My hair had been completely shaved off. My head was red and purple, swollen, and bandaged. A crooked railroad line of stitches ran across my forehead and below the bandage over my right eye. One especially nasty gash ran roughshod across my face and chin, held together with gnarly-looking stitches. My nose had been broken and was flat, as if it had been mashed down by some irrepressible force. And burns from the airplane fuel had swollen my skin, discoloring it and distorting it hideously.

This was no six-million-dollar man staring back at me. This was Frankenstein's monster—the work of a mad scientist—an utterly grotesque assemblage of parts, held together by wires and screws, stitches and bandages, rods and plaster casts.

I didn't even look human. I certainly bore no resemblance to the young man with a bright future ahead of him who had boarded that ill-fated plane. The injuries were so severe, the burns so pervasive, the gashes so deep, that all hope for a somewhat normal appearance left me. This was not the kind of thing that cleared up in a few months of bed rest. This was horrifying. This was permanent. This was me.

Now I knew why my brother had thrown up.

I was surprised more people hadn't.

Body building, one of my favorite pastimes, was definitely out. I couldn't even lift my arms. And what about baseball and football? It would be a real surprise if I ever walked again. Forget about diving to catch a pass or going after a hard-hit ground ball. It was over.

I was forever being examined, X-rayed, probed, and injected. An entourage of doctors came through, discussing my case among themselves, asking each other questions and talking about me in the third person as if I weren't in the room.

Results from the tests trickled in, but none of them trickled down to me. I was left in the dark. No one told me the extent of my injuries or the prognosis for my recovery.

Then, finally, after a week of tests, Dr. Graham came to my room and talked to me about the results. "When you first arrived in the hospital after the accident," he said, "we assumed your internal injuries to be severe. And we were particularly concerned about your head injuries and potential brain damage."

As I mentioned before, Dr. Graham was a renowned orthopedic surgeon. I learned from the hospital staff that he was known as the doctor of the stars, having treated a number of celebrities. His best-known patient was Evel Knievel, whose fame was built around daredevil stunts with his motorcycle—everything from jumping over a world's record number of cars to jumping over the Snake River Canyon.

Dr. Graham continued: "I'm aware of the fact that you're still experiencing memory loss, but everything else with regard to your brain looks pretty good. Though we don't understand why, we see no indication of internal injuries. Most of your injuries are related to bone, ligament, and muscle problems. That's *good* news. Anyway, I've talked with your parents and we're going to let you go home tomorrow."

Tomorrow! I thought. *That's a miracle! The original estimate was eight months! And I'm going home in eight days?!* I was stunned.

Later that day my parents and my brother Don arrived. They were overjoyed at the news. And they were fully committed to whatever it took—however long—for me to recover.

"You know, Dale," my dad said, "one big reason this is possible is because your mom has decided to take a leave of absence from the family business so she can take care of you full time."

My brother chimed in with his characteristic sense of wry humor. "And don't worry, Dale, we've hired three drivers to take your place at the plant."

I laughed. And boy did it hurt. My face, my ribs, everything hurt. But a laugh never felt so good.

When I woke up the next morning, my first thought was *I'm getting out of here! I'm going home!*

I could hardly wait. The check-out procedures took forever, but a nurse finally arrived with a wheelchair and painstakingly worked me into it.

As my brother wheeled me down the hallway, I asked my dad, "Would you mind driving by the place where the plane crashed? I'd like to see what it looks like."

Dad was walking to my left; my mom, to the right. Neither said a word.

My brother broke the silence: "Are you sure you can handle that right now? It's only been a little over a week since the crash."

"Yeah. I'd really like to see it for myself." And then I said, trying to reassure them, "I'll be OK."

"Alright, Dale," Dad said with a sigh, "if you're sure."

No sooner were the words out of my mouth than I wondered if I *would* be OK. Wondered what it would be like seeing the grim monolith that was the face of death for Chuck and Gene. Wondered what memories would come back.

Feared what memories would come back.

When we were finally outside the hospital, the warmth of the morning sun was the first thing I felt. It seemed as if I had been in an artificially lit cave for the past eight days, with artificially cooled air mingled with smells of all things sterile. I took a deep breath of fresh air. It brought life . . . and hope.

I was out of the hospital and on my way to recovery. However hard it would be, however long it would take, I was on my way. And it felt great.

As they wheeled me to the car and settled me into the front seat, I took a final look at the hospital. A well of emotions rose to the surface. So much had happened there in just a week. So much death. So much life. So many experiences. So many changes.

We drove north on Hollywood Way from St. Joseph toward Hollywood-Burbank Airport. The cemetery lay just south of it. We turned on a tiny street called Valhalla Drive, which came to an abrupt dead end.

"There's the mausoleum ahead of us, Dale." Dad parked the car along the curb.

I strained with my good eye to focus on the concrete-and-marble domed building that rose seven stories high. It was a drab structure surrounded by a black fence. I don't know what I was expecting, but it wasn't this. I was told we had hit a monument in the center of the cemetery, and I had imagined a large tombstone of some kind or a small mausoleum for a family. I wasn't prepared for anything this size. It was huge. More than huge, it was massive.

None of us got out of the car. None of us spoke. For several minutes we sat in silence, until at last my brother made a comment.

"Except for the engines and the tail, you could have picked up any piece of that airplane with one hand," he explained in a voice barely above a whisper.

Dad raised his arm and pointed. "Your plane sheered off those trees just before impact. Apparently, that's what turned your plane into the monument." He pointed to the crater in the concrete dome, just five feet from the top. "The damage to the air memorial is minor compared to your aircraft. They haven't even finished cleaning up everything yet," he said, indicating the debris on the ground.

What was left of the plane had been removed. I could see gouges in the ground where the plane had dug in. Then I noticed the gilded letters on the side of the memorial:

PORTAL OF THE FOLDED WINGS

The scene spun in my head, and turbulent emotions surged within me, followed by a series of questions: *What is wrong with my memory? Why can't I remember this? How does someone forget something so huge? What really happened barely a week ago?*

Then the big question, the one that loomed over me like some haunting apparition: *Why was I the only survivor?*

I couldn't sort it all out. My mind hurt. It felt as if it were going to explode. I started to panic, and so I took slow, deep breaths to stave off the attack. I hung my head, noticing the grass for the first time. It was dingy and ugly, browned by the scorch of the mid-summer sun. I looked up again. The monument looked old and a little dingy itself, having weathered decades of summer suns.

I couldn't stop looking at the structure, marveling at it, wondering about it. I was drawn to it in ways I couldn't understand, like a curious insect drawn to a glowing bulb.

The irony was impossible not to notice—this memorial to deceased aviators had taken the lives of two more. Inside the structure were plaques to their memory. Outside, where Chuck and Gene had died, there were no plaques.

I had flown over it scores of times. Even that seemed mysterious to me. A sense of destiny came over me as I sat there in the car staring. It was intriguing. At the same time it was indicting. I felt as if it were taunting me somehow. As we sat at the end of Valhalla Drive, everyone had something to say. I was quiet, my mind busy with its own questions, all of which eventually came around to one: *Could it be true that I had caused the crash?*

7

DESTINED FOR THE SKY

It was good to be home. Good to be pampered by my mom instead of the nurses. Not to mention the food. There's nothing like your mother's cooking, especially when you're sick. I ate it up. The food. The pampering. The familiar surroundings. It was wonderful.

I was in a hospital bed, which they had placed in the den. I had lots of time to think, pray, dream. Invariably all my dreams led to one: flying.

I mentioned my dream of becoming an airline pilot began when I was fourteen.

Since the age of twelve, I had been working at my grandfather's business, "the plant," as we called it, and at my father's Long Beach Redwood Corporation, the landscaping products and trucking company next door. I loved working in the family business. I felt like royalty, part of a rich bloodline with the secure destiny of being one of the heirs to the throne, possibly running it all someday along with my brothers.

I had started with the most menial tasks, working my way up through the ranks. There were no special privileges, no fast track to success, despite my pedigree as one of the boss's sons. I swept, I cleaned, I sacked sawdust, I baled shavings. Then I began doing truck maintenance on my dad's 18-wheelers. Small repairs at first and routine maintenance, but gradually I took on more and more responsibility. Later, I logged a million miles driving the big rigs throughout the state delivering the products the business produced.

I also worked hard in order to learn Spanish and could talk with some of the workers, which they appreciated. It bonded us in a special way. It felt like one big hardworking family. And I was a part of it.

There was no job too small for me to do and no job too big that I couldn't someday do it. I felt confident working there. There was a lot of hope in the business. My dad had a can-do attitude. "If you can dream it, you can achieve it," he was fond of saying. Earl Nightingale, the motivational speaker, had been a big influence in his life. Dad had listened to all his tapes. His if-you-think-you-can-you-can philosophy permeated the company. Dad wouldn't allow the word *can't* in our vocabulary. He had always encouraged his workers to bring him their problems, but they had to first write out the problem and have two possible solutions written out with it. "Think it out, then write it out" was another thing you would hear him say. Dad was an outstanding businessman with impeccable integrity.

It's hard to think of a fourteen-year-old as having a philosophy of life, but all those things worked themselves into my thinking and set my course from that time forward.

That same year, something happened that changed who I was and what I wanted to do with my life. My grandfather received an unexpected financial bonus and decided to take the family on a trip around the world. We were in no way a wealthy family, but that summer it felt like we were. We traveled to Berlin and saw the Berlin Wall. We toured the Middle East. We went to Paris. France was so old and so beautiful in contrast to the United States. Paris at night was magical, quite possibly the most beautiful city in the world. And the girls. You can't imagine the effect the French girls had on the pubescent boy I was then. I felt I was becoming a man. And that felt really good. Because of the magnificent lights, the lure of Paris at night was almost addictive. Being there planted seeds within me to want to travel and see the world.

We flew everywhere and saw as much of that world as we could see in a three-week period. Switzerland was my favorite. But there was Austria. Italy. Lebanon. Syria. Egypt. We traipsed through the ruins of an empire in Rome and traveled through the pages of the Bible in Jerusalem. We saw the *Mona Lisa* in the Louvre and the most beautiful women in the world in Italy and Scandinavia.

Everywhere we went, we were treated royally. We were looked up to because we were Americans, and the rest of the world still treasured the memories of our involvement in World War II. England, France, Denmark, Italy, they were all so appreciative, mainly because there were so many people still alive who had fought in that war, who had lost fathers and sons in that war, who had cheered American soldiers as they liberated Europe, city by war-torn city.

Pretty amazing experiences for a kid on the cusp of growing up. The most amazing experience, though, was not any one place we traveled to or any particular sight we saw when we got there. The most amazing things to me were the TWA Boeing 707s we traveled on and the pilots that flew them.

The size of the jet, the sheer power of its engines, the thrill of liftoff, the sound of the landing gear being retracted, the ease at which the massive machine cut through the air, these were all mesmerizing. And then, before you knew it, you were at thirty thousand feet, looking down on fleecy expanses of clouds, and through breaks in the clouds to cities, farmlands, oceans that spread as far as the eye could see, sunlight glinting off their scalloped surfaces.

The pilot behind all this power stood so tall and nonchalant in his crisply pressed uniform as you boarded his plane, smiling, greeting us as if we were someone special. His demeanor was a picture of confidence and control, someone who was trained and could be trusted. Then there was the thrill of hearing his voice over the loudspeaker telling us what we could see out the left window. Or letting us know when we were about to encounter turbulence and not feeling the least bit worried because his voice was so calm and reassuring.

When our travels were over, I was a different person, with new dreams that captivated me, new sights on my horizon, new adventures that stretched ahead of me.

I wanted to be one of those pilots, flying one of those jets to exotic parts of the world. But it seemed out of reach for a teenager who sacked his granddad's wood sawdust and repaired his father's trucks in what now seemed a small and shop-worn part of the world.

Then at that pivotal age of fourteen, something else happened. Someone I had always known, who was an engineer and vice-president of our company, helped me look at my life differently. His name was Ron Davis, one of my dad's best friends, who that year became *my* best friend. My dad was a responsible, hardworking man, intent on building a business to provide for his family and to pass it on to his sons. He was not a pal-around kind of guy, not one who would play catch with you in the backyard. Usually at the end of the day he was spent, with the best of himself left behind at the office. And even at his best at the office, he was fairly aloof to me anyway.

Ron was just the opposite. He may have sensed in me a need to connect with an older man. That year Ron took me backpacking up to the top of Mt. Whitney. On that trip we saw a lot of amazing sights on our way to what seemed to be the top of the world. We talked a lot about science, laughed a lot, and in the process he became a little like a father to me, filling a void that my father was either unable or unwilling—or simply too busy—to fill.

And then the question: "Have you ever thought about flying?"

He had listened to me talk about our trip around the world, listened to my farfetched fantasies of flying jets, my admiration for the pilots who flew them, my desire to use my mind in a profession, my apprehensions about the boredom of sacking sawdust or being stuck in an office doing the same things day in and day out for the rest of my life.

"Have you ever thought about flying?"

The question followed me like a stray, not only for the next few days but for the next few years. His brother Paul, whom I also knew well, had been taking flying lessons and loved it. "Try it," he said. "I think you would be good at it."

It seemed a wish-upon-a-star type aspiration. Something right out of a fairy tale. After all, I was just a kid. And flying was a man's job. Where would I get the training? Where would I get the money for the training?

Ron was thirteen years older than I was, a genius with a near-photographic memory. He was quiet and humble yet had a prodigious grasp of scientific things, which made him fascinating to listen to. Talking with Ron stimulated my inquisitive young mind. I was full of questions, and he was full of answers. Yet he never made me feel stupid for asking or for not knowing something. I respected him. And I took everything he said seriously. But nothing more seriously than the words "Try it. I think you would be good at it."

Ron's brother Paul began to fan the flames of the burning desire to fly that was smoldering under the surface. I feared talking about it with my parents. Mom would be fearful. Dad would be practical. I also feared talking about it with my granddad, whom I adored. He had started the business that I was now a part of. Nothing would please him more than to see me follow in his footsteps. Nothing would disappoint him more than for me to follow another set of footsteps.

It would be another four years, the summer of 1968, before I got up the courage to take my first lesson.

My instructor was a man named Terry, an airline pilot who had given up a safe and secure job as a banker for the adventure of flying. One day I met Terry at Brackett Airfield, bought a pilot's logbook, gave him thirty dollars, and we took off.

I had always been good with machines. I was driving tractors at age ten, then forklifts, then giant Caterpillar front-end loaders, then 18-wheelers. I loved the feel of machines. They felt like an extension of who I was. But no machine prepared me for the Cessna 150 we flew that day.

I sat beside Terry in the cockpit as we flew around the Southern California city of Ontario. It was an oh-my-gosh moment. A moment I never forgot. And a moment that kept me coming back, plunking down another thirty dollars, and another and another, to recapture that thrill.

I felt free when I was flying. Above the fray of traffic. Above the worries of the workaday world. Above the boundaries of stop signs and double lines, signs that signaled No U-turns or Speed Limit 35. Here I was untrammeled by the rules and regulations of everyday life. Here I was free to be me. Here was where I belonged. And I knew it on the first flight.

I learned everything I could as fast as I could. I took as many lessons as I could afford, learning how to taxi, steer the rudders with my feet, take off, guide the aircraft with fingertip pressure on the controls, everything.

Nothing felt as good as being in the cockpit, lifting off from earth, and taking flight. Nothing. And now nothing could stop me from becoming a professional pilot.

I would drive a truck at night, earning a decent income. I took aviation ground school between my afternoon classes and work—went to school during the day—and flew every chance I got in between. After I had taken twenty hours of flight instruction from Terry, I met Chuck and took the rest from him.

Finally, in June 1969, after logging sixty hours in the air, I was ready for my test with the FAA, the regulatory board that issues licenses for pilots. Chuck and I were taking one of our routine flights with a stop in Visalia. It was there we parted ways and I hopped into the Cessna 150 that I had rented for the short fifteen-minute flight to Tulare, where I was scheduled to meet the flight examiner for my private pilot flight test. Chuck had signed me off for a solo flight so I could make the hop to my flight check destination. His last-minute instruction replayed in my mind as I taxied over to the hangar. "Relax, you're more than ready," he had said. "And remember, when he asks a question, just give him the exact answer. No more and no less. And treat him with respect." That's all the advice Chuck gave me. But it proved to be enough.

After I landed the airplane, I taxied to the large former WWII hangar where I was to meet the man who had the power to approve my pilot's license. The examiner was a relaxed fiftyish WWII veteran. We quickly exchanged preliminary information, strapped ourselves into the aircraft, and proceeded with my flight exam. My attention was so focused that it seemed like only moments before we were again landing and taxiing to the hangar. The check ride was over. The examiner shook my hand in congratulations and signed my log book. I was now a licensed pilot.

That was the biggest day of my life. I could fly alone. I was a pilot on my way to living my dream.

"Have you ever thought about flying?" Ron had asked four years before.

And I haven't stopped thinking about it since.

⑧
SECRET PLACE OF THE MOST HIGH

A shooting pain in my shoulder brought me back to earth.

It was no longer June of '69. It was July. What a difference a month makes.

In the days that followed, friends were still coming by to visit. Now it was more friends from our church and less from school. Howard and Ginny Dunn were two of them. They were friends of our family for a long time and it lifted my spirits to see them.

"How are you doing, Dale?" Howard asked.

"Thankful to be alive and happy to be home."

"I think God gave me a Scripture He wants me to share with you."

What does God have for me? I wondered.

He paused, waiting for my permission.

"Please. Go ahead."

He picked up his Bible and thumbed through its well-worn pages. "Psalm 91," he said, and started reading:

> "He who dwells in the secret place of the Most High
> Shall abide under the shadow of the Almighty.
> I will say of the Lord, He is my refuge and my fortress;
> My God; in Him I will trust.
> Surely He shall deliver you from the snare of the fowler,
> And from the perilous pestilence.

He shall cover you with His feathers,
And under His wings you shall take refuge:
His truth shall be your shield and buckler.
You shall not be afraid of the terror by night;
Nor for the arrow that flies by day,
Nor of the pestilence that walks in darkness,
Nor of the destruction that lays waste at noonday.
A thousand may fall at your side,
And ten thousand at your right hand;
But it shall not come near you.

Psalm 91:1–7"

Tears burned my eyes. I had never heard that before. As he read, it was like the first light of dawn in my spirit, a spirit that had been wandering in the dead of night trying to find answers.

I was alive not because I had been living a good life for Him. To the contrary, I was living my own life for me. I had a deep sense that the prayers of my parents and grandparents over the years had somehow protected me. I wasn't certain, but I thought so. All I was certain of was that it wasn't anything *I* had done.

Why me? was the question that burned within me. And now this psalm shed light on a possible answer. Why was *I* spared? I think it had something to do with God's sovereign purpose. It wasn't only because He loved me. It was because He had plans for me. What those plans were wasn't clear at the time. What was clear was that He had been my fortress against the blunt force trauma that had killed the other pilots. I hit the same dome my friends hit and at the same speed. We all impacted the monument within inches of each other. I needed the strength of a fortress to survive the crash. But I needed the softness of feathers to survive the fall.

Why was I allowed to get on that flight in the first place? If God was providentially protecting me, why not keep me from the accident altogether?

Because I think there were more important things that needed protecting than my physical being or my vocational dreams. The broken bones would lead to a broken spirit. God loved the heart of the little boy I once was. Somewhere along the way to growing up, my heart lost its way. He was turning me back, showing me where I had lost my way, and letting me begin again from where I had started, back in the fifth grade when I surrendered my life to God and invited Jesus into my heart.

It was a piece of the larger puzzle. A big piece. It was what I needed at the moment. Everything wasn't clear, but clear enough that I could take the next step. Which was good, because that's all the strength I had.

I didn't have strength for the entire journey. Just enough for the next step.

The next step landed me in the backyard.

I had wheeled myself there to soak up some summer sun and to read what I could of the Bible my parents had given me at graduation. If God had a plan for me, I wanted to know about it. More important, I wanted to know *Him*.

Even though I was an athlete who had driven trucks and flown planes, traveled the world and achieved a lot of success, there was so much in me that hadn't matured. I had the body of a well-developed man. I had been a body builder. I could walk up and down stairs on my hands, do somersaults off the high dive; I excelled at sports. Yet if you had put a mirror up to my spiritual life, I was the proverbial ninety-eight-pound weakling. I had no spiritual strength, no stamina, nothing at all to rely on in the spiritual realm.

If indeed there is a spiritual battle going on all around us, I was not a warrior but a water boy.

And I didn't want that. I wanted to be a warrior, one of the King's men. But first I had to know the King. And I started getting to know Him that afternoon in the backyard.

I used my good eye to read. The Bible lay on my lap, flopped open. I read as the sunlight danced through the trees, as the wind whispered through its branches, sometimes turning the pages for me. It was so peaceful back there. My life had been so busy chasing my dreams that I never had time like this, just to sit and read and think, to enjoy the warmth of the sun on my arms, the breath of the sky against my face.

I desired a friendship with the God who had spared my life. If I were ever to walk again, it would be with Him on His path, not mine. If I were ever to run again, it would be for Him, on the course He set before me. And if I were ever to fly again, it would be with Him at the controls. He would not be *my* copilot; I would be *His*. Who knows where we would go together; but wherever it was, it would be together. No more flying solo.

It was during these visits with God that I began to realize that if I were ever going to be normal again, God would have to do the miraculous and I would have to do the arduous.

There was a lot of hard work ahead. It would be all uphill with the wind in my face. But I wouldn't be going it alone.

I couldn't really do anything in the way of physical therapy. I was still in casts, a wheelchair, and a lot of pain. Where to start when everything is broken?

I started with my eye. Somehow I got the idea that my damaged eye needed exercise. The doctor had told me I would not regain sight in that eye. At best, I would be able to distinguish light from darkness. Without telling anyone, and when no one was around, I taped my good eye shut and forced myself to use my injured eye.

It was painful at first. I could only see shadows. Light and darkness registered, but nothing else. Day after day I did this. And day after day I thanked Him. I thanked Him for what I saw, and I thanked Him in advance that someday I would see normally again. I clung to the Scripture "For we walk by faith, not by sight" that I found in 2 Corinthians 5:7. It was going to take faith to get my sight back. I wasn't going to get faith by simply praying for it. Faith would come by believing and then acting upon what God said in His Word.

During that time I began to realize that if I was ever going to be normal again, it would require two things: First, the hand of God to perform a series of miracles on my body. And second, an enormous amount of effort on my part.

One day while trying to read the Bible with my injured eye, my brother walked up behind me. I was straining so intently to read that I hadn't noticed him.

"What are you doing, Dale? Why do you have tape over your left eye?"

His questions felt like an inquisition, and I felt like a fool. I wasn't about to explain. My faith was growing, but still I was timid and self-conscious.

"I was just experimenting, that's all. I wanted to see how much I could see with my right eye. I think it's a little better."

"Did you have to tape your good eye shut to find out?" His chiding stung, and he pulled off the tape.

After that I was more careful about doing my exercises. And I was more careful about what I said and to whom I said it. My faith was fragile but growing. As it grew, I began to feel more confident that God was going to heal me, that I would be normal again, that I would walk again, run again, fly again.

Eventually I got to the point where I could go to church. That wasn't something high on my list before the crash. Now it was. It wasn't a religious routine I sought. It was a relationship with the Most High, the Almighty, the One who had been my refuge and my fortress, the One who had delivered me from the snare, who had covered me with His feathers.

God wasn't theoretical anymore. He was personal. And now my relationship with Him was personal.

I had a lot of attention that first Sunday I went back, both from the pulpit and from the pews. But gradually I began to blend in. As I did, I noticed something I had never given a second thought to before. There were other people at church in wheelchairs: a person who had been crippled in an accident, one from a disease, another from a disability. I felt enormous compassion for them, seeing them from the vantage point of someone who was also disabled. I found myself wheeling my way over to them, striking up a conversation, asking about their lives. It was the first time that had ever happened. Sunday after Sunday they had come. And Sunday after Sunday I had ignored them. *How many others have ignored them?* I wondered. How hurtful that must have felt, being marginalized like that. Sitting while everyone else was standing. Listening to fragments of conversations that others were having. No one stooping to talk with you, ask how *you* were doing, let alone ask you over for a meal or out to a movie.

It broke my heart . . . in places I didn't know needed breaking.

⑨
FEAR AND MEMORY LOSS

Since I couldn't fly yet, I thought it would be a step forward to audit the aviation ground school at a local junior college. Several of my high school peers were attending there, and Anna, my long-time girlfriend, was willing to regularly drive me to the college and even wheel me into the class. I couldn't do much but listen, learn, and use my right hand to turn the pages of my book and take notes. I thought a few sessions would get me thinking in the right direction again.

The instructor took me under his wing and encouraged me in my commitment to aviation. Since everyone in the class was an aspiring pilot, they had all heard about the crash, and I was somewhat of a celebrity. The instructor approached me and asked me to speak to the class about aviation safety. It was a great opportunity to express some of the concerns I'd developed since the crash.

"Intersection departures should not be made for any reason," I began. "The pilot in command should take control immediately if he senses any problems. Learn the FAA regulations—always obey the regulations. . . ." I droned on with my newfound convictions. But before long I found it impossible to stick to my well-rehearsed speech.

Then I remembered the boldness of Peter and John when they answered a disbelieving team of religious leaders who had commanded them not to speak about Jesus anymore. Peter and John answered and said, "Whether it is right in the sight of God to listen to you more than to God, you judge.

For we cannot but speak the things which we have seen and heard" (Acts 4:19–20).

I'm not leaving this classroom without telling these people what God has done for me, I decided. I felt the same overwhelming love in my heart for these students as I did for the hospital staff and the people in the cars on the freeway when I awoke from the coma months earlier. I thought of Chuck Burns, my flight instructor and friend, whom I never told about Jesus. I reflected on the pain and guilt of his eternal loss. These thoughts were enough to stop me in the midst of my "better safe than sorry" message.

"There is only one reason that I am alive and talking to you today..." As my eyes flooded with tears, I paused to regain control of my voice. "God saved my life. God loves me very much, but He loves each of you no less. Jesus Christ came into this world to die so that you can live." I looked around the room and noticed that every eye seemed intently focused on me.

"I challenge each of you to read what Jesus said and taught in the Bible. You can do it quickly and easily. Get a red-letter edition of the New Testament, and just read the red letters, the words Jesus spoke. You owe it to yourself to find out if Jesus is the Son of God. He either is or He isn't. You decide. But if you find that He truly is the Son of God, wouldn't you want to learn more about Him?"

I continued, "I've done this exact exercise, and I don't believe for a moment that any mere man, no matter how great or educated, could say and do the things Jesus did. It wouldn't be possible. I challenge you to learn about the free gift of eternal life with God, which you only receive by believing on Jesus Christ. You see, Jesus came into the world not to condemn the world, but that the world through Him might be saved."

As I rolled back to my desk, my classmates erupted first with loud applause, and then a standing ovation. The response only brought more tears to my eyes. But I could tell by the teacher's expression that my lesson was not quite the one he'd had in mind.

A few days later I had another idea. "You want to do *what*?" Mom asked, stopping her dinner preparations.

"I want to go back to Pasadena College. I need to get back into school so I can finish my degree and move on to becoming an airline pilot. The airlines need pilots real bad right now."

I knew she didn't want to discuss my flying again. It had brought her too much pain. So she avoided that part of my statement.

"Dale, it's only been a few months since the crash. You need to get stronger before you tackle a goal like that. How would you get around? How would you carry your books, get up the stairs, and accomplish all the other things you'd need to do? You're still in a wheelchair, and you've only got one arm to wheel yourself around."

"I'm stronger now, Mom. Besides, I feel I need to tell my friends about the changes God has made in my life. It might help them."

"You were pretty rebellious when you were there before," she said.

"Well, yeah. I didn't exactly like all the rules."

"You don't have to like them; you just have to follow them."

"How much trouble can a guy in a wheelchair get into? Look at me."

She smiled. And she talked to Dad. My parents made some calls; I wrote a letter and had a tearful meeting with Dr. Shelburne Brown, the president of the college, who saw the change in me, and Dr. Lewis Thompson, the dean of students, who was especially kind and understanding. Dr. Thompson went above and beyond the call of duty, helping make arrangements for my return.

It was October when I returned, and classes had already started. Getting around was a pain. Still as stubborn as ever, I usually refused help. It didn't matter how many books I had to carry, how many flights of stairs I had to hop up with my one good leg, I was going to do this. I was late for every class, sopping wet with sweat, and could hardly concentrate. I had trouble following the teacher, trouble taking notes, trouble remembering the notes I had taken.

I had been something of a big man on campus before the crash, and

I expected to be an even bigger man, commanding even more attention after it. But the old crowd I used to hang out with began to thin. After all, I was in a wheelchair, wrapped in bandages, and weighed down with casts. I wasn't as mobile as I used to be, wasn't as fun as I used to be. On top of that, I was pretty off-putting to look at. And I wasn't sporting around in my MGB, giving rides to my buddies.

I had experienced a lot of things on that campus, but this was the first time I experienced loneliness. It hurt, especially when the same people that had sought me out before were now seeking ways to avoid me.

Even my former college roommate avoided me. I could hardly blame him, but I could also hardly bear it.

My entire identity had been built around the physical, from body building to athletics to my appearance. Because of those things, I had an aura of attractiveness about me. Now the aura was gone, and I was alone.

As I was wheeling myself across campus, feeling a little sorry for myself, I heard a small plane flying overhead. I was gripped with an unexpected longing. *I've got to get out of this wheelchair and back in the sky,* I thought. *I don't care how beat-up my body is, I'm going to be a pilot again. Someday. Nothing is going to stop me!*

I stopped in my tracks and wheeled myself to the first pay phone I could find. I called Capt. Fred Griffith, a veteran professional pilot I had become acquainted with. He had been a test pilot for Lockheed Aircraft and was one of the best instructors in the country. Fred was a true aviator. He also knew something of what I was going through. Years earlier he had had his own brush with death. He ejected from a test flight, and his parachute failed to open properly. He survived the fall but was severely injured. He knew firsthand the fear of flying after an accident. *Who better to turn to?* I thought.

I told him of my desire to get back into flying again and particularly to fly over the air memorial that we had crashed into. "But I don't want anyone else to know," I told him. I asked if he would fly with me, and he agreed.

The next day I managed somehow to get to the airport. I shouldn't have been driving, but I was desperate. And desperate people do desperate things. Fred met me there and wheeled me out to his single engine Cessna 182. I hadn't been back at the terminal since the day of the crash. Rolling up to the terminal, I saw the sign over the large glass entry: *Pacific Aeromotive*. Seeing it, I had a strange, unsettled feeling.

Fred helped me into the cockpit, and I perched in the left seat, feeling cramped and awkward.

"Would you like to conduct the Before Start Checklist?" Fred asked.

I stared at the instrument panel with all its dials and levers, and for the first time I realized I had no idea how to operate them.

I started to read the checklist out loud. "Flap handle."

I paused. I couldn't remember what a flap handle was. I had arrived at the airport believing I was capable of piloting the Cessna 182. After all, I had my pilot's license and had even finished training for my multiengine rating. But as I scanned the dials and levers, everything looked foreign to me. I felt like it was the first time I'd ever been in the cockpit of an airplane. I simply couldn't remember how to fly! Two years of information and experience had been wiped from my mind.

Fred patiently went over the checklist and then started the engine. When it roared to life, I felt out of control. I wanted to stop and do it another day. My heart was pounding so hard I could barely hear Fred speak. Fred had wanted to let me make the takeoff, but he changed his mind when he saw how fearful I was.

"Relax, Dale. I'll do the flying. You just sit back and enjoy the ride."

Fred taxied the Cessna down to Runway 15, just as we had done the day of the crash. He pushed the engines full throttle and took off, just as we had done the day of the crash.

It was so traumatic I could hardly breathe. We ascended rapidly, and in the blink of an eye we were soaring over the dome-shaped monument. My heart pounded and my forehead dripped with sweat as I watched the Portal of the Folded Wings disappear beneath us.

"You did it, Dale! Congratulations!" he said. "Is that going to do it for you?" Then he looked at me. I had a white-knuckled grip on the seat and my shirt was soaked in sweat.

"Are you going to be alright?"

I was at a loss for words and an even greater loss of confidence. Finally I spoke. "I'd like you to land and then go around once again, Fred, if that's OK with you. The sooner I get over this, the better."

Fred understood. But the second time around was no easier. I was limp with terror. I couldn't move, I couldn't engage. I felt so ashamed. *Go on,* I told myself. *Get over it. It's like getting thrown off a horse. You've got to get back on and ride or you'll never overcome the fear.*

When we landed, I was relieved but embarrassed. I felt like I had let Capt. Fred down. He told me my reaction was normal for what I had been through and reassured me that I would conquer my fears. I just had to keep facing them.

And that's what I was determined to do. The next day I made arrangements to enroll in the aviation ground school at the nearby junior college—the same course I had audited and where I had spoken to fellow students. It would help me relearn what I had forgotten. The next class started in mid-January, which would give me a little more time to recover.

Shortly after the flight with Fred, I dropped out of Pasadena College. Mom was right. It was too much, too soon.

And it was too lonely.

⑩
A FUTURE AND A HOPE

The remainder of the fall of 1969 was even lonelier. I had become disillusioned with my friendships, which one by one fell away during that season of my life. I became weary of the well-wishers, the Hallmark-card greetings, the hang-in-there sentiments. I became suspicious of the smiles, the promises to come and see me that never materialized, and the call-me-if-you-need-anything good-byes.

One friendship, however, didn't disappoint. I looked forward to time alone with God—reading my Bible, praying, thinking, which I did a lot in our backyard, our suddenly leafless backyard.

Up till then, I had always been a doer; now I was learning just to be. Not that I really had a choice in the matter. It was as if there had been an untimely frost and the seasons changed overnight. I went from the summertime of my life to the dead of winter without so much as a storm warning.

Someone once said, I forget who, "In October, when the leaves fall, you can see deeper into the forest." It's true. So much foliage had fallen from my branching ambitions, and as a result, I *could* see deeper into the forest that was my life.

I didn't feel I needed to be doing anything—playing among the trees or gathering firewood or trying to find some way of making money out of the forest. I could just be there and rest. It was good. It was part of my restoration.

Trees need the winter. I never knew that before. They need time to strengthen for the growth they experience in springtime. All that green, pulpy growth has to harden, or the tree would not be able to withstand the seasonal winds that whip against it.

I had experienced a lot of growth. Now was the time for the energy to be diverted from the branches to the roots. The roots of my faith were going deeper. Much of what was going on with me was going on underground, so to speak, beneath the surface, unseen.

Growth can be a lonely place, but it is a necessary place.

That's what I learned in the fall of '69, there in my wheelchair, in the backyard with the bare branches—and my Bible.

Initially my parents, as well as my doctor, had not revealed the full extent of my injuries. They told me things like "your ankle is broken" or "your shoulder is dislocated" or "your back is broken in a few places." But they never went into detail. Later I learned that Dr. Graham had advised my parents not to discuss my injuries with me until I asked. In this way, he believed I would learn of their seriousness as I was emotionally able to handle the information.

I had been talking about and praying about my physical restoration for several weeks, when my dad sat down with me for a man-to-man talk.

"You've got a lot of work ahead of you, Dale. And you need to understand that it may be years before you'll be able to function normally, even somewhat normally. You'll not be able to regain the use of everything, you know. The doctor says you'll never walk again."

I wasn't prepared for what he said and couldn't respond.

He explained, "We didn't want to tell you everything too soon. You had enough trauma those first few weeks."

I don't know if it was for my benefit or his, but I said, "Don't worry, Dad. It will all come back. You'll see. God will restore me to the way I was. And on the anniversary of the crash, I'm going to fly over that monument as pilot in command. With God's help we'll do it. He and I are a team now. Just wait, you'll see."

Dad sat back in his chair and said nothing, which was uncharacteristic of him. He had always been a can-do kind of guy, always looking on the bright side. But Dad had been apprehensive about my flying. It wasn't a career choice he could fully support. And now, after the crash, he could muster no enthusiasm at all. He couldn't even fake it.

That was the last time I spoke to him about flying over the monument, the last time I spoke to him about a lot of things.

Ever since my release from the hospital, we had been making numerous trips to Burbank for additional surgeries, postoperative checkups, and treatments. Day after day we threaded our way along the freeways to Dr. Graham's office, located just across the street from St. Joseph. We averaged three trips a week. Then we were down to two.

On one of those visits in early November, my grandparents joined my parents and I to talk with Dr. Graham together. First there was the usual routine of X rays, and then the doctor examined my eye, head, face, back, legs, and ankles. Then we waited in the lobby for the X rays to come out.

When Dr. Graham called us in to his office that day, he was unusually animated as he pointed to my X rays. "I can't believe this," he said.

"Praise the Lord!" Grandpa declared under his breath as he characteristically rattled the coins in his pocket.

I wheeled myself in for a closer look. "What's going on?" I asked.

Dad spoke first. "Dale, when the doctors examined you at the hospital, they told us your left ankle was so severely shattered it would never heal properly. The bone had exploded on impact. Without blood circulation, there is no healing."

"It's called *avascular necrosis*," the doctor said. "It means bone death."

Dad continued. "The doctors recommended operating on your ankle to remove the shattered bone and move your foot up against your leg bone, supporting it with metal braces and pins. That way you could still put weight on your foot. The only problem is your left leg would be three or four inches shorter than your right leg. You'd have to wear an elevated shoe, and without an ankle joint, you would have a severe limp."

A chill crept through me as he spoke. I had no idea such a possibility existed. I shivered at the thought.

"Your grandpa and I talked it over," my dad said, "we prayed about it, and we felt we should give God an opportunity to work in the situation."

Dr. Graham listened as my dad spoke, his face reflecting no emotion. Then he interjected, "The risk was that once the bone died, it would likely collapse. We would not be able to do anything at that point. And you would be unable to walk at all. Ever. From my perspective, it was a big gamble."

Tears filled my eyes. "So what did you find on the X rays today?"

"The bone has begun to vascularize," the doctor said. "For some reason blood is beginning to circulate. The bone is beginning to heal." He looked at the X rays and shook his head. "I can't explain it, but here it is."

"Praise the Lord!" Grandpa said again, a little more emphatically.

You can imagine the ride home. We were all filled with joy—and gratitude. As the familiar green freeway signs flew past, the visual of a checklist came to mind:

1. God spared me from certain death.
2. My vision is changed. Nothing looks the same to me.
3. God has given me a renewed spirit.
4. There are no internal injuries.
5. I was released from the hospital in eight days.
6. Now God is healing my dead ankle.

There is a pattern here, I thought. *God is doing something. Even the crazy idea to exercise my eye is part of it.*

With that thought, I closed my left eye. It was true. The vision in my injured eye was becoming clearer.

My faith was doing handstands. I could hardly contain myself. That's when I prayed, *God, I'm going to get to know You better. I'm going to work with You to get the job done that You have in mind for my life. I don't know what Your plan is exactly, but I have a feeling it's something special. I'll tell You this: I'm going to stick close enough to You to find out exactly what it is.*

⑪
SURVIVING THE UNSURVIVABLE

It was late November. I had to get out—out of the backyard, out of the house, out of town. I asked a friend to take me to the Portal of the Folded Wings in Burbank.

I had to see it again, this time up close and personal. I had to see the place where my pilot friends had died and where I had lost so much of my life, so much of my memory. Maybe something would come back. An image. A feeling. A missing piece to the puzzle my life had become.

We drove to North Hollywood, where Valhalla Memorial Park Cemetery was located, just off the flight path of Runway 15. After we parked, I eased into the wheelchair, and my friend wheeled me to the memorial.

The closer we got, the larger it loomed.

The larger it loomed, the smaller I felt.

It was massive, a huge cube of a building topped with a colorful dome. As we approached it, I saw a large bronze plaque that read:

WELCOME TO THIS SHRINE OF
AMERICAN AVIATION.
THE PLAQUES HEREIN MARK
THE FINAL RESTING PLACE
OF PIONEERS IN FLIGHT.

On each side there were sculpted cherubs and female figures lifting their hands skyward. It felt strangely comforting, this lifing of hands. My prayers to God were for clarity about the crash. They were questions I raised to Him. I came empty-handed. Would I leave the same way? I didn't expect all my questions to be answered, but I expected to leave with something.

We looked at the dome. The place of impact was still being repaired. I didn't say much that day, but I did a lot of thinking. *The FAA classified our accident as non-survivable.*

At that moment I asked God, *Did I survive only to find out that I caused the accident, the deaths of Chuck and Gene? Will that be the outcome, once the investigation is complete? Do I need to learn to live with the guilt and the shame? How can I live with it? How can I move on? Was it a blessing that I lived, or a curse? Perhaps the investigation will reveal I wasn't to blame, I wasn't at all responsible. Perhanps the crash was caused either by mechanical or pilot error.*

As we got closer, I saw another plaque identifying the Italian-American artist who created the sculptures and ornamentation:

Frederico Augustino Giorgi
PORTAL SCULPTOR
1878–1963

I later learned the sculptor considered this work to be his masterpiece. It was beautiful in one sense. In another sense, it was grotesque—a hulk of a building standing so stoically; an immovable object that had snatched our plane out of the sky and threw it to the ground. An unchanging structure that forever changed three lives. Without apology or the slightest show of remorse.

We went inside to see plaques of remembrance for the fallen pioneers of aviation. The ashes of fifteen of them were buried there. Sensing I needed time to process my thoughts, my friend left me alone. I looked up to see that the dome was a mosaic of stars—a portal to the heavens. All of my thoughts were drawn there, all my empty-handed prayers.

The questions that had hounded me before, the ones I thought had been held at bay, came back at me in a vicious assault.

Why did I live? Why me and not the others? Why, God?

I sat beneath the dome of stars, wondering with my questions, waiting for His answers.

Was I spared because God had a special plan for me? *Is that true, God? Do You? Did You save me so I could serve You? God, almost all of my friends have left me. I am no longer popular. I'm the guy in the wheelchair who survived "that crash." I can't play sports. I can't remember what was said in class, no matter how hard I try. How am I going to do this, God? How am I going to go through life with this limp body and this lame brain?*

I paused, waiting for something, unsure what it was. Was I waiting for one of the angels on the shrine to come down and explain it all? Was I hoping for heaven to open and spill out the answers like gum balls? Was I waiting for a sign? A word? An audible voice? An inner conviction? I had no idea. Not even a clue.

But I was there. I showed up. And I was there with my one hand raised to heaven. I was not one to beg, but I was begging. *I've never known loneliness before, God. Is this a season in my life when You want it to be just You and me? If so, just say so. I'll be fine if that's what You want. Is that what You want? Please, do something, say something. Anything. Just don't leave me alone.*

During those weeks I made many visits to the memorial, by myself mostly. Sometimes I would get in the car and drive there at night. The cemetery was closed at night, and I would drag my bent and broken body to the fence, crawl under it, casts and all, in order to spend a few hours alone there. I prayed there, flat on my back, looking up at the dome. I thought there, trying to dredge up something from my subconscious. And I cried there. For Chuck. For Gene. For the robust person I once was. For the shell of a person I was now.

Dale and the Piper Aztec that he and Chuck flew regularly before the crash. Photo taken November 1969.

I think I used the memorial as a focal point to help get my memory back.

Doctors who worked on me talked with me only briefly about my memory loss. Dr. Graham didn't seem as concerned with it as with the other losses I had suffered. Maybe it was because he felt he could help with the ankle and the shoulder and the face but not with the memory.

Doctors explained that there are different types of amnesia. The two most common are retrograde and anterograde. The former type involves memory loss before the cause, such as a motorcyclist not remembering driving his motorcycle prior to his head injury. The latter has to do with the inability to store new memories after the cause, such as the motorcyclist not being able to recall his hospital experiences or conversations with family and friends who visited him there.

Posttraumatic amnesia, which affects memory before and after head trauma, can be transient or permanent, depending on the severity of the brain damage. Some of my memory loss has proven to be permanent, some of it transient.

The transient losses return at the oddest times and in the oddest ways, with no particular pattern. The memories are random. *When* they return and *why* they return are also random.

The depth and duration of this kind of amnesia are related to how severe the injury is. Often people with head trauma may remember events, but they will not remember the faces of the people in the events. Another type of amnesia, called source amnesia, is when people can recall certain information, but they don't know where or how they obtained the information.

Since different parts of the brain store different types of memories, the more pervasive the damage, the more types of memories are affected. All this to say I suffered a lot of damage and as a result experienced a lot of memory loss.

At the memorial that November day when my friend took me, I still had no memory of the crash. No memory of the three days in a coma. There were only sketchy memories of people and events in my past. There were no words from heaven. No answers. But it was important for me to be there. I'm glad I went. Something had drawn me there—it was almost a gravitational pull. I felt as if I were some small, inconsequential planet orbiting closer and closer to the sun, and the closer I got the more of me was being burned away.

Somehow—in ways I can't understand, let alone express—it felt good. Cleansing. Cathartic. And in some way necessary.

I would be back.

And I would keep going back until the shrine gave up the secret it was keeping.

Or until I was burned away completely.

(12)

GOOD NEWS AND BAD NEWS

The crash was almost six months behind me now. I had faithfully made the pilgrimage to Dr. Graham's office more times than I could count. They were mostly routine visits. Routine X rays. Routine checks to see how I was healing, how I was holding up.

Today was different. Today he brought out the usual X rays, but he said something most unusual. "Well, Dale, I've got good news and bad news."

I perked up, all ears.

"The good news is that your ankle is doing surprisingly well."

"Great," I said. "What's the bad news?"

"Well, it's not really news to us, but it will be to you. It's your shoulder." Dr. Graham looked me straight in the eye, as if to see how I would take the news.

"My shoulder? I know that I can't move my arm now, but it's going to be OK someday, isn't it? It was just dislocated, right?"

"It wasn't dislocated, Dale, it was disintegrated. In fact, on the medical report I described your ball-and-socket joint as having exploded. We even found shoulder bone throughout your back, neck, and chest. It had blown to bits. And the muscles and ligaments all around that area were stretched way beyond their elasticity."

"So that's why I can't lift my arm."

"That's exactly why. When we did the surgeries, we put all the pieces of the bone back together the best we could. We hoped that eventually

287

you might gain some mobility. At this point, I'm pessimistic. You have no strength in that shoulder, and no control of it. We hoped by now you would. Not only that, Dale, but your shoulder muscles have been inactive for almost six months now. In that amount of time, injured, unused muscles grow brittle. Before much longer, you'll have virtually no chance of ever using your shoulder and most of your arm again."

Not the news I was prepared to hear. Questions raced through my mind. *What about my plans for flying, for ground school, for flight instruction?*

"So, what can we do?" I asked tentatively.

Dr. Graham spoke enthusiastically now. "If we can go back a third time into the left shoulder area and take out some more slack muscle, I think you might have a 10 percent chance of lifting your arm about 45 degrees someday. That's the best we can hope for, Dale."

My heart sank. "Ten percent?" I took a deep breath and with it came a surge of faith. "Well, Doc, a ten percent chance of success is ten percent more than God needs. Let's go for it."

Dr. Graham looked at me soberly. "OK. There really is no other choice. The muscles are deteriorating rapidly. To tell you the truth, I'm very concerned about what we're going to find when we get in there. It could be too late."

Dr. Graham had only one date open for surgery. If I didn't take it, I would have to wait another month, which he thought was perilously late.

This will be the last operation, I vowed to myself. But I had made that same vow so many operations before. I had already had twelve surgeries, and here I was agreeing to go under the knife again.

When I checked in to St. Joseph Hospital, the staff was eager to see me, see the progress I had made, and was ready to help me get through the next phase of my recovery. In spite of the cheerful staff, the place had been a prison to me, a place of pain and shadows and horrible memories. I arrived as late as I could.

When I got to my room, I noticed the curtains were drawn between me and my roommate. It wasn't long before I learned why.

"Nurse!" an angry voice blurted out. "Get in here! Can you hear me? Nurse!"

When the nurse came in, you could see the weariness on her face from having to answer endless calls like this from the crabby old man. He rattled off a litany of complaints: Dinner was cold. The meat was tough. Everything tasted bland. The TV wasn't working right. The volume was set too low. Then another diatribe about his medication.

Congratulations, Dale, I thought. *You've got yourself a real winner this time.* I wondered whether I would have to put up with this all night.

Then, unexpectedly, the gentlest of thoughts came into my mind. I began to wonder about this man, his life, where he was spiritually. I wondered why he was so angry. An overwhelming love for him came over me and I felt compelled to speak to him. I prayed silently for him. Then I maneuvered myself out of bed, let go of the railing, and hopped across the room. I grabbed the curtain that separated us and wiggled it.

"Hello, sir," I said. "What's your name?"

The pause stretched for what seemed an eternity. Then he spoke, his words bristling with irritation.

"Name's Green. Joel Green."

"Well, my name is Dale Black, Mr. Green. I guess we'll be sharing the same room. Nice to meet you."

He pulled back the curtain. A leathery, saddlebag of a face glared at me. "What are you in the hospital for? You're just a kid."

I chuckled. "Yeah, I don't know if you remember a plane crash back in July..."

I went on to give him the short version of the story. He did, in fact, recall hearing about it on the news. And he recalled one of the headlines in the newspaper: "Fate? Coincidence? or Cruel Irony?" We talked about the aircraft, about the monument, and about the miracle of my surviving. And then I just blurted it out...

"Mr. Green, do you know Jesus Christ? He's the reason I'm alive. He

289

has given me joy like I never knew before. I have purpose in my life now, Mr. Green. Do you know Jesus as your Lord and Savior?"

He looked away. No answer.

"Mr. Green, do you know about the free gift of salvation through Jesus Christ?"

Silence. Then a softening of the face. Then tears. Lots and lots of tears. At last he spoke.

"I'm a minister's son." His voice trembled. "I'm seventy-seven years old, and I've been running from God all my life." He sniffed in the emotion and said with sadness in his voice, "It's too late for me now, Dale."

"It's never too late, Mr. Green. It's never too late to allow God to take your life and turn it into something beautiful. God's time is now. Let's get forgiveness for the past mistakes. God says in His Word that when you ask Him to forgive you, your sins are thrown away, as far as the east is from the west. In other words, He forgets them! It's great, Mr. Green. Give God your life now and you'll forever be glad you did."

Again, silence. I wondered about his reaction, wondered if I had been too bold, too brash. But the love I had for him was overwhelming, just like the love I had for people the first week after the crash. A lot was at stake, I thought. *Everything* was at stake.

At last, I spoke again: "Mr. Green, would you like to pray to God now and ask Him to forgive you?"

Again, silence. Then softly, "I, eh . . . I'd like that."

Mr. Green didn't quite know what to say, I sensed that. I also sensed that the walls of bitterness were coming down. I wasn't quite sure what to do next, what to say, or how to say it. I wasn't experienced at things like this.

"Just repeat after me, Mr. Green."

He nodded, and I just relaxed and tried not to get in the way of what God wanted to do.

"Dear God." He repeated after me. "I'm sorry I've been running away from You." And he repeated that too. "I should have been running *to* You." He continued, word for word. "Lord, I'm a sinner, and I'm tired of running."

As soon as those words came from his mouth, he broke down and wept, then sobbed. I waited until the tears ran their course.

"Father," I said.

"Father," he said.

"Thank You for Your unending love."

"Thank You for Your unending love."

"And for sending Your Son to die on the cross for me."

"And for sending Your Son to die on the cross for me."

"I invite Jesus into my life right now."

"I invite Jesus into my life right now."

"Take over the controls of my life."

"Take over the controls of my life."

"Thank You, God. Amen."

"Thank You, God. Amen."

He dried his tears, thanked me, and we talked awhile until the nurse came to check on him. I could tell by how he treated her that he was a changed man. The nurse could tell too. He was polite and gentle with her. And with me. After she left, he told me to call him by his first name. "Joel," he reminded me. We talked into the night and became friends. More than friends . . . buddies.

Bright and early in the morning I was prepped for surgery. Joel's side of the room was quiet, and I didn't disturb him. I was wheeled away. The last thing I remember is the nurse giving me a needle in the hip, and my words, which this nurse was used to hearing from me: "Carol, did I tell you that this is my last surgery?" She smiled. The smiled blurred. And I was out.

"Wake up, Dale! Dale, wake up!" Dr. Graham was patting me firmly on the face. When at last I opened my eyes, he was smiling down at me. "Dale, listen! I can hardly believe it! There was no deterioration in your shoulder muscles at all. I had little to do but shorten the muscles. They were healthier than I could ever have imagined." The doctor was so excited he couldn't contain himself. "I think you may eventually have up to 45 degrees mobility out of that shoulder. I can hardly believe it!"

"No, Doc," I managed to say in my groggy state. "My . . . God . . . is a God . . . of completeness. . . . He *will* . . . restore my shoulder. I'll be able to lift my arm over my head someday. You watch. You'll see."

When I was finally wheeled back to my room, I added my shoulder to the list of wonders that God had performed in my life.

A nurse came in to fluff my pillow and pull a blanket over me. I glanced over to say hello to Joel. His bed was empty.

"Hey, where's my buddy?" I asked, motioning to the other side of the room.

The nurse shook her head. "Joel's gone, Dale. I'm sorry. He died early this morning."

I was stunned. My breath left me. My thoughts left me. Then it hit me. Joel was in heaven. And I wasn't sad. I vowed then and there never to be timid about sharing the Good News of Jesus Christ again.

Suddenly I realized another reason why I was in the hospital. I thought of how intricate and complete God's love truly is.

It wasn't just for me and my shoulder.

It was also for Joel.

(13)

FROM HORRIFIC TO HEAVENLY

In March 1970, I re-enrolled at Pasadena College, attending classes during the day. It was there in the dorm, around 2 a.m. on the sixteenth that I awoke with a start, drenched in sweat. The dream was so vivid that for several seconds I thought it was real. I was in the cockpit of the Navajo just as it slammed into the monument at an incredible speed. I was hurled through the air, falling several stories to the ground. My arms whirled violently in circles, trying to keep my balance so I would land on my feet. Before hitting the ground, I woke up.

I had had this dream before—probably a hundred times. This time it was different. This time I felt it. I heard it, I smelled it, and I tasted it. The noise of the crash hurt my ears. The smell of burning oil filled my nostrils. The heat from the engines burned my flesh, and the taste of concrete filled my mouth. It was all so real. I was actually trying to spit pieces of concrete and marble from my mouth as I woke up. The smell lingered in my nose.

I lay in my bed, terrified. I sat up and looked across the room at my roommate to see if the sound of the crash had wakened him, but he was fast asleep. I had to get up. I had to get out of there. It was too intense.

I put on a heavy jacket, got my crutches, and maneuvered myself to the nearby football field. When I reached the 50-yard line, I put down my crutches and eased onto my back. Looking up at the stars, I paused to catch my breath. The starry sky seemed so immense, the glittering wonder of it all blinking down on me. This time, though, was different from the other

293

times I had gone there to process my life. This time it felt as if God were reaching down to me, trying to speak through the silence.

I had prayed so long for God to restore my memory. Was He at last beginning to answer that prayer? It felt like He was. And part of it felt reassuring. Another part felt unsettling. The crash had been horrific. And every cell within me, every space between the cells, had experienced the trauma. My body had become a projectile, traveling at 135 mph, and then stopping suddenly. Abruptly. Violently. And after the initial impact there was another—the seventy-foot free fall to the ground.

Nothing more came that night.

The next night, though, in the very same bed, more of my memory came back to me. I had been asleep and woke up with a start. Sitting up, I remembered some of the names of the people who had come by the hospital, names I had forgotten. My memory was coming back in fragments. I couldn't control when they came, how many came, or in what order they came.

The third night I remembered loading the plane the day of the crash. I recalled that we had performed two engine run-ups that day. I remembered the sound of the engines screaming at high rpms with the propellers out of sync. I remembered Chuck yelling at the last moment while trying to correct the erratic pitch of the plane.

When the memories started coming back, they came back with a heightened sense of awareness. I felt the bumps in the ambulance ride, for instance. I heard the desperate wail of the siren. I smelled aviation fuel everywhere. In the ambulance, the smell of fuel was almost suffocating.

I saw myself inside the ambulance. Then suddenly, I was outside the ambulance, chasing it. Chasing it for what seemed forever. I remember the stark terror I felt on that ride. It was too much for me. It was just too much.

The fourth night I couldn't sleep for fear of what I would remember. I called my parents, telling them I needed to talk. I was so overwhelmed by the horror of the memories that I didn't know what to do. We arranged to meet at a restaurant near the college, but during the time it took for them to make the drive, I had second thoughts. The memories were too raw, I was too fragile to recount them, and I wasn't sure they could help anyway. By the time they arrived, I decided not to share any of it.

On the fifth night the memories returned. This time they were stronger. This time I was leaving my body and floating just below the ceiling in the emergency room. I hadn't remembered it at the time it happened. I remembered it now. And in vivid detail.

Now it was clear these were not dreams, because they were now coming to me while I was wide awake.

During the following week I remembered something so amazing it took my breath away. Images of heaven started coming back. Images and sounds. Sounds and feelings. In the order that they happened. And in intricate detail.

Before the crash I had thought of myself as a realist and a pragmatist, much like my father. I loved science and statistics and things you could touch, hold, quantify, and contain. So my initial reaction to my journey to heaven was one of questioning. But in my heart there was no doubt about it. Whether I liked it or not, the memories were real, and they continued to pour back.

Finally everything started making sense. So many questions were answered. Although my mind had been unable to remember the experiences of leaving my body and visiting the entrance of heaven, my heart had remembered everything, storing it deep within me for the right time to reveal it.

Now was the time.

Gradually the rapid recall slowed. Within a few weeks it was down to a trickle. The picture became clear as each piece of the puzzle was turned over and put into place.

My experiences in heaven, as I have come to understand them, were embedded in me, almost like a memory chip. I say that because they have become so much more than memories. They have become permanent, life-changing events that have reprogrammed my values, my beliefs, the very way I live my life.

Just as it was time for the memories to come back to me, now is the time for them to be shared with you.

(14)

JOURNEY TO HEAVEN

I kept waking up. And I kept coming back to midfield. If ever there was a field of dreams, that football field in the middle of the night was it. It was the place where my most wonderful and horrible memories collided at the 50-yard line.

My last memories were when I had been in the hospital, seeing myself in the operating room from a vantage point near the ceiling. I remember feeling lighter and lighter, being drawn down the hallway and swept out the door of the hospital, and then suddenly I was gone.

The first memory of where I had gone when I was in a coma made no sense to me. It was a looping memory that replayed itself over and over again. The memory was of this stunningly beautiful light that permeated everything, going out in every direction but not expanding.

How could it be? I wondered. *How could light do that? I've never seen light like that.* My mind refused to cooperate. What I was seeing defied logic, defied rational analysis, let alone rational explanation.

Something was beginning to reveal itself, I was sure of that. I didn't know exactly what, but I did know that my prayers were being answered. God *was* restoring my memory. At first the memories came in fragments, then in a flood. Unlike the earlier memories, which came out of sequence, the memories I am about to share came back sequentially.

These are not memories I could summon on command. They bypassed my conscious brain. If I thought too much, they resisted revealing themselves.

297

I had to let my brain relax and allow my heart to take over. I wasn't used to giving up control easily, but I had no alternative. They wouldn't come if I didn't let go and tune in to my heart.

So I would go and lie down in the middle of our football field, in the middle of the night, gazing at the starry wonder of the Milky Way, where I would relax, let go, and . . .

Now it was coming back . . . where I had gone.

The more it came back, the more I let go, until the memories replayed themselves like one long, continuous movie.

Leaving the hospital, I sped through what appeared to be a narrow pathway. An incandescent-like beam of light, almost like a searchlight, originated from me and illuminated my path. It wasn't a tunnel of light that I was traveling through. It was a path in the darkness that was delineated by the light. Outside of this pathway was total darkness.

But in the darkness millions of tiny spheres of light zoomed past as I traveled through what looked like deep space, almost as if a jet were flying through a snowstorm at night, its lights reflecting off the flakes as they blurred past.

The speed at which I traveled was blinding, and the path narrowed to twice the width of my body. I had no pain, no discomfort whatsoever. No high-altitude ear-popping. No queasy stomach. No headache. And I had no worries, not even the least concern. Only questions.

What happened to me? Why is this happening to me? Where am I going? What is going to happen next?

What happened next is beyond my ability to describe. I will use the best words I can, yet the best words pale in the presence of what I experienced.

I was still traveling at enormous speed, all the while feeling no sensation of movement. No wind in my hair. No g-forces distorting my face. No pressure against my eyes, making them close.

At this time, I became aware that I was not traveling alone. Accompanying me were two angelic escorts dressed in seamless white garments woven with silver threads. They had no discernible gender but appeared masculine and larger than I was. Their skin tone was light golden brown and their hair fairly short. I could see their emotions, clearly delighted to be ushering me through this wonderland. They moved just behind me, one to the left of me, one to the right. Remarkably, my peripheral vision was enhanced, and I could see both of their glowing faces at the same time. I could even see behind me while hardly moving my head.

I was fast approaching a magnificent city, golden and gleaming among a myriad of resplendent colors. The light I saw was the purest I had ever seen. And the music was the most majestic, enchanting, and glorious I had ever heard.

I was still approaching the city, but now I was slowing down. Like a plane making its final approach for landing. I knew instantly that this place was entirely and utterly holy. Don't ask me how I knew, I just knew. I was overwhelmed by its beauty. It was breathtaking. And a strong sense of belonging filled my heart; I never wanted to leave. Somehow I knew I was made for this place and this place was made for me. Never had I felt so "right" anywhere. For the first time in my life, I was completely "whole."

The entire city was bathed in light, an opaque whiteness in which the light was intense but diffused. In that dazzling light every color imaginable seemed to exist and—what's the right word?—*played*. If joy could be given colors, they would be these colors. The colors were pure and innocent, like children playing in a fountain, splashing, chasing each other, gurgling with laughter. Water everywhere sparkled in the sunshine.

The colors seemed to be alive, dancing in the air. I had never seen so many different colors. If the brightest light on earth could shine through the most magnificent chandelier with tens of thousands of flawless crystals, it would appear as dirty glass in comparison to the amazing brightness and colors that entranced me.

It was breathtaking to watch. And I could have spent forever doing just that. The closer I got to the city, the more distinct the illumination became. The magnificent light I was experiencing emanated from about forty or fifty miles within the city wall.

I saw a great phosphorescent display of light that narrowed to a focal point that was brighter than the sun. Oddly, it didn't make me squint to look at it. And all I wanted to do was to look at it. The light was palpable. It had substance to it, weight and thickness, like nothing I had ever seen before or since.

The light from a hydrogen bomb is the closest I can come to describing it. Just after the bomb is detonated—but before the fireball that forms the mushroom cloud—there is a millisecond of light that flashes as the bomb releases its energy. It was something like that but much larger.

The glow and energy of this light radiated in all directions, upward and outward. It wasn't something you shielded your eyes from; it wasn't something you even flinched at. Just the opposite. It was warm and inviting. Almost hypnotic in its ability to draw you in to it.

Somehow I knew that light and life and love were connected and inter-related. It was as if the very heart of God lay open for everyone in heaven to bask in its glory, to warm themselves in its presence, to bathe in its almost liquid properties so they could be restored, renewed, refreshed.

Remarkably, the light didn't shine *on* things but *through* them. Through the grass. Through the trees. Through the wall. And through the people who were gathered there.

There was a huge gathering of angels and people, millions, countless millions. They were gathered in a central area that seemed over ten miles in diameter. The expanse of people was closer to an ocean than a concert hall. Waves of people, moving in the light, swaying to the music, worshiping God. Holiness hovered over them the way I imagine the Spirit of God brooding over the surface of the deep at the beginning of time. During priceless moments of worship you are so enraptured by it that you don't miss the moment before or long for the moment after.

Somehow the music in heaven calibrated everything, and I felt that nothing was rushed. Nothing waited for you, because you weren't late for anything. You weren't early either, having to wait for what was to happen next. Everything happened right when it was supposed to happen, and you were right there to experience it. In sync. With everything. Never hurried or stressed.

Time was clearly evident. But it, too, was perfect. The music was in perfect timing. The songs and hymns had a beginning and an ending. Yet in heaven I was certain that time was stable, nothing dying or decaying, nothing hurried and nothing late.

Time seemed relaxed, comfortable, and natural. The limitations and consequences of earthly time did not apply here. Heavenly time and order were intertwined as part of the perfect whole.

I was outside the city, slowly moving toward its wall, suspended a few hundred feet above the ground. I'm not sure how I knew directions there, but I had a strong, almost magnetic sense, that it was northwest. Which meant I was approaching the city from the southeast.

A narrow road led to an entrance in the wall, which led into the city. I moved effortlessly along the road, escorted by my two angelic guides, on what seemed to be a divine schedule. Below me lay the purest, most perfect grass, precisely the right length and not a blade that was bent or even out of place. It was the most vibrant green I had ever seen. If a color can be said to be alive, the green I saw was alive, slightly transparent and emitting light and life from within each blade.

The iridescent grass stretched endlessly over gently rolling hills upon which were sprinkled the most colorful wild flowers, lifting their soft-petaled beauty skyward, almost as if they were a chorus of flowers caught up in their own way of praising God. The fragrance that permeated heaven was so gentle and sweet, I almost didn't notice it amid all there was to see and hear. But as I looked at the delicate, perfect flowers and grass, I wanted to smell them. Instantly, I was aware of a gentle aroma. As I focused, I could tell the difference between the grass and the flowers, the trees and even the air. It was all so pure and intoxicating and blended together in a sweet and satisfying scent.

In the distance stood a range of mountains, majestic in appearance, as if they reigned over the entire landscape. These were not mountains you wanted to conquer; these were mountains you wanted to revere.

It seemed that my vision had been extremely enhanced. How otherwise could I see the colors I was seeing or the light that was in everything? It was something like being in a 3-D movie and then putting on the 3-D glasses. Or being outside in the darkest night and putting on night goggles. Suddenly everything has more dimensions, more richness. But that is an understatement. Multiply that by ten thousand and it would be like what I was experiencing. There are no words that capture the scenes that were before me. Utterly breathtaking.

My body was elevated above the ground and moved effortlessly to whatever location my escorts determined. My energy seemed boundless, and even though I had always worked hard to be in excellent condition, I had never come close to feeling as strong and healthy as I felt now. It was as though I could accomplish anything.

The road was only wide enough for two people and followed the contours of the hills. Then it began sloping upward toward the huge wall that encircled the city. I gazed again at the light, which stunned me with its glorious brightness and drew me toward it. I wanted to take everything in, to see it all, absorb it all, and remember it all.

Next I heard the faint sound of water rushing in the distance. I couldn't see the water, but it sounded as if it were rivers cascading over a series of small waterfalls, creating music that was ever-changing.

Music was everywhere. The worship of God was the heart and focus of the music, and everywhere the joy of the music could be felt. The deepest part of my heart resonated with it, made me want to be a part of it forever. I never wanted it to stop. It swelled within me and without me as if it were inviting me into some divine dance.

The music was a seamless blend of vocals and instrumentals, the voices enhancing the instruments, and the instruments enhancing the vocals. Neither diminished the other but rather enriched the other. There was no competition, only cooperation. Perfect harmonic order. I had the feeling—and it was the most satisfying of feelings—that I was made for the music, as if each muscle in my body were a taut string of some finely tuned instrument, created to play the most beautiful music ever composed. I felt part of the music. One with it. Full of joy and wonder and worship. Perhaps this is what love sounds like when put to music. It felt so. And every part of me felt it.

I was in complete harmony with it, and it accompanied me, beguiling me onward throughout my journey. I thought I would burst with exuberance as I found myself included in such sacred and joyous melodies. I wanted to pause and let the music resonate so I could savor the glorious experience. But it never stopped. It just kept on playing.

The music of praise seemed to be alive and it passed through me, permeating every cell. My being seemed to vibrate like a divine tuning fork. I felt all this, every ecstatic moment of it. And I never wanted it to end. The music there, like the light that was there, existed in everything, and everything felt in perfect harmony. There was not a note of discord. Not a trace of someone playing his own music. Not a bit of competition anywhere. This was perfect unity. Expressed toward one focus—God.

It was as if all of heaven knew the beat, the tempo, the words, the pitch, the tone, and all participated in their unique way but in a way that all was united into one song. There were not different songs playing together; it was all one song, sung by everyone, simultaneously.

It was beautiful beyond belief. And it was blissful beyond belief. I never felt such overwhelming peace.

(15)
CELESTIAL PERFECTION

While in heaven, I somehow realized that knowledge is flawed and did not seem to be of great significance. Truth is what prevails and has supremacy in heaven. When I had questions or needed understanding it seemed to be imparted automatically and directly into my heart.

Just one of the things I somehow seemed to "understand" was that heavenly order was everywhere and in everything. I understood in my heart that God's will was perfection and His Word was the source of all creation. As I considered all that I had seen, I understood that the Word of God was and is the foundation for everything. God was the heart of heaven, His love, His will, His order.

Somehow I recognized that Jesus, the Word, was the structure that held it all together. Like the rib cage around the heart. He was the creative power that brought everything that I saw into place and stabilized it.

The multitudes of angels and people were responding to the will of God and acting in perfect order to accomplish His will. Even light—the way it traveled and reflected—was highly complex, yet mathematical and precise. The melodies and rhythms of the music were all in perfect order. Nothing out of sync. No part of heaven was independent of the whole. There was complete unity.

Between the central part of the city and the city walls were groupings of brightly colored picture-perfect homes in small, quaint towns. I'll call them townships, because I can't think of a better word for them. I focused on only three townships, but certainly there were more. A lot more, no doubt. The dwellings in these townships were not arranged in a uniform or symmetrical manner but appeared perfectly balanced somehow. Each home was customized and unique from the others yet blended harmoniously. Some were three or four stories, some were even higher. There were no two the same. If music could become homes, it would look like these, beautifully built and perfectly balanced.

The flowers in heaven fascinated me. Again, a delightful and delicate balance between diversity and unity. Each was unique. All were one. And they were beautiful to behold. Each petal and leaf illuminated with that glorious light and added just the right splashes of color to the velvety expanse of green grass.

As I described previously, the grass, the sky, the walls, the houses, everything was more beautiful than I ever dreamed anything could be. Even the colors. They were richer, deeper, more luminescent than any colors I have ever seen in the farthest reaches of earth or in the most fantastic of dreams. They were so vibrant they pulsated with life. Each and every color, no matter how varied, took its color from the glistening whiteness that permeated heaven.

If millions of jewels had been gathered into one place and the brightest sunlight shone through them, it wouldn't begin to describe the colors I saw. Heaven was filled with a rainbow of hues and provided me with a sensory feast.

My eyes were next drawn to a river that stretched from the gathering area in the middle of the city to the wall. It flowed toward the wall and seemed to end there, at least from my vantage point. The river was perfectly clear with a bluish-white hue. The light didn't shine on the water but mysteriously shone within it somehow.

The wall to the city was not a single wall but rather a series of walls layered next to each other. The wall was made of three outer layers, three inner layers, and one higher wall in the center. The outer layers of the wall were about forty feet tall. Each layer of the wall was taller as it got closer to the center, like a stairstep. At its tallest point the wall was a couple hundred feet. And surprisingly, it was as thick as it was tall. The wall was massive and stretched out to my left and right as far as I could see in both directions.

The outer wall was greenish in color with a hint of blue and a hint of black mingled within it. It was made entirely of translucent stones. Large multicolored stones were built into the base of the wall in layered rows. A powerful light permeated the wall, and you could see all the colors of the rainbow in it. Strangely, whenever I moved, the colors moved ever so slightly as if sensing my movement and making an adjustment.

The two angels that had escorted me there were still with me, moving me along, the three of us in sync, making sure I was *where* I should be, *when* I should be there.

I was eye-level with the base of the wall now and no longer hovering above it, but standing in front of an impressive opening. It was an archway that seemed to be approximately forty feet high and thirty to thirty-five feet wide.

A tall, majestic angelic being stood to the right side of the gate, dressed similarly to my escorts with the exception of the golden belt wrapped around his upper waist. A large emblem was located on the belt where a buckle would normally be. He appeared very strong and masculine. His hair was either white or it was the light radiating from him. But his entire being, and his head, specifically, was illuminated in bright white light. His face seemed to light up with love and joy at seeing me.

The entrance, or gateway, was opalescent in color, as if it had been made of pearls that had been liquefied, and then solidified onto the wall. The entrance was completely composed of this mesmerizing substance that also coated the entire inside of the opening as far as I could see. The ornamentation around the entrance included phenomenal detail. It was the most astounding sight I had ever seen. As I basked in the beauty that adorned the gateway, I noticed large gold letters emblazoned above the opening. They seemed to quiver with life. The single line of letters formed an arch over the entrance. I didn't recognize the letters but knew the words were as important as any words could be. Other letters were written in honey-colored gemstones on the ground in front of the entrance and included several lines. The entrance through the thick wall was breathtaking. The opening seemed filled with light that was the purest of white, yet it seemed to have countless hues that changed with even my slightest movement. I was filled with excited anticipation of entering that beautiful gate.

I was immersed in music, in light, and in love. Vibrant life permeated everything. All these weren't just *around* me, they were *inside* me. And it was wonderful, more wonderful than anything I had ever experienced. It felt as if I belonged there. I didn't want to leave. Ever. It was as if this was the place I had been searching all my life to find, and now I'd found it. My search was over!

A smaller group of people in soft-white robes had congregated to my left in the lush grass just off the roadway. It now seemed as if the music was orchestrating the event, moving people to their proper places. They had just arrived and were waiting in the wings, on time and in place, as if they followed a director's cue.

Who are these people? I wondered. *And why are they here?*

As suddenly as I had wondered, the answer came. They were here *for me*. Wherever they had traveled from and however far they had traveled, they had traveled *for me*. The looks on their faces, their excitement at seeing me, at welcoming me, was overwhelming. I felt so special, so loved. I had never felt such a deep sense of belonging. They radiated profound joy at seeing me. Everyone smiled, their eyes warm and kind; their hearts so filled with unconditional love that it spilled out of them onto me. No one was recognizable as an earthly acquaintance, but all seemed remarkably familiar. I didn't know these people, but somehow I knew they were my family—my spiritual family, my brothers, my sisters, spanning generations.

Although I didn't know them, somehow they knew me. They knew Dale Black. They knew my name. And they knew the *real* me, not the one I tried to project on earth to be accepted by someone I wanted to be friends with or to be validated by some group of peers I wanted to be part of.

They not only knew my name but somehow they knew the story behind my name. I was unaccustomed to such love and acceptance. I began to understand that this love is what God had designed for me from the beginning. These people had come to welcome me, include me, and communicate to me that I was a valuable part of the family of God. I had never felt so loved in my life, yet I had never done anything for these people. This was unconditional love. They were vessels of God's love. Both individually and collectively.

For some reason I clearly understood that I should not be touched, at least not yet. No one tried to touch me, and I didn't have a need to be embraced. The love I received from my spiritual family was so fulfilling and satisfying that no human touch could rival how loved I felt.

As I gazed into the radiant faces of these precious people, I looked into eyes that were more colorful than any on earth. Their smiles were brighter. Their countenances more alive. Each person was a living, vibrant, eternal being, exuding the very life of God.

I didn't think about whether they were male or female, although there were both. I saw them for who they were. None were skinny, none overweight. None were crippled, none were bent or broken. None were old, none were young. If I had to guess, I would say they appeared to be somewhere around thirty years old. They had no wrinkles, no signs of shifting or sagging, no signs of aging at all. I somehow understood that time was not an enemy here. Although some form of time does seem to exist in heaven, no one aged. No one died. Nothing decayed.

They wore soft-white seamless robes. Their skin tones were different but blended together so that no single person stood out. I did not notice racial differences, but I was aware that they had come from many tribes and nations.

None were recognized by the physical or social distinctions that we recognize on earth. All were recognized by their spirit, by the essence of who they were. Everyone and everything was full of pure life and was connected to the light somehow, and everything that was connected led to God.

Part of the joy I was experiencing was not only the presence of every-thing wonderful but the absence of everything terrible. There was no strife, no competition, no sarcasm, no betrayal, no deception, no lies, no murders, no unfaithfulness, no disloyalty, nothing contrary to the light and life and love.

In short, there was no sin.

And the absence of sin was something you could feel. There was no shame, because there was nothing to be ashamed of. There was no sadness, because there was nothing to be sad about. There was no need to hide, because there was nothing to hide from. It was all out in the open. Clean and pure.

Here was perfection. Complete and utter perfection. The revelation of sin's absence was astounding and exhilarating. This is where I belonged. I was made to be in heaven. In a perfect place where there is no sin.

I had been in heaven for some time before I recognized sin's absence. Now I contemplated the one thing that *dominated everything* on earth . . . that *infected everything* on earth, but was missing here. It can be compared to oxygen. I went through life not really thinking about the air I was breathing while I worked, slept, ate, and drove. But take that air away and I would think about nothing else. Similarly, I was so accustomed to sin that I hadn't even recognized its far-reaching effects in every part of life. But nothing had been tainted in heaven by sin's destructive touch. This perfection I experienced was largely due to the absence of sin.

The best unity I have ever felt on earth did not compare with the exhila-rating oneness that I experienced with my spiritual family in heaven. This love . . . God's love, was transforming. To experience something so sacred, so profound as the boundless love of God was the most thrilling part of heaven. It satisfied a longing in the deepest part of me. My spiritual family had shared God's perfect love with me. How could I ever be the same?

My attention was diverted to the beautiful entrance. I was certain I was going through the gate. Again I turned back toward my precious fam-ily and did not want to leave that perfect love. But because of the highly expectant look on their smiling faces, it seemed as if they knew I would be given a gift and what that gift would do for me.

I felt so special, you can't believe how special. After all, all this was *for me*. Everyone there was there *for me*. I had no idea what gift I was to receive, but the anticipation on the faces of the people let me know that it was something extraordinary.

I felt like a kid again, like that fifth-grade kid who loved God. Like that kid who used to look forward to Christmas like you wouldn't believe. I couldn't wait to open the gifts that waited for me under the tree. And I couldn't wait for the gift that waited for me now.

The music continued, such beautiful music, and I became even more excited. It swelled and with it so did my anticipation.

And then, as I was about to travel through the entrance and receive the gift . . .

I was swept away.

16

ASK AND RECEIVE

It was springtime, and I was back for yet another visit with Dr. Graham. This time I brought flowers for his receptionist.

"Oh, Dale! What a surprise!"

"It's the least I can do for all you have done for me."

"Well, it's no secret that you are our favorite patient." She winked and lowered her voice. "Even Doc has a special place in his heart for you, Dale. But, of course, he'll never let *you* know."

My weekly checkups had grown into pleasant afternoon diversions. I felt such gratitude for Dr. Graham's staff. They were so caring, so loving. The quiet, reserved concern of the doctor touched me even more.

This particular day I was feeling on top of the world. After the routine X rays and exam, the doctor simply said, "Dale, I'd like to meet with you in my office next week." His face was as inscrutable as ever.

"Great! See you next week, Doc!"

He left the room, and I picked up my crutches and walked down the hall, where I went past autographed photographs of Evel Knievel, Peggy Fleming, and dozens of other sports figures and television celebrities.

All the way down the hall I wondered what he wanted to see me about, why he didn't say more. I couldn't imagine what it might be. Nothing serious, surely. After all, I was out of the woods on all the serious stuff.

The following week I returned with new gifts in hand. After the X rays, which he normally went over with me in the examination room, he took me to his private office. The stuffed chair was stiff, and I felt even stiffer. He sat at his desk, quietly looking over my file as I fidgeted in anticipation.

"OK, Dale. I've got good news and bad news."

"Where have I heard that before?" A big smile stretched across my face and pulled painfully at my stitches.

"Your shoulder is doing well," he said matter-of-factly. "Have you been exercising it?"

I chuckled. "I guess you can call it that. I call it T-A-S . . . training in aeronautical sciences! When I'm driving my car, I stick my arm out the window and let the wind lift it. I can't move it on my own yet, but depending on the angle of my hand, I get quite a bit of elevated movement and stretching from the wind. I know it's making the shoulder stronger."

He cracked his first smile. "You're right. It is getting stronger. In fact, your shoulder is the most amazing thing I've seen in my medical career."

"I'm guessing that's not the reason you wanted to meet with me."

"No. The reason is your ankle."

"My ankle? I thought it was healing just fine."

"When we observed the blood beginning to circulate in your ankle, I really believed that your faith played a part in that. Regrettably, the blood supply hasn't increased beyond the 15 percent I observed when we examined it last."

He paused, as if trying to find the right words. But no words came.

"What do you recommend?" I asked.

He got up from his desk and pulled a thick leather-bound medical book off the shelf, opening it to a page he had marked. He looked at the page, then at me.

"I believe we need to operate on your ankle immediately. There is no time to lose. We need to perform a bone fusion, removing pieces of the bone from your hip and attaching them to your leg and foot bones. This will result in permanent immobility of the ankle, but it will allow you to at least put weight on it in the future."

His finger conspicuously tapped at a picture in the medical book. I don't know what I said next. But I knew I needed time to process what Dr. Graham had said.

It was a big decision. A permanent decision.

I left the office quickly, without small-talking with the receptionist or the usual chorus of good-byes to the staff.

My plans that afternoon included another flight with Capt. Fred Griffith, the test pilot who had flown me over the monument for the first time after the crash. He was going to take me flying again. I was more prepared for it this time, both emotionally and physically . . . until my visit with Dr. Graham. His news knocked the wind out of me. The last thing I felt like was getting into a plane, a plane I would never again fly if I had the operation that Dr. Graham felt was so critical.

I was confused and angry. I pulled my car over to use a pay phone and canceled the flight with Fred. I drove and drove and drove, trying to get it out of my system. *How could God do this? I mean, good grief, what does He want from me? I've sought Him. I've taken care of myself, followed the doctor's orders. I've shared His love with others. I believed God's Word, believed He would heal me. Now this.*

I caught the Ventura Freeway, wound around the interchange, and drove south to Long Beach. I needed a second opinion.

I respected my grandpa enormously. As I closed the door to his office, I hadn't even sat down before the news spilled out of me. I repeated what Dr. Graham had said.

Fusion is permanent. And permanent is a long time. If I got the ankle fused, walking would be difficult, sports would be something I watched on TV, and flying . . .

Forget flying.

Forever.

One question seemed paramount. *Why?*

Grandpa leaned forward, looking directly into my eyes. "Dale, you receive healing by faith, not by sight!" Those were Grandpa's first words.

"It's not what you see on the X-ray machine that matters. What matters is what God says about it and then what you're going to believe in your heart."

Grandpa and I continued our discussion as I wiped the stream of tears from my eyes.

"Dale, the Bible says in Hebrews the eleventh chapter, that 'faith is the substance of things hoped for, the evidence of things not seen.' That means that what you see, feel, or hear isn't the final word. Don't be moved by your physical senses or the circumstances around you. I'm not saying to ignore what the doctors say. Not at all. They are professionals, and they are here to help, and God uses doctors in mighty ways. But above all else, when push comes to shove, believe what God has said. Do what God's Word says to do. Do what you believe in your heart God is telling you to do."

I stared blankly at the tough, stubborn man of faith who sat across from me. His face was flushed with the intensity of his words. Yet I simply could not grasp the full impact of all that he was saying. I still didn't know if God wanted me to have the surgery.

At last, in a burst of frustration, I said, "Look, Grandpa. I'm going to take this piece of paper." I ripped a sheet off a legal pad that he'd placed next to his open Bible. "I'm gonna write down everything you say. . . ."

"Dale, don't put your faith in me. That will never work. Eventually all men will fail. But God cannot fail. And it is impossible for God to lie. Dale, your faith must be in God and in His Word." His voice was kind but firm.

I responded, "No, don't worry, Gramps. I'm not putting my faith in you, it's just that you've been a DOER of God's Word a lot longer than I have, and I know you can help direct me to the right principles in the Bible. But I will guarantee you this: Whatever I write on this list, I am going to do. After I have done everything that I write down, then all I have to do is wait on God."

"OK, Dale, you work that out between God and yourself. But here is what I recommend for you because this has been my experience." And so Grandpa began to list the principles he had learned while seeking the will of God.

"First of all, pray. Pray alone, pray with the elders, and pray with your friends. Just make sure that your prayer partners really believe and agree with you that God *will* answer your prayer."

I carefully wrote down everything on my checklist. Pray. Pray alone and in a group of only those who believe.

"Second, Dale, read your Bible."

I interrupted. "Read what? Where do I begin?"

"Let God show you, Dale; just start reading," Grandpa replied. "Something in the Bible will jump out at you as if it were printed in big red letters. God will have special chapters and verses for you. Special words will speak directly to your heart. He will lead you to them if you will ask and then expect Him to lead."

Being a young, underdeveloped Christian, I thought this all sounded pretty mysterious. "But I am going to do every last thing on this list. I refuse to be a hearer only! I will become a doer of God's Word!"

Grandpa hesitated for a moment, then continued. "Third, Dale, do exactly what God says in the Bible. Be on guard and ready, however, because in my experience I've learned that your faith will be tested in order to be strengthened. Understand, it is not God testing your faith, but He is allowing it to be tested to determine whether you really believe in your heart what God has promised. And remember, Dale, God's will is what you're looking for, and His will is found in His Word. He will never violate His Word."

Grandpa's words burned into my heart, and I was sure that I would never forget a single thing he had said. Nevertheless, I carefully folded the piece of paper with my checklist on it and tucked it securely into my shirt pocket, determined to follow each bit of instruction to the letter.

Now that I had discussed my fears and hopes about my ankle with Grandpa and had a plan to follow, I needed to talk to him about another equally difficult subject. I shifted in my chair, adjusted my cast and braces, trying to find a comfortable position. He leaned forward, peered deep into my eyes, and asked, "What else is troubling you, Dale?"

I had spent a lot of time with my grandfather. We were very close, and I knew my grandfather loved me. He communicated his love by listening well and giving me his time when I needed it.

Russell Price commanded a great deal of respect among his peers and was known by all as a man of principle who possessed a strong backbone. He was a man of his word. He lived in a world governed by principles. The most important things in his life were God, his family, his church, and his business . . . in that order.

Of course I loved Grandpa, and respected him too. That's why I found myself in his office that spring afternoon. I now told him about the returning memories of the crash. Next, I nervously confessed to him that I had observed my body on the operating table. Timidly I began to share vivid memories of heaven but only in a brief, general way. First I wanted to "test the waters" to see how he'd react. I briefly explained the wall, the people, the music, but did not go into much detail.

"Dale, before you go on, may I say a few things?" he asked.

I nodded. "Sure, of course, that's exactly why I'm here."

"In my lifetime, Dale, I've observed many people before you who have used supernatural experiences to gain accolades from others. Many books have been written about this, and these people go around the country speaking on the subject to fan the flame of self-promotion. But in my opinion, most of this is done for financial gain or recognition and is not pleasing to the Lord. Dale, when you're dealing with things like heaven and eternity, you're operating in God's realm. That realm is the spiritual, and I think you need to be cautious. If God has truly given you these experiences, then those experiences are sacred, aren't they?"

I looked into his well-wrinkled, warm, and kind face but didn't say a word.

"Dale," he continued, "I don't hesitate for a second to believe that the experiences you have now remembered are real. I've known you all your life and I know your heart. If God has allowed you to see a glimpse of heaven, even if you were in heaven for a time, then you have a couple of options. You can speak about your experience, or you can treat the experience as sacred and let your life be a reflection of your experience. By that I mean, if you really did see the other side, then live out whatever you believe you saw. Live what you believe you heard. Just live what you learned. Your life's actions will speak louder than your voice."

Moments passed and neither of us said a word. He was giving me time to think and process.

Finally, my grandfather muttered while staring out his office window, "That might explain why you had no internal injuries or major brain damage." He wiped tears from his eyes and said, "Well, praise the Lord."

I had asked Grandpa specific questions hundreds of times before and was always glad that I had. I decided to ask another one. "Grandpa, what would you do if you were in my shoes?"

"Dale, let me say, if it were me, I would not use the experience for personal gain. Look, I'm not faulting others, and I'm not judging what others do. But you asked me my opinion, and I'm giving it to you. Live what you saw, Dale. Live what you believe you've learned from those experiences. I wouldn't go around telling anyone anything until God has specifically instructed you to. If your experience in heaven was real, then let your life say so. And if the experiences were really from God, they will not go away. They will become a permanent part of you.

"You can do what you want with this, Dale, and I'll not judge you one way or the other. You can write about it, speak about it, or you can quietly live it instead. It's totally up to you. But make sure that you hear from God. Spend enough time in prayer to know what He's telling you to do."

Of course, none of what Grandpa shared surprised me; I knew him well. Finally, I thanked him for taking the time and hobbled out of his office.

As I drove home, I began to talk to God. I felt as if He were right there with me. My problem was His problem.

"Lord," I prayed as I drove. "You made the world. You made the stars and everything in the universe. You created everything in existence." I paused and unconsciously held my breath. I felt as if God had just shown me how the power of His spoken Word created all things in existence. It seemed to suddenly all make sense.

"O God, You are so completely awesome!" I pondered these thoughts as I made my way southbound on the 405 bound for the Seal Beach Boulevard off-ramp. "And God, You made my ankle too. You know exactly what is wrong with it and how to fix it again. Father, I've read in the Bible that Jesus healed everyone that asked. He didn't turn anyone down. It seems clear to me, Lord, that the Bible indicates that healing is available to everyone. Therefore, I believe it is Your will to heal me too. I believe without doubt that You want me healed and that You want to restore my ankle."

After parking my MGB, wanting to give the raw skin under my arms a needed reprieve from the constant use of crutches, I hopped on my right leg into the house. Without a moment's hesitation, I made my way to my room and picked up my Bible. I held it in my hands for a few minutes, wondering where to turn and what to read.

"God, You have something special to say to me through Your Word, right?" I held the Bible in both hands. "Lord! Please tell me where to read. Where should I begin?"

I waited for a moment. Suddenly the number *seven,* then Matthew, chapter 7, entered my mind as if it were a photograph. At first I assumed this was just my imagination. But the mental picture could not be erased. Matthew, chapter 7, persisted.

Somewhat skeptically, I turned the pages until I found the seventh chapter of Matthew: *"Judge not, that you be not judged. For with what judgment you judge, you will be judged. . . ."* As I read, I thought, *What does this have to do with my ankle?*

Verse by verse I read on. And then it happened, just like Grandpa had said it would. My eyes were fixed on the verse, and the words leapt out at me as if they had my name printed all over them. The words seemed to grab me by the neck and shake me.

Matthew 7:7–8, *"Ask, and it will be given to you; seek, and you will find; knock, and it will be opened to you. For everyone who asks receives, and he who seeks finds, and to him who knocks it will be opened."*

God had led me to this simple statement of faith that had challenged His people for centuries. Was I any less likely to receive or find or enter into His dwelling place than any other of His children?

Then I said, "God, You said that everyone who asks, receives, and he who seeks, finds. God, that means me! And I ask You right now to heal my ankle so I can walk and run someday. Thank You, God. I believe You are answering this prayer even now."

The decision was made, then and there. "Lord, I am making a choice. I'm deciding to believe that You are going to answer my prayers and heal my ankle. I am asking You to do what is impossible in the natural realm.

"God, if I'm ever going to walk again, if I'm ever going to play sports again . . ." By now tears were streaming down my face. I could barely see, but my prayer poured out like a river. "God, if I'm ever going to fly again . . ." I choked in my emotion. "Lord, if I am ever going to walk or play sports or fly, it will be for one reason. That reason will be that You healed me according to Your Word. I trust You, Lord, and I believe in You and Your Word! And I'll be careful to give You the glory."

I stood up as if to deliver the final verdict. "God, I believe that it is not Your will for me to have this bone fusion operation! I respect Dr. Graham and I appreciate him, but You will be the one to perform this operation in Your way. And with You as my Physician, I will have normal use of my ankle someday."

"Thank You, God . . . thank You, Father," I whispered, wiping my eyes. With that, I closed my Bible. From that moment on, the course was set . . . the flight plan was filed. Under His wings I would be carried to the destination of His choosing.

Over the next few days, I confirmed another decision in my mind and settled it in my heart. I would live what I learned from my experiences in heaven. I decided not to share my sacred experiences with anyone—not my parents, not my girlfriend, not even my wife or children, should I ever have them. Until God clearly instructed me otherwise, these experiences would be kept between Him and me alone. And I knew Gramps would keep my secret. I asked God for the strength to live a life that would reflect the experiences He blessed me with. I would need His power and strength to bring glory to Him by becoming that reflection of His faith, hope, and love.

The next day I phoned Grandpa. He seemed pleased to hear my decision but reminded me not to get my eyes off God's Word and His promise. Then I phoned Dr. Graham. That was entirely another story.

"Dale, you're making a mistake, a *serious* mistake. You are gambling with your ability to walk again, to *ever* walk again. If the circulation in your ankle doesn't improve, you won't be able to move it, let alone put any weight on it. Your ankle will collapse. Arthritis will set in. And you will be in severe pain the rest of your life. With no cure. Am I making myself clear? Do you understand, Dale?"

The words were hard to hear. The tone was even harder. I told him how much I respected him, how much I appreciated all he had done for me, but my decision was final.

I believed God was going to let me fly again. If I was ever to do that, it wouldn't be with a fused ankle. I made the decision in faith. I'm sure Dr. Graham thought I had made it in presumption. Regardless, I was the one who had to live with the consequences.

✈

"Hello, Mrs. Ferguson? This is Dale Black." I felt a little foolish making the call, but I was determined to do it anyway. "In James, the fifth chapter, the Bible instructs us to call for the elders of the church and have them pray, if any is sick. I wanted to ask you and your husband to pray about something for me."

She didn't hesitate at all. "Sure, Dale. What is it?"

I read from the scribbled notes I'd made on the paper in Gramps' office.

"Well, it's about some things that I'm asking God to do in my body. He started a miracle in my ankle, but then it seemed as if He quit! But now I believe He is going to restore my ankle all the way, 100 percent. I need some believers to pray in agreement with me. Would you pray for me and specifically ask God to restore blood circulation in my left ankle?"

Grandpa had specifically said to make sure that those I asked to pray truly believed that God would do what He says. I knew that the Fergusons and my uncle and aunt, Jerry and Verna Price, would be the ones to ask for prayers of faith. They sincerely loved me, but, more important, they had faith in an all-powerful God who desires to heal and answer prayer.

After speaking to them, I went outside to catch some fresh late-afternoon air. There stood a familiar smiling face. It was our friendly next-door neighbor, young Terry Smith. Terry's father was a retired airline pilot. "How are you getting along, Dale?"

Here was my first opportunity to speak about my faith in God's Word regarding my ankle. "Well, Terry, I'm getting along great! God is completely healing my ankle. He's producing another miracle in my body, and I'm very grateful. And Terry, how's it going with you?"

Within two hours of reading the seventh chapter of Matthew, I had made a decision not to have the operation of fusing bone from my hip into my ankle. Four people were now praying in faith for my ankle to be restored. Yet I began to realize the first person that needed to be convinced that God's Word was true in my life was the one looking back in the mirror—me. I didn't completely understand it all at first. But as I repeated promises from the Bible and spoke out loud about those words to myself and to others, something wonderful was happening. Those Bible promises began to take root in my heart.

"Now faith is the substance of things hoped for," I reminded myself, "the evidence of things not seen." Evidence—that's the kind of hard facts lawyers present that must stand up in a court of law. I was beginning to understand.

There was a kind of exhilaration to this new experiment in obedience to God's Word. I felt as if I were beginning an adventure with the God who created me. And that's exactly what it was. He and I were going to travel together. He would instruct; I would obey and learn.

Because of my inexperience, though, I had not counted on discouraging words, disappointing circumstances, or devastating medical reports. My first unexpected detour came when my father heard that I had decided not to have the bone-fusion surgery recommended by Dr. Graham. "Dale, I think you're being unrealistic," he said.

It was difficult to disagree with my dad. He was a strong individual and a successful businessman, president of his own company, one of the spin-offs of the family business. He had also seen me through the entire airplane crash ordeal, and he had shared my burden without complaint. It was Dad and Grandpa who had believed that prayer would heal my ankle in the first place. On my behalf they rejected one operation just after the crash and their decision turned out to be the best one for me. But now I felt sad saying, "No, Dad, I've made up my mind. I've already asked God to heal my ankle, and I'm going to believe that He will."

When I returned to the college campus, I had dozens of opportunities to verbally confirm my newfound perspective.

When friends asked how I was doing, I had a standard reply: "God has healed me. Praise the Lord! Soon I'll have new X rays to prove it! You watch. You wait. You'll see."

As the time of my next doctor's appointment came around, I gathered up five friends who wanted to see the miracle firsthand. We piled into an old green Cadillac and headed for Burbank. As we drove, I reminded them of our purpose: "You guys are going to be eyewitnesses to an awesome miracle."

We cruised happily along the freeway, parked, then descended upon the medical building like a small, loyal regiment of soldiers. We were full of youthful zeal. Dr. Graham's staff, somewhat used to my eccentric behavior, graciously welcomed my friends.

"They're here to see that God has healed my ankle," I explained.

The X rays were taken. We waited anxiously until Dr. Graham emerged with them in hand. "Wait, Doc. Before you put up the X rays, would you mind if we prayed together and thanked God for what He has already done?"

Doctor Graham nodded OK to my request. The six of us held hands as we gathered around the viewing screen to pray. We thanked the Lord for what He had done and for what we were about to see. After we said amen, Dr. Graham placed the negatives on the screen to begin his analysis.

He paused a long time before he spoke. At last, and with some difficulty, he broke the news. "There is absolutely no progress. I'm sorry, Dale, the blood is not circulating in your ankle."

Even though the war was far from being over, that little battle marked a heavy defeat. My friends and I were an untrained unit. Our equipment and weapons had not been previously tested. As for me, I was only beginning to learn how to put on the full armor of God. I had a long, long way to go.

Subdued and thoughtful, we headed back to the car. "Don't worry, Dale, God is certainly not finished yet!" Dave patted me on the back as he spoke. Gene, Larry, Jerry, and others offered their own guarded condolences.

I told my friends that I didn't want to talk. I turned and gazed out the window, discouraging further communication. It was uncomfortable for everyone anyway. And it was a good thing, because inside I was becoming self-centered again. In my heart, thoughts that I was ashamed of exposed themselves. *Don't give me all those neat little answers and clichés. It's my life, not yours. You have no idea how I feel!* The cold fact was this: *God did not do what He told me He would do. God let me down. He blew it and I don't like it at all! I have acted like a fool by trusting Him!* My thoughts riveted to the possibility that maybe Dr. Graham was right. Maybe I had made a choice that would leave me more crippled than I had dared believe. Was God that unfair? Was He that hard to figure out? What was I going to do now?

All at once I remembered—the checklist! Had God allowed my faith to be tested? I recalled Grandpa Price cautioning me that once my faith was put into action, I would be tested back. I had told hundreds of people that my ankle was healed. I wasn't playing games. I had truly believed it to be so. But what had happened? When the X rays came back with a negative report, I had believed them more than God's Word. I listened to the wrong voice. I believed in circumstances and let go of the promise of God! How could I have let it happen?

My faith grew as I studied the Bible and replaced my doubt with increasing faith in the promises of God.

Within days I was standing in the college chapel service, giving my testimony again. I shared my renewed faith in God's Word, and the importance of patience and long-suffering with faith in prayer. After sharing my experience, Rev. Reuben Welch anointed me with oil and prayed for me while others prayed for the bones in my ankle to be restored.

I invited any who were interested to return the next morning to Dr. Graham's office for another opportunity to see a miracle. I explained to them that my faith had been put to the test. "Come and see the miracle!" I announced to the students in the chapel. This time, the well-worn green Cadillac and a second car made their way to Burbank, loaded with high-strung Christian students who believed in a miracle-working God.

Before our group got out of the car, we had a word of prayer and thanked God for what He had already done. The last episode had been a test of my faith. I had clearly flunked. But now I knew where I had made my mistake. Most people have heard the phrase "seeing is believing." But according to the Bible I had now learned that "believing is seeing." Now was the time for what I believed would become something we could all see.

I thought I finally understood. I was certain I had uncovered the keys to finding the will of God—by *knowing* the promises in the Word of God. Little did I know that the most important lessons about God and His will lay just ahead of me. What I was to learn about myself in the process would not only surprise me but would change me forever.

"Now faith is the substance of things hoped for, the evidence of things not seen."—Hebrews 11:1

⑰
LOSING LIFE TO FIND IT

Once again in Dr. Graham's office, we went through the same procedures. The X rays were taken, and as before, we gathered around the viewing screen. I explained to the doctor briefly what had gone wrong the last time. I told him how I had failed to realize that my faith must be in the promises of God and not in circumstances. We held hands and prayed, thanking God for His love and for His Word.

Dr. Graham placed the negatives on the screen. On this occasion, it took the long-suffering doctor even longer to speak.

Finally, he turned to me and revealed his findings. "Dale, I'm sorry." He was clearly struggling. "Not only is there no progress, but now we have waited too long. There is no blood circulation in your ankle. There is nothing we can do to reverse the situation. The bone is completely dead."

I was stunned. How could this be? I had done what I was supposed to do. I had corrected my error. This was not the way things were supposed to work. I had followed the checklist perfectly. My thoughts and questions could not be contained. As far as I was concerned, the news was as bad as it could be, and I was devastated. If I could not trust God, then I could never trust anyone or anything. Ever.

As we made our way back toward campus, no one said a word. I wanted it quiet and everyone knew it. After an hour of tense silence in the car, we finally arrived back on campus. No one was more relieved than I was. I hurried as quickly as my crutches could carry me to my dorm room, where

I shut and locked the door. I didn't want to see anyone. I was assaulted with such immense, overwhelming doubts and fears that I crumbled beneath them. *You're a fool, Dale Black. You're a stupid fool to put your complete trust in God. You obviously don't know what you're doing, and now you'll never walk again. You can forget about sports. Flying is out of the question, forever. All because of your idiotic faith experiment. God doesn't heal everybody. You can't make the decision to have God heal you. It was a big mistake not to have had that bone fusion operation. At least you could have walked again. But no, you had to act like some big man of faith. Welcome to the world of lifetime cripples. How could you be so foolish? Now you've lost everything, Dale.*

It was extremely difficult for me to sit comfortably. I didn't like to lie down because of my various casts and braces. But it also hurt to sit upright for very long. The most practical place for me to spend any amount of time was on my knees. The next day that's exactly where I found myself, on my knees at the side of my bed. Desperate. And alone.

I had locked the door because there wasn't a person on the face of the earth that I wanted to talk to. I only wanted to talk to God, but what I had to say was not particularly reverent. "God, You have blown it! I have made an absolute fool of myself in front of the medical staff and in front of my friends. Not only that, but we've made a real mess of making my life into one that gives You glory. Worst of all, my vocational goals have come to a dead end. I am crippled for life. Severe arthritis is just around the corner."

What I was saying was incorrect and I knew it, but I continued anyway. "Why didn't You do what You said You would do in those promises from the Bible? Are You playing some kind of game with me? I did everything on the list, right? I did everything. But You didn't keep Your part of the bargain, God. Could You explain why? What else do You want from me? Do You really want me in a wheelchair for life? Is that it? Well that's exactly what You've got!"

After I finished my selfish temper tantrum, I heard a clear yet gentle voice in my heart. In the exhausted quietness of my spirit, I sensed the tender voice of God's Spirit. "Dale, why do you want to be healed so badly? *'Seek*

326

first the kingdom of God, and His righteousness, and all these things will be added to you.'"

I had read that Scripture recently, several times, but somehow I had just passed by the part about "His righteousness." Now tears began to flow down my face and once more I sensed Him speaking to me. "Seek Me first. And My righteousness, Dale. And all these things will be added to you."

I knew exactly what He meant. I should have been seeking the Healer before the healing. I wanted a miracle more than I wanted the Miracle Worker. And His other words rang in my spiritual ears. "*His* righteousness... *His* righteousness."

Despite my outspoken faith, despite my Christian words, despite my best efforts, I knew very well that I was not leading a completely pure life. There were still hidden sins in my life that I didn't want to deal with. My stubborn demands for a miracle were right at the top of the list. I knew that the answer to my prayers would glorify God, but I was really more interested in what it would do for me.

In those moments, everything changed. I finally gave up *all*. I surrendered *all* my life to God. I invited Him into every part of my life and asked Him to take complete control. "Lord, I'm so sorry. I'm living on borrowed time anyway. Every day of life is a gift from You. It is so obvious to everyone, especially me, that Dale Black should have died in that plane crash. I have nothing to lose, wheelchair or not."

If I've seen heaven, why am I still so self-centered? I couldn't understand it. I fell before the Lord and just wept.

I wept as if my tears could wash away all the dreams I had treasured for a unique, adventurous life. "I give up my obsession to walk again. I give up flying, sports, my quest for respect from others, everything. Lord, it's up to You. I will still pray for healing because I believe that is what Your will is for me according to Your Word. But this time I'll put You first in my life. First place in my dreams."

Then and there I decided that no matter what the cost, I would serve Him. I gave up my selfish goals and plans. "God, if You can use me better

327

as a twenty-year-old in a wheelchair, as a cripple, then not my will but Yours be done."

At that moment I experienced something that had never happened to me before in my young life. I had a physical sensation that felt as if a heavy, rich substance, like oil, was being poured upon my head and was flowing over every part of me. The feeling was overwhelming and unforgettable. I was filled with joy and peace, and I felt completely free!

Within a few days I was asked to share once again in the Wednesday night chapel service. I shared a very simple message about submitting to God in every area of our lives. I didn't mention my ankle—or anything about me, for that matter. My conversations with everyone changed from talk of miracles on the outside to talk of a broken will and submitted heart on the inside.

When it came time for my next appointment with Dr. Graham, I did not invite anyone to join me. Instead, I went alone.

It had been two weeks since I had surrendered my entire will to God. Two weeks since I had felt the warm "oil" upon me. Two weeks since I had resigned myself to a life in a wheelchair, if that was what God wanted for me.

On the way to the doctor's appointment my car found its way to the familiar Valhalla Memorial Park, and I pulled over and stopped just a few feet from the Portal of the Folded Wings. On countless occasions since the crash I had spent time there with God. There I asked Him questions. There I reviewed in my mind the sequence of the aircraft smashing into the monument and my body falling to the ground. There at the monument I again sat in wonder of what He had done in sparing my life.

On this day I reviewed the checklist of the previous months. But this time I renewed my love for God and vowed to serve Him for the remainder of my days. The borrowed old green Cadillac then weaved through traffic along the familiar trek to Dr. Graham's office.

I quietly entered the doctor's waiting room. I whispered a prayer in my heart: *I give myself to You, God.* I had no expectations. Just a desire to be all that God wanted me to be.

After a review of all my injuries, Dr. Graham took the normal X rays of my ankle. He placed them up on the viewing screen to look at them. His voice was strangely soft and characteristically monotone. "Your ankle is healing, Dale. The blood has started circulating again." He paused as he pointed to the screen. "I don't understand it." His focus dropped to the floor as he shook his head in wonder. "I cannot tell you why, Dale, but your ankle has healed more in the past two weeks than it has in the entire past six months combined."

He lifted his eyes to look into my face as if he might find the answer there. Then he shook his head one last time. "I don't understand it at all. . . ."

In the quietness of that moment, deep within my spirit, there was a resounding echo, *"He who loses his life for My sake will find it."*

(18)

ON WINGS LIKE EAGLES

It was a long, hard spring. I had dropped out of Pasadena College after six grueling weeks. I pushed my body too hard, and it pushed back, refusing the rigorous schedule I was putting it through.

As the sap returned to the trees and their branches began to bud, I felt my body was going through a springtime of its own. One by one, the bandages came off. The stitches. The wires. I was down to one cast. The one on my left leg and ankle.

I continued ground-training classes at the junior college. And I continued flying lessons.

I also started working out at the gym. All my muscles had atrophied, but I couldn't do anything about that until my bones healed. The progress was slow. I did curls with my right arm, and gradually the strength came back. My left arm was another story. I was able to raise it to about a 45-degree angle, but it took a lot of effort and the pain was excruciating.

That was all the encouragement I needed. I hit the gym that much harder, hit the books that much harder, hit everything harder and faster.

Now that the vertebrae in my back had mended, I was doing sit-ups. I was wearing my patch on my good eye, forcing me to work the muscles in the injured eye.

Two weeks before the anniversary date of the crash, the cast came off. The leg looked like a toothpick, the foot was shriveled up, and the ankle, well, it looked pathetic.

But I was determined to make that date with the monument, and I worked hard, pushing myself through the pain. The back pain. The shoulder pain. The ankle pain.

As it turned out, I had pushed too hard.

The closer I got to the anniversary of the crash, the more the ankle swelled. And the more it swelled, the more painful it became, until I could hardly walk. I was trying so hard to do everything I could to get my body ready for the anniversary flight. I had promised myself and anyone who would listen that I would fly again over the monument as pilot in command. Now it was just days away. Even though my body was making amazing progress, it would take a miracle to pass an FAA medical in time to keep that date.

FRIDAY, JULY 17, 1970

The day before the anniversary of my crash.

No way. Who am I kidding? Me? Getting in a plane and flying over the crash site?

Tomorrow I'll look like a fool. A braggart full of myself. What was I thinking?

I'm not a teenager any longer. I'm twenty years old. I should know better. I should have listened to the doctor. I should have—

Incriminating thoughts cornered me, wagging their accusatory fingers.

Who do you think you are?

The problem isn't the swelling in your ankle; it's the swelling in your head.

I looked at the mirror. The patch mocked me. I took off my clothes, getting ready for bed. My right arm looked like it belonged to a Titan; the left arm, to a wimp. I tried to raise it. The pain was excruciating. I managed to lift it to about a 60-degree angle from my body, but only for a second and it took every ounce of strength I had.

I looked down at my legs. My right one looked like it was chiseled from a quarry; my left one, gimpy and discolored. I followed the grotesque sight down to my ankle. It was the size of a large grapefruit.

The ankle that refused to die!

I might be able to squeak my arm past the medical examiner, but not this. It would look as though I were trying to smuggle some kind of contraband fruit past customs.

Stripped not only of my clothes but also of any selfish pride, I knelt beside the bed. Like I had done so many times before, I bowed my head and prayed out loud a child's prayer.

"Lord, tomorrow is the anniversary of the plane crash, July 18. It's been a whole year. I am in such better shape than I was just after the crash last year. Better physically. Better spiritually. More than anyone could have dreamed. I praise You for that. I thank You for that. And I give You the glory."

I paused, wondering what the next thought should be, wondering if I could even put it into words.

"God, so many times in the Bible I've read about the way You speak to people in dreams."

And I felt awkward asking this, the way a child feels awkward about asking for something that's not his but that he wants really, really bad.

"Would You give me a special dream tonight? Talk to me, please? Tell me . . . whatever You want to tell me, OK?"

Again I paused, like a kid collecting his thoughts, then, with his arms full, realizing he has forgotten one.

"Oh, and Father, I promised a lot of people that I would fly over the air memorial as pilot in command on the first anniversary. It's not humanly possible, I know that. I can see that. My ankle would have to be almost normal to pass the exam. And I would have to convince someone to allow me to rent their aircraft. And fly by myself. On crutches and all. God, this would require a couple more miracles from You. And all within twelve hours. But Lord, if this would bring glory to You, or if for some other reason You want this to happen . . . please work it out."

Then I prayed something uncharacteristic of me, something Jesus prayed in the garden of Gethsemane; and in doing so, I exchanged more of my self-will for surrender.

"I would sure like to fly tomorrow, if You would allow it. But Your will be done, not mine."

A peace I can't describe came over me.

"Father, thanks for life. Thanks for Your unending love."

I took a deep breath, not quite sure how to end. Feeling a little clumsy with my words, but also feeling an enormous tenderness toward Him.

"I love You, dear God. And I promise to always serve You."

I felt I had just crawled onto His lap, and now He was tucking me in for the night. I was full of love and peace and joy. And those were the feelings that sang me to sleep.

The next morning I awoke, rested, but not quite ready to jump out of bed. He had indeed spoken to me in a dream that night. The "secret place of the Most High" became real to me. I knew what it was like to "rest in the shadow of the Almighty."

To rest.

Not only to strive, but to rest. That's what I had missed out on so much over the past year. I had worked really, really hard. I had believed really, really hard. But I had not rested in God nearly enough.

That night I experienced what it was like to be nested *under* Him. To be covered with *His* feathers. To find refuge under *His* wings.

I wasn't afraid.

I wasn't anxious.

I wasn't ashamed.

I was *His*. His child. His baby bird. And He was going to help me fly. Maybe not today, but someday. I wasn't destined for the nest. I felt destined for the sky. He knew that about me long before I knew it about myself.

I didn't want to get out of bed. I had been embraced in a dream. By Him. Have you ever felt that way? Ever felt that a dream was so good, so beautiful, you didn't want to wake up?

That's how I felt. As if some of heaven had opened and spilled itself onto me. Drenched in love. Like the loving arms of my heavenly Father were embracing me.

"Our Father . . . who art in *heaven*."

Whatever else heaven is, it is where the Light and Love and Life exist at the center of the universe. I felt as if heaven opened, and I saw my Father's face looking down on me. Looking down at me in delight. Loving me unconditionally.

I basked in that. It wasn't because of anything I had done. It wasn't because I had earned it. He just loved me.

Smells from the kitchen made their way into my room. It was a lazy Saturday morning, but Mom was up early as usual, making breakfast. The smell of coffee perking on the stove, bacon crackling in the pan, and French toast. Mmm.

I threw off my covers and followed my nose to the kitchen.

"Morning, Mom."

"Good morning, Dale."

It *was* a good morning.

I sat down and started to eat. A bite, two bites, three. Savoring each one when . . .

. . . a thought—as white and hot and fast as lightning—bolted across my mind.

I walked *out here. Without crutches!*

I raised my pant leg. The swelling had gone down! I was so excited I couldn't take another bite. But I couldn't share my excitement with my mom. This time I wasn't going to make a parade out of my faith. If I was going to do this, I was going to do it differently, quietly, unpretentiously.

Careful not to overdo it, as I had done in the previous weeks, I hopped back to my room on my good leg. I sat on my bed, looking at my ankle, touching it, rubbing it.

For the first time in a year the ankle looked almost normal. The pain was still there, but the swelling was gone. And with the swelling gone, maybe, just maybe, I could squeak by the FAA physical.

I looked at the clock. A little past eight. *A lot to do,* I thought. *Take the physical. Rent a plane. Talk the person I rent it from into letting me fly it. Alone. Could get one from my aeronautics teacher, maybe, at Compton Airport. Fly to Burbank. Take off from Runway 15. That was crucial.*

Quickly I put on a suit and tie, grabbed my crutches, and hopped to the door. I decided not to call ahead to schedule an appointment. On this short notice, they'd probably not see me. I'd just show up and see if the doctor could work me in.

I never appreciated my MGB more than I did that day. It ate up every straightaway; took every turn in stride. Arriving at the office of an FAA medical examiner in Long Beach, I left my crutches inside the car and hopped on my good leg to the entrance, saving my tentative left foot for the exam. I took a deep breath before opening the door.

This is it, I told myself.

I walked through the door, slowly and steadily, trying to walk as normally as possible. It hurt so bad. I limped slightly into the waiting room as I walked to the front desk and asked for an application.

Have you ever had a concussion? the form asked.

Yes, I answered, determined to tell the whole truth.

Have you been hospitalized within the past five years?

Yes.

Have you had surgery within the past five years?

Yes.

Have you at some time lost consciousness?

Yes.

The questions were getting harder, more probing. And then the last question.

Have you ever been the pilot in command at the time of an airplane crash?

No.

Passenger, yes. Pilot, no.

Nervously I handed back the form and prayed under my breath, "God, You have brought me this far . . . would You please allow the paperwork to go through?"

No questions were asked.

The paperwork went through!

Now the physical. The doctor was formal, somewhat impersonal. Another day, another exam. Which, thank God, was cursory. He looked at my head, but he didn't seem to notice the scars. The hair had grown back nicely enough to cover them pretty well.

Whew!

Now the eyes. He looked at both, then examined my good eye, had me read the eye chart. Everything OK there. Now the right eye. And I was praying my heart out between each line. Although I could see pretty well with both eyes, when I closed my good eye, it was quite fuzzy. I could read the larger lines fine, but then came the last line, and I could barely make out the letters.

I knew I could see well enough to fly.

I read the letters the best I could.

Another big but unspoken *Whew!*

"I need you to hop on one leg for two minutes so I can check your heart rate," the doctor said.

"Sure," I said, and you can guess which leg I chose.

The results?

I passed! I walked out of the office with a limp, but I walked out with a First Class medical certificate, dated July 18, 1970.

Under the heading LIMITATIONS, they typed the word *None*.

Later next to that word I typed *Thank GOD!!!!!*

I called my aeronautics professor and asked if I could rent his single-engine Piper Cherokee.

"When?" he asked.

"Now."

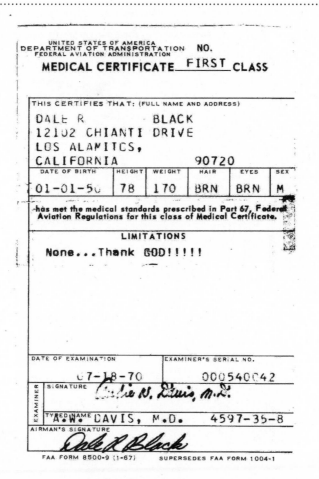

UNITED STATES OF AMERICA
DEPARTMENT OF TRANSPORTATION **NO.**
FEDERAL AVIATION ADMINISTRATION

MEDICAL CERTIFICATE FIRST **CLASS**

THIS CERTIFIES THAT: (FULL NAME AND ADDRESS)

DALE R   BLACK
12102 CHIANTI DRIVE
LOS ALAMITOS,
CALIFORNIA   90720

DATE OF BIRTH	HEIGHT	WEIGHT	HAIR	EYES	SEX
01-01-50	78	170	BRN	BRN	M

has met the medical standards prescribed in Part 67, Federal Aviation Regulations for this class of Medical Certificate.

LIMITATIONS

None...Thank GOD!!!!!

DATE OF EXAMINATION	EXAMINER'S SERIAL NO.
07-18-70	000540042

EXAMINER SIGNATURE

TYPED NAME A.W. DAVIS, M.D.   4597-35-8

AIRMAN'S SIGNATURE

FAA FORM 8500-9 (1-67)   SUPERSEDES FAA FORM 1004-1

This certificate was acquired exactly one year after the crash. The doctor's office incorrectly typed Dale's height at 78 inches, which went unnoticed until the next year. Dale's actual height is 72 inches

We arranged to meet at Compton Airport, where his four-seater was hangared. I had spoken to him months earlier. Of course he knew about the crash, my injuries, my goals, my faith. I had spoken in his class at the junior college and he had been watching my progress with keen interest and a lot of encouragement.

My MGB ran with the wind and got me to Compton Airport in record time. Mr. Travis, my professor, gave me the customary in-flight exam that was required to prove I was again capable of flying an aircraft and flying it solo.

Once in the air, he had me stall the aircraft several times, take some steep turns, some takeoffs and landings, a complete check ride.

Back on the ground, he had me fill out some rental forms and then he signed my logbook. He looked at it before giving it to me. "Looks like you haven't flown in a while," he said, knowing the full reason why.

"You're right, sir. I've been busy with college. You see, I've got this aeronautics professor . . ." I looked at Mr. Travis, grinning. "He's incredibly demanding."

He smiled back, endorsing my logbook to fly the Piper Cherokee 140 with the words, "Safe to operate PA-28-140 as Pilot in Command. July 18, 1970."

He handed me the book and placed a hand on my shoulder. "Welcome back, Dale."

It felt great to *be* back.

I hopped back to the small plane. My ankle was hurting pretty bad by now. Cleared for takeoff, I taxied to the runway and took off for Burbank. By the time I landed, the pain was severe from using my left foot for braking and my left arm for landing. Even though I was compensating by using my heel only for rudder and braking, my ankle was getting more of a workout than it had in over a year, and it was throbbing.

In spite of the pain, though, I felt great. Captain of my own airplane again.

Moments after landing in Burbank, I was ready to take off again and complete my mission. I taxied to the runway and stopped at the intersection of Runway 15. I picked up the microphone and radioed the control tower.

"Burbank Tower, this is Cherokee 37 November, over."

"37 November, this is Burbank Tower, go ahead."

"Burbank Tower . . . this is 37 November. One year ago today . . ."

I released the mic button, ending the transmission. Overwhelmed with emotion, I lowered my head and cried. I cried so hard I wasn't sure I could go on.

"37 November, this is Burbank Tower, go ahead . . ."

I dried my eyes with my shirtsleeves, then looked around the cabin for something to *keep* them dry.

"37 November, this is Burbank Tower, how do you read?"

I took several deep breaths, yanked off my dress shirt, and blotted my face. *I'm going to fly this flight,* I said to myself. *And I'm going to do it now.*

"Cherokee 37 November, this is Burbank Tower, how do you read?"

I took a deep breath and pressed the button on the mic.

"Burbank Tower, this is Cherokee 37 November. One year ago today a Piper Navajo crashed into the air memorial Portal of the Folded Wings, just south of the airport. Two pilots were killed. I alone survived. I dedicate this anniversary flight to the glory of God."

The tower was silent. I wondered if they had heard me. But they were fighting emotions of their own.

"37 November, stand by."

Another pause, and then the words "37 November, two of us were on duty that day . . . we didn't think anyone survived."

Again a pause.

"37 November, we're glad you made it! Congratulations!"

A fresh flood of emotion washed over me. I was shocked anyone even remembered.

"37 November is requesting to use the full length of runway one-five. Negative intersection departure."

"Roger, 37 November. You're cleared to cross runway one-five. Taxi to the approach end, hold short . . . monitor this frequency."

While holding at the approach end of the runway, I completed the engine run-up . . . once . . . twice . . . three times.

Looking across the airport, I focused on the southern end of the runway.

The air memorial stood indifferently against a hazy sunset sky. I glanced at the runway . . . back to the memorial . . . then to the cockpit instruments. There was nothing else to check.

"Burbank Tower, 37 November, ready for takeoff. I'd like to remain in the pattern."

"Roger, 37 November, you're cleared for takeoff runway one-five. Report right downwind. Have a *very* safe flight."

Suddenly I was terrified. This time I was flying over the monument alone. I paused a moment to regain my composure. *No,* I reminded myself. *I wasn't flying alone. I had never flown alone.* A calm assurance came over me.

I pushed the throttle forward, heard the familiar rev of the engine, felt the power under each wing, the familiar bouncing, and in a moment I was airborne.

My eyes found the huge ornate dome, glinting in the sun, and they fixed on it. With unblinking determination, I stayed the course, taking the same route the Piper Navajo had taken a year earlier. The closer I got, the harder my heart beat. Then, barely a hundred feet over the dome, I passed it.

As it vanished beneath me, tears streamed down my face. I mopped them with my shirt.

That day I took three passes over the Portal of the Folded Wings. As I did, I softly said, "Thank You, God. Thank You. Thank You. Thank You."

When the sun fell below the horizon, I banked toward the airport. I did a touch-and-go landing and radioed for permission to go home.

"Burbank Tower, this is 37 November, requesting a straight out departure."

"37 November, roger. Straight out departure, approved."

A pause, and then the microphone crackled one last time.

"37 November, Burbank Tower. A very . . . big . . . congratulations to you . . . from all of us."

I was so overwhelmed I couldn't speak. More tears. So many tears they seemed to be running not only out of my eyes but out of my nose, my mouth, every pore on my face.

I wanted to say something to them, but I couldn't find the words. I didn't want to give the impression that I alone had accomplished this feat. I knew that if God hadn't reached down and performed a series of miracles on my broken body over the last twelve months I couldn't be flying now. And if God hadn't orchestrated today's new answers to prayer, this anniversary flight as pilot in command never could have taken place. I knew then and have always known since that although I am small, I am connected to a very big God.

As the single-engine plane climbed, my eyes fell on the lush green grasses of the Hollywood Hills Forest Lawn Cemetery, where Chuck was buried. I thought about Chuck and Gene, how they died, and how I should have died along with them. I stared down at St. Joseph Hospital and Dr. Graham's office. I thought of the thirteen surgeries, all the people I had met—the doctors, nurses, friends who came to visit. I remembered Joel Green, who took his own flight to heaven just hours after we met. So much flashed through my mind. And with those images came the words I wanted to say to the men back at the control tower.

"Burbank Tower, thank you for your help today. This is 37 November, reminding you that with God . . . nothing shall be impossible."

(19)

ANNIVERSARY SURPRISE

Once I touched down at Compton Airport, I climbed into my car and headed for home. *How will I tell my parents?* I wondered. How could I find the words to tell them how much this meant to me, why I had to do it? How could I tell them that I wouldn't be going into the family business, that for some reason I was going to fly. I had to fly, had to or something essential would die in me?

How do you say things like that to your mom and dad? How do you speak your heart without breaking theirs? How do you tell them you have to leave the nest? That even though your wings aren't healed you have to stretch them? You're grateful, but you've got to get on with your life. How do you look your mom in the eye and say those things when she knows that every time you get into a plane, you put your life at risk? You risk another crash. Risk hurting her all over again. Risk inflicting a wound that may never heal.

How do you do that?

I didn't know.

I pulled into the driveway, careful how I got out of the car. It had been a long day, and my body felt it. I left my crutches in the car. I wanted to end the day walking through the door on my own two legs.

My steps grew slower the closer I got to the front door, putting off the inevitable as long as possible, steeling myself for their reaction.

I opened the door.

342

"SURPRISE!"

The house was filled with friends and family. And my mom and dad—whose hearts I feared breaking—had arranged a One-Year Survival Anniversary party. My brothers were there. My college roommate was there. My next-door neighbor. My girlfriend, Anna, and her sister Susan. Gramps. Grandma. Jerry and Verna. The people who had prayed for me. Cried with me. Encouraged me. Visited me. They were all there. All there and cheering me home.

Grandma pulled me to the sofa and snuggled next to me, nuzzling me, holding and rubbing my hands. Mom played the piano. Everyone patted me on the back. Loving me.

It was a bit of heaven, one of the closest I've experienced on earth.

As people were enjoying the festivities, my mother went to the kitchen. I followed her, knowing I had to tell her, knowing she would want to be told.

"Mom, I, uh . . . I need to tell you something."

She braced herself.

"I need to tell you where I was today, what I did."

I paused, looking into her eyes. I was so excited, but I didn't want to hurt her, didn't want her to feel that I was rejecting my home, the family business, everything she and dad had done for me.

"I passed the FAA medical today. I flew over the memorial. And I did it as the command pilot. Three times."

Her face registered shock. She gazed at me for a long time, speechless.

"I'm proud of you, Dale!" Tears fell from her eyes. She gave me a hug, my wilted T-shirt blotting her tears. "I know that was important to you," she said, knowing full well that my choice would take me away from her, possibly forever, possibly leaving a hole in her heart that could never be filled.

She pulled away and wiped her tears, looking at me tenderly.

"I guess you're just destined to fly."

My secret was no longer a secret. She ushered me into the living room and shared it with everyone.

That's when the real party began.

✈

God loved the tenderhearted boy who somewhere along the way to growing up had lost his way. He remembered the boy and the boy's prayers as he knelt beside his bed. He went after the little boy and brought him the last part of the way home.

And the two of us—the boy I once was and the man I had become—knelt together to pray. They prayed about how much the boy needed his Father . . . and how much the man needed him still.

A year before I wanted to be a pilot.

And I wanted it bad.

A year later, I wanted a Father. My heavenly Father.

And I wanted Him bad.

That is the difference between who I was then and who I am now. A boy wanting so badly to be a man. A man wanting so badly to be a boy. A boy who could sit on his Father's lap and just be held.

Psalm 103 says that God has compassion on us the way a father has compassion on his children. The reason? Because He knows our frame and He knows that we are but dust.

My frame had been wrecked, just like the airplane I crashed in. A joint or two had been ground to dust. And with each passing year I feel the earth making its claim on me.

What I felt in the dream that night before my anniversary flight was not a Father's criticism but a Father's compassion.

I felt so whole, so happy, so healed. So loved. So totally and un-conditionally loved.

I felt something else too. I felt peace. The peace a child feels when held in the strong arms of his father, seeing the smile on his face, the glint in his eye, and hearing tender words from his lips.

I realize that I was held by those same strong arms the year before when the wings broke and I fell to the ground. God's hand was in all of it in some mysterious way that has taken a lifetime to understand.

Little by little my life would come back to me. It would take several years of recuperation before I would be back to normal. Someday there would be no more wheelchairs. No more crutches. No more braces. No more eye patches.

I would be back on the baseball team too. I was no longer quick enough to play shortstop, so the coach moved me to outfield.

My body came back, a little at a time.

So did my memory.

And so did the little boy.

The little boy who dreamed of flying.

We're all home now. My body, my memory, the boy I once was. At least we're as close to home as we will be this side of heaven.

INVISIBLE CITY

"Captain, do you copy that?"

A jolt on my arm from First Officer Steve Holmes snaps me back to reality, my senses flooding with cockpit sights and sounds that demand immediate attention. Suddenly I am again alert with a burst of adrenaline.

"Say it again, Steve?"

"We're established at the Outer Marker, level at one-two thousand. What do you want to do now?"

The tension in Steve's voice is thick and real, and in a nanosecond my mind is again aware that we are streaking across the night sky in our glistening white-and-blue-striped corporate jet somewhere over south central Africa. Having just descended from 41,000 feet, I slow the jet from nearly the speed of sound to just over two hundred knots. Low on reserve fuel, we are established in a holding pattern over what we think—what we hope—is Lusaka International Airport.

For only the second time in my more than twelve thousand hours of flying, the option of diverting to our alternate airport is no longer viable. In my seventeen years of flying hundreds of Christian ministry flights to over fifty countries, many unusual, awesome, and wonderful things have occurred. But never anything like this.

I stare out the window into the darkness. I can't comprehend what I am *not* seeing. In spite of the lack of apparent weather, we aren't seeing anything. No runway, no airport—not even a city—a city of over a million people that should be right below us.

For the first time ever, our long-range navigational instruments are not working at all. The communication radios are out as well. With the short-range navigational aids that do work, we assume we are flying over the capital of Zambia, but nothing is certain.

"Steve, we're going to stay in the holding pattern until I'm ready to shoot this approach."

Chewing on my words, Steve wipes the sweat from his palms.

"OK, fine, but we're not going to be able to stay here long, right?"

"Absolutely, but by staying high and clean earlier, we've got a little more fuel than I thought we would have. Here's what I need now. Confirm again that we're holding over Joppa, the Outer Marker for Lusaka, Zambia. Check the ADF on your RMI and, using your number two radio only, go ahead and triangulate with two remotely located VORs and of course your DME. Make sure you verify, very carefully, the frequencies using the AUDIO IDENT. I want to know if you believe—without doubt—that we're holding over Lusaka."

"You got it."

"I'm going to check my instruments the same way using the number one radio. I'll do the same thing you're doing but independently. Try the COMM radios one last time."

"You know, Dale, we've been checking all those things during the last hour."

"I know, but I still have some doubt about our location. I mean, look outside, Steve. Have you ever seen or heard of anything like this before?"

Steve slowly shakes his head, squeezing the arm of his copilot's chair as he shifts uncomfortably in his seat.

"See, that's my point. I want you to use all three frequencies, approach control, the tower, and emergency one-twenty-one point five. And recycle the transponder; make sure we're squawking 7-7-0-0, the emergency code. Also, don't click just five times, but seven or more times with your MIC button on the tower frequency—just in case the runway lights can be activated that way."

"We've done all that before too, you know."

"Steve, come on, let's work together. Let's do it all again. I want to know we'll be shooting our last approach into a runway environment—not into oblivion, or into that lake . . . what's it called?" I glance again at the navigational charts. "Yeah, Lake Kariba."

My pulse quickens as I scan the instruments while we both go to work twisting dials and penciling marks on charts to calculate our position independently.

Another part of my brain is reflecting on the combination of events that have brought us to this in-flight emergency. Our alternate airport was Livingstone. There we had adequate runway, good elevation, and a good place to RON (Remain Over Night) if necessary. Only thirty minutes' flying time from Lusaka.

We departed Sudan with tanks topped, enough fuel to fly to Lusaka, execute a full approach with a Missed Approach, then fly to Livingstone, our alternate, and then hold for one hour if we needed to. That should have given us adequate fuel reserves. But things started going wrong an hour or so after takeoff. First, we were required to hold over southern Sudan because the air traffic controllers, who don't have radar, got confused. That used twenty-eight minutes of our fuel reserves. Shortly thereafter we lost the first, then a second Global Navigation System. The GNS units help us navigate, with pinpoint accuracy, to anywhere on the globe. Plus they provide invaluable fuel management and winds aloft data. It's highly unusual for either unit to malfunction, but we've lost both and don't know why.

We then flew via Dead Reckoning navigation over Uganda and Rwanda.

We had no permission to land in either place. We still had no reason to believe things would deteriorate any further. But due to the inaccuracies of our limited means of navigation, we had burned nine more minutes of our precious fuel reserves.

Next, we lost total radio communication over Northern Zambia. This, again, made no sense. We have three COMM radios onboard. All indications from the cockpit indicate our radios are working just fine. Still, no one has responded to our calls. Without the GNS systems giving us the jet stream wind information, we lack valuable flight planning data. The high altitude winds, stronger than expected, accounted for consuming another eleven minutes of reserve fuel.

All these factors taken one by one would be relatively minor and normally wouldn't pose a serious threat to the safety of this flight. But combined, they become a viable force against our fuel supply and our flight-planning options. That's exactly how aviation accidents happen. I know all too well. And it's generally not just one factor, but a combination of factors, that cause aircraft accidents.

This most recent factor, certainly not one we had ever considered, was that now flying over the Lusaka area, we cannot see a runway, an airport, or even the lights of the city. The weather report and forecast called for clear skies with visibility of over fifty miles. So why can't we see Lusaka? It's the capital. But there are no lights coming from any direction, not from Lusaka or from any of the three adjacent cities, as far as the eye can see. Through the cockpit window there is only blackness beneath us.

Steve and I compare our findings.

"Captain, I show we're holding at Joppa, directly over Lusaka, Zambia."

"OK, Steve, I concur."

Even though there still exists some disturbing, unanswered questions, we believe we are flying nine miles southeast above Lusaka's International Airport.

Looking down at the fuel gauges, I verify that we have enough fuel for another turn in the holding pattern, plus one full approach, and a little extra. There's not enough fuel for another Missed Approach. There is not enough fuel to fly to an alternate airport. But there is enough for another turn and one slow, deliberate and controlled precision ILS approach into Lusaka. Presuming it is there. It has to be.

"Steve, we'll do one more turn in the hold."

"Are you sure?"

"I am. Steve, you've got the aircraft."

"Roger, I have the controls."

"Steve, I'm going to dim my instrument lights even further. You stay in the hold, level at twelve thousand—use the autopilot."

"May I hand-fly it instead?"

"Negative. Stay on autopilot, and make sure you select and remain on Altitude Hold."

I want to know that we won't unknowingly drift from our safe altitude of twelve thousand feet. I want the assurance that by using the autopilot, if we drift from our assigned altitude, an aural warning horn will sound, and a very bright light in the center of both instrument panels will illuminate. That will alert us that we are not where we need to be.

My mind immediately references one of the aviation accidents I studied. In 1972, an Eastern Airlines L-1011, holding near the Miami International Airport late at night, crashed into the Florida Everglades partially due to both pilots not knowing that the autopilot Altitude Hold function had been inadvertently disengaged. If Steve varies from our altitude, I will hear the audible warning horn, plus Steve will see the Master Warning Light Illumination.

"Steve, I'm going to close my eyes for the next turn."

I grab my uniform jacket from the coatrack and pull it over my head, making it even darker. Allowing my eyes every opportunity to adjust to the utter blackness outside, I'm hoping that in a few moments my dilated pupils will be better able to pick up any small light on the ground that might be visible.

"OK, Dale, turning right heading one-one-zero degrees, level at one-two thousand, speed two-one-zero knots—established in the hold. I'm on autopilot."

Although it takes about thirty minutes for the human eye to fully adjust for maximum night vision, I only have a fraction of that much time. *But five or ten minutes of complete darkness will certainly help. At least, I hope it will.*

After a few minutes I remove my jacket and rub my eyes. I focus outside with the interior cockpit lights at full dim. Moving my eyes side to side, up and down, I strain to allow my peripheral vision to pick up any sort of light. Even the faintest, tiniest light will help.

I jerk forward. "Wait a minute, Steve."

"Do you see something?"

"I think I see something . . . wait. Yeah, it's a light . . . maybe a flashlight . . . maybe a lantern. OK, I just saw another flash of light. It's gone now, but it was a light.

"There is a small light that is still on," I continue, as I stretch and twist my neck, now looking far back through the cockpit's left side window panel. The light is extremely dim and visible only in the periphery. "But I'm satisfied, Steve. We are over land."

We still, however, have no clue as to why we can't see the city.

By switching the fuel selector on the jet's pedestal, I make a quick study of the fuel levels in the Learjet's five tanks. I'm mortified. I try to swallow but can't. My mouth is completely dry. Taking a deep breath while leaning to my right, I speak matter-of-factly. "We will land this Learjet now, Steve—no matter what. If we don't see the airport by two hundred feet above the ground, we'll descend below minimums. Do you understand? Steve, I will descend below minimums."

"Roger, understand. We'll fly below minimums, regardless."

"Correct. I'll land on a street, a field, sand, or anything. And if for some reason we see only water, then I'll spend three minutes searching for land. If we don't see land within three minutes, I'll make a gear-up, controlled landing into the water. Make sure you look for anything. . . . And all outside lights are ON. Landing, RECOG, NAV, and Strobe lights. Make sure all remain on."

Then in a voice just above a whisper, "Be on the lookout for buildings, you know."

My voice is strangely calm, but internally I am almost in shock. I can hardly believe this flight has deteriorated to this nightmarish level.

Steve squirms and shakes his head. "Roger, you've got it."

I crack open the door into the cabin and look back at the passengers, huddled in the center of the cabin, praying as a group. No one looks up, but I overhear one of the prayers.

". . . and Father, we know that if we pray according to Your will, You hear us, and if You hear us, whatever we ask, we know that we already have, in faith, the petitions we asked of You. We thank You, Lord, for a safe landing. Father, use this experience for our good and Your glory."

Then, turning my attention to the passengers in as calm a voice as possible, I speak: "Make sure you guys are strapped in tightly for landing. And please, continue with your prayers, OK?"

Another shot of adrenaline fires through my veins, knowing that the next few minutes will be the most crucial minutes of my life. This is it. There is no turning back now.

"OK, Steve, let's do it."

"Now?"

"Now. I have the flight controls."

"Roger, you've got the controls."

"Give me the Before Landing Checklist."

With sweat pouring down his face, Steve goes into action, performing the checklist and the many duties required of him before landing.

I am once again flying inbound on the electronic beams of the runway's ILS approach. All checklists are now complete. The sleek, glistening jet is in the landing configuration. The flaps are down; the landing gear, down and locked, verified by three green lights. Both engine igniters are ON as they should be, helping prevent possible engine flameout. I double-check everything again, especially that all our outside lights are ON. I want every available light ON to hopefully reflect off of any early sign of the ground or surroundings. I want to see something—sand, pavement, anything. Hopefully not water. Hopefully not a skyscraper.

"A thousand feet above minimums." Again Steve makes first officer callouts as we descend, following both horizontal and vertical electronic guidance to some invisible runway. Still we see nothing but blackness.

"Five hundred feet above minimums."

Moments later . . . "One hundred feet above."

A second passes.

"Minimums, no ground contact. Minimums."

"Can you see anything?"

"Negative."

"Going below minimums, Steve."

"Roger, no contact."

Suddenly, warning tones and commands from the flight instruments scream out from the cockpit speakers overhead: *GLIDE SLOPE, GLIDE SLOPE—PULL UP.*

"Below minimums, one hundred feet below."

"Can you see anything?"

"Negative. No contact."

GLIDE SLOPE, GLIDE SLOPE—PULL UP.

I try hard to ignore the automatic warnings built into our executive jet.

"Leveling at one hundred feet, Steve. Can't go lower. Keep your eyes outside. Advise when you see something."

I can't take my eyes off the instruments; we're too close to the ground. I can't take my eyes away from the cockpit.

"Steve, tell me you see something. We can't stay here, not at this altitude."

"Steve, I need an answer . . . NOW."

The instruments scream out again.

GLIDE SLOPE, GLIDE SLOPE—PULL UP.

"Steve!"

Out of the corner of my eye I see that Steve's face is only inches from the windshield, yet he isn't making a sound. The shock of what he *doesn't* see freezes him in place. I feel as if the wind has been knocked out of me.

For a split second I glance outside into the darkness, wince, and hold my breath. Nothing. Complete blackness. Just as quickly I bring my eyes back to the instruments inside the cockpit.

Frozen in disbelief, Steve can barely think, barely speak, barely move.

"Wait! I have contact. Ground contact!" Steve shouts while pointing. "There's a road, a parking lot—straight ahead. Speed one-twenty-nine, V-Ref plus two."

I tear my eyes from the instruments again to see us flying just above the blurring desert. Ahead and barely visible is a paved surface that is as dark as the back side of the moon. There are no familiar lines, numbers, or stripes on the pavement, but there it is, a solid surface, the lights of our jet now shining all over it. Not water, not sand—a solid surface.

Steve winces again and screams, "Abort! Vehicles on the runway. Abort!"

My eyes dart from side to side along the makeshift runway and find it lined with a dozen military vehicles.

"We're landing, Steve."

I don't have the time to look at everything going on outside, but in my split-second view I see military jeeps loaded with soldiers in full battle gear, half-tracks, and other military vehicles. They are scrambling all over the place.

They better get out of the way, I silently demand as I prepare to bring the jet gently onto the solid surface. Still concerned about fuel, I try to assure myself. *Just another few seconds, and we'll be OK.*

I feel the wheels greet the long-awaited surface, transferring the full weight of the jet from the wings to the landing gear. In that instant my fear throttles down with the engines. My index finger flips a small toggle switch, and spoilers rise above the wings. Panels deploy, adding drag and killing much of the remaining lift. With the palm of my hand resting on top of both thrust levers, I smoothly and quickly pull upwards and aft on the reverse thrust levers, and two jet engines scream again into high rpm. The aircraft's frame vibrates and shudders from nose to tail as engine thrust is directed forward, helping slow the jet. A sudden applause erupts behind me, coming from the passengers in the cabin, no doubt expressing their relief and joy at the answer to their prayers.

I try to maintain smoothness in controlling the aircraft, but my concerns for a smooth deceleration dissolve in an instant as Steve points, shouting: "Stop! They've blocked the runway. Emergency stop!"

Abruptly yanking the reverse thrust levers even farther back while slamming on the wheel brakes with my toes, I hear everything loose in the cabin crashing against the closed cockpit door. The Learjet skids to a halt, stopping cold, just a few feet from two combat readied military vehicles, each brimming with soldiers.

Almost in shock, my trembling hand reaches for and sets the parking brake. Instinctively, I study the fuel gauges, curious to know how little fuel remains. An involuntary chill shudders through my body. With adrenaline racing, Steve's eyes and mine lock for a second, then we look away, shaking our heads, neither of us saying a word.

We made it. Thank God, we made it.

I take a deep breath and expel it loudly. As I sit motionless in the cockpit, I am amazed as dozens of tall black fully armed soldiers in battle fatigues scurry into position and surround our aircraft, all wielding rifles that are pointing directly at me. Steve stares in disbelief. In the center and on top of each vehicle is a single-barreled 50-caliber machine gun, each manned by two towering soldiers, again, pointing directly into the cockpit.

My mind is racing for options as I bring the throttles to cut-off, starving the engines of what little fuel remains. Both engines spool down, and finally . . . it's over.

This flight is now at an end.

But as I peer down the barrels of manned rifles and machine guns . . . I realize another adventure has just begun.

(21)
ADVENTURES OF FAITH

Powerful lights from every direction light up our jet, almost turning the night into day. It feels as if we are on a Hollywood movie set with the lights blaring, the cameras running, and everyone cued for action.

We are on the ground, half a world away from home. But on precious pavement. And no one has been injured—yet. The thought crosses my mind of the tragic irony—to narrowly escape disaster by landing on unlighted pavement in central Africa, only to be machine-gunned to death by soldiers who misunderstand our purpose.

"Take over the aircraft operations, OK? Keep passengers inside and calm. Release the parking brake when the *After Landing Checklist* is done, and caution on battery power."

Steve sits shivering with fear. "What are *you* going to do?"

"Talk. And follow instructions."

"Good luck."

"Thanks. I'll be back."

My heart is racing as I open the top half of the passengers' cabin door and shield my eyes from the intense lights; I notice that the rifles follow me. The twenty-five to thirty soldiers I can see are wielding weapons pointing directly at my heart and head. The soldiers are backlit, and it's hard to see their faces, but it's clear that each vehicle is equipped with enough firepower to start a small war.

As usual I have no planned speech. I simply pray silently as I have done

357

thousands of times before. *God, Your Word says You'll give me the words to speak when needed . . . so give me those words now . . . please.*

I open the lower half of the door and exit the aircraft alone. Dressed in full uniform, I slowly raise my hands, indicating I am unarmed and submissive; I speak so calmly that even I am surprised.

"Please, don't shoot. We are here to help. We bring the love of Jesus Christ, our Lord and Savior, to the African continent."

I have never said anything like that before, and the words just tumble from my lips. I wonder if they've heard me . . . understood me.

What language do they speak here? I ask myself.

Suddenly, a spotlight from one of the military vehicles turns in my direction, jarring and blinding me. Then, in the most official and distinguished use of the English language I have heard since my last visit to London, comes a commanding voice.

"Why did you land at this airport? No one is permitted to land here. This airport is closed."

With my hands still high in the air, I respond, "Sir, I am so sorry to ask this question, believe me, and I'm embarrassed at the same time. But where are we? Is this Lusaka?"

There is a pause. Some of the soldiers look at each other, then look back at me.

His voice booms. "Yes, Lusaka International Airport. The capital of Zambia. This airport is closed to all civilian aircraft. The runway is being repaved. It has been closed for many months."

"Sir," I reply, deferring to his authority, "will you allow me to reach into my left jacket pocket and pull out a simple piece of paper that we believe gave us permission to land here? Sir, I am unarmed and would never try to hurt anyone. We have flown many miles, all the way from America to visit your wonderful country. Maybe we can offer some assistance."

Although no permission is officially granted, I slowly move my right hand into my uniform jacket. The soldiers' rifles follow my every move with eager fingers on the triggers.

"When we left the United States, we were given written permission to land here in Lusaka."

With the flight plan in my hand, I carefully open it, revealing its contents to my captors.

"Walk forward with your hands above your head."

As I do, I become increasingly amazed with each step. I see a sight I will never forget. Approaching the soldiers, I become aware of how small a person I truly am. The soldiers tower over me as if they are part of an NBA team. No one in the group appears less than six and a half feet tall. A couple of them have to be over seven feet.

I focus on the leader of the group, smile at him, and slowly extend my hand. I am relieved as an ever-so-slight smile creeps across his face. Some of the guns are lowered. From somewhere in the crowd a few soldiers chuckle. A couple of dozen soldiers then huddle together and begin to converse. To my relief, the group seems to have relaxed. Then an unexpected announcement from the leader.

"You must all go to jail," we are told. "Now."

"Sir, in all due respect, I am the one responsible for landing here. They"—I point to the passengers in the aircraft—"are not to blame in any way."

"Get everyone off the airplane. Leave your things. You will walk to jail."

"Walk to jail?"

The passengers deplane, and we are ushered on foot down the airport taxiway.

I wonder what awaits us. I assume we will never see the personal belongings we are leaving behind. But I don't care. I am glad to be safe on the ground. Beyond that, I don't know what to expect.

Eventually our walk brings us to the edge of the airport, where a guard tower stands sentry on the perimeter of a barbed-wire fence with searchlights glaring down at us. A few dozen soldiers surround the building, all wearing green woolen uniforms and matching caps with red bands, toting rifles and tugging at taut leashes that hold German shepherds barking and bearing angry teeth. It reminds me of a scene from a World War II movie. Except there are no stunt doubles!

As the soldiers check our passports and luggage, I ask one of them, "Why are there no lights in your city? In fact, the whole country seems to have no lights at night. Why?"

"Our country has security problems. The whole country is blacked out at night."

Nearer to the terminal I see old, rusting vehicles around the buildings that seem to be throwbacks to an earlier, bygone era.

We are told we can't do anything but stay in jail until the general comes the next day to determine our fate. In the meantime, some of the passengers settle into chairs for the night. Others find other places to sit and rest.

The "jail" is actually a guarded terminal building that has been secured and used as a holding area. Many of the soldiers have living quarters in a portion of this same building. We are allowed to mingle and talk to the troops within the confines of the building.

Before long, several of us get acquainted with some of the soldiers. We talk about music, sports, language, where they were born, things like that. Then we meet several of the wives who live on the compound with their soldier husbands. I am six feet tall, and not one woman is shorter than I am. It's surprising. And remarkably, it's fun. Everyone speaks such proper English that at times I'm a little embarrassed at how undignified we Americans sound.

It's amazing. Ever since Joel Green, I haven't had to worry about what to say to people when it comes to spiritual things. I've learned to just smile, listen to God, and answer the questions I am asked.

The whole world is thirsty for unconditional love. Only God can provide that. My job, I've come to learn, is not to provide the water but simply to point the way to the well—the well of Living Water that God offers each of us through a relationship with His Son, Jesus Christ.

My encounter with the soldiers is no different from the one I had with

360

Joel Green in the hospital bed next to me. The conversations start with a simple introduction. After that all I do is answer questions, pointing the way to the well.

One of the passengers and I walk over to one of the soldiers who is standing alone, guarding the building. "Hello," we say with a smile. "What is your name?"

"Mwelwa."

We shake hands. "My name is Dale. I'm glad to meet you. So, Mwelwa, where were you born?"

"Ndola is where I was born."

"Where is that?"

"A little north of here."

We continue talking, genuinely interested in this man's life. We ask about his family, his interests, and gradually get acquainted with him.

"Mwelwa," I say. "What's the most important thing in your life?"

He seems surprised by my question, and before he answers, I ask him another question: "Do you know Jesus? I mean, He is the most important thing to me, Mwelwa, but do you know Him? Do you know Jesus Christ as your personal Savior?"

"Well, no, I don't think so."

"Mwelwa, if you died tonight—you do know that someday you will die; I will die. Everyone will, right?" He nodded. "So, Mwelwa, if you were to die tonight, do you know for sure that you would spend eternity with God in heaven?"

"No."

"Would you like to know that?"

"Yes. Of course."

"Mwelwa, the Bible says that there is only one way. . . ."

For the next several hours we have one conversation like that after another, soldier after soldier, wife after wife, on into the wee hours of the morning. By dawn almost all the soldiers and their wives have come to Jesus, praying for forgiveness and receiving the free gift of eternal life. Just as with the woman at the well, it all starts with a simple conversation. One thing leads to another, and all things lead to the well where Jesus is waiting with a cup of Living Water.

Countless men and women are gathered around that well in Lusaka, smiling, their hearts full of joy. You can see it in their eyes. It's almost like those I saw gathered at the gate of heaven eighteen years before, awaiting my arrival. This time *I* am at the gate, so to speak, waiting for *them* to arrive, smiling at them, welcoming these new brothers and sisters at the entrance of heaven.

I am awake the entire night, reveling in the wonder of it all. *This* is why we are here. It isn't a mistake. And we aren't in any danger. We are, in fact, in the safest place we can be—the center of God's will. He has led us here, to *these* people whose lives were so parched, whose souls were so thirsty. In this case, though, I didn't so much lead them to the well as He led me to them.

Others in our group, those who are provided blankets, sleep only an hour or two, but as captain, I feel responsible to be vigilant and keep watch. Around ten the next morning, I am approached by a soldier named Robinson. He says the general is in his office and demands to speak with me. I am ushered about two hundred yards away to another building at the airport. I put my tie back on, still wearing my pilot's uniform.

It is not a pleasant meeting. I take some verbal abuse and apologize profusely for landing without permission, even though as far as I am concerned, I did have permission. Once on the ground, though, it is an entirely different story. And so, with a written apology to the government of Zambia, and after paying a moderate fine, I am given permission to refuel and take off.

When I arrive back at the jail I find Steve praying with a member of the mission team. I pause and bow my head as I hear Steve asking God to forgive him of his sins. I listen with great joy as Steve invites Jesus Christ into his heart and life.

Like my grandfather in years past, it is now I who whisper, "Well, praise the Lord."

Steve is wonderfully transformed by the same love that God had shown to the soldiers and their wives. The same love He makes available to all who will believe.

To God, it doesn't matter if you are black or white, Zambian or American, a soldier named Mwelwa or a copilot named Steve. All are one in Christ. And all are now booked on the same flight to heaven.

As we board the plane, I realize I have a "new" copilot. Steve realizes it too. He has seen firsthand the love of God in action. And seeing it, he has decided to experience it for himself. It both fills him and makes him thirsty for more.

For me, Steve's entry into the family of God is just another of the many answers to my prayers. This time watching God turn a co-worker into a brother.

TUESDAY, MAY 22—16:10—LUSAKA, ZAMBIA

As we taxi the 18,500-pound Learjet to the runway, we get through our routine Before Takeoff Checklist and set up all navigation radios. I rev the engines and the airplane shudders to life, eager to take flight. The soldiers on the tarmac wave enthusiastically, sorry to see us go. As we depart "the surly bonds of earth," the hum of the well-tuned engines is heavenly music to my ears.

Leaving the sea of soldiers behind, it reminds me of my return flight from heaven—how quickly I was swept away, how everything grew smaller until at last it was out of sight. Memories of how wonderful it felt to be in heaven, surrounded by such love, flooded my mind. It was a lot like the love we were surrounded by in the Lusaka Airport.

When we got back to the States, we sent Bibles to Mwelwa and the other soldiers and their wives. After all, they were family now.

That family has grown with each one of the hundreds of mission trips we have flown, with each Bible sent, each gospel tract, each showing of the

Jesus film, each clinic we helped build, each shipment of medical supplies we helped deliver.

A Learjet similar to the one flown on Dale's missionary flight to Zambia. Photo taken and provided by Andrei Bezmylov (as seen on *www.airliners.net*).

I glance past the wing for a final glimpse of the Lusaka International Airport, reflecting on my life before that fateful crash so many years ago ... and my life after it. As the airport becomes a dot on the landscape, above me only clouds, I realize how much I have changed. For me, airplanes were once symbols of status; now they are symbols of service.

How I used to love the thrill of flight then.

Now it is a different thrill that excites me.

Now it is the thrill of seeing the love of God in action, where I can quench my thirst, if only for a moment, with a little sip of heaven.

A sip that fills me and at the same time makes me thirsty for more.

I feel so full. So satisfied.

Thank You, God. Thank You ...

For sparing my life.

For healing my broken body.

For giving me new dreams.

But most of all, for allowing me the privilege of serving You and experiencing Your love over and over again.

As we level off at 37,000 feet, heading for South Africa, I select autopilot ON.

Turning to Steve, I say, "You know, we're brothers now."

"What? What do you mean?"

"Well, when two people have invited Jesus Christ into their lives, it means that they are both re-born children of God. That makes you and I brothers in Christ."

"Wow, Dale. You know, I don't really have any close family."

"Well, now you have millions of brothers—and millions of sisters—in Christ, all over the world. And Steve, if you only knew of the family that awaits you in heaven . . . I'll explain more later, OK?"

"Yeah, sure. Thanks. And thanks for choosing me for this trip."

"Steve, I honestly believe it was God who picked you for this flight." I put a gentle hand on his shoulder. "I do have a question for you, though."

Straightening his posture, getting ready to assume some new first-officer duty, Steve responds, "Roger, go ahead."

I smile with a light chuckle. "What do you suppose God has in store for us next?"

He grins, "I can't wait to find out . . . *brother* Dale."

✈

✈

AFTERWORD

PORTAL OF THE FOLDED WINGS

The Portal of the Folded Wings is the massive shrine that our twin-engine Piper Navajo hit that fateful morning of July 18, 1969.

The Spanish Mission Revival structure was built in 1924 by American architect Kenneth McDonald Jr. and Italian sculptor Frederico A. Giorgi.

It was designed as the entrance to Valhalla Memorial Park Cemetery, Valhalla being the mythological palace of Odin, the Norse god of slain warriors.

Originally, visitors drove from Valhalla Drive into the cemetery through the arches that led under the rotunda, past three reflection pools and exquisite garden walls. After it was dedicated, the shrine was used for public events from picnics to concerts to radio broadcasts extending well into the 1930s.

The shrine was built to memorialize the passing of aviation's greatest pioneers, from aviators to engineers to inventors.

James Floyd Smith has a plaque there—the person who, in 1918, invented the manually operated parachute for the U.S. Army.

Charles Lindbergh is also remembered there as the person who, in 1927, flew the first solo flight across the Atlantic.

Amelia Earhart has a plaque in the monument as well, the first woman to fly solo across the Atlantic, disappearing in 1937 over the central Pacific, attempting to circumnavigate the globe.

General Billy Mitchell, the American Army general who is regarded as the father of the U.S. Air Force, is likewise remembered there.

Dale Black will also soon have a plaque there.

My achievement? I survived.

I survived in order to dedicate my career to improving aviation safety.

I survived to train scores of professionals to become better and safer pilots.

I survived a crash that took the life of two pilots and caused $70,000 worth of damage to the shrine.

After the first anniversary flight, still haunted by feelings of guilt, wondering if I had in any way been responsible, I tracked down the remains of the plane that had been taken away for salvage. The tail was in Van Nuys. The cockpit and engines were in Long Beach. So was the throttle quadrant. But the pieces of wreckage did nothing to solve the mystery that still haunted me.

I was finally able to retrieve a copy of the FAA accident report, and scoured it for answers. That official report revealed that both fuel selectors were in the ON position at the time of the crash. My feet had *not* turned them off. Also, both engines had been operating at full power on takeoff and on impact, so the problem wasn't with the engines. I pored over the report of the accident, which cited "pilot error" as the cause of the crash.

Several factors contributed to the fatal crash that day. The intersection departure made for an unforgiving takeoff. The plane never increased to the proper speed. Gene had pulled the controls back too quickly and too sharply, lifting off the runway prematurely. The plane momentarily seemed to be airborne due to what is called "ground effect," which is a false feeling of lift created by the plane's proximity to the ground. When you climb to approximately one hundred feet, the ground effect goes away. When Gene noticed he didn't have enough power to keep climbing, he applied full-throttle to the engines. Chuck stepped in, but he was too late. He tried to lower the nose to pick up speed, but it wasn't soon enough to clear the trees. The left wing of our plane clipped the trees at eighty feet, which turned the aircraft just enough for a direct impact into the dome of the mausoleum.

We slammed into the memorial at 135 mph, hitting it just five feet from the top. It was that combination of factors that caused the crash.

The crash was chronicled in all the newspapers in surrounding cities, and I've been told it was later memorialized in *Ripley's Believe It or Not.*

Not quite the epitaph I was hoping for.

The epitaphs of others are noted on tombstones that fill Valhalla like so many tabs on file folders of the fallen.

Aviators are memorialized there, but also athletes like Gorgeous George, the wrestler. And countless actors. From Oliver Hardy of Laurel and Hardy fame to Ruth Robinson, one of the Munchkins in *The Wizard of Oz.* Even the voice of Jiminy Cricket is buried there, Cliff Edwards. Countless others are there, too. Who even remembers their names? Let alone the lives behind the names.

Located in North Hollywood, the cemetery is just off the end of Runway 15 at Burbank Airport, directly in the flight path. Since the opening of the airport, a new entrance to the cemetery was designated. Cars no longer drive through the shrine's arches. An iron fence has been erected around the plaques inside the dome. And the three reflection pools have long since been filled in.

For the first couple of years after the accident, I went to the memorial every chance I got. Sometimes with family or friends, sometimes alone, about every two weeks.

During that time of change in my life, I found a new girlfriend. She looked beyond my broken body and limitations, and loved me for who I was and what I'd become. Her name is Paula, a tall blonde who loves God in an extremely personal way. We were married in 1972.

The last time I revisited the memorial was on July 18, 2009, with Paula. She arranged for a special flight that day. Our daughter, Kara, took pictures as I flew a small single-engine Cessna 172 from the French Valley Airport in Southern California. After the flight, we drove our car to Burbank. We toured Dr. Graham's old office and St. Joseph Hospital, and spent some time at the grave of Chuck Burns. As always, we prayed together at the Portal of the Folded Wings.

I'm not sure why I keep going back. I have no unfinished business there. I have closure now, and peace. But I still return regularly.

I just turned sixty, and the shrine is more than eighty years old. It underwent a facelift in 1994, covering the gaping cracks, replacing the fallen tiles—a poignant reminder of the decay that will make dust of buildings and people alike, in the end.

Architecturally, the shrine lifts our eyes toward the sky, as if to say, "This is not their final resting place."

The remains of fifteen pioneers of aviation are buried within the shrine, from the first dirigible pilot to the machinist who made the Wright brothers the fathers of modern aviation. His plaque reads:

Charles E. Taylor
ASSISTANT TO WRIGHT BROTHERS IN
BUILDING FIRST ENGINE AND
FLYING MACHINE
May 24, 1868–January 30, 1956

My favorite plaque is the one over the remains of the chaplain at the site:

John F. F. Carruthers
AUGUST 31, 1889–JANUARY 13, 1960
CHAPLAIN, PORTAL OF THE FOLDED WINGS
AIR HISTORIAN

AT THE GRAVE, WHEN MY WARFARE IS ENDED
THOUGH NO FLOWERS EMBLAZON THE SOD
MAY A PRAYER MARK THE GOOD I INTENDED
LEAVING ALL DECORATIONS TO GOD.

With more life behind me than ahead of me, I wonder how my memorial will one day read. Not the one someone inscribes on a plaque, but the one my Father God writes.

COMMUNION ON THE MOON

The headlines immediately before and after my crash were all about the Apollo 11 flight. John F. Kennedy's dream of putting an American on the moon was first publicly voiced by the president in 1961, and it was voiced with resolve. His speech left an indelible impression on me. By the end of the decade, he vowed, the U.S. would have a man on the moon. Here we were at the end of the sixties, and it appeared as if that dream was going to come true. After several preliminary missions that put men into orbit around the moon, this was to be the first mission to put them on the moon.

It seems ironic to me that while I was in a coma and visiting the splendors of heaven, astronaut Buzz Aldrin was leading Neil Armstrong and the NASA team in the first official, or maybe not so official, activity on the moon's surface. Buzz conducted Holy Communion. Talk of what they did was hushed for many years but is now public knowledge. Still inside the newly arrived lunar module, Buzz Aldrin believed the best way of showing respect and celebration was to thank God for their safe arrival by acknowledging Him in taking communion as the first human act on the moon's surface. He chose to honor God for this human victory, and he did so against much resistance. In some way, I have felt connected to Buzz Aldrin ever since.

ANNIVERSARY FLIGHTS

Working enormously hard through my injuries, I eventually, and gratefully, became a commercial pilot for TWA. I also became an FAA check airman for the Boeing 737, Learjet, and the Cessna Citation. I spent my career helping train airline pilots and tried my best to improve aviation safety as a ground, simulator, and flight instructor, as well as a flight examiner.

Each year on July 18, for the first twenty-five years, I flew as pilot in command over the Portal of the Folded Wings, with two exceptions. In 1971, I was a volunteer missionary in the jungles of northern Peru. The next year, Paula and I, newly married, returned to those same Peruvian jungles to share the love of God and the gospel message with the Aguaruna Indian tribe. What an experience. But that's another book.

Dr. Graham was a regular passenger for many of my anniversary flights over the years. So was Ron Davis, my best friend and the one most instrumental in me becoming a pilot in the first place. Friends from college or from the family business often joined me, and later other pilots or missionary friends.

On those flights I flew an assortment of airplanes. From the Cherokee 140 to the Cherokee Six, Piper Seneca, Aztec, and of course the Navajo on anniversaries 1977 and 1978. Later I flew the Cessna Citation I, Citation II, the Learjet 24, Learjet 35, MU-2, Piper Cheyenne II, and Learjet 55. Some years I was able to radio the tower and give them my traditional transmission, publicly dedicating the flight to God. Other years the tower appeared too busy, so I didn't attempt the radio announcement.

On the eighth anniversary of the crash, Dale was finally able to fly a Piper Navajo (the same type that crashed) as pilot in command over the Portal of the Folded Wings.

Of all the anniversary flights flown on July 18 over the monument, one is burned in my memory like it happened yesterday. Paula and I had arranged for a small prayer service near the Portal of the Folded Wings, led by our family friend and pastor of my youth. The control tower allowed us to park our jet at the southern end of Runway 15, off to the side. From there the monument and cemetery are close and clearly visible. Our son, Eric, and daughter, Kara, now old enough to comprehend so much more, seemed moved by the experience. Dr. Graham was there, along with several others.

We read from Psalm 91, then prayed and thanked God for answering so many prayers. Next we boarded the twin-engine Learjet that my company managed, this one called *Lady Barbara,* Frank Sinatra's private jet.

As usual, Paula took charge of the passengers and got everyone seated while I taxied the airplane to the approach end of Runway 15. I set the parking brake prior to takeoff.

What is so memorable to me is what happened when I took a peek into the cabin prior to making the traditional call to the control tower. Somehow I connected all the dots again. Dr. Graham's smiling eyes met mine. Here was the man who had helped put my body back together. The man I had seen from outside of my body in the emergency room, the man for whom I was filled with an overwhelming love within minutes of my awaking from the coma, even before I could talk. Dr. Graham winked and gave me a thumbs-up.

I saw the expectant faces of our precious children. If God hadn't spared my life, Eric and Kara wouldn't be there. I remember watching Paula, seeing her so full of God's love and wisdom, as gorgeous as ever, and knowing she'd drop anything, anytime, to obey God. Another happy face that day was my pastor, Mark Smith, who had baptized me when I was twelve years old. I remember the joy, the unity, the peace. But primarily, it is the love I will never forget. It is the love from and for others that reminds me more of heaven than anything else on earth.

Dale and Dr. Graham in a TWA Boeing 747 at Los Angeles International Airport. Photo taken on the tenth anniversary of the crash, July 18, 1979.

I called the tower: "Burbank Tower, on this day in 1969, a Piper Navajo crashed just south of the airport. Two were killed. I alone survived. I dedicate this flight to the glory of God." The throttles were advanced and the jet screamed into the air barely above the monument. As I looked down, I reflected on the familiar Scripture we had just read minutes earlier: "He who dwells in the secret place of the Most High shall abide under the shadow of the Almighty" (Psalm 91:1). The secret place for me was the relationship between my loving heavenly Father and me.

It was an understanding that He and I have. This is because of my uniqueness as His creation, and because of His amazing capacity to love me as a single individual.

And just think . . . if God loves me this way, imagine how much He loves you.

....

For God so loved the world that He gave His only begotten Son, that whoever believes in Him should not perish but have everlasting life. For God did not send His Son into the world to condemn the world, but that the world through Him might be saved. He who believes in Him is not condemned; but he who does not believe is condemned already. . . . —JOHN 3:16–18

....

On the twenty-fifth anniversary, I guess you could say I had a climatic moment. I was able to fly captain in a United Airlines Boeing 747 from Denver to Burbank and back. My son, Eric, was the copilot and my wife, Paula, and daughter, Kara, were able to sit in the cockpit for the entire round-trip flight, right next to the UAL instructor pilot. (Oh, did I mention this was a United Airlines, $120 million Boeing 747-400 six axis flight *simulator?*)

Following the twenty-fifth anniversary flight in the simulator, Paula had arranged for a surprise celebration backyard barbecue. Many friends from the airlines and the local church, plus our children and relatives, were in attendance, and it was a complete surprise to me. During the festivities, Paula came over to me, pointed skyward, and asked, "Dale, what kind of airplane is that?"

I looked up and for once was not exactly sure. But it was circling right above us, so I had time to study it.

"Take a good look, Dale."

"Well, I think it's a uh—uh."

I was so focused on trying to determine the aircraft type, I couldn't see anything else. (Has that ever happened to you? Happens to me a lot.) Then Paula, who knows me so well, said, "Dale. What is the airplane *pulling?*"

Finally I saw it. Behind the aircraft, a large banner read, "Dale— Celebrating 25 years. Praise God!"

My mouth dropped open and my eyes filled with tears.

All I remember next was bowing my head, hugging Paula, and thanking God again for sparing my life.

Dale and Paula on the twenty-fifth anniversary of the crash, 1994, at the United Airlines Training Center in Denver.

DR. GRAHAM—SPECIAL FRIEND

One of the last things Dr. Graham cautioned me about in 1970 was not to injure my left ankle again. Although it was an answer to prayer on so many levels, the blood circulation in the talus bone remained at only 40 percent after two years.

Within a few years, Dr. Graham and I didn't see much of each other. He was busy with a thriving practice as well as traveling the country, giving lectures and attending Evel Knievel's events.

I was still working to regain what I had lost in the accident. Due to the head injuries, my short-term memory had been permanently impaired. For years I studied everything I could on how to improve my memory. I discovered that anything I wanted or needed to learn now had to be placed into my long-term memory, or I simply couldn't recall it. This required an extraordinary amount of study, review, and more review to get things to "stick."

In the midst of this new way of living, I was hard at work in flight training, gaining more aviation certificates and ratings, and busy finishing college; I was now married and raising a family, and also worked full time at the family business to pay for it all.

I've mentioned that before the crash I had been very active as an athlete. Afterward, I returned slowly to a variety of sports. I played softball, swam regularly, played tennis. I even got back to water-skiing, lifting weights, and some boxing. These activities helped me keep my focus on recovery instead of falling into self-pity about the things I couldn't do.

Then one day in 1976, while playing sandlot tackle football, I blew it. I pulled back to throw the pass, but my wide receiver wasn't open (at least that's my story, and I'm sticking to it). I had to run the ball for the first down. A would-be tackler forced me to jump over him. When I landed, I was pretty sure I'd broken my left ankle.

For three months it hurt horribly. I continued to work and acted as normal as possible in public. But at home, I used my old crutches from after the crash. (I still have those crutches, by the way.) Paula tried repeatedly to get me to go see Dr. Graham. For two more months I refused. "It'll be fine," I'd say.

Not only was I in excruciating pain, but I had never told Paula that my ankle was only 40 percent vascularized—that the rest of the ankle bone had no blood circulation and was considered dead.

After her persistence, I finally broke the news to Paula. I also shared about Dr. Graham's warning not to run or jump, and my foolish disregard of the doc's advice.

Paula handled the news amazingly well, but she still encouraged me to see Dr. Graham. He had the talent, the experience, and all my files. He'd know exactly what was wrong and what to do about it.

Finally, five months after the football injury, I conceded. Paula made the appointment, and I went to visit Dr. Graham.

As I sat in the examining room, it was as if I had gone back in time. Seven years after the crash everything was still familiar. When Dr. Graham finally walked in he didn't even say hello or make eye contact. His hands went immediately to my left ankle and he held it warmly, like it was something precious to him.

"What brings you in here today, Dale?"

I explained what had happened.

He took X rays, and a few minutes later we were standing in front of the familiar screen.

Silence.

He said nothing. He didn't even look at me. Then he gazed out the window for a moment, then back to the X rays.

More silence.

It was more than enough time for somebody to say something.

"Doc? What is it?"

"It's normal." He slowly shook his head, rubbed his chin.

"What do you mean?"

"Your ankle is normal."

More silence.

"Doc, you used to talk to me in percentages. You used to say, 20 percent healed, 30 percent, or 40 percent vascularized. So what percentage are you seeing today?"

He paused, looking for the right words.

"Dale, your ankle is *100 percent*. Completely vascularized."

The doctor walked out of the room. I wasn't sure what he was feeling, what it all meant to him.

I borrowed the office phone, called Paula and broke the news. She was amazed and relieved. Together we thanked the Lord.

About ten minutes after my phone call, the doctor came back into the room, composed and warmer this time.

"Dr. Graham, if my ankle is healed, then what is causing all the pain?"

He pointed to the X rays as he spoke in medical terms I couldn't follow. The bottom line was that although my ankle was 100 percent vascularized, many bones inside the ankle needed relief by repositioning. He picked up my shoe and showed me where it was putting pressure on some of the bones in my ankle. He suggested that I get special orthopedic shoes.

He wrote down the name of a podiatrist and had his secretary make an appointment for me. Then he started fashioning a handmade insert with a pair of surgical scissors.

"In the meantime, put this in your left shoe. It'll take some pressure off the talus." Even though I never kept my podiatrist appointment, I did buy some new shoes and kept the insert inside, and the pain slowly faded away. But this whole event seemed to have a wonderful purpose.

About two weeks later, back at our home in Long Beach, we got a call from Dr. Graham. He invited Paula and me to his home for dinner.

Dr. Graham gave us a tour of his luxurious estate, which overlooked the city of Burbank and the San Fernando Valley. I could easily see Hollywood-Burbank Airport, and my eyes gravitated to the newly installed red light on top of the Portal of the Folded Wings.

During our wonderful dinner overlooking the city lights, Dr. Graham showed signs of vulnerability. I had seldom seen this softer side. After dinner we discussed the many miraculous events that he had been witness to throughout the aftermath of the crash. Dr. Graham had a front-row seat, observing a personal, loving God who had revealed himself over and over throughout the days and years following the accident. Ultimately that evening, I was able to share the free gift of pardon made available to us through Jesus Christ. A short time later Dr. Graham surrendered his life to the Lord. His search was over and we became more than doctor and patient. We became brothers in the family of God.

About a month later, back home in Long Beach, another phone call came from Dr. Graham. He wanted me to meet with his photographer at the airport for pictures, and he asked me to dress in my pilot's uniform. I had no clue what he was up to, but I complied. The next day Paula and I met the photographer at the airport, and she took several pictures of me standing in front of different types of airplanes.

A few weeks after that, Dr. Graham's office called, asking me to come in for follow-up X rays. Although surprised, I agreed.

Returning to the familiar office once again, Dr. Graham met me in the waiting room wearing a good-sized smile. Without a word, he grabbed my shoulder and turned me into the hallway past the front reception desk. I shuffled in front of him.

Evel Knievel's framed photo had always been the first portrait in a hallway gallery of celebrities, patients of Dr. Graham. But now, to my complete amazement, my photo hung in that prestigious first position. A large color portrait of yours truly, standing next to a Piper Navajo, hung on the gallery wall.

Needless to say, I was stunned and humbled to be worthy of such an honor.

Then three years later, on July 18, 1979, Dr. Graham and his photographer friend met Paula and me in Los Angeles at my favorite restaurant, the Proud Bird. The aviation-themed restaurant is situated on the approach end of Runway 25 at LAX. The big jets land right in front of you. By then I was a pilot for TWA.

After dinner, we toured TWA's facilities and I showed them the inner workings of the airline. We talked, we laughed, and we fellowshiped.

Although Dr. Graham was my grandfather's age, he and I had become close friends. If you wonder how this could happen, it's because all over the world, every day, people from all ages, nationalities, and races share the most amazing relationship on planet earth. They are one in a bond of love—the love of God flowing among brothers and sisters in Jesus Christ.

The most awesome, glorious experience on earth, next to our

relationship with God through Jesus Christ, is being a part of the family of God.

Only a few months later, just after finishing initial pilot training on the Boeing 707 with TWA, 111 pilots were laid off. I was one of them. This was a huge shock and disappointment.

Due to the fact that I had failed the flight physicals while interviewing with a couple dozen other airlines previously, I couldn't just go fly with another airline. Dr. Graham, knowing this, thought I might be devastated. So he came by to offer encouragement.

"You know, Dale and Paula," he said, "God can use this furlough for good."

I smiled. "You're right, Doc."

"He's done that so many times before. So don't worry about this. You and God, together, you'll bounce back." Now Dr. Graham was the one saying God would take care of it.

The doctor was right. With that furlough came the birth of our jet charter, jet pilot training, and jet aircraft sales company—and a very different future. Years later, I was recalled by TWA.

Dr. Graham has finished his race. I'm so grateful that heaven is his home now. I look forward to our wonderful reunion.

LIVING A DIFFERENT DREAM

Some would say I have lived my dream. I see it a little differently. I did not so much live my own dream as I lived the dream God had when He dreamed of me.

I have flown with Him on over a thousand mission trips, plus the thousands of professional flights. Here and there on those trips I have seen reflections of heaven in the tens of thousands of faces of strangers who became family to me. Brothers and sisters in Christ, so full of love and joy and unity that it seemed like echoes of the love I felt in heaven.

I have experienced so much.

What an adventure!

I tend to think in aviation images. One image that comes back often is the one-year anniversary flight that I described earlier. The words are crystal clear in my memory: "Burbank Tower, this is 37 November, ready for takeoff."

"37 November, roger, you're cleared for takeoff, runway one-five."

A pause, then the words "37 November, this is Burbank Tower. A very . . . big . . . congratulations to you . . . from all of us!"

Tears fill my eyes as I remember my takeoff on that emotional flight. Greater tears come when I realize that the words I most long to hear are not theirs . . . but His: "Well done, good and faithful servant. Enter into the joy of your Lord."

Enter into the joy . . .

For three days in a coma I experienced something of that joy. Both the experience of it then—and the anticipation of it now—have charted the course of my life.

I emerged from that coma to see again . . . walk again . . . fly again.

And most important, to live again.

SIGNING OFF

This is your captain speaking: Before I sign off, I want to thank you for taking this trip with me. May the Lord's protection be upon you wherever you go. Wherever it is, may God go with you. May *He* be your Captain, and *you* the copilot. And when at last your journey is over and it's time for your wings to be folded, know this: Your homecoming will be worth the trip it took to get you there, however bumpy the ride, whatever "crashes" you experience along the way.

Yes, it will be *so* worth it.

You can trust me on that!

HOW THIS BOOK CAME ABOUT

When people find out my husband was the only survivor of a horrific airplane crash and that he also experienced a journey to heaven, they are often curious about how these events have impacted my life and our marriage. They also like to know how this book came about. Let me explain.

Dale and I met at college in Pasadena, California, almost two years after the crash. My dorm mate had a crush on him, and Dale was the one person I heard "all about." He was known as the reformed campus rebel, having been expelled the year before the accident for disciplinary reasons. But due to his remarkably changed life since the crash, college authorities allowed him to return, still in a wheelchair.

Dale was an enigma. He was still a rebel, yet he possessed a strong and tender heart for the things of the Lord. His faith in a God who cared and interacted with him on a personal and intimate level was unique, powerful, and attractive.

A year after we met, Dale and I were married. He continues to be my best friend. We've raised a family together. We've started businesses together. We've traveled the world together. We've experienced wonderful successes as well as severe challenges . . . but always together. For almost forty years we've also ministered side by side. I know him extremely well, and he tells me I'm the only one who truly understands him.

Throughout the years Dale told me several times that he had had an out-of-body experience following the crash. I strongly suspected he had visited heaven, but for some reason he would not talk about it. Why was I suspect? Simple. All the signs were there.

What I didn't know about was Dale's commitment not to share about his journey to heaven with anyone other than his grandfather unless God clearly instructed him otherwise. And when Dale commits to something, he is unbendable.

A few years ago, while Dale was starting to write about his life experiences, we were discussing the moments immediately following the crash. As I had done before, I began to ask probing questions about what he remembered. This time he was unusually quiet. So I asked more questions. He got up and walked around the room. I pressed harder. Suddenly he stood still and silent for several minutes. Then in the greatest emotional response I'd ever seen from him, he let it spill out. He finally revealed to me what I had suspected all along. Dale had visited heaven after all.

As Dale recounted his amazing journey, he paced the floor. I grabbed a pen and paper. He talked. I scribbled notes. This went on and on into the night. The intricate details, the intensity of the concepts, the incredible descriptions . . . I was stunned. His recall was so precise and so completely aligned with the Bible, I knew immediately his experience was not only real but also sacred.

Dale answered each of my questions quickly, but always with great emotion. There were no pauses, no hesitations to his story. His entire awesome journey to heaven was there buried deep in his heart. I was so astounded by his descriptions that at times I froze in place, in awe of what God had revealed to, of all people, my own husband. I have never been more convinced of Dale's honesty and sincerity as when he finally unloaded the secrets of his heavenly journey, the secret he had kept for almost forty years.

For the next several days, hundreds of dots started to connect in my head. So many things I had thought were strange about my husband now made sense. These quirks were, and still are, some of the leftover effects of his heavenly journey.

Dale's values and priorities completely changed after the airplane crash.

That's the primary reason he is dramatically different from anyone I have ever known. He is sensitive toward and strongly drawn to relationships where there is unity and love at the core. Dale doesn't look for facts but the truth in each situation. He sees under the surface of things. He studies the Bible from his heart rather than his head and knows it intimately. Since the crash, he is drawn toward certain types of music. He has a quest to understand order in science, but only to understand more about God. He is fascinated with light and the properties of light as well as space and astronomy. And the list goes on and on. Without question Dale has been profoundly and permanently affected by his visit to heaven.

After much prayer, Dale finally agreed to write about his heavenly journey, but only for immediate family. At the time neither of us dreamed it would ever go beyond that. However, over the next several months, God used a series of events to clearly confirm it was time to share not only about Dale's amazing survival and recovery, but also about his journey to heaven and back.

You should know that his story is verifiable. There are medical records, witnesses, and the lasting results of Dale's changed life. I am probably the best witness to the validity of this story because I've studied the documents and I know almost everyone in this story personally. I still have the X rays, the letters, the newspaper articles, hundreds of photos, the FAA reports, and more. I also know the man. And I, too, have been impacted by the life-changing experience that has affected Dale each and every day of the last four decades.

Due to the injuries sustained in the crash, primarily his difficulty with short-term memory, Dale has had to work enormously hard to accomplish his vocational dreams. But the physical limitations that still challenge him also serve as blessed reminders of his miraculous survival. He's learned several creative "tricks" to compensate for his injuries and, incredibly, has flown for over forty years as a professional pilot following the accident that almost took his life. And probably because of the crash, Dale spent most of his professional career as an award-winning flight instructor and examiner, trying to do his part to improve aviation safety. He is respected by colleagues as one of the best pilot instructors and safest professional aviators in the business.

It has taken a lifetime to more fully reveal God's faithfulness in Dale's life. And that faithfulness has culminated in this book.

I hope you have enjoyed Dale's story and that some part of it has encouraged you in your own journey. God continues to direct our lives, and believe me, after four decades, it is still quite a ride.

—Paula Black

ABOUT THE AUTHOR

Capt. Dale Black is a retired airline pilot who has dedicated his career to professional pilot training and aviation safety. Capt. Dale has flown for over forty years and has more than seventeen thousand hours of flying experience in a variety of two-, three-, and four-engine commercial jets, as well as many corporate jets and general aviation aircraft. He is a former aircraft systems instructor for the Boeing 747, Boeing 727, Boeing 737, and Boeing 707 aircraft. He has been a senior simulator and flight instructor on the Boeing 737, the Learjet 35/36, Learjet 24/25, Learjet 55, and Cessna Citation I and II. He has been a flight examiner for the Airline Transport Pilot Certificate, the Boeing 737, and a variety of jet-type ratings. Additionally, he has been a certified flight engineer on a variety of commercial jets. Dale is also a former flight standards captain, safety consultant, accident prevention counselor, and regular speaker in aviation seminars. He founded and operated a jet pilot training and jet aircraft sales company. He has been a pilot and instructor for many celebrities as well as executives of several Fortune 500 companies.

Dale has an MA in Theology and a PhD in Business with an emphasis in airline management and marketing. He is founder of Eagle International Ministries, where he has led scores of teams on short-term Christian missionary projects to over fifty countries since 1981.

He is a regular speaker on topics regarding life after death, heaven, and Bible prophecy.

Dale and his wife, Paula, own a real estate company. They are the parents of two grown children and live in Southern California.

He can be contacted at CaptDale@DaleBlack.org or by visiting *www .DaleBlack.org.*

You are invited to share the
life-changing story and message of
Flight to Heaven

- Give this book as a gift. As you have discovered, not only will you be sharing a suspenseful real-life adventure, but friends and family member are sure to be impacted by the inspirational story and glorious glimpse of heaven.

- Write a book review on your favorite Web sites or your own site or blog. Another idea is to suggest that your local newspaper or radio station do an interview or book review.

- Reach out to those in need by providing copies of the book to places where people often need encouragement and inspiration (retirement homes, hospitals, jails and prisons, and anywhere an uplifting story is needed).

- Encourage your church or organization to request the author as a speaker.

- Consider setting up a personal book study, and invite your friends and neighbors to meet together and discuss the book.

For more information and ideas, visit
www.flighttoheaven.org

90 MINUTES IN HEAVEN

DON PIPER
WITH CECIL MURPHEY

To the prayer warriors . . .
You prayed; I'm here!

ACKNOWLEDGMENTS

I wrote this book in self-defense. In the years since 1989 I have seldom satisfied anyone with quick answers or brief encounters retelling my experiences. On radio, on TV, in newspapers, and from countless pulpits and other speaking engagements, I have generally left more unanswered questions than satisfactory responses. People consistently have wanted to know more . . . always more. I wrote three different manuscripts about this experience to satisfy inquiring minds. None of them satisfied me. That's when I prevailed upon one of America's distinguished authors to partner with me to write a book that would answer the most compelling issues concerning my death and life. Cecil Murphey, author of very successful biographies of such luminaries as Franklin Graham, Truett Cathey, B. J. Thomas, Dino Karsanakas, and Dr. Ben Carson, gave me the perspective I wanted to write the book I needed to write. You're holding it now.

Cec has become a devoted friend, confidant, and mentor. Indeed, one of the blessings of writing this book has been to know Cec Murphey. His passion for this project is felt on every page. Thank you, Cec! You are deeply appreciated. Likewise, the Knight Agency's Deidre Knight's belief in this project is much appreciated. And Dr. Vicki Crumpton of Baker Publishing Group is a person I have grown to admire. Her dedication to seeing this story in print is cherished.

I want to thank the staff of both Memorial Hermann Medical Center's Trauma Unit and St. Luke's Episcopal Hospital in Houston for their devotion to the healing arts. Special thanks to Dr. Thomas Greider, my orthopedic surgeon since that fateful night of January 18, 1989.

Precious people of God from many churches have allowed me to serve them. Not only were their prayers crucial to my survival but their presence has been a blessing to my ministry. Deep gratitude goes to South Park Baptist Church of Alvin, Texas, God's great prayer warriors. I would like to acknowledge the special contributions of First Baptist Church, Airline Baptist Church, and Barksdale Baptist Church, all of Bossier City, Louisiana. My father in the ministry, Dr. Damon V. Vaughn, former pastor of the first two of those churches is owed an immeasurable debt.

For standing faithfully with me in the days since my accident I express undying love for the First Baptist Church of Rosharon, Texas, along with Hunters' Glen and Murphy Road Baptist Church of Plano, Texas. Since 1996 I have called First Baptist Church of Pasadena, Texas, my place of service. Your support for this project has been sweet and unwavering. Thank you all for your patience, forbearance, prayers, and love.

To Anita Onerecker and her late husband, Dick, thank you for allowing God to use you so dramatically. To all my friends, brothers and sisters in Christ, who prayed so passionately, I thank you. Only God knows your sacrifices and kindnesses. Most of all, I thank my friends of many years, Cliff McArdle and David Gentiles, true gifts from God. Whether day or night, convenient or imposition, expedient or sacrificial, you have always been faithful. And thank you all for encouraging me to see this book to fruition.

Finally, I want to express profound gratitude to my wife's parents, Eldon and Ethel Pentecost, and my own parents, Ralph and Billie Piper, for their incalculable sacrifices and faithful support. To my three children, Nicole, Chris, and Joe, I say . . . God has given me children so much better than I could have ever deserved. I am highly blessed. How can I say thank you for all you have meant to me, even more so since that Wednesday so long ago? And to my wife of thirty years, Eva, no one should ever have had to do the things you've had to do for me. But you did them, faithfully, compassionately, and without hesitation. Of all my family and friends, only Eva comes closest to really knowing how painful this journey has been each day, for she has endured it with me. Eva, you are a gift from God.

Lord, you know I haven't always understood the whys of what has happened, but I've never stopped trusting you. I pray, Abba Father, that this humble effort to tell my story pleases you and blesses many. Amen.

DON PIPER
FEBRUARY 2004

Don with sons Chris and Joe in 1982.

PROLOGUE

I died on January 18, 1989.
Paramedics reached the scene of the accident within minutes. They found no pulse and declared me dead. They covered me with a tarp so that onlookers wouldn't stare at me while they attended to the injuries of the others. I was completely unaware of the paramedics or anyone else around me.

Immediately after I died, I went straight to heaven.

While I was in heaven, a Baptist preacher came on the accident scene. Even though he knew I was dead, he rushed to my lifeless body and prayed for me. Despite the scoffing of the Emergency Medical Technicians (EMTs), he refused to stop praying.

At least ninety minutes after the EMTs pronounced me dead, God answered that man's prayers.

I returned to earth.

This is my story.

THE ACCIDENT

That is why we can say with confidence,
"The Lord is my helper,
so I will not be afraid.
What can mere mortals do to me?"

HEBREWS 13:6

The Baptist General Convention of Texas (BGCT) holds annual statewide conferences. In January 1989, they chose the north shore of Lake Livingston where the Union Baptist Association, composed of all Baptist churches in the greater Houston area, operates a large conference center called Trinity Pines. The conference focused on church growth, and I went because I was seriously considering starting a new church.

The conference started on Monday and was scheduled to end with lunch on Wednesday. On Tuesday night, I joined a BGCT executive and friend named J. V. Thomas for a long walk. J. V. had become a walker after his heart attack, so we exercised together the last night of the conference.

Months earlier, I had begun thinking that it was time for me to start a new congregation. Before embarking on such a venture, I wanted as much information as I could get. I knew that J. V. had as much experience and knowledge about new church development as anyone in the BGCT. Because he had started many successful churches in the state, most of us recognized him as the expert. As we walked together that night, we talked about my starting a new church, when to do it, and where to plant it. I wanted to know the hardships as well as the pitfalls to avoid. He answered my seemingly endless questions and raised issues I hadn't thought about.

We walked and talked for about an hour. Despite the cold, rainy weather, we had a wonderful time together. J. V. remembers that time well.

So do I, but for a different reason: It would be the last time I would ever walk normally.

_____ ᏩᏇ _____

On Wednesday morning the weather worsened. A steady rain fell. Had the temperature been only a few degrees colder, we couldn't have traveled, because everything would have been frozen.

The morning meetings started on time. The final speaker did something Baptist preachers almost never do—he finished early. Instead of lunch, the staff at Trinity Pines served us brunch at about ten thirty. I had packed the night before, so everything was stowed in my red 1986 Ford Escort.

As soon as we finished brunch, I said good-bye to all my friends and got into my car to drive back to the church where I was on staff, South Park Baptist Church in Alvin, a Houston bedroom community.

398

When I started the engine, I remembered that only three weeks earlier I had received a traffic ticket for not wearing a seat belt. I had been on my way to preach for a pastor friend who was going to have throat surgery. A Texas trooper had caught me. That ticket still lay on the passenger seat, reminding me to pay it as soon as I returned to Alvin. Until I received the ticket, I had not usually worn a seat belt, but after that I changed my ways.

When I looked at that ticket I thought, *I don't want to be stopped again.* So I carefully fastened my seat belt. That small act would be a crucial decision.

There were two ways to get back to Houston and on to Alvin. As soon as I reached the gates of Trinity Pines, I had to choose either to drive through Livingston and down Highway 59 or to head west to Huntsville and hit I-45, often called the Gulf Freeway. Each choice is probably about the same distance. Every other time to and from Trinity Pines I had driven Highway 59. That morning I decided to take the Gulf Freeway.

I was relieved that we had been able to leave early. It was only a few minutes after 11:00, so I could get back to the church by 2:00. The senior minister had led a group to the Holy Land and left me responsible for our midweek service at South Park Church. He had also asked me to preach for the next two Sundays. That night was a prayer meeting, which required little preparation, but I needed to work on my sermon for the following Sunday morning.

Before I left Alvin, I had written a draft for the first sermon titled "I Believe in a Great God." As I drove, I planned to glance over the sermon and evaluate what I had written so far.

Many times since then I've thought about my decision to take the Gulf Freeway. It's amazing how we pay no attention to simple decisions at the time they're made. Yet I would remind myself that even the smallest decisions often hold significant consequences. This was one of those choices.

I pulled out of Trinity Pines, turned right, and headed down Texas Highway 19. That would take me to Huntsville and intersect with I-45, leading to Houston. I didn't have to drive far before I reached Lake Livingston, a man-made lake, created by damming the Trinity River. What was once a riverbed is now a large, beautiful lake. Spanning Lake Livingston is a two-lane highway whose roadbed has been built up above the level of the lake. The road has no shoulders, making it extremely narrow. I would have to drive across a long expanse of water on that narrow road until I reached the other side. I had no premonitions about the trip, although I was aware of the road's lack of shoulders.

At the end of the highway across the lake is the original bridge over the Trinity River. Immediately after the bridge, the road rises sharply, climbing the bluff above the Trinity's riverbed. This sharp upturn makes visibility a problem for drivers in both directions.

This was my first time to see the bridge, and it looked curiously out of place. I have no idea of the span, but the bridge is quite long. It's an old bridge with a massive, rusty steel superstructure. Other than the immediate road ahead, I could see little, and I certainly didn't glimpse any other traffic. It was a dangerous bridge, and as I would learn later, several accidents had occurred on it. (Although no longer used, the bridge is still there. The state built another one beside it.)

I drove at about fifty miles an hour because it was, for me, uncharted territory. I braced my shoulders against the chill inside the car. The wind made the morning seem even colder than it was. The steady rain had turned into a cloudburst. I would be happy to finally reach Alvin again. About 11:45 A.M., just before I cleared the east end of the bridge, an eighteen-wheeler driven by an inmate, a trusty at the Texas Department of Corrections, weaved across the center line and hit my car head-on. The truck sandwiched my small car between the bridge railing and the driver's side of the truck. All those wheels went right on top of my car and smashed it.

I remember parts of the accident, but most of my information came from the accident report and people at the scene.

From the description I've received from witnesses, the truck then veered off to the other side of the narrow bridge and sideswiped two other cars. They were in front of the truck and had already passed me going in the opposite direction. The police record says that the truck was driving fast—at least sixty miles an hour—when it struck my car. The inexperienced driver finally brought the truck to a stop almost at the end of the bridge.

A young Vietnamese man was in one vehicle that was hit, and an elderly Caucasian man was in the other. Although shaken up, both drivers suffered only minor cuts and bruises. They refused help, so the paramedics transported neither man to the hospital.

Because of the truck's speed, the accident report states that the impact was about 110 miles an hour. That is, the truck struck me while going sixty miles an hour, and I was carefully cruising along at fifty. The inmate received a citation for failure to control his vehicle and speeding. Information later came out that the inmate wasn't licensed to drive the truck. At the prison, supervisors had asked for volunteers to drive their truck to pick up food items and bring them back. Because he was the only volunteer, they let him drive their supply truck. Two guards followed close behind him in another state-owned pickup.

After the accident, the truck driver didn't have a scratch on him. The prison truck received little damage. However, the heavy vehicle had crushed my Ford and pushed it from the narrow road. Only the bridge railing stopped my car from going into the lake.

According to those who were at the scene, the guards called for medical backup from the prison, and they arrived a few minutes later. Someone examined me, found no pulse, and declared that I had been killed instantly.

I have no recollection of the impact or anything that happened afterward.

In one powerful, overwhelming second, I died.

2
MY TIME
IN HEAVEN

He was afraid and said, "How awesome is this place! This is none other than the house of God; this is the gate of heaven."

GENESIS 28:17

When I died, I didn't flow through a long, dark tunnel. I had no sense of fading away or of coming back. I never felt my body being transported into the light. I heard no voices calling to me or anything else. Simultaneous with my last recollection of seeing the bridge and the rain, a light enveloped me, with a brilliance beyond earthly comprehension or description. Only that.

In my next moment of awareness, I was standing in heaven.

Joy pulsated through me as I looked around, and at that moment I became aware of a large crowd of people. They stood in front of a brilliant, ornate gate. I have no idea how far away they were; such things as distance didn't matter. As the crowd rushed toward me, I didn't see Jesus, but I did see people I had known. As they surged toward me, I knew instantly that all of them had died during my lifetime. Their presence seemed absolutely natural.

They rushed toward me, and every person was smiling, shouting, and praising God. Although no one said so, intuitively I knew they were my celestial welcoming committee. It was as if they had all gathered just outside heaven's gate, waiting for me.

The first person I recognized was Joe Kulbeth, my grandfather. He looked exactly as I remembered him, with his shock of white hair and what I called a big banana nose. He stopped momentarily and stood in front of me. A grin covered his face. I may have called his name, but I'm not sure.

"Donnie!" (That's what my grandfather always called me.) His eyes lit up, and he held out his arms as he took the last steps toward me. He embraced me, holding me tightly. He was once again the robust, strong grandfather I had remembered as a child.

I'd been with him when he suffered a heart attack at home and had ridden with him in the ambulance. I had been standing just outside the emergency room at the hospital when the doctor walked out and faced me. He shook his head and said softly, "We did everything we could."

My grandfather released me, and as I stared into his face, an ecstatic bliss overwhelmed me. I didn't think about his heart attack or his death, because I couldn't get past the joy of our reunion. How either of us reached heaven seemed irrelevant.

I have no idea why my grandfather was the first person I saw. Perhaps it had something to do with my being there when

404

he died. He wasn't one of the great spiritual guides of my life, although he certainly influenced me positively in that way.

After being hugged by my grandfather, I don't remember who was second or third. The crowd surrounded me. Some hugged me and a few kissed my cheek, while others pumped my hand. Never had I felt more loved.

One person in that greeting committee was Mike Wood, my childhood friend. Mike was special because he invited me to Sunday school and was influential in my becoming a Christian. Mike was the most devoted young Christian I knew. He was also a popular kid and had lettered four years in football, basketball, and track and field, an amazing feat. He also became a hero to me, because he lived the Christian lifestyle he often talked about. After high school, Mike received a full scholarship to Louisiana State University. When he was nineteen, Mike was killed in a car wreck. It broke my heart when I heard about his death, and it took me a long time to get over it. His death was the biggest shock and most painful experience I'd had up to that time in my life.

When I attended his funeral, I wondered if I would ever stop crying. I couldn't understand why God had taken such a dedicated disciple. Through the years since then, I had never been able to forget the pain and sense of loss. Not that I thought of him all the time, but when I did, sadness came over me.

Now I saw Mike in heaven. As he slipped his arm around my shoulder, my pain and grief vanished. Never had I seen Mike smile so brightly. I still didn't know why, but the joyousness of the place wiped away any questions. Everything felt blissful. Perfect.

More and more people reached for me and called me by name. I felt overwhelmed by the number of people who had come to welcome me to heaven. There were so many of them, and I had never imagined anyone being as happy as they all were. Their faces radiated a serenity I had never seen on earth. All were full of life and expressed radiant joy.

Time had no meaning. However, for clarity, I'll relate this experience in terms that refer to time.

I saw my great-grandfather, heard his voice, and felt his embrace as he told me how excited he was that I had come to join them. I saw Barry Wilson, who had been my classmate in high school but later drowned in a lake. Barry hugged me, and his smile radiated a happiness I didn't know was possible. He and everyone that followed praised God and told me how excited they were to see me and to welcome me to heaven and to the fellowship they enjoyed.

Just then, I spotted two teachers who had loved me and often talked to me about Jesus Christ. As I walked among them, I became aware of the wide variety of ages—old and young and every age in-between. Many of them hadn't known each other on earth, but each had influenced my life in some way. Even though they hadn't met on earth, they seemed to know each other now.

As I try to explain this, my words seem weak and hardly adequate, because I have to use earthly terms to refer to unimaginable joy, excitement, warmth, and total happiness. Everyone continually embraced me, touched me, spoke to me, laughed, and praised God. This seemed to go on for a long time, but I didn't tire of it.

My father is one of eleven children. Some of his brothers and sisters had as many as thirteen children. When I was a kid, our family reunions were so huge we rented an entire city park in Monticello, Arkansas. We Pipers are affectionate, with a lot of hugging and kissing whenever we come together. None of those earthly family reunions, however, prepared me for the sublime gathering of saints I experienced at the gates of heaven.

Those who had gathered at Monticello were some of the same people waiting for me at the gates of heaven. Heaven was many things, but without a doubt, it was the greatest family reunion of all.

Everything I experienced was like a first-class buffet for the senses. I had never felt such powerful embraces or feasted my eyes on such beauty. Heaven's light and texture defy earthly eyes or explanation. Warm, radiant light engulfed me. As I looked around, I could hardly grasp the vivid, dazzling colors. Every hue and tone surpassed anything I had ever seen.

With all the heightened awareness of my senses, I felt as if I had never seen, heard, or felt anything so real before. I don't recall that I tasted anything, yet I knew that if I had, that too would have been more glorious than anything I had eaten or drunk on earth. The best way I can explain it is to say that I felt as if I were in another dimension. Never, even in my happiest moments, had I ever felt so fully alive. I stood speechless in front of the crowd of loved ones, still trying to take in everything. Over and over I heard how overjoyed they were to see me and how excited they were to have me among them. I'm not sure if they actually said the words or not, but I knew they had been waiting and expecting me, yet I also knew that in heaven there is no sense of time passing.

I gazed at all the faces again as I realized that they all had contributed to my becoming a Christian or had encouraged me in my growth as a believer. Each one had affected me positively. Each had spiritually impacted me in some way and helped make me a better disciple. I knew—again one of those things I knew without being aware of how I had absorbed that information—that because of their influence I was able to be present with them in heaven.

We didn't talk about what they had done for me. Our conversations centered on the joy of my being there and how happy they were to see me.

Still overwhelmed, I didn't know how to respond to their welcoming words. "I'm happy to be with you," I said, and even those words couldn't express the utter joy of being surrounded and embraced by all those people I loved.

I wasn't conscious of anything I'd left behind and felt no regrets about leaving family or possessions. It was as if God had removed anything negative or worrisome from my consciousness, and I could only rejoice at being together with these wonderful people.

They looked exactly as I once knew them—although they were more radiant and joyful than they'd ever been on earth.

My great-grandmother, Hattie Mann, was Native American. As a child I saw her only after she had developed osteoporosis. Her head and shoulders were bent forward, giving her a humped appearance. I especially remember her extremely wrinkled face. The other thing that stands out in my memory is that she had false teeth—which she didn't wear often. Yet when she smiled at me in heaven, her teeth sparkled. I knew they were her own, and when she smiled, it was the most beautiful smile I had ever seen.

Then I noticed something else—she wasn't slumped over. She stood strong and upright, and the wrinkles had been erased from her face. I have no idea what age she was, and I didn't even think about that. As I stared at her beaming face, I sensed that age has no meaning in heaven.

Age expresses time passing, and there is no time there. All of the people I encountered were the same age they had been the last time I had seen them—except that all the ravages of living on earth had vanished. Even though some of their features may not have been considered attractive on earth, in heaven every feature was perfect, beautiful, and wonderful to gaze at.

Even now, years later, I can sometimes close my eyes and see those perfect countenances and smiles that surprised me with the most human warmth and friendliness I've ever witnessed. Just being with them was a holy moment and remains a treasured hope.

When I first stood in heaven, they were still in front of me and came rushing toward me. They embraced me, and no matter which direction I looked, I saw someone I had loved and who had loved me. They surrounded me, moving around so that everyone had a chance to welcome me to heaven.

I felt loved—more loved than ever before in my life. They didn't say they loved me. I don't remember what words they spoke. When they gazed at me, I *knew* what the Bible means by perfect love. It emanated from every person who surrounded me.

I stared at them, and as I did I felt as if I absorbed their love for me. At some point, I looked around and the sight overwhelmed me. Everything was brilliantly intense. Coming out from the gate—a short distance ahead—was a brilliance that was brighter than the light that surrounded us, utterly luminous. As soon as I stopped gazing at the people's faces, I realized that everything around me glowed with a dazzling intensity. In trying to describe the scene, words are totally inadequate, because human words can't express the feelings of awe and wonder at what I beheld.

Everything I saw glowed with intense brightness. The best I can describe it is that we began to move toward that light. No one said it was time to do so, and yet we all started forward at the same time. As I stared ahead, everything seemed to grow taller—like a gentle hill that kept going upward and never stopped. I had expected to see some darkness behind the gate, but as far ahead as I could see, there was absolutely nothing but intense, radiant light.

By contrast, the powerful light I had encountered when I met my friends and loved ones paled into darkness as the radiance and iridescence in front of me increased. It was as if each step I took intensified the glowing luminosity. I didn't know how it could get more dazzling, but it did. It would be like cracking open the door of a dark room and walking into the brightness of a noonday sun. As the door swings open, the full rays of the sun burst forth, and we're momentarily blinded.

I wasn't blinded, but I was amazed that the luster and intensity continually increased. Strange as it seems, as brilliant as everything was, each time I stepped forward, the splendor increased. The farther I walked, the brighter the light. The light engulfed me, and I had the sense that I was being ushered into the presence of God. Although our earthly eyes must gradually adjust to light or darkness, my heavenly eyes saw with absolute ease. In heaven, each of our senses is immeasurably heightened to take it all in. And what a sensory celebration!

A holy awe came over me as I stepped forward. I had no idea what lay ahead, but I sensed that with each step I took, it would grow more wondrous.

Then I heard the music.

3
HEAVENLY MUSIC

Then I looked again, and I heard the singing of thousands and millions of angels around the throne and the living beings and the elders.

REVELATION 5:11

As a young boy I spent a lot of time out in the country and woods. When walking through waist-high dried grass, I often surprised a covey of birds and flushed them out of their nests on the ground. A whooshing sound accompanied their wings as they flew away.

My most vivid memory of heaven is what I heard. I can only describe it as a holy swoosh of wings.

But I'd have to magnify that thousands of times to explain the effect of the sound in heaven.

It was the most beautiful and pleasant sound I've ever heard, and it didn't stop. It was like a song that goes on forever. I felt awestruck, wanting only to listen. I didn't just hear music. It seemed as if I were part of the music—and it played in and through my body. I stood still, and yet I felt embraced by the sounds.

As aware as I became of the joyous sounds and melodies that filled the air, I wasn't distracted. I felt as if the heavenly concert permeated every part of my being, and at the same time I focused on everything else around me.

I never saw anything that produced the sound. I had the sense that whatever made the heavenly music was just above me, but I didn't look up. I'm not sure why. Perhaps it was because I was so enamored with the people around me, or maybe it was because my senses were so engaged that I feasted on everything at the same time. I asked no questions and never wondered about anything. Everything was perfect. I sensed that I knew everything and had no questions to ask.

Myriads of sounds so filled my mind and heart that it's difficult to explain them. The most amazing one, however, was the angels' wings. I didn't see them, but the sound was a beautiful, holy melody with a cadence that seemed never to stop. The swishing resounded as if it was a form of never-ending praise. As I listened I simply *knew* what it was.

A second sound remains, even today, the single, most vivid memory I have of my entire heavenly experience. I call it music, but it differed from anything I had ever heard or ever expect to hear on the earth. The melodies of praise filled the atmosphere. The nonstop intensity and endless variety overwhelmed me.

The praise was unending, but the most remarkable thing to me was that hundreds of songs were being sung at the same time—all of them worshiping God. As I approached the large, magnificent gate, I heard them from every direction and realized that each voice praised God. I write *voice,* but it was more than that. Some sounded instrumental, but I wasn't sure—and I wasn't concerned. Praise was everywhere, and all of it was musical, yet comprised of melodies and tones I'd never experienced before.

"Hallelujah!" "Praise!" "Glory to God!" "Praise to the King!" Such words rang out in the midst of all the music. I don't know if angels were singing them or if they came from humans. I felt so awestruck and caught up in the heavenly mood that I didn't look around. My heart filled with the deepest joy I've ever experienced. I wasn't a participant in the worship, yet I felt as if my heart rang out with the same kind of joy and exuberance.

If we played three CDs of praise at the same time, we'd have a cacophony of noise that would drive us crazy. This was totally different. Every sound blended, and each voice or instrument enhanced the others.

As strange as it may seem, I could clearly distinguish each song. It sounded as if each hymn of praise was meant for me to hear as I moved inside the gates.

Many of the old hymns and choruses I had sung at various times in my life were part of the music—along with hundreds of songs I had never heard before. Hymns of praise, modern-sounding choruses, and ancient chants filled my ears and brought not only a deep peace but the greatest feeling of joy I've ever experienced.

As I stood before the gate, I didn't think of it, but later I realized that I didn't hear such songs as "The Old Rugged Cross" or "The Nail-Scarred Hand." None of the hymns that filled the air were about Jesus' sacrifice or death. I heard no sad songs and instinctively knew that there are no sad songs in heaven. Why would there be? All were praises about Christ's reign as King of Kings and our joyful worship for all he has done for us and how wonderful he is.

413

The celestial tunes surpassed any I had ever heard. I couldn't calculate the number of songs—perhaps thousands—offered up simultaneously, and yet there was no chaos, because I had the capacity to hear each one and discern the lyrics and melody.

I marveled at the glorious music. Though not possessed of a great singing voice in life, I knew that if I sang, my voice would be in perfect pitch and would sound as melodious and harmonious as the thousands of other voices and instruments that filled my ears.

Even now, back on earth, sometimes I still hear faint echoes of that music. When I'm especially tired and lie in bed with my eyes closed, occasionally I drift off to sleep with the sounds of heaven filling my heart and mind. No matter how difficult a day I've had, peace immediately fills every part of my being. I still have flashbacks, although they're different from what we normally refer to as flashbacks. Mine are more flashbacks of the sounds than the sights.

As I've pondered the meaning of the memory of the music, it seems curious. I would have expected the most memorable experience to be something I had seen or the physical embrace of a loved one. Yet above everything else, I cherish those sounds, and at times I think, *I can't wait to hear them again—in person.* It's what I look forward to. I want to see everybody, but I know I'll be with them forever. I want to experience everything heaven offers, but most of all, I want to hear those never-ending songs again.

Obviously, I can't really know how God feels, but I find joy and comfort in thinking that he must be pleased and blessed by the continuous sounds of praise.

414

In those minutes—and they held no sense of time for me—others touched me, and their warm embraces were absolutely real. I saw colors I would never have believed existed. I've never, ever felt more alive than I did then.

I was home; I was where I belonged. I wanted to be there more than I had ever wanted to be anywhere on earth. Time had slipped away, and I was simply present in heaven. All worries, anxieties, and concerns vanished. I had no needs, and I felt perfect.

—⁓⁓—

I get frustrated describing what heaven was like, because I can't begin to put into words what it looked like, sounded like, and felt like. It was perfect, and I knew I had no needs and never would again. I didn't even think of earth or those left behind.

I did not see God. Although I knew God was there, I never saw any kind of image or luminous glow to indicate his divine presence. I've heard people talk about going inside and coming back out the gate. That didn't happen to me.

I saw only a bright iridescence. I peered through the gate, yearning to see what lay beyond. It wasn't an anxious yearning, but a peaceful openness to experience all the grace and joy of heaven.

The only way I've made sense out of that part of the experience is to think that if I had actually seen God, I would never have wanted to return. My feeling has been that once we're actually in God's presence, we will never return to earth again, because it will be empty and meaningless by comparison.

For me, just to reach the gates was amazing. It was a foretaste of joy divine. My words are too feeble to describe what took place.

415

As a pastor, I've stood at the foot of many caskets and done many funerals and said, "To be absent from the body is to be present with the Lord to those who love him and know him." I believed those words before. I believe them even more now.

—✦✦—

After a time (I'm resorting to human terms again), we started moving together right up to the gate. No one said it, but I simply knew God had sent all those people to escort me inside the portals of heaven.

Looming just over the heads of my reception committee stood an awesome gate interrupting a wall that faded out of sight in both directions. It struck me that the actual entrance was small in comparison to the massive gate itself. I stared, but I couldn't see the end of the walls in either direction. As I gazed upward, I couldn't see the top either.

One thing did surprise me: On earth, whenever I thought of heaven, I anticipated that one day I'd see a gate made of pearls, because the Bible refers to the gates of pearl. The gate wasn't made of pearls, but was pearlescent—perhaps *iridescent* may be more descriptive. To me, it looked as if someone had spread pearl icing on a cake. The gate glowed and shimmered.

I paused and stared at the glorious hues and shimmering shades. The luminescence dazzled me, and I would have been content to stay at that spot. Yet I stepped forward as if being escorted into God's presence.

I paused just outside the gate, and I could see inside. It was like a city with paved streets. To my amazement, they had been constructed of literal gold. If you imagine a street paved with

416

gold bricks, that's as close as I can come to describing what lay inside the gate.

Everything I saw was bright—the brightest colors my eyes had ever beheld—so powerful that no earthly human could take in this brilliance.

In the midst of that powerful scene, I continued to step closer to the gate and assumed that I would go inside. My friends and relatives were all in front of me, calling, urging, and inviting me to follow.

Then the scene changed. I can explain it only by saying that instead of their being in front of me, they were beside me. I felt that they wanted to walk beside me as I passed through the iridescent gate.

Sometimes people have asked me, "How did you move? Did you walk? Did you float?" I don't know. I just moved along with that welcoming crowd. As we came closer to the gate, the music increased and became even more vivid. It would be like walking up to a glorious event after hearing the faint sounds and seeing everything from a distance. The closer we got, the more intense, alive, and vivid everything became. Just as I reached the gate, my senses were even more heightened, and I felt deliriously happy.

I paused—I'm not sure why—just outside the gate. I was thrilled at the prospect and wanted to go inside. I knew everything would be even more thrilling than what I had experienced so far. At that very moment I was about to realize the yearning of every human heart. I was in heaven and ready to go in through the pearlescent gate.

During that momentary pause, something else changed. Instead of just hearing the music and the thousands of voices praising God, I had become part of the choir. I was one with them, and

417

they had absorbed me into their midst. I had arrived at a place I had wanted to visit for a long time; I lingered to gaze before I continued forward.

Then, just as suddenly as I had arrived at the gates of heaven, I left them.

FROM HEAVEN TO EARTH

4

Even when I walk
    through the dark valley of death,
I will not be afraid,
    for you are close beside me.
Your rod and your staff
    protect and comfort me.

PSALM 23:4

The EMTs pronounced me dead as soon as they arrived at the scene. They stated that I died instantly. According to the report, the collision occurred at 11:45 a.m. The EMTs became so busy working with the others involved, that it was about 1:15 p.m. before they were ready to move me. They checked for a pulse once again.

I was still dead.

Above: Don's Ford Escort after the accident. The roof was removed to extract Don and was laid back on top after the car arrived at the wrecking yard. Below: The accident scene.

The state law said they had to pronounce me dead officially before they could remove my body from the scene of the accident. Unless they declared me dead, an ambulance would have to transport my body to a hospital. That county didn't have a coroner, but I learned later that a justice of the peace could declare me dead, and then they could remove my body.

Ambulances had come from the prison, the county, and Huntsville. Except for one, all of them left without taking back any patients. The last one was preparing to leave. From information I've pieced together, someone had arranged for an unmarked vehicle to take my body to a mortuary.

They had called for the Jaws of Life[1] to get me out of the smashed car. Because I was dead, there seemed to be no need for speed. Their concern focused on clearing the bridge for traffic to flow again.

When the truck came in at an angle and went right over the top of me, the truck smashed the car's ceiling, and the dashboard came down across my legs, crushing my right leg. My left leg was shattered in two places between the car seat and the dashboard. My left arm went over the top of my head, was dislocated, and swung backward over the seat. It was still attached—barely.

That left arm had been lying on the driver's side door, because I had been driving with my right hand. As I would learn later, the major bones were now missing, so my lower left arm was just a piece of flesh that held the hand to the rest of the arm. It was the same with the left leg. There was some tissue just above my knee that still fed blood to the calf and foot below. Four and a half inches of femur were missing and never found. The doctors have no medical explanation why I didn't lose all the blood in my body.

421

Glass and blood had sprayed everywhere. I had all kinds of small holes in my face from embedded glass. The steering wheel had pounded into my chest. Blood seeped out of my eyes, ears, and nose.

Just from seeing the results of the crash, the EMTs knew I had to have sustained massive head injuries and that my insides were completely rearranged. When he first felt no pulse, one of the EMTs covered me with a waterproof tarp that also blocked off the top of the car. They made no attempt to move me or try to get me out immediately—they couldn't have anyway, because it would have been impossible for them to drag or lift me out of the vehicle without the Jaws of Life.

One thing that sped help to the scene was that the two prison guards in the pickup truck immediately called for emergency assistance from the prison. Otherwise, we would have been too far away for any emergency vehicle to get to us quickly.

They examined the drivers of the other two cars; both of them were uninjured and refused medical attention. The prisoner who drove the truck sustained no injuries. As soon as the EMTs determined he was all right, they transported him back to the prison. Police halted all traffic on the bridge and waited for the ambulance to arrive. While they waited, traffic backed up for miles in both directions, especially the direction I had come from. It was only a narrow two-lane bridge, not wide enough for a car to turn around. Even if the waiting traffic could have turned around, they would have had to drive an extra forty or fifty miles around the lake to reach another road leading to their destination.

From the backed-up traffic, Dick and Anita Onerecker walked at least half a mile to the scene of the accident. Dick and Anita had started a church in Klein, which is north of Houston. Both had spoken at the conference I'd just attended. I'm not positive we actually met at Trinity Pines, although we may have. For years I had heard of Dick Onerecker, but that conference was the first time I had ever seen him.

On Wednesday morning, the Onereckers left Trinity Pines a few minutes before I did. By Houston standards, that January morning was extremely cold. As they sped along, Anita said, "I'm really chilled. Could we stop for coffee? I think that would warm me up."

Dick spotted a bait shop right on Lake Livingston, so they pulled over. Apparently, while they were buying coffee, I drove past them.

Many times afterward, Dick would bury his face in his hands and say, "You know that could easily have been us. It should have been us, but because we stopped and you drove past us, you got hit."

Before the Onereckers reached the bridge, the accident had occurred and traffic had started to back up. People got out of their cars and milled around, asking questions and sharing their limited information.

After Dick and Anita got out of their car, they asked fellow drivers, "What's going on up there?"

The word had passed down that there had been a serious auto accident. "A truck crashed into a car" was about all anyone knew.

Dick and Anita stood around a few minutes, but nothing happened, and more cars lined up behind them. Sometime between 12:30 and 12:45, they decided to walk to the accident site. When they saw a police officer, Dick said, "I'm a minister. Is there anybody here I can help? Is there anyone I can pray for?"

423

The police officer shook his head. "The people in those two cars," he said and pointed, "are shaken up a little bit but they're fine. Talk to them if you'd like."

"What about the other vehicle? The one with the tarp over it?"

"The man in the red car is deceased."

While Dick talked to the officer, Anita went over to the other vehicles. She gave her barely touched coffee to the old man.

Dick would later tell it this way: "God spoke to me and said, 'You need to pray for the man in the red car.'" Dick was an outstanding Baptist preacher. Praying for a dead man certainly ran counter to his theology. *I can't do that,* he thought. *How can I go over there and pray? The man is dead.*

The rain had become a light drizzle, but Dick was oblivious to his surroundings. Dick stared at the officer, knowing that what he would say wouldn't make sense. Yet God spoke to him so clearly that he had no doubt about what he was to do. God had told him to pray for a dead man. As bizarre as that seemed to him, Dick also had no doubt that the Holy Spirit was prompting him to act.

"I'd like to pray for the man in the red car," Dick finally said to the officer.

"Like I said, he's dead."

"I know this sounds strange, but I want to pray for him anyway."

The officer stared at him a long time before he finally said, "Well, you know, if that's what you want to do, go ahead, but I've got to tell you it's an awful sight. He's dead, and it's really a mess under the tarp. Blood and glass are everywhere, and the body's all mangled."

Dick, then in his forties, said, "I was a medic in Vietnam, so the idea of blood doesn't bother me."

"I have to warn you—" The man stopped, shrugged, and said, "Do what you want, but I'll tell you that you haven't seen anybody this bad."

"Thanks," Dick said and walked to the tarp-covered car.

From the pictures of that smashed-down car, it's almost impossible to believe, but somehow Dick actually crawled into the trunk of my Ford. It had been a hatchback, but that part of the car had been severed. I was still covered by the tarp, which he didn't remove, so it was extremely dark inside the car. Dick crept in behind me, leaned over the backseat, and put his hand on my right shoulder.

He began praying for me. As he said later, "I felt compelled to pray. I didn't know who the man was or whether he was a believer. I knew only that God told me I had to pray for him."

As Dick prayed, he became quite emotional and broke down and cried several times. Then he sang. Dick had an excellent voice and often sang publicly. He paused several times to sing a hymn and then went back to prayer.

Not only did Dick believe God had called him to pray for me but he prayed quite specifically that I would be delivered from unseen injuries, meaning brain and internal injuries.

This sounds strange, because Dick knew I was dead. Not only had the police officer told him but he also had checked for a pulse. He had no idea why he prayed as he did, except God told him to. He didn't pray for the injuries he could see, only for the healing of internal damage. He said he prayed the most passionate, fervent, emotional prayer of his life. As I would later learn, Dick was a highly emotional man anyway.

Then he began to sing again. "O what peace we often forfeit, O what needless pain we bear, all because we do not carry everything to God in prayer!"[2] The only thing I personally know

425

for certain about the entire event is that as he sang the blessed old hymn "What a Friend We Have in Jesus," I began to sing with him.

In that first moment of consciousness, I was aware of two things. First, I was singing—a different kind of singing than the tones of heaven—I heard my own voice and then became aware of someone else singing.

The second thing I was aware of was that someone clutched my hand. It was a strong, powerful touch and the first physical sensation I experienced with my return to earthly life.

More than a year would lapse before I understood the significance of that hand clasping mine.

5
EARTH TO HOSPITAL

But they were looking for a better place, a heavenly homeland.
That is why God is not ashamed to be called their God, for he
has prepared a heavenly city for them.

HEBREWS 11:16

I 'm not certain what the world record is for exiting a wrecked
car, but Dick Onerecker must have surely broken it that
Wednesday afternoon. When a dead man began to sing
with him, Dick scrambled out of that smashed car and raced
over to the nearest EMT.

"The man's alive! He's not dead! He's alive!"

Who would have believed him? A preacher had started to
pray for a man who had been dead for an hour and a half. Then
he dashed across the road shouting, "That man has come back
to life!"

The EMT stared.

"He's alive! The dead man started singing with me."

The words didn't make sense as Dick thought of them later, but he could only keep yelling, "He's singing! He's alive!"

"Oh really?" a paramedic asked.

"I'm serious, this man's alive."

"We're medical professionals. We know a dead guy when we see him. That guy is *dead*."

"I'm telling you, that man just sang with me. He's alive."

"The justice of the peace is on his way here." He explained that although they knew I was dead, they couldn't move my body until someone in authority actually declared me dead. "But I can tell you this much: He is dead." The man turned away from Dick and refused to go over to my car.

Several ambulances had already arrived and departed.

Dick walked up in front of the remaining ambulance and said to the driver, "That man is alive. Go look at him."

The EMT began to act as if he handled feebleminded people all the time. "Please, we know our business. That man is—"

"Listen to me! I'm going to lie down on this bridge, and if you don't come over here, you're going to have to run over me."

"He's dead."

"Then humor me. Just feel his pulse," Dick pleaded.

"Okay, we'll check on him for you," the man said, mumbling under his breath. He walked over to the car, raised the tarp, reached inside, and found my right arm. He felt my pulse.

Everyone leaped into action. They began trying to figure out how to get me out. They could have taken me out on one side, but it would have been without my left leg. There was no clearance from the dashboard between my left leg and the seat, so they would have had to amputate. My leg was barely hanging on to my body anyway. I'm not sure they could have gotten my right leg out either. The point is that even though they could have gotten me out without the equipment, they would have left some of me in the car. They decided to wait on the proper equipment. They got on the phone and ordered the Jaws of Life to hurry from Huntsville, which was at least thirty miles away. I'm sure they did whatever they could for me, but I remember nothing. I remained vaguely conscious of people moving around me, touching me, and talking. I heard voices, but I couldn't make sense of anything they said. Dick refused to leave me. He got back inside the car, where he was able to kneel behind me, and he continued to pray until the Jaws of Life arrived. Only after they lifted me into the ambulance did he leave my side. When the EMTs lifted me out of the car, I remember that it involved a number of men—at least six or seven. As they moved me, I heard them talking about my leg. One of them said something about being careful so that my left leg didn't come off.

My system was in shock, so I felt no pain—not then, anyway. That came later.

They laid me on a gurney and started to roll me toward the ambulance. A light mist sprayed my face, and I saw nothing except the superstructure of the bridge above me. I was unable to move my head. I heard people walking around and glass crunching under their feet. They kept their voices low, so I had trouble following what they were saying.

I remember thinking, *Something terrible has happened here, and I think it's happened to me.* Even when I knew they were moving me into the ambulance, I felt weightless.

I don't remember anything about the ambulance ride, but later I learned that we went to two hospitals, both of which were little more than rural clinics.

"There's nothing we can do for him," I heard one doctor say as he examined me. "He's not going to make it. You may have gotten him out of the car alive, but it won't do any good. He's past hope."

They put me back inside the ambulance and drove away. I vaguely remember when they pulled up at the Huntsville Hospital, a fairly large regional medical center. It was about 2:30 P.M.

By then the authorities had notified my wife, Eva. She teaches school, and someone had called the school to tell her about the accident. Someone else called the schools where our three children attended. Church members picked up our children and took them to their homes to keep them until they heard from Eva.

No one knew then that I had died hours earlier. For the first hours after I returned to earth, they had no idea how extensive my injuries were. Even though they knew nothing specific, church people began to pray for my recovery. They called others to join with them.

Eva found out I had died from Dick Onerecker almost two weeks after the accident on one of Dick's visits to see me in the hospital. It was only then that she understood just how bad it had been. Also, by that time our insurance agent, Ann Dillman, a member of South Park, had brought pictures of the wreckage after it had been moved from the bridge. Eva says it was quite some time before she really understood how bad it was. She says she probably didn't pay attention to the bad news on purpose because she was trying to focus on immediate matters at hand.

Our children, other family members, and friends then began to piece together just how horrendous the accident was and how close I came to not surviving it.

One of the EMTs said, "We're here now. You're going to be all right."

I was aware of being wheeled into the hospital. I stared uncomprehendingly at a large number of people who pulled back to make space and watched the gurney roll past them. Faces stared down at me, and our eyes met for a split second as the gurney kept moving.

They took me into a room where a doctor was waiting for me. It's strange, but the only thing I recall about the doctor who examined me was that he was bald. He spent quite a while checking me over. "Mr. Piper, we're going to do everything we can to save you," he must have said three times. "You're hurt bad, seriously hurt, but we'll do all we can." Despite his words, I later learned that he didn't expect me to survive. But he did everything he could to give me hope and urge me to fight to stay alive. Several people moved around me. They were obviously trying to save my life, but I still felt no pain. It was like living in some kind of twilight state where I could feel nothing and remained only vaguely aware of what went on around me.

"We have your wife on the phone," someone said. They patched her through on the telephone to the emergency room. A nurse laid the phone beside my ear, and I remember talking to Eva, but I can't recall one word either of us said.

Eva remembers the entire conversation. According to her, the only thing I said was, "I'm so sorry this happened."

"It's okay, Don. It's not your fault."

Over and over I kept saying, "I'm so sorry. I just wanted to come home. Please bring me home." In some kind of childlike

431

way, I suppose I felt that if I couldn't be in my heavenly home, I wanted to be back in my earthly one.

_____ (꒳◡꒳) _____

I was alert enough to know that they wanted to transport me on a Life Flight helicopter to Hermann Hospital Trauma Center in Houston. But they decided that the weather was too bad and the cloud ceiling too low, so their helicopter couldn't take off.

My condition was deteriorating rapidly, and they didn't know if I was going to survive the afternoon. Despite that, the medical team made a significant decision: They decided to put me back inside an ambulance for the eighty-mile trip to Houston. They didn't have the facilities to take care of me. Hermann Hospital was the only place for me if I was to have any chance to survive.

They brought around a new ambulance. It's amazing that as injured as I was—and they still thought I could "expire" at any second—I became aware of little things such as the fresh odors of a new vehicle, especially the fresh paint.

"You're our first patient," the attendant said as we drove away.

"What?"

"You're the first person to ever ride in this ambulance," he said. "We're going to take you to Houston. We'll get you there as fast as we can."

"How fast do I go?" the driver asked the attendant who sat next to me.

"As fast as you can."

"How fast is that?" the driver asked again.

"Put the pedal to the metal! We've got to get there—*now!*"

Before we started the trip, I still had felt no pain. I was in and out of consciousness. I felt weightless, as if my mind had no con-

432

nection with my body. However, about ten minutes down the road, a slight throbbing began. At first, I became aware of a tiny pain in my left arm. Then my left leg throbbed. My head started to ache. Within minutes I hurt in so many places, I couldn't localize any of it. My entire body groaned in agony and screamed for relief. The full force of the trauma invaded my body. It felt as if every part of my body had been wounded, punched, or beaten. I couldn't think of a single spot that didn't scream out in pain. I think I cried out but I'm not sure. Every beat of my heart felt like sledgehammers pounding every inch of my body.

"You've got to do something! Please!" I finally pleaded. That much I remember. "Medicine—just something to—"

"I've given you all I can."

"You've given me all you can?" His words didn't make sense. If they'd given me medication, why was I feeling so much pain? "Please—"

"I can't let you go unconscious," the attendant said. "You have to remain awake."

"Please—just something to—"

I couldn't understand why I had to remain awake. If they'd just knock me out, the pain would go away. "Please," I begged again.

"I'm sorry. I really am, but I can't give you anything else. You've already had enough to throw most people into a coma. You're a fairly big guy, but I just can't let you go unconscious."

I'm sure I whimpered, moaned, or even screamed several times during the rest of the torturous ride. The vehicle rocked back and forth, in and out of traffic, and the entire time the siren blared. It was the most painful, nightmarish trip of my life.

Even now I can close my eyes and feel the ambulance vibrating and bumping on the shoulder of the road as it took the curves.

One of the EMTs said something about rush-hour traffic just getting heavy, so I assumed it must be around 5:00. Momentarily, I wondered how it could be so late in the day.

The drive seemed interminable, although I think I passed out several times from the pain. We finally arrived at the emergency room in Houston at Hermann Hospital.

It was 6:20 P.M. Six and a half hours had passed from the time of the accident.

By the time I reached the hospital in Houston, thousands of people were praying. They spread the word so that members in hundreds of churches also prayed for my recovery. For the next few days, word spread about my injuries, and more people prayed. Over the years, I've met many of those who asked God to spare my life. Perhaps some of you reading this book prayed for my survival and recovery. I can only add that the prayers were effective: I lived, and I'm still alive.

As the EMTs lifted my gurney out of the ambulance, I spotted Eva's face. Next to her stood a deacon from our church. I felt as if they were looking at some lost puppy, given my pathetic appearance. They were amazed, gawking, but saying nothing.

Eva stared at me. Until that moment, I had been only vaguely aware of what was going on with my body. The pain had not abated, but I still had not reasoned out that I had been in an accident. It didn't occur to me that I was dying.

As I stared into her face, I recognized the anguish in her eyes. She probably said something to try to comfort me, I don't know. What stays with me is that I sensed her pain and that she feared I wouldn't live.

That's when I knew I must have been in really bad shape—and I was. My chest had already turned purple, and medics had bandaged almost every part of my body. Tiny pieces of glass were embedded in my face, chest, and head. I was aware that tiny shards had fallen out of my skin and rested on the gurney next to my head.

No one had to tell me that I looked hideous. Anyone who knew me wouldn't have recognized me. I wondered how Eva had known who I was.

My pain was off the scale. Once inside the trauma center, a nurse gave me a shot of morphine—and then followed up with several more shots. Nothing helped. Nothing dulled the pain.

Shortly after my arrival at Hermann, they sent me to surgery, where I remained for eleven hours. Under anesthesia, I finally felt no pain.

Our dear friend Cliff McArdle valiantly stayed with Eva throughout the night. Cliff, my best friend David Gentiles, and I had been ministry friends since our graduation from seminary and remain close to this day.

By the time I was conscious again, it was Thursday morning. When I opened my eyes, somehow I knew that I had become the first patient in a newly opened ICU pod. One nurse was cleaning my wounds while another was putting me into traction. I could feel that she was putting rods between my ankle and my arm. I heard myself scream.

"We've done an MRI on you," the doctor said. Until then I wasn't aware that he was also in the room. "You're very seriously injured, but the good news is that you have no head or thoracic injuries."

At the time, I didn't care where my injuries were. The throbbing pains were racing through my body. I hurt more than I thought was humanly possible.

I just wanted relief.

When Dick Onerecker came to see me two weeks after the accident, I had just been moved from the ICU to a hospital room. He told me about God telling him to pray for me and that he had done that for several minutes.

"The best news is that I don't have any brain damage or any internal injuries," I said.

Dick chuckled. "Of course you don't. That's what God told me to pray for, and God answered."

"You believed that? You believed that God would answer that prayer?"

"Yes, I did," he said. "I knew with all the other injuries you had incurred that God was going to answer my prayer."

It took a few seconds for me to absorb what he'd said. From the force and intensity of the impact, I would have had internal injuries. Even the doctor had commented—in amazement—that I had neither head nor thoracic injuries.

"I'll tell you this," I said. "I know I had internal injuries, but somewhere between that bridge and this hospital I don't anymore."

Tears ran down Dick's face, and he said, "I know. I wish I could pray like that all the time."

THE RECOVERY BEGINS

And we can be confident that he will listen to us whenever we ask him for anything in line with his will. And if we know he is listening when we make our requests, we can be sure that he will give us what we ask for.

1 JOHN 5:14–15

Pain became my constant companion. For a long time I would not know what it was like not to hurt all over my body.

Despite that, within a few days of the accident, I began to realize how many miracles had occurred. I refer to them as miracles—although some may call them fortunate circumstances—because I believe there are no accidents or surprises with God.

First, I wore my seat belt. I shamefully admit that I had not "bothered" to wear one until I got ticketed. That morning, I had consciously belted myself in.

Second, the accident happened on the bridge. What if it had happened on the open highway across the lake when I was headed toward the bridge? My car would have plunged down at least thirty feet into the lake, and I would have drowned.

Third, I had no head injuries. Anyone who saw me or read the medical report said it was impossible that I suffered no brain damage. (Eva still jokes that on occasion she's not so sure I didn't.) Just as bewildering to all the medical people was that the accident affected none of my internal organs. That fact defied all medical explanation.

Fourth, orthopedic surgeon Dr. Tom Greider, who was on duty at Hermann Hospital that day, saved my leg. Dr. Greider "just happened to be" one of the few experts in the United States who deals with such bizarre trauma. He chose to use a fairly new, experimental procedure, the Ilizarov frame. He performed the surgery one week after my accident. The implanted Ilizarov not only saved my leg, but also allowed them to lengthen the bone in my left leg after I had lost four inches of my femur in the accident. The femur is the largest bone in the human body and quite difficult to break.

When Dr. Greider examined me, he faced a choice. He could use the Ilizarov frame or amputate. Even if he chose to use the Ilizarov frame, there was no guarantee that I would not lose the leg. In fact, at that stage, he wasn't even certain I would pull through the ordeal. A less-skilled and less-committed doctor might have amputated, assuming it wouldn't make much difference because I would die anyway.

Fifth, people prayed for me. I have thousands of cards, letters, and prayer-grams, many from people I don't know in places I've never been who prayed for me because they heard of the accident. I've since had people tell me that this experience changed their prayer lives and their belief in the power of prayer.

On the night I entered Hermann Trauma Center, I was in surgery for eleven hours. During that operation, I had the broken bone in my right leg set. My left forearm had to be stabilized because two inches of each bone were missing. My left leg was put into traction because four and a half inches of femur were missing. During the operation, an air tube was mistakenly inserted into my stomach. This caused my stomach to inflate and my lungs to deflate. It would be several days before they discovered that this was the cause of the swelling in my stomach. Further complicating my breathing, I was unable to be elevated, and I developed pneumonia. I nearly died a second time.

Because of many bruises and the severity of my obvious wounds, my doctors hardly knew where to start. Other less serious problems became obvious weeks later. Several years passed before they discovered a fractured pelvis that they had missed initially.

I lay on my bed with needles everywhere, unable to move, dependent on the life-support apparatus. I could barely see over the top of my oxygen mask. During most of those days in the ICU, I was in and out of consciousness. Sometimes I'd wake up and see people standing in front of my bed and would wonder, *Am I really here or am I just imagining this?*

Monitors surrounded me, and a pulse oximeter on my finger tracked my oxygen level. Because I wasn't getting enough oxygen, the alarm went off often, bringing nurses racing into my room.

The ICU in Hermann is near the helipad; helicopters took off and landed at all hours of the day. When I was awake, I felt as if I were in a Vietnam movie. There were no clocks in the room, so I had no concept of time.

Other people lay in beds near me, often separated by nothing more than a curtain. More than once I awakened and saw orderlies carrying out a stretcher with a sheet over the body. As a pastor, I knew that many people don't leave the ICU alive.

Am I next? I'd ask myself.

Although I asked the question, the pain prevented my caring. I just wanted not to hurt, and dying would be a quick answer.

I had experienced heaven, returned to earth, and then suffered through the closest thing to hell on earth I ever want to face. It would be a long time before my condition or my attitude changed.

Nightmarish sounds filled the days and the nights. Moans, groans, yells, and screams frequently disrupted my rest and jerked me to consciousness. A nurse would come to my bed and ask, "Can I help you?"

"What are you talking about?" I'd ask. Sometimes I'd just stare at her, unable to understand why she was asking.

"You sounded like you're in great pain."

I am, I'd think, and then I'd ask, "How would you know that?"

"You cried out."

That's when I realized that sometimes the screams I heard came from me. Those groans or yells erupted when I did something as simple as trying to move my hand or my leg. Living in the ICU was horrible. They were doing the best they could, but the pain never let up.

"God, is this what I came back for?" I cried out many times. "You brought me back to earth for this?"

My condition continued to deteriorate. I had to lie flat on my back because of the missing bone in my left leg. (They never found the bone. Apparently, it was ejected from the car into the lake when my leg was crushed between the car seat and dashboard.) Because of having to lie flat, my lungs filled with fluid.

Still not realizing my lungs were collapsed, nurses and respiratory therapists tried to force me to breathe into a large plastic breathing device called a spirometer to improve my lung capacity.

On my sixth day, I was so near death that the hospital called my family to come to see me. I had developed double pneumonia, and they didn't think I would make it through the night.

I had survived the injuries; now I was dying of pneumonia. My doctor talked to Eva.

"We're going to have to do something," he told her. "We're either going to have to remove the leg or do something else drastic."

"How drastic?"

"If we don't do something, your husband won't be alive in the morning."

That's when the miracle of prayer really began to work. Hundreds of people had been praying for me since they learned of the accident, and I knew that. Yet, at that point, nothing had seemed to make any difference.

Eva called my best friend, David Gentiles, a pastor in San Antonio. "Please, come and see Don. He needs you," she said.

Without any hesitation, my friend canceled everything and jumped into his car. He drove nearly two hundred miles to see me. The nursing staff allowed him into my room in ICU for only five minutes.

Those minutes changed my life.

I never made this decision consciously, but as I lay there with little hope of recovery—no one had suggested I'd ever be normal again—I didn't want to live. Not only did I face the ordeal of never-lessening pain but I had been to heaven. I wanted to return to that glorious place of perfection. "Take me back, God," I prayed, "please take me back."

441

Memories filled my mind, and I yearned to stand at that gate once again. "Please, God."

God's answer to that prayer was "no."

When David entered my room, I was disoriented from the pain and the medication. I was so out of it that first I had to establish in my mind that he was real. *Am I hallucinating this?* I asked myself.

Just then, David took my fingers, and I felt his touch. Yes, he was real.

He clasped my fingers because that was all he could hold. I had so many IVs that my veins had collapsed; I had a trunk line that went into my chest and directly to my heart. I used to think of my many IVs as soldiers lined up. I even had IVs in the veins in the tops of my feet. I could look down and see them and realize they'd put needles in my feet because there was no place left on my body.

"You're going to make it," David said. "You have to make it. You've made it this far."

"I don't have to make it. I'm not sure . . . I . . . I don't know if I want to make it."

"You have to. If not for yourself, then hold on for us."

"I'm out of gas," I said. "I've done all I can. I've given it all I can. I don't have anything else to give." I paused and took several breaths, because even to say two sentences sapped an immense amount of energy.

"You have to make it. We won't let you go."

"If I make it, it'll be because all of you want it. I don't want it. I'm tired. I've fought all I can and I'm ready to die."

"Well, then you won't have to do a thing. We'll do it for you."

Uncomprehending, I stared at the intensity on his face.

442

"We won't let you die. You understand that, Don? We won't let you give up."

"Just let me go—"

"No. You're going to live. Do you hear that? You're going to live. We won't let you die."

"If I live," I finally said, "it'll be because you want me to."

"We're going to pray," he said. Of course, I knew people had been praying already, but he added, "We're going to pray all night. I'm going to call everybody I know who can pray. I want you to know that those of us who care for you are going to stay up all night in prayer for you."

"Okay."

"We're going to do this for you, Don. You don't have to do anything."

I really didn't care whether they prayed or not. I hurt too badly; I didn't want to live.

"We're taking over from here. You don't have to do a thing— not a thing—to survive. All you have to do is just lie there and let it happen. We're going to pray you through this."

He spoke quietly to me for what was probably a minute or two. I don't think I said anything more. The pain intensified—if that was possible—and I couldn't focus on anything else he said.

"We're going to take care of this." David kissed me on the forehead and left.

An all-night prayer vigil ensued. That vigil marked a turning point in my treatment and another series of miracles.

The pneumonia was gone the next day. They prayed it away. And the medical staff discovered the error with the breathing tube.

On that seventh day, in another long surgery, Dr. Greider installed the Ilizarov device so that I could sit up and receive

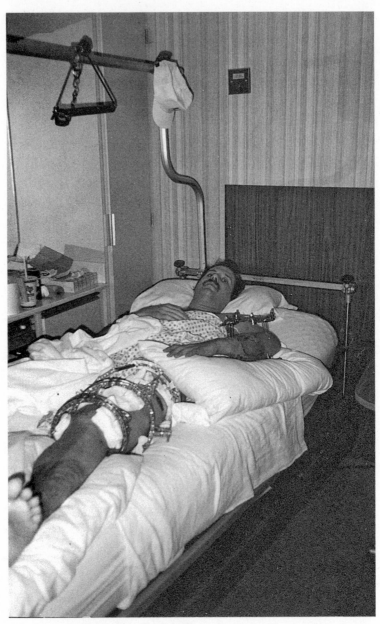

Don wearing the Ilizarov bone growth device.

breathing treatments. They also deflated my stomach, which allowed my lungs to inflate.

Normally, hospitals require six months of counseling before they will authorize the use of the Ilizarov frame. In my case, the medical staff could give Eva no guarantee that the experimental procedure would work. They also told her that using the Ilizarov frame would cause me considerable physical pain as well as extraordinary emotional and psychological distress. Worse, they warned that even after going through all of that, I might still lose my leg.

"This is extremely painful and takes months—maybe years—to recover," the surgeon said to Eva. Again he reminded her of the worst that could happen—that I might still lose the leg. "However, if we don't go this route, we have no choice but to amputate."

He quietly explained that if they amputated they would fit me with a prosthesis, and I'd have to learn to walk with it.

Eva had no illusions about the extent of my injury or how long I would have to endure excruciating pain. She debated the pros and cons for several minutes and prayed silently for guidance. "I'll sign the consent form," she finally said.

—⟨⟩⟨⟩—

The next morning, when I awakened after another twelve hours of surgery, I stared at what looked like a huge bulge under the covers where my left leg had been. When I uncovered myself, what I saw took my breath away. On my left leg was a massive stainless steel halo from my hip to just below my knee. A nurse came in and started moving around, doing things around my leg, but I wasn't sure what she did.

445

I became aware of Eva sitting next to my bed. "What is that?" I asked. "What's she doing?"

"We need to talk about it," she said. "It's what I agreed to yesterday. It's a bone-growth device. We call it a fixator. It's the only chance for the doctors to save your left leg," she said. "I believe it's worth the risk."

I'm not sure I even responded. What was there to say? She had made the best decision she could and had been forced to make it alone.

Just then, I spotted wires leading from the device. "Are those wires going through my leg?"

"Yes."

I shook my head uncomprehendingly. "They're going *through* my leg?"

"It's a new technique. They're trying to save your leg."

I didn't know enough to comment. I nodded and tried to relax.

"I believe it will work," she said.

I hoped she was right. Little did I know that nearly a year later I would still be staring at it.

DECISIONS AND CHALLENGES

7

Can anyone ever separate us from Christ's love? Does it mean he no longer loves us if we have trouble or calamity, or are persecuted, or are hungry or cold or in danger or threatened with death? (Even the Scriptures say, "For your sake we are being killed every day; we are being slaughtered like sheep.")

ROMANS 8:35–36

One of the most difficult things for me—aside from my own physical pain—was to see the reaction of my family members and close friends. My parents live in Louisiana, about 250 miles from Houston, but they arrived the day after my first surgery. My mother is a strong woman, and I always thought she could handle anything. But she walked into the ICU, stared at me, and then crumpled in a faint. Dad had to grab her and carry her out.

Her collapse made me aware of how pitiful I looked.

447

Most of those first days remain a blur to me. I wasn't sure if people really visited me or if I only hallucinated—and from what Eva and the nurses told me, I sometimes was delirious.

The hospital allowed visitors to come in each day, a few at a time. Even when they said nothing, their sad, pitying eyes made it clear to me how they felt. I write *clear to me* because I know how I perceived them. In retrospect, I may have been mistaken. I suspect I was so positive I would die—and I wanted to—that I saw in their eyes what I was feeling about myself.

Accurate or not, I felt as if they were staring at a mangled body and not a living person, that despite the assuring and comforting words they spoke, they expected me to die at any moment. I wondered if they had come to pay their last respects before I closed my eyes forever.

Though my pneumonia was gone, we still had to treat its aftermath. Nurses came in every four hours for respiratory therapy treatments. They beat on my chest and forced me to breathe through a plastic mouthpiece an awful-smelling, terrible-tasting stuff that was supposed to coat my lungs. This treatment would prevent the pneumonia from recurring and help restore my lungs. I'd wake up and see people coming in, and I'd think, *Oh no, here we go. They're going to make me breathe that stuff and pound on me and try to get the phlegm dislodged.* As painful as they were, the treatments worked. Dr. Houchins, the head of the Hermann trauma team, came in several times a day. What Dr. Houchins may have lacked in bedside manner, he made up in sheer bulldog determination not to lose any of his patients.

He demanded that I breathe. "Don't quit now. Don't quit. Keep trying." It wasn't just the words he spoke, but—as sick as I was—I felt as if he fought right alongside me. "Don't give up. Keep trying."

Often I didn't have the energy to breathe and just stopped trying.

I saw the pained expression on his face and then watched his features contort into an angry intensity. "Did you hear what I said? Do it! Now! Breathe and cough! Do it."

I shook my head. I just didn't have the strength to do anything more.

"This is not negotiable. Do this right now! Breathe!"

"I can't."

"All right, don't do it. You're dead. You're going to die if you don't do it. Can you get that into your mind?"

I didn't want to live, but something happened when he yelled at me.

I breathed.

Shortly after that, the staff figured out how to elevate my leg so I could sit up. Just to sit up was a great step forward. I didn't think I'd ever get to lie on my side or stomach again.

—⟡⟡—

Once while I was still in the ICU, it seemed as if every time I opened my eyes and blinked, within seconds someone thrust a spoon filled with food about six inches from my mouth.

"Just open up."

One time it was a man's voice.

I opened my eyes and stared. Holding the spoon was a burly man. He lifted my oxygen mask and gently poked the spoon into my mouth. "That's it, just take a bite."

I obeyed and swallowed while my drugged mind tried to figure out what was going on.

Slowly I realized that the voice belonged to Stan Mauldin, head football coach and athletic director of the Alvin High School Yellow Jackets. Our daughter would live with Stan and Suzan and their two children during my convalescence. Coach Mauldin had heard that because I wouldn't eat, I was losing weight at an alarming rate. (Although I had lost only a few pounds then, within my first six weeks in the hospital I lost nearly fifty pounds.)

As soon as Stan heard about the situation, he made time in his demanding schedule to show up at Hermann Hospital. He didn't just drop in to visit. He asked the nurses to give him my food, and he sat beside my bed until I awakened.

As soon as he realized I was fully awake, Stan shoveled in the food and talked while I did my best to chew and listen. That gentle act of sacrifice by a bear of a man was one of the most thoughtful acts I witnessed during my days of recovery. Stan epitomizes strength and tenderness combined in one exceptional person.

—◌◌◌—

I've referred to the Ilizarov frame, which may have sounded like a common procedure. It was far from that. Eva had to make a decision no one should have to make alone. She had to decide whether to allow the then-experimental Ilizarov process.

Initially this device was used to stretch legs. Its invention came about to help individuals who have a congenital condition where one leg is shorter than the other—some as much as twelve inches—and have to rely on wheelchairs, calipers, or crutches. The Ilizarov frame forces the bone in the leg to grow while keeping the surrounding tissue intact. The body can form new bone between gaps in response to the mechanical force of the Ilizarov frame.

450

The Ilizarov bone growth device is what they call an external fixator. A Siberian doctor named Ilizarov invented it.

Dr. Ilizarov experimented on sheep to develop a way to grow missing bones or lengthen congenitally short bones. For missing bone cases like mine, the application involves breaking a limb with a clean break. Wires about the size of piano wire are placed through the skin and bone, and they exit out the other side.

The femur Ilizarov device is anchored in the hip by rods about the size of pencils. The doctors drilled holes for four large rods from my groin to the side of my left hip. After they did that, I had at least thirty holes in my left leg. Many of them went completely through my leg and out the other side. The larger ones just went into the flesh, and rods were embedded in the pelvis. After about six months passed, I could actually see down inside my leg as the pinholes stretched out.

Every day someone would come in and turn the screws on the Ilizarov device to stretch the bones. Most of the time the nursing staff took on this task. After I came home, Eva did it. For nearly a year, my left femur bone would regrow and replace the missing piece. It's an ingenious device, although terribly painful, requiring an arduous, lengthy recovery. I called it "hideously wonderful."

Six rods also went through the top of my left arm and came out the other side. Big stainless steel bars were placed above and below the arm to stabilize it, because both forearm bones were missing. The rods were the size of a pencil and allowed Dr. Greider to harvest bones from my right pelvis and place them in my left forearm. The doctor explained that this was like taking core samples when drilling an oil well. They also harvested about thirty-two square inches of skin from my right

451

leg to place over the enormous wound in my left arm. Then they embedded a Teflon strip between the newly constructed bones in my forearm in order to prevent the new bones from adhering to each other—that is, attaching themselves and growing together.

Unfortunately for me, that part of the technique didn't work—the bones healed, but they attached themselves to each other. Consequently, I have no pronation or supination in my left arm—my arm does not straighten out at the elbow, and I can't turn palms up or palms down. When I extend my arm, my hand is always in a hand-shaking position. My hand cannot twist either right or left. I know all this seems barbaric, and at the time it felt like it. But like the Ilizarov, it works.

Yes, the Ilizarov device worked—and it was also the most painful process I endured as part of my recovery.

The stainless steel Ilizarov on my leg weighed about thirty pounds, and the external fixator on my arm probably weighed another twenty. Whether I was in my wheelchair (about eight months), on my rolling walker (three more months), or eventually my crutches (four more months), I carried that extra weight around for nearly a year.

Can you imagine the strange stares I received everywhere I went? People gasped and gawked at a man in a wheelchair with steel rods sticking out all over his body.

Virtually every time I made my routine visit to Dr. Greider's office in my wheelchair, the reaction of the other patients was universal. Though each wore casts or braces or walked on crutches, all of them would stare at me and my rods and halos. Then without fail, someone would say somewhat sardonically, "Wow, and I thought I was bad off." Occasionally, someone would even add, "After seeing you, I feel better." For a long time, I became the standard by which painful injury was judged.

I've often kidded others that because of all this "metalwork," if archaeologists discover my body years from now, they'll think they've found a new species! My anatomy has been completely rearranged.

Never again will I take simple physical ability for granted. During my recovery, even the tiniest movement was a miracle. Every time I relearned how to do something, it felt like an achievement.

Only later did I understand how hard Dr. Greider had worked to find a way to save my left leg and arm. I'll always be grateful that he didn't just give up on me.

My right knee was crushed, and I wore a cast on it for quite some time. They put a small, mesh basket around the kneecap so it would heal. My right arm was the only limb that didn't break.

Even with the success of the Ilizarov frame, however, the pain didn't leave—not for one minute.

I wonder how many times I asked, "How long?" I wanted to know how long I'd have to endure the device, how long before I'd know if it worked, how long before I'd walk again.

No one would—or could—give me an answer, but I kept asking anyway.

"A few months," was the usual answer.

"How few?" I persisted.

One of the doctors finally said, "Many months. Maybe longer."

"You mean possibly a few years?"

"Yes, perhaps years."

"And there's no guarantee that I'm going to be able to keep these limbs?"

"There's no guarantee. An infection could come on suddenly, and we'd be forced to remove your leg."

"You mean I could endure this for months and still end up with no leg?"

He nodded.

Obviously, that wasn't what I wanted to hear. Even though Eva had told me the same thing, denial must have set in. I kept seeking a guarantee that I would fully recover.

I wanted answers, but perhaps even more than that, I wanted assurance that I would be well. I wanted to be normal again. I wanted to be able to walk out of the hospital on my own two legs and go back to my former way of life. No one was willing—or able—to give me those assurances.

Many months passed, but one day I did walk back into that hospital and hug all those nurses.

During the months after I received the Ilizarov frame, I had other problems. I developed infections—several times. Each time, I faced the reality that it might rage through my body and I would wake up without my leg.

I also had infections after they released me. Three times I had to be rehospitalized, put in isolation, and receive massive amounts of antibiotics to cure the infections.

Even then, many nights I prayed, *God, take me back to heaven. I don't know why you brought me back to earth. Please don't leave me here.*

God's answer to that prayer was still "no."

I still don't know all the reasons, but in the months and years ahead, I slowly understood at least some of the reasons I had returned to earth.

The healing process had begun. As I lay in that hospital bed day after day, I slowly acknowledged that God had sent me back to earth. I couldn't figure out why I had to endure the physical suffering, but I kept thinking of the words of David Gentiles. He and others had cried out in prayer for me to live. Because God had answered them, there had to be a purpose in my staying alive.

Through days of intense agony, I would remember David's words. Sometimes the sense that God had a purpose in my being alive was all that kept me going.

I was in Hermann ICU for twelve days. Then I stayed four to five days in Hermann Hospital before they transferred me down the street to St. Luke's Hospital. Both hospitals are part of the world's largest medical center. I remained in St. Luke's for 105 days. Once I was home, I lay in bed for thirteen months and endured thirty-four surgeries. Without question, I am still alive because people prayed for me, beginning with Dick Onerecker and other people around the country, many of whom I've never met.

That's perhaps the biggest miracle: *People prayed and God honored their prayers.*

As I look back, I see how many people God used to save me. Dick Onerecker saved my life by his continued praying. Dr. Greider saved my leg and my arm and got me through that initial surgery. Dr. Houchins saved my life after the surgery because of his bulldog determination to keep me alive. The courageous nurses of the orthopedic floor of St. Luke's Hospital cared for me day and night. Each of them played a vital role.

I attribute leaving ICU alive to the prayers of David Gentiles and the others. "We're taking over from here. You don't have to do a thing to survive. We're going to pray you through this."

I knew I wasn't going to die.

God's people wouldn't let me.

8
PAIN AND ADJUSTMENTS

Don't be afraid, for I am with you. Do not be dismayed, for I am your God. I will strengthen you. I will help you. I will uphold you with my victorious right hand.

ISAIAH 41:10

E ven though they didn't realize it, visitors made my situation worse. They cared for me and wanted to express that concern. Because they cared, they did the most natural thing in the world—they visited my hospital room. That was the problem.

The constant flow in and out of my room exhausted me. I couldn't just lie there and allow them to sit with me or talk at me. Maybe I needed to function in my role as pastor or felt some kind of obligation to entertain them. I didn't want to hurt anyone's feelings by asking him or her to leave or not to come.

Many days, I smiled and chatted with them when all I really wanted to do was collapse. Sometimes the intense pain made it almost impossible for me to be a good host, but I still tried to be gracious. I kept reminding myself that they cared and had made an effort to see me.

Between friends, relatives, and church members, I felt as if a line stretched from the front door of the hospital to my room. Eva came in one afternoon and realized how much the visitors disturbed me. She chided me for allowing it.

I think she figured out that I wouldn't tell anyone not to come back, so she asked the nursing staff to cut back on the number of visitors they allowed. It didn't stop everyone from coming, but it did cut down the traffic in and out of the room.

Besides the pain and the flow of people in and out of my room, I lived in depression. A large part of it may have been the natural result of the trauma to my body and some of it may have been my reaction to the many drugs. I believe, however, that because I faced an unknown outcome and the pain never let up, I kept feeling I had little future to look forward to. Most of the time I didn't want to live.

Why was I brought back from a perfect heaven to live a pain-filled life on earth? No matter how hard I tried, I couldn't enjoy living again; I wanted to go back to heaven.

Pain has become a way of life for me since the accident, as I am sure it has for many. It's curious that we can learn to live with such conditions. Even now, on rare occasions when I am lying in bed after a good night's sleep, I will suddenly notice that I don't hurt anywhere. Only then am I reminded that I live in continuous pain the other twenty-three hours and fifty-five minutes of each day.

It took a while for me to realize how profoundly my condition affected my emotions.

I prayed and others prayed with me, but a sense of despair began to set in. "Is it worth all this?" I asked several times every day.

The doctors and nurses kept trying to push medications on me for my depression, but I refused. I'm not sure why. Perhaps because I had so much medicine in me, I didn't want any more. Besides, I didn't think more medicine would do any good.

I wanted to be free from my miserable existence and die. Obviously, I felt wholly unequipped to deal with that turn of events. I now know that I was a textbook depression case.

Soon everyone else knew it too.

"Would you like to talk to a psychiatrist?" my doctor asked.

"No," I said.

A few days later, one of the nurses asked, "Would you like me to call in a therapist? Someone you could talk to?"

My answer was the same.

Because I didn't want to talk to anyone, what I called "stealth shrinks" began to creep into my room.

"I see you've been in a very severe accident," one undercover psychiatrist said after reading my chart. He tried to get me to talk about how I felt.

"I don't want to talk about the accident," I said. The truth is, I couldn't. How could I possibly explain to anyone what had happened to me during the ninety minutes I was gone from this earth? How could I find words to express the inexpressible? I didn't know how to explain that I had literally gone to heaven. I was sure that if I started talking that way, he'd know I was crazy.

He'd think something had gone dreadfully wrong with my mind, that I had hallucinated, or that I needed stronger drugs to take away my delusions. How could I put into words that I had had the most joyful, powerful experience of my life? How could I sound rational by saying I preferred to die? I knew what was waiting, but he didn't.

I had no intention of talking to a psychiatrist (or anyone else) about what had happened to me. I saw that experience as something too intimate, too intense to share. As close as Eva and I are, I couldn't even tell her at that time.

Going to heaven had been too sacred, too special. I felt that talking about my ninety minutes in heaven would defile those precious moments. I never doubted or questioned whether my trip to heaven had been real. That never troubled me. Everything had been so vivid and real, I couldn't possibly deny it. No, the problem was I didn't want to share that powerful experience with anyone.

That didn't stop the psychiatrists from coming into my room and trying to help me. After a few times, they didn't tell me they were psychiatrists. It's humorous now, but the hospital psychiatrists were determined to help me. After I refused to talk to them, they would sneak into my room and observe me. Sometimes they came in while a nurse was working on me. Other times they came in and studied my chart and said nothing, and I assumed they expected me to start a conversation.

Often they'd walk in and say something like, "I'm Dr. Jones," but nothing else. The doctor might check my pulse and ask, "How's your stomach?" He'd examine my chart and ask pertinent questions. Eventually, he'd give himself away with a simple question such as "How do you feel today?"

"About the same."

"How do you really feel about all of this?" No matter how they varied the routine, they always asked how I *really* felt.

"You're a psychiatrist, aren't you?" I'd ask.

"Well, uh, actually, yes."

"Okay, what do you want to know? You want to know if I'm depressed? The answer is I'm very depressed. And I don't want to talk about it."

The conversations went on, but I've blotted most of them from my mind. Even though I knew Dr. Jones and the others were trying to help me, I didn't believe there was any hope. I hated being depressed, but I didn't know what to do about it.

The longer I lay in bed, the more convinced I became that I had nothing to look forward to. Heaven had been perfect—so beautiful and joyful. I wanted to be released from pain and go back.

"Why would anyone want to stay here after experiencing heaven?" I asked God. "Please, please take me back."

I didn't die, and I didn't get over my depression.

I didn't just refuse to talk to psychiatrists; I didn't want to talk to anyone about anything. I didn't want to see anyone. I would have been fine if no one visited me—or so I told myself.

In my depression, I just wanted to be left alone so I could die alone, without anyone trying to resuscitate me.

I also had enough pride as a professional and as a pastor that I didn't want anyone to see how bad off I was. I don't mean just the physical problems; I didn't want them to know about my low emotional state either.

When people did get into the room to see me, of course, their words and gazes made me feel as if they were saying, "You're the most pitiful thing I've ever seen."

I guess I was.

461

And so the depression continued. It would be a long time before God would give me another miracle.

_____

I was the father of three children, the husband of a wonderful wife, and until the accident, a man with a great future. I was thirty-eight years old when the accident happened and until then, the picture of health and in great physical shape. Within days after my accident, I knew I would never be that virile, healthy man again. Now I was utterly helpless. I couldn't do anything for myself, not even lift my hand. Deep inside, I feared I would be helpless for the rest of my life.

As an example of my helplessness, I had not had a bowel movement for the first twelve days in the hospital. Knowing my system would turn septic, they gave me an enema, but that didn't do much good.

I say "not much good" because I would pass a tiny amount and the nurse or nursing assistant would smile with delight.

One day I managed to squeeze out a tiny bit. "Oh, that's so good. We're so happy for you. Let's wait. Maybe there'll be more."

In my depression, I'd think, *This is the most pitiful experience in my life. I'm like a baby and everybody gets excited over a tiny bowel movement.*

I don't remember what I said to the nursing assistant, but I'm sure I wasn't pleasant.

She left the room. That was one of those rare times when no one was visiting. I was totally alone and glad for the peace and quiet.

Within minutes after the nurse left, the enema took effect.

I exploded. I had the biggest bowel movement I've ever had in my life. The odor overwhelmed me.

In my panic, I clawed through the sheet and my fingers finally found the call button. Seconds later, the young nursing assistant raced into the room.

"I'm so sorry, I didn't mean to do this," I said. "I'll help you clean it up." The words had no sooner left my mouth before I realized I couldn't help her. I felt terrible, helpless, and loathsome.

I started to cry.

"No, no, no, don't worry about a thing. We're just so happy that you did it. This is good because it means your system is beginning to work again."

In humiliation, I could only lie there and watch the poor young woman change everything. It must have taken her at least half an hour to clean up and then at least twice that long for the odor to vanish.

My embarrassment didn't leave me, even though my mind tried to tell me differently. I had barely taken in any food for twelve days and this was a real breakthrough. I, however, could only think that this was one of the most embarrassing events in my life.

As awful as it seemed to me, more embarrassing, helpless experiences caught up with me. I had to have a urinal; I couldn't wipe myself; I couldn't shave. I couldn't even wash my hair. They had to bring special devices to lay my head in and pour water over my hair and then drain it down a tube to a garbage can. In yet another act of incredible kindness, Carol Benefield, who had cut my hair for years, came to trim my hair several times while I was confined to my bed. For these sixty-mile round-trips, Carol would accept no money whatsoever.

Friends, family, and medical personnel found ways of providing for all of my physical needs, but I could only think of myself as being completely, utterly helpless. My right arm, the one that hadn't been broken, had so many IVs in it that they had a piece of wood taped to me so I couldn't bend the arm.

I had IVs everywhere. They ran into my chest and entered the tops of my feet. They lined up in a major tube that went directly to my heart through my chest. Many of my veins collapsed. I was so completely incapacitated they had to lift me off the bed with chains to change my bedding or do anything else that required moving me.

I was losing weight at an alarming rate, which scared the doctors. I just couldn't eat anything and atrophy had set in. During the nearly four months I stayed in the hospital, I lost about sixty pounds. Before the accident I had weighed 210, and I got down to less than 150. The only way they could determine my weight was to put me in a sling like a baby to lift me up off the bed and weigh me. They tried to coax me into eating and tempted me by preparing my favorite foods, but nothing tasted good. Just the smell of food nauseated me. I had no appetite. I tried to eat, I really did, but I couldn't handle more than a few bites.

I assumed that depression stopped me from eating, although I don't know if that was the cause. I do know that when I tried, I couldn't force myself to chew anything. I didn't even want to swallow.

They attached me to a morphine pump they called a PC. Whenever the pain was really bad, I pushed a button to give myself a shot. I had to have pain medication constantly. At first I tried to resist taking more painkillers, but the doctor rebuked me for that. He said that my body was tensing from the pain and that retarded my healing.

At night they gave me additional medication to try to make me sleep. I write *try* because the additional medicine didn't work. Nothing they did put me to sleep—not sleeping pills, pain shots, or additional morphine. I had no way to get comfortable or even to feel relieved enough from pain to relax.

I've tried to explain it by saying it this way: "Imagine yourself lying in bed, and you've got rods through your arms, wires through your legs, and you're on your back. You can't turn over. In fact, just to move your shoulder a quarter of an inch is impossible unless you reach up and grab what looks like a trapeze bar that hangs above your bed. Even the exertion to move a fraction of an inch sends daggers of pain all through your body. You are completely immobile."

Because I began to break out with bedsores on my back due to being in one position too long, the hospital finally provided a special waterbed that constantly moved. That did take care of the bedsores.

The only time I ever left the room was when they wheeled me down to X-ray, which was always an adventure. Because of all the metal parts and equipment on me, they had trouble figuring out how to x-ray me. Three or four men wore lead suits in the X-ray room and held the lens and plates behind my steel-encased limbs, because no machine was designed to x-ray those types of things.

That also meant that some days I spent two or three hours in X-ray while the technicians tried to figure out how to take a picture so the doctors could see whether the bones were knitting. They had no precedent for a case such as mine.

When someone came to wheel me to X-ray, he'd always say, "We're taking a trip down the hall."

That was all they had to say, because I knew what they meant. To distract myself as the gurney cruised down the long hallways, I played a game of connect-the-dots with the ceiling tiles. I started that the day I came back from the first surgery. I was probably hallucinating, but I remember the ICU unit was brand-new, and I was the only patient. When they brought me in, I was moaning and couldn't stop. Then I saw the ceiling tiles, and as I stared at them, it seemed as if they were running together and forming some kind of pattern that I couldn't figure out. In my mind, I began making pictures and designs out of them. As I did that, I'd also think, *I'm going completely crazy.* But I did it anyway. Eventually, connecting the dots became a form of distraction allowing me to focus, if only momentarily, on something other than my pain.

The worst daily torment took place when a nurse cleaned the pinholes where the wires went into my skin. All the nurses that treated me on the orthopedic floor, the twenty-first floor of St. Luke's Hospital, had to be taught how to clean those pinholes. Because they didn't want the skin to adhere to the wire, they had to keep breaking the skin when it attached itself—as it did occasionally. Then the nurse forced hydrogen peroxide down each pinhole to prevent infection. I could think of nothing worse to endure, and it happened every day.

That wasn't all. Four times a day, every six hours, they'd take an Allen wrench and turn screws on the device. The idea was that this would stretch the ends of the bones inside the leg and eventually cause the growing bone to replace the missing bone. The turn hurt beyond description, even though each turn was very slight, less than half a millimeter. It didn't matter whether it was day or night, every six hours someone came into my room to turn the screws.

As a pastor, I had visited many hospital rooms, including trips to the ICU. I had seen agony on many faces, and I had frequently winced in sympathy. Even so, I couldn't imagine anything on a day-to-day basis that could be more painful.

Perhaps the worst part for me was that I never slept. For eleven and a half months I never went to sleep—I just passed out. Even with megadoses of morphine, I was never pain free. When they decided it was time for me to go to sleep, a nurse injected me with three or four shots of either morphine or another sleeping medicine. I'd lie in bed, and no matter how much I told myself to relax, I couldn't. I fought the pain and then, apparently, I passed out. My next conscious moment would be an awareness of intense pain. I felt nothing else in between.

Eventually, family members and even hospital personnel left me alone because they knew I didn't have a functioning body clock. I had no sense of time, and I couldn't relax, because I was under such tension. If I made the slightest effort to move, a wire embedded in my flesh would tear my skin at the point of entry. I could move, but the wires didn't. With even the tiniest movement, excruciating pain slashed through my entire body.

After a while, I learned to live with that situation, but I never got used to it.

The first person I "met" (we never saw each other in person) for whom the Ilizarov frame was used for its original purpose was Christy. The Ilizarov procedure was created to lengthen bones for people born with congenital birth defects. However, the device could not be attached until the bones had stopped growing. Especially during adolescence, bones grow at a very rapid pace, so doctors must carefully choose the right time for the procedure.

Christy, a teenage girl, was in the room next to mine. She had been born with one leg shorter than the other. Once her bones had matured, she had chosen surgery to attach the Ilizarov frame to have her bones lengthened so that both legs would be of normal size.

Because Christy's surgery was elective, she had some idea about the pain and the length of recovery she would have to go through. For months, she had gone through extensive counseling, and her family knew how to take care of the wounds. They also knew approximately how long it would take and the commitment they had to make to care for her.

The difference between Christy and me was that she knew what she was getting into—at least to the extent that anyone can. I woke up with the device already attached. In my depressed state, that made me feel even worse. Even though I knew they had put the Ilizarov frame on me to save my leg, I could only see it as the major source of my agony.

Another problem arose, although a minor one. Even though we had different doctors, the same staff people came into Christy's room and mine to turn the screws. Sometimes the wrenches got misplaced, and the attendant couldn't find them in my room so they'd rush over to Christy's for hers. Or they'd come and borrow mine. Fortunately for both of us, our fixators were interchangeable and someone could borrow wrenches from one room to adjust screws in the other room.

That's how I first learned about Christy—the borrowing of wrenches. We never saw each other face-to-face, but we did see each other's doctor, and somehow that, plus our common problem, created a bond between us.

Christy and I shared something else—pain. Many times I heard her crying. I don't mean weeping, but a cry, or a scream, and sometimes just a low moan. She probably heard similar sounds from my room as well. I wasn't as likely to cry because that's not my nature. One of the nurses suggested it might be better if I did let go and scream. Even though she may have been right, I never did—at least not consciously.

When I was in control of my faculties, I never cried out. I had heard others scream from their pain and their cries disturbed me greatly. Also, I had learned to keep my hurts and emotions to myself. I believed at that time that moans, wails, and screams did no good. The only times I screamed, I was either unconscious or heavily medicated. I learned about those outbursts because other people told me.

Although Christy and I never met during the twelve weeks we lived next door to each other, we corresponded by sending letters back and forth, and the nurses willingly acted as our mail carriers.

I tried to encourage Christy. She told me her story and was very sympathetic to my accident. She was also a believer. We corresponded on that level as well.

In some of my worst moments of self-pity, however, I would think that when all the pain was over, Christy would be a normal young woman; I would never be normal again. She could play and run and do everything a normal teen did. Even then I knew I would never run again.

I had many, many times of self-pity, reminding myself that she chose her pain, while I had no warning and no options. She knew in advance what she was getting into; I had no idea. She was doing something that positively impacted the rest of her life;

469

I was doing something just to save my life. Yes, self-pity filled my mind many, many days.

Always, however, I came back to one thing: God had chosen to keep me alive. Even in my worst moments of depression and self-pity, I never forgot that.

Christy and I shared similar pain. We also shared a faith that reminded us that our loving God was with us in the most terrible moments of suffering. Just having her in the next room comforted me, because I'd think, *I'm not the only one; somebody else understands how I feel.*

That's when I began to think of being part of an exclusive fraternity. In the years since my release, I've met other members of this reluctant and small fellowship. Because I knew what it felt like to suffer, I could understand their pain, just as Christy had felt mine and I had understood hers.

—ᏮᎧ—

More than enduring, eventually I was able to do something doctors said I would never be able to do: I learned to walk again. I can stand on my own feet, put one foot in front of the other, and move.

They had warned me that because of the broken knee in my right leg, and the loss of the femur in my left (even with a replaced-and-stretched bone in place), I would not walk again, and if I did, I would be wearing heavy braces. More than once, I came close to losing my left leg, but somehow God took me through each crisis.

Therapy began on my arm about four weeks after the initial operation and on my legs two weeks after that.

470

About the same time, they put me in what I referred to as a Frankenstein bed. They strapped me to a large board and turned the bed so that my feet were on the floor and I was in a standing position, although still strapped to the bed. Two physical therapists placed a large belt around my waist and walked on either side of me. My legs had atrophied and grown extremely weak, so they helped me take my first steps. It took me days to learn to stand again so that I could put weight on my own legs. My equilibrium had changed because I had grown used to a horizontal position. I became incredibly nauseous each time they raised me into a vertical position. Days passed before I was used to that position enough to take my first step.

I didn't really learn to walk until after the hospital discharged me. A physical therapist came in every other day to help me. Six months would pass before I learned to walk on my own more than a few steps.

My doctor removed the Ilizarov device eleven and a half months after the accident. After that, I could use a walker and eventually a cane. I didn't walk without leg braces and a cane for a year and a half after the accident.

My accident occurred in January 1989. They removed the external metal work from my arm fixator in May, but they put internal metal plates down both of the bones of the forearm. Those metal plates stayed there for several more months.

In late November, they removed the fixator from my leg, but that wasn't the end. After that, I remained in a cast for a long time, and they inserted a plate in my leg—which stayed there for nine years. I was content to leave it there, but they said they had to take it out. My doctor explained that as I aged, the bones, relying on the plate for strength, would become brittle. As I learned, our bones become and remain strong only as a result of tension and use.

During those years with the fixator and the subsequent metal plates, whenever I had to fly, I set off metal detectors from Ohio to California. Rather than go through the customary walk-through detector, I would say to the security people, "I have more stainless steel in me than your silverware drawer at home."

They would wand me and smile. "You sure do."

My children took pride in referring to me as "Robopreacher" after the title character in the movie *Robocop*. After a horrible incident, doctors used high technology and metal plates to restore the policeman so he could fight crime.

Regardless of how barbaric all these rods and wires and plates might have seemed, they worked. People gasped when they saw them embedded in my flesh. Those same people are now awed at my mobility. But under this thin veneer of normalcy, I'm still a work in progress, always adjusting.

9
ENDLESS
ADJUSTMENTS

A friend is always loyal, and a brother is born to help in time
of need.

PROVERBS 17:17

I t's amazing how differently people responded after the accident. Several friends and members of South Park Church
saw me during those first five days after my accident. Many
of those same people saw me after the all-night prayer vigil that
David Gentiles instigated. As they watched each tiny step of my
recovery, they rejoiced. I saw everything in my recovery happening
so slowly that acute depression continually gripped me. After the
ICU, I stayed in the hospital 105 days the first time. I suppose
depression would strike anyone who has been confined that long.

During the months of my recovery, the church worked hard
to make me feel useful. They brought vanloads of kids to the

hospital to see me. Sometimes committees met in my hospital room—as if I could make any decisions. They knew I couldn't say or do much, but it was their way to affirm and encourage me. They did everything they could to make me feel worthwhile and useful.

Much of that time, however, I was depressed and filled with self-pity. I yearned to go back to heaven.

—ᏻᏊ—

Beyond the depression, I had another problem: I didn't want anybody to do anything for me. That's my nature.

One day Jay B. Perkins, a retired minister, came to visit me. He had served as pastor of several south Texas churches before his retirement and had become a powerful father figure in the ministry for me. South Park hired him as the interim while I was incapacitated.

Jay visited me faithfully. That meant he had to drive more than forty miles each way. He came often to see me, sometimes two or three times a week. I wasn't fit company, but I smiled each time anyway. I'd lie in bed and feel sorry for myself. He'd speak kindly, always trying to find words to encourage me, but nothing he said helped—although that wasn't his fault. No one could help me. Not only was I miserable but, as I learned later, I made everyone else miserable.

My visitors tried to help me, and many wanted to do whatever they could for me. "Can I get you a magazine?" someone would ask.

"Would you like a milkshake? There's a McDonald's in the lobby. Or I could get you a hamburger or . . ."

"Would you like me to read the Bible to you? Or maybe some other book?"

"Are there any errands I can run for you?"

My answer was always the same: "No, thanks."

I don't think I was mean, but I wasn't friendly or cooperative, although I wasn't aware of how negatively I treated everyone. I didn't want to see anyone; I didn't want to talk to anyone; I wanted my pain and disfigurement to go away. If I had to stay on earth, then I wanted to get well and get back to living my life again.

Because Jay visited often, he noticed how detached I was from friends and family. One day he was sitting beside me when one of the South Park deacons came for a visit. After ten minutes, the man got up and said, "I just wanted to come by and check on you." Then he asked the inevitable question, "Is there anything I can get for you before I leave?"

"Thank you, no. I appreciate it, but—"

"Well, can I get you something to eat? Can I go downstairs and—"

"No, really. Thanks for coming."

He said good-bye and left.

Jay sat silently and stared out the window for several minutes after the deacon left. Finally he walked over to the bed and got close to my face and said, "You really need to get your act together."

"Sir?" I said like anyone would say respectfully to an eighty-year-old preacher.

"You need to get your act together," he repeated. "You're just not doing a very good job."

"I don't understand what—"

"Besides that," he said and moved even closer so that I couldn't look away. "Besides that, you're a raging hypocrite."

475

"I don't know what you're talking about."

"These people care about you so much, and you just can't imagine how deeply they love you."

"I know they love me."

"Really? Well, you're not doing a very good job of letting them know you're aware. You're not treating them right. They can't heal you. If they could heal you, they would do it. If they could change places with you, many of them would. If you ask them to do anything—anything—they would do it without hesitating."

"I know—"

"But you won't let them do anything for you."

"I don't *want* them to do anything." Without holding anything back, I said as loudly as I could, "The truth is I don't even want them to be here. I'd just as soon they didn't come. I know it's inconvenient. They must have better things to do. I know that—why would I want anybody to come and see me like this? It's just awful. I'm pathetic."

"It's not your call."

I stared back, shocked at his words.

"You've spent the better part of your life trying to minister to other people, to meet their needs, to help them during times of difficulty and tragedy and—"

"I . . . I've tried to—"

"And now you're doing a terrible job of letting these people do the same thing for you." I'll never forget the next sentence. *"Don, it's the only thing they have to offer you, and you're taking that gift away from them."*

Not ready to surrender, I protested and tried to explain. He interrupted me again.

476

"You're not letting them minister to you. It's what they want to do. Why can't you understand that?"

I really didn't get the impact of his words, but I said, "I appreciate them, and I know they want to help. I think that's very fine and everything but—"

"But nothing! You're cheating them out of an opportunity to express their love to you."

His words shocked me. In my thinking, I was trying to be selfless and not impose on them or cause them any trouble. Just then, his words penetrated my consciousness. In reality, I was being selfish. There was also an element of pride there—which I couldn't admit then. I knew how to give generously to others, but pride wouldn't let me receive others' generosity.

Jay didn't let up on me. After all, I was a completely captive audience. He stayed at me until he forced me to see how badly I distanced myself from everyone. Even then I found additional excuses, but Jay wore me down.

"I want you to let them help you. Did you hear me? You will allow them to help!"

"I can't—I just can't let—"

"Okay, Don, then if you don't do it for yourself, do this for *me*," he said.

He knew I'd do anything for him, so I nodded.

"The next time anyone comes in here and offers to do something—anything, no matter what it is—I want you to say yes. You probably can't do that with everyone, but you can start with just one or two people. Let a few of the people express their love by helping you. Promise me you'll do that."

"I'm not sure I can."

"Yes, you can."

"I'll try, but that's just not me."

"Then make it you." His gaze bored into me. "Do it!"

I'm amazed now as I think of Jay's patience with me. His voice softened, and he said, "Just try it for me, would you? You have to get better at this. Right now you're not doing very well. This is one of the lessons God wants you to learn. You're going to be hurting a long time. It'll feel longer if you keep on refusing help."

"Okay," I said, unable to resist any longer.

I promised. I didn't think he would leave until I did.

My first reaction had been irritation, maybe even anger. I thought he had stepped over the line, but I didn't say that. After he left, I thought about all the things he had said. Once I overcame my anger, my pride, and my selfishness, I realized he had spoken the truth—truth I needed to hear.

Two days passed, and I still couldn't do what he asked.

On the third day, a church member popped into my room, greeted me, and spent about five minutes with me before he got up to leave. "I just wanted to come by and check on you and see how you were doing," he said. "You're looking good."

I smiled; I looked terrible, but I didn't argue with him.

He stood up to leave. "Is there anything I can do for you before I go?"

I had my mouth poised to say the words, "No, thank you," and an image of Jay popped into my mind. "Well, I wish I had a magazine to read."

"You do?" He had the biggest grin on his face. "Really?"

"I think so. I haven't read one in a while—"

"I'll be right back!" Before I could tell him what kind, he dashed out the door so fast it was like a human blur. He had to go down twenty-one floors, but it seemed as if he were gone less than a minute. When he returned, he had an armload of magazines. He was still grinning as he showed me the covers of all of them.

478

I thanked him. "I'll read them a little later," I said.

He put them on the table and smiled. "Is there anything else?"

"No, no, that's all I need. Thank you."

Once I had opened the door and allowed someone to do something kind for me, I realized it wasn't so hard after all. After he left, I began skimming through the magazines. I wasn't really reading, because I kept thinking about what had happened.

Jay was right. I had cheated them out of the opportunity to express their love and concern.

About forty minutes later, a woman from the singles group came to see me, and we went through the regular ritual of chatting. "How are you doing?"

"Fine."

"Well, can I get you anything?"

"No, I . . . I—" Again, Jay's words popped into my head. "Well, maybe a strawberry milkshake."

"Strawberry milkshake? I'd love to get one for you." I don't think I had ever seen her smile so beautifully before. "Anything else? Some fries, maybe?"

"No."

She dashed out the door and came back with the strawberry milkshake. "Oh, pastor, I hope you enjoy this."

"I will," I said. "As a matter of fact, I love strawberry milkshakes."

Later, I imagined members of the congregation standing outside my door comparing notes. "He asked me to get a strawberry milkshake."

"Yes, and he let me run an errand for him."

Just then I realized how badly I had missed the whole idea. I had failed them and myself. In trying to be strong for them, I had cheated them out of opportunities to strengthen me. Guilt overwhelmed me, because I could—at last—see their gifts to me.

The shame flowed all over me, and I began to cry. *This is their ministry,* I thought, *and I've been spoiling it.* I felt such intense shame over not letting them help. When I finally did open up, I witnessed a drastic change in their facial expressions and in their movements. They loved it. All they had wanted was a chance to do something, and I was finally giving that to them.

You need to get your act together. For the next several hours those words of loving rebuke from Jay wouldn't go away. Tears flowed. I have no idea how much time passed, but it seemed hours before I finally realized God had forgiven me. I had learned a lesson.

In spite of my condition, not many people could have pulled off what Jay did. That experience changed my attitude. Even now, years later, I still fight with allowing others to help, but at least the door is now ajar instead of locked shut.

Sometimes when I'm emotionally low or physically down, I tend to brush people off or assert that I don't need anything. Yet when I can open up and allow others to exercise their gifts and help me, it makes such a difference. Their faces light up as if they're asking, "Will you really let me do that for you?"

I had seen my refusal as not wanting to impose; they saw my change as giving them an opportunity to help.

I'm eternally grateful for that lesson of allowing people to meet my needs. I'm also grateful because that lesson was learned in a hospital bed when I was helpless.

Someone brought a plaque to me in the hospital. At first, I thought it was supposed to be some kind of joke because it contained the words of Psalm 46:10: "Be still, and know that I am God" (NIV '84). Perhaps it was meant to console me. I'm not sure the person who gave it to me (and I don't remember who it was) realized that I couldn't do anything *but* be still.

Yet that plaque contained the message I needed; it just took me a long time to understand.

Weeks lapsed before I realized that part of what I needed was to be still—inwardly—and to trust that God knew what he was doing through all of this. Yes, it was a verse for me, even though it wasn't one I would have chosen.

God forced me to be still. By nature I'm not particularly introspective, but I became increasingly so; I had no choice. I could do little else—other than feel sorry for myself. The longer I lay immobile, the more open I became to God's quietness and to inner silence.

Eva found a beautiful version of that same verse engraved in gold and gave it to me as a gift. The plaque is now in my church office; I see it every time I look up from my desk.

Day after day I lay in bed, unable to move. I lay on my back a total of thirteen months before I could turn over on my side. Just that simple action made it one of the best days of recovery. "Oh, I had forgotten how good this feels," I said aloud.

During that long recovery, I learned a lot about myself, about my attitude, and my nature. I didn't like many things I saw in Don Piper. In the midst of that inactivity, however, the depression persisted.

I began to wonder if that depression would ever go away.

Then God provided another miracle.

10
MORE MIRACLES

I will praise the LORD at all times.
   I will constantly speak his praises.
I will boast only in the LORD;
   let all who are discouraged take heart.
Come, let us tell of the LORD's greatness;
   let us exalt his name together.
I prayed to the LORD, and he answered me,
   freeing me from all my fears.

PSALM 34:1–4

Sometimes the depression became so bad I didn't think I could breathe. It carried me back to the days in the ICU when I received breathing treatments because my lungs had collapsed. Except now my lungs weren't collapsed, only my spirit. Few things sap the human spirit like lack of hope. For weeks and months, no one could tell me when or even if I would ever be normal again. As a result, I went into a full-scale depression.

483

As my horribly mangled body mended, I needed spiritual mending as well. I began to think of it this way: The Greek word for "spirit" is *pneuma*. The word can also mean "wind" or "breath." That Greek word is the root for what we call *pneumonia*. Just as it was necessary to reinflate my lungs to overcome pneumonia, I needed the breath of God to help me overcome the depression of my spirit.

I don't know when I became aware of that depression. In the first few weeks of my recovery, I was in such constant physical pain I couldn't hold any thoughts in my mind for more than a second or two.

I also battled a lot of anger during those first weeks. I wasn't angry with God, though I often wondered why God had sent me back to earth and why I had to go through such intense physical agony. But even being in pain was not the issue for me. From my first day in the hospital, pain has always been present. Like many others, I've learned to live with that reality. My struggle is that I had experienced the glory and majesty of heaven only to return to earth. In my weaker moments, I didn't understand why God would return me to earth in such awful condition. Many live in greater pain, but few—if any—have experienced heaven.

Instead, my anger focused primarily on the medical staff. I suppose it was because they were there all the time. Deep inside, I seethed with an inner rage, perhaps at myself as much as the medical staff. Why wasn't I recuperating faster? I blamed them for the slowness of my recovery. In my rational moments, I knew they did the best they could. Despite my antagonism and irritation—which I'm sure they sensed—they stayed right with me and constantly encouraged me.

I didn't want encouragement—I wanted results. I wanted to be healthy again. Why couldn't my life be the way it used to be? I wanted to walk by myself, and I didn't want to depend on others all the time.

The medical staff wouldn't give me any definite answers, and that sent fresh waves of rage through my system. In retrospect, I'm sure they told me what they could, but I was anything but a typical case. No one knew my prognosis. In fact, for several weeks, they weren't even sure if I would live, let alone make a significant recovery.

I became paranoid—I knew I wasn't rational even when I complained and demanded more attention or additional medication to alleviate the pain. Nothing suited me. The pace was too slow. They made me wait too long before responding to my bell. No one wanted to answer questions.

"How long will I have to wear this Ilizarov frame?" I asked almost every medical person who came into my room.

"I don't know," was the most common answer.

"But I want to know something," I finally said.

"A long time, a very long time," was the only other answer a nurse or doctor would give me.

A couple of times I just had to have an answer, so I kept pressing the doctor.

"Weeks. Months," he said. "We can't tell you because we don't know. If I knew, I'd tell you."

Common sense said they were doing their best, but in those days, I didn't have much common sense. Part of it was the pain, and perhaps the mammoth doses of medications affected me as well, but I wasn't a good patient. Instead of being satisfied, I kept asking myself, *Why won't they tell me? What do they know that they're hiding? There are things they're not telling me, and I have a right to know what's going on.*

During many sleepless nights, I would lie in bed, convinced that the nurses conspired against me. It never occurred to me to wonder why they would want to do that.

Then why don't they tell me anything? I'd rail as I lay there. *What can they possibly do that will hurt more than this?*

The answer was *nothing.* I endured additional pain that resulted not from the accident itself but from the process of healing. For instance, when they harvested bones out of my right hip and put them in my left arm, they made an incision six inches long—and closed it up with metal staples. When the day came for them to take out the staples, they pulled them out of my skin. As they pulled each one, I winced in pain and steeled myself so that I wouldn't scream at the top of my lungs. I couldn't remember hurting that excruciatingly. I had, of course, but I had forgotten how much torture my body could take.

The poor nurse who was extracting the staples stopped after each one. Sadness filled her eyes, and I knew she sensed how deeply the procedure hurt me. She was a large woman and always treated me as gently as she could. "I'm so sorry, Reverend," she said softly.

"I know," I mumbled. "You can't help it." Momentarily, I lapsed into my pastoral role of trying to console her. I didn't want her to feel bad for the torture I felt.

"Reverend, why don't you just haul off and yell?"

"It wouldn't do any good."

"If it was me, I'd be yelling."

"Yeah, I bet you would." I offered a faint sense of humor. "And you'd wake up every patient in the hospital."

486

I just never could yell voluntarily. Maybe it was a fear of losing control. Perhaps I feared that if I did scream, she and others
would consider me as weak. I'm not sure of the reasons, even
now. I know only that I couldn't scream like others on my floor.
From several other rooms, every day I heard patients scream out
in agony. I just couldn't let go like that. Instead, I'd hold my
breath and sometimes break out in a cold sweat, but I wouldn't
scream purposely.

Though I know I wasn't the easiest of patients in demeanor or
medical requirements, the nurses of the orthopedic floor treated
me with kindness and much compassion. I learned to care a great
deal for them and admire their dedication. I guess they must
have seen something in me as well. I know the nursing staff often
bent the rules when well-wishers showed up to see me, no matter
what time of day or night they came. But the sweetest moment
came when I was discharged from my 105-day stay at St. Luke's.
Apparently, arrangements were made with nursing staffs of other
hospital floors to cover for them as the nurses from my floor all
accompanied me down the elevator and to my waiting ambulance
on the day of my discharge. Being surrounded by nurses that fed
me, medicated me, bathed me, and did only the Lord knows what
else, made my going home that day so wonderful. It was as if they
were saying, "We've done our best. Now you've got to get better
and come back and see us." I can only imagine how different I
must have seemed to them that going-home day from the day I
had arrived wavering between life and death.

───෴෴───

In spite of my stubborn resistance to showing emotion, before
I left St. Luke's, the months of intense pain finally crumbled my

resolve. I broke down and cried. I felt worthless, beaten down, and useless. I was convinced I would never get any better.

"God, God, why is it like this? Why am I going through this constant pain that never seems to get any better?" Again I prayed for God to take me. I didn't want to live any longer. I wanted to go back home, and now for me, home meant heaven.

I prayed that way for days, and usually, I'd fall asleep from exhaustion. When I'd awaken, a cloak of hopelessness would spread over me again. Nothing helped.

Just before the accident, I had ordered several cassette tapes of popular Christian songs originally recorded during the 1960s and '70s by people like the Imperials and David Meece. Eva had brought them to the hospital along with a tape player, but I had no interest in listening to them.

Instead, I watched TV. I once told a friend, "I've watched every *Brady Bunch* episode at least eight times, and I know all of the dialogue by heart."

One morning between three and five o'clock, I couldn't bear to watch another TV rerun, so I decided to play the cassettes. A nurse came in and helped me set up the first cassette to play.

The first song had been recorded by the Imperials, and it was called "Praise the Lord." The lyrics suggest that when we're up against a struggle and we think we can't go on, we need to praise God. As preposterous as that prospect seemed at three o'clock in the morning in a hospital bed, I continued to listen for any help to bring me out of my deep heartache. There was a phrase in the next verse about the chains that seem to bind us falling away when we turn ourselves over to praise. The whole song centered on praising God in spite of our circumstances.

The instant the Imperials sang the second chorus about the chains, I looked down at my chains—pounds of stainless steel

488

encasing my arm and leg. Before my accident, I'm sure I'd heard and sung that song hundreds of times. I had even played it myself. Just then, those words became a message from God—a direct hit from on high.

Before they had finished singing the song, I lay there and heard my own voice say, "Praise the Lord!"

No sooner had that song ended than David Meece sang, "We Are the Reason." His words reminded me that we are the reason Jesus Christ wept, suffered, and died on the cross. Meece sang about how he finally found that the real purpose in living was in giving every part of his life to Christ. That wasn't a new song to me, but something happened during those predawn hours. Other than music, I heard nothing else—no moaning from other rooms or footsteps of nurses in the hallway. I felt totally isolated from the world around me.

Then the dam broke. Tears slid down my cheeks, and I couldn't wipe them away—and I didn't even want to try. They just flowed. The tears wouldn't stop, and I cried as I had never wept before. I'm not sure, but I think the crying lasted for about an hour.

Slowly the sobbing subsided. Calmness swept over me, and I lay relaxed and very much at peace. That's when I realized another miracle had taken place: My depression had lifted. Vanished.

I had been healed. Again.

Stark reminders from some simple songs had changed me. The Imperials reminded me that Satan is a liar. He wants to steal our joy and replace it with hopelessness. When we're up against a struggle and we think we can't keep going, we can change that by praising God. Our chains will fall from us.

Meese encouraged me by reminding me of the real reason we have for fully living this life. It's to give everything we have to God—even the heartbreaks and pain. God is our reason to live.

That morning I determined to get on with living the rest of my life, no matter what. I made that decision with no psychiatric help, no drugs, and no counseling. As I listened to those two songs, God had healed me. The despair lifted. My mental chains had broken. I also knew that nothing I had gone through—or would endure—was as horrific as what Jesus suffered.

I'm not trying to imply that I'm against psychological help. Before and since my accident, I've sent many people for counseling. But because I wasn't open to help of any kind, God healed me in a dramatic and unexplainable way.

As I lay there, my attitude changed. I had no idea when my physical pain would end or how long I'd have to wear the Ilizarov frame, but I knew Jesus Christ was with me. I still didn't understand why God had sent me back to live with all of this agony, but that no longer mattered.

Now I was free. He had healed my mind. My body would mend slowly, but I had experienced the major victory. Never again would depression afflict me. It was just one more miracle from heaven.

BACK TO CHURCH

11

So humble yourselves under the mighty power of God, and in his good time he will honor you. Give all your worries and cares to God, for he cares about what happens to you.

1 PETER 5:6–7

Some people who have known me for a long time see me as some kind of courageous figure. I certainly haven't seen myself that way—not for an instant—because I know too much about the real me. I also know how little I did to get through my ordeal.

Despite my own perceptions, friends and church members say they received encouragement by watching me as I progressed from a totally helpless state and gradually moved toward a fairly normal lifestyle. A number of individuals have said to me in the midst of their own difficult times, "If you could go through all you endured, I can go through this."

I'm glad they've been heartened by my example, but I've had a great deal of difficulty accepting myself as a source of inspiration and courage. I don't know how to cope with their admiration and praise, because I didn't do anything. I wanted to die. How uplifting can that be?

When people tell me how inspiring I've been, I don't argue with them, of course, but I remember only too well the time David Gentiles told me that he and others would pray me back to health. I lived because others wouldn't let me die. Those praying friends are the ones who deserve the admiration.

Most of the time when people have that if-you-can-do-it attitude, I nod, acknowledge what they're saying, and add, "I'm just doing the best I can." And really, that's all I did during the worst days. Sometimes "the best I can" was nothing but to endure. Even when I struggled with depression, it was still the best I could do. Maybe that's what God honors. I don't know.

By nature, I'm a determined individual, which I admit can sometimes be a first cousin to stubbornness. Yet many times I felt terribly alone and was convinced that no one else understood. And I still think that's true. When our pain becomes intense and endures for weeks without relief, no one else really knows. I'm not sure it's worthwhile for them to know what it's like.

They care. That's what I think is important.

—꙰꙰—

After I came home from the hospital in the middle of May, I still had to sleep in a hospital bed until February 1990—a total of thirteen months. Even after sleeping in my own house, I had setbacks of various kinds or developed infections. Back to the hospital I'd go, and some of those trips, especially in the early days, were for life-threatening infections. Sometimes I stayed two weeks and other times three. On most occasions Eva drove me there, but I always came home in an ambulance.

After they initially released me from the hospital, church members kept telling me how good I looked "considering all that's happened." No one actually said the words, but I imagined them saying, "We prayed for Don. We can't believe how well it turned out. We asked for him to live, and we asked for him to be better." That is, I was a pitiful mess, but I was alive and that's what they had asked for.

My twin sons, Joe and Christopher, were only eight at the time of the accident, and our daughter, Nicole, was twelve. One of the things that hurt me most during my recovery was the sense of pain my children had to cope with. They didn't say a great deal, but I knew how they felt.

This is a handmade card from my son Joe, written to me in February 1989 while he was living with his grandparents. (I didn't correct the spelling.)

hi dad,

You are the best. I love you and I hope you like the cards. I whish this never hapined
I love you Dad,

Joe

Months later when I finally came home, most afternoons, Joe's twin, Chris, came in from school and into the large living room where my bed was. Without saying a word, Chris would walk over and lay his head on my chest. I don't know how long his head lay there, probably not more than a full minute.

He never said a word.

He didn't need to. That simple gesture was enough. I felt so loved by my son.

After a minute or so, Chris would go into his room, get out of his school clothes, change into his play clothes, and then go outside and play. That's the way he greeted me almost every day.

I know it was hard on him—really hard on him—and he expressed his grief in the only way he knew how.

—–⌒⌒—–

Just six months after the accident, I was able to participate in a very special moment for Nicole.

Southern Baptists have mission organizations for young people. The most well-known are the Royal Ambassadors for boys and Girls in Action (GAs) and Acteens for girls. As soon as she was old enough, Nicole participated in GAs and Acteens. She fulfilled all the requirements, such as Scripture memorization, various service projects, and mission trips. When she was fourteen, she learned she would be awarded the honor of Queen with Scepter at a coronation ceremony at South Park Baptist Church in June 1989.

This award is the pinnacle of Acteen participation and is presented during a church ceremony. Her receiving the award was a tribute to her own utter determination. During the time she threw herself into those activities, she wasn't able to live at home. Our friends Suzan and Stan Mauldin had opened their home to her, and she lived with them. Nicole received no emotional or physical support from me, because I was barely surviving in the hospital. She received little support from her mother, because Eva's

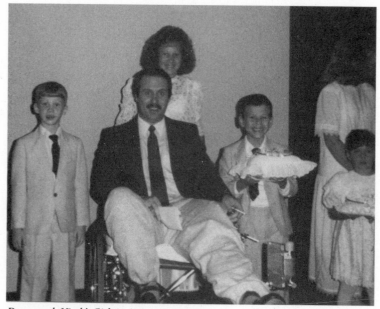

Don attends Nicole's Girls in Action coronation.

life consisted of leaving school every afternoon and rushing to the hospital, where she stayed with me until she went home to bed.

The challenges made us all the more proud of Nicole.

One of the traditions associated with the coronation is that fathers escort their daughters down the aisle. Brothers, if the girls have any, follow and carry the crown and scepter.

Because of the timing of South Park's annual coronation, there was great doubt about my being able to be present, much less escort her down the aisle.

I'm grateful that my doctors discharged me from the hospital in time to be present for the coronation. I really wanted to be there. This wasn't her wedding, but it was the biggest thing so far in her young life, and I wanted to share the moment with her.

I was in a wheelchair, and Nicole held my arm as I rolled down the aisle. Chris and Joe walked behind us, carrying her

495

crown and scepter on pillows. They also helped roll my chair down the aisle. I wore a suit coat and tie (my first time since the accident) along with my warm-ups split down the sides to allow for my Ilizarov.

Not only was Nicole absolutely elated that her daddy could be present for her extremely important occasion, she was thrilled that her father could "walk" her down the aisle.

Tears filled my eyes as I maneuvered down the aisle. I heard others sniffling. But I also knew that we wept tears of joy over this wonderful moment in Nicole's life.

—⟨⟩ ⟨⟩—

The doctors sent me home initially, I believe, because they thought I'd recover faster in an environment with family around me. It may also have cost a lot less for me to be home. I'm not sure, but I was glad to be out of the hospital. Insurance didn't pay for any of my treatment. The bill was covered at first by workmen's compensation, and ultimately the State of Texas, because a federal court found them at fault.

Still, being in my own home wasn't much easier for me or my family, especially Eva. Every day someone had to give me shots. I had to have physical therapy treatments—all done to me and for me at home. Our living room looked like a hospital room. I did feel better being out of that sterile environment. Just being around familiar things lifted my spirit. I enjoyed being able to look out the window at my neighborhood or having people drop in to see me who didn't wear white uniforms.

The medical team sent my bed and a trapeze contraption—just like what I had used at the hospital. Nurses visited every day; physical therapists came every other day.

Some of the sweetest memories I have are of the kind people who simply spent each day with me while Eva went back to work. When church members heard that she had to return to teaching or lose her job, they decided to do what they could.

Ginny Foster, the senior pastor's wife, organized a group of people to stay with me each day. Ginny organized what she laughingly called the "Don Patrol"—mostly women from the church, along with a few retired men.

It was about seven hours from the time Eva left in the morning until she returned. My sleep habits depended on when I could fight the pain no more and would pass out. But gradually, a pattern began to emerge. I would generally go to sleep about two or three o'clock in the morning and wake up around ten. The Don Patrol arrived about nine o'clock while I was still asleep. They either prepared lunch for me or brought it with them.

Often I would awake to find a charming woman knitting at the end of my bed. Or perhaps an older man would be reading the *Houston Chronicle*. He'd lower the newspaper and grin at me, "Good morning. Do you need anything?"

The parade of sweet faces changed every day. Although the volunteers were different, the goals remained the same: Take care of Don and keep him company.

As I lay in bed day after day, I realized how much others had done for us. While I was still hospitalized, friends from the Alvin church had packed up our furniture and moved us to a new house, where I could be on the ground level with no stairs to worry about.

During the day, I would look through the patio window from my "hospital room." Often I spotted high schoolers Brandon and Matt Mealer and their buddy Chris Alston mowing our lawn. Chris arranged to borrow our van one night and surprise me by

497

taking me to a movie. I don't even remember what the movie was, but I will never forget his thoughtfulness. Once when our fence blew down during a windstorm, it was back up before we could call anyone to help. Only God knows all the kindnesses shown to us during my recovery.

——⟨⟩⟨⟩——

As I began to stir in my bed each morning, my "keeper" would get up and bring me a toothbrush and a pan to brush my teeth and wash my face. I'd have a glass of juice held to my lips and later a huge lunch ready for me.

After feeding me, washing up, and making sure I was as comfortable as my physical condition would allow, they all asked the same question: "Is there anything else I can get for you before I leave?"

My answer was always the same: "No, thanks." I would muster what I hoped was my best smile. It probably wasn't, but they always smiled back.

"It's all right. I'll be fine."

The capacity for sacrifice and service that human beings have for one another knows no bounds. With all our faults, surely God must have meant that the kindnesses shown to me during my injury and recovery were paramount examples of us being created in his image.

Within an hour or so after my daily Don Patrol angel quietly exited, the door would open, and Eva would enter from a long day at school. She always gave me a big smile and kissed me.

"Are you all right?" she would ask.

"I'm fine," I would say, meaning it.

498

I couldn't put my feelings into words then, but the assurance that I had been visited by an angel from the Don Patrol caused my spirit to soar.

_____ ᘒᘖ _____

For months after I came home, good-hearted members of the Don Patrol transported me back and forth for water therapy, which was done near our home in Alvin. During the first thirteen months, if I wasn't inside the hospital, I was lying in the hospital bed at the house. For months, I probably wasn't out of the bed more than five minutes a day except for therapy. Some days I didn't even get out of bed.

The worst part is that once I was in the hospital bed, I was completely incapacitated. I couldn't get up or do anything for myself. Without the help of the therapist, I never would have sat up or been able to move on my own again.

Slowly, gradually, I learned to walk again. The first day I got out of bed on my own, I took three steps. I slumped back onto the bed, feeling a wave of exhaustion overwhelm me. But I smiled. *I had walked.* Three steps sounds like so little, and yet I felt a powerful sense of accomplishment.

So much of recovery from a trauma of this magnitude has a striking similarity to training a child in infancy. I had been helpless for such a long time that when I could finally go to the bathroom by myself, it felt like a remarkable accomplishment. Walking again was a stark reminder of what we all take for granted every day as we talk, move, and live.

When I could walk again, it was not only a singular accomplishment but a tribute to hundreds of medical people who worked tirelessly to help me. It was also a tribute to my friends and family who believed in me, although they couldn't have known just how difficult it would be for me to put one foot in front of the other.

While I suppose walking represented a certain triumph of will, it also meant I could begin to live in relative normalcy. I often thought of the last night at Trinity Pines when J. V. Thomas and I took our walk around the camp. That was my last normal walk ever. For many months no one was sure I'd ever walk again. For a long time, taking just three shaky steps seemed like climbing Mount Everest.

"I did it!" I shouted to the silent room. "I walked! I walked."

Taking those first steps at home on my own remains one of the best moments of my recovery. Those few steps convinced me that I was getting better. Now I had goals to work toward. I had gone through the worst part of the recovery. I knew I would continue to improve. Each day I took a few more steps. By the end of the week, I had made a complete circle of the living room.

When Eva came home and watched me demonstrate my daily progress, her smile made me feel as if I had won a marathon. She reacted with absolute joyful delight the afternoon I showed her that I could walk throughout the house all by myself.

———❦❦———

A week after I came home from the hospital, I had decided I wanted to go to church on a Sunday morning.

In retrospect, it was premature, but I felt a burning desire to be back with people I loved and to worship with them. With the help of a small group, we planned for them to help me get there. In case I couldn't make it, we didn't want to disappoint anyone, so we decided not to announce it to the congregation.

By then I could sit in a wheelchair—as long as someone was there to lift me out of bed and into it—but I still couldn't stand up. Six friends from church came to our house and took the seats out of one of the church vans. At the church, they had constructed a ramp so they could roll me up to its doors.

I kept thinking of all the work I had laid on them, and several times I started to apologize, but they assured me it was their pleasure.

Then I remembered Jay's words. My family and friends saw me the first day of the accident. I never saw what I looked like. They endured the shock and the fear. They had to come to grips with the possibility of my death or my long-term disability. In some respects, this ordeal was more difficult for my family and friends than it was for me. They loved being able to help me. In a way, this was part of their own recovery, and they were glad to be able to do something special for me.

Yet, as much as I wanted to attend the worship service that morning, it was still hard to let them do everything for me. I felt totally helpless and absolutely dependent on them. As I realized that once again, I smiled.

"Thank you," I said and then allowed them to take care of me.

They carefully put me into the van, drove me to the church, and pulled up at the side door. When one of the men in the van opened the door, church members on their way into the sanctuary saw me.

"Look! It's Pastor Don!" someone yelled.

I heard cheering and clapping as people stood around and made way for the men to wheel me up the ramp.

Just then, everything turned chaotic. People rushed toward me. Several cheered. It seemed as if everyone wanted to touch me or shake my hand. I could hardly believe the fuss they made over me.

Finally someone wheeled me inside and stopped my chair in front of the platform near the church organ. It wasn't possible to lift me up.

By then the entire congregation had become aware that I was in front of the sanctuary. I smiled as I thought, *It's only taken me five months to get from the conference at Trinity Pines back to church. I may be slow, but I'm faithful.*

Just then someone whispered in my ear, "We want you to say something to the congregation." He got behind me and steered me toward the center of the sanctuary, right in front of the pulpit.

By then exhaustion had begun to seep in. It had probably nagged at me all along, but I had been so determined to get back to church, I refused to admit how tired I felt. I had been out of bed more than two hours. That was the longest time I had been out of bed up to that point, and also the longest time I had spent in a wheelchair.

In that moment I realized I had been foolish in wanting to come, because I wasn't up to the physical demands on my body. My stubbornness had overestimated my endurance.

Perhaps just as bad, I became completely overwhelmed at the congregation's loving response. I didn't know if I could speak. What could I say after all those weeks of absence and all I'd been through?

While I was still trying to figure that out, someone thrust a microphone in my hand. As I clutched it, I kept thinking, *You people really have no idea how little I contributed to my recovery. You see it as a triumph. I see it merely as survival.*

Just then spontaneous applause broke out. I had expected them to be glad to see me; I had not been prepared for the avalanche of praise to God. Every person in that building stood, and the applause began—and it kept on for a long time. I finally waved them to stop.

As I stared at them, I felt guilty about their applause and excitement. I couldn't believe those people were applauding me. *If they only knew*, I thought. *If they only knew.*

Then God spoke to me. This was one of the few times in my life when I heard a very clear voice inside my head.

They're not applauding for you.

Just those words, but it made a difference and I could speak. Finally, I had it straight. They were giving thanks to God for what he had done for me. God had brought me back from death to life once again. I relaxed. This was a moment to glorify God. This wasn't praise for me.

I still had to wait for what seemed like a long time until the applause ceased. I spoke only four words. Anyone who was there that glorious day can tell you what they were: "You prayed. I'm here."

The congregation erupted in spontaneous applause again. If I had said anything else, I'm sure they wouldn't have heard it anyway.

I couldn't say it, but I believed then—and still do—that I survived only because a number of people wanted me to. They were relentless, passionate, and desperate, and they believed God would hear them. People prayed for me who had never seriously prayed before; some who hadn't uttered a word of petition in years cried out to God to spare me. My experience brought people to their knees, and many of them had changed in the process of praying for me to live.

503

When I did live, those same people—especially those who hadn't been in the habit of praying—said the experience revolutionized their lives. In some instances, individuals I had never met—from Cottonwood, Arizona, to Buffalo, New York—heard my story second-, third-, and fourthhand. Over the next three years, people would approach me and say, "I saw you on a video interview. You're the man! I prayed for you." Or they heard one of the audiotapes of my testimony distributed by my church and would say, "You just don't know what it means. God heard *our* prayers, and we're so happy you lived."

To some individuals, I'm not really a person but a symbol. For them, I represent answered prayer. They may remember my ministry at South Park Church or even some of the messages I preached, but what they remember most is that they sought God's face in deep, sincere, earnest prayer. They pleaded for me to survive, and I did. I don't know what to make of it, except to say that this is something outside of and beyond me.

I think I'm also a human response to some of the questions people wanted answered. Since I began to tell others about my experience in heaven, I can't begin to count the people who have come to me and asked such questions as, Is heaven real? What is heaven really like? Or they'll ask specific questions about the praise or the streets of gold. Someone seems to always mention a recently departed loved one.

Just to know that I've been there and come back to earth and am able to talk to them seems to bring deep comfort to many. Sometimes it amazes me.

Others look at the marks on my body even today and say, "You're a miracle because of all you went through. You're a walking miracle."

12
OPENING UP

For we know that when this earthly tent we live in is taken down—when we die and leave these bodies—we will have a home in heaven, an eternal body made for us by God himself and not by human hands. We grow weary in our present bodies, and we long for the day when we will put on our heavenly bodies like new clothing. For we will not be spirits without bodies, but we will put on new heavenly bodies. Our dying bodies make us groan and sigh, but it's not that we want to die and have no bodies at all. We want to slip into our new bodies so that these dying bodies will be swallowed up by everlasting life.

2 CORINTHIANS 5:1–4

God used my closest friend, David Gentiles, to keep me alive, and I'm grateful. He also used David again in my life nearly two years after the accident.

Until then I had never talked to anyone about my heavenly experience. In a general sense, I had talked to Eva, but I always closed off the conversation before she asked questions. She tacitly understood that part of my experience was off-limits. To her credit, she never pressured me to say anything more.

505

It wasn't that I wanted to withhold anything from Eva; I just couldn't talk about the experience. At times I felt that it had been too sacred and that to try to explain it would diminish the incident.

Nearly a year and a half after my release from the hospital, David came to the Houston area for a discipleship weekend. He used that as an excuse to come to the house and spend time with me.

When the two of us were alone, I had a flashback to the time when I had been lying in ICU and had told him that I couldn't go on. That's when he had told me that he would pray me through. We talked about that day, and I thanked him again for his friendship and relentless commitment to prayer.

"How are you feeling now?" he asked.

"I'm in pain." I tried to laugh and added, "I'm always in pain, but that's not the worst part for me right now."

He leaned closer. "What is the worst part?"

"I just don't know where I'm going. I lack any clear direction about my future."

David listened as I talked about the things I would like to do, the things I couldn't physically do, and how I wasn't sure that God wanted me to continue at South Park. I felt loved and needed there, but I wasn't sure that was where I should be.

He listened for a long time and then asked gently, "What did you learn from your accident and recovery experience?"

For three or four minutes I shared several things, especially about letting other people inside and allowing them to help me. Then I said, "But in the midst of all this suffering and despondency, I have learned that heaven is real."

He raised his eyebrows. "What do you mean by that?"

Slowly, hesitantly, I shared a little—very little—about my brief visit to heaven. "Tell me more," he said, and I didn't hear it as prying. He was my friend and wanted to know. I also sensed that I could speak about heaven to David and that, as much as any human being was able, he would understand.

"I died in that accident. The next moment I stood in heaven," I said.

He leaned forward, and although he waited silently for me to continue, I saw the excitement in his eyes.

The more I shared, the more animated he became. In retrospect, I believe David's exuberance was a combination of my personal confirmation of heaven's reality and his relief in knowing something good had come out of my long nightmare.

After I had shared my experience in heaven, he said nothing, and a peaceful silence filled the room. Our friendship was such that we didn't have to fill the gap with words.

David finally nodded slowly and asked, "Why haven't you talked about this before?"

"I have two very good reasons. Number one, if I go around talking about having been in heaven, people will think I'm nuts."

"Why would you think that? I heard you, and I didn't—"

"Number two," I said, interrupting him, "I don't want to go over that experience again. It's . . . well, it's just too personal. Too special. This is something I haven't even processed enough to understand it myself. It's not that I don't want to share it, but I don't think I can."

"Why do you think you experienced heaven if you're not supposed to share it?"

"I don't have an answer for that question."

"Why?"

507

"I'll tell you a better question I've asked myself—Why did I experience it and have it taken away from me? What was that all about?" Months of pent-up anger burst forth, and all the interior pain spewed out. "Okay, why did I have to go through this? I saw the glory and the beauty—the most powerful, overwhelming experiences in my life—and then I had to come back. Why? For this?" I pointed to my arm and leg. "Listen. I was in an accident that took my life. Immediately I went to heaven, and it was greater and more wonderful than anything I've ever imagined. I had a magnificent taste of heaven, and then I was pulled back to this life again. My body is a mess. I'm constantly in pain. I'll never be healthy or strong again. I'm still processing this because—because, frankly it all seems cruel to me."

David stared at me and asked again, "Why do you think you experienced it if you're not supposed to share it?"

"Like I said, I don't have an answer for that question."

"Is it possible that God took you to heaven and brought you back for you to share what happened to you? Don't you realize what a powerful encouragement you can be to others?"

His words shocked me. I had been so focused on myself, I hadn't thought about anyone else.

I broke down as I tried to relate to him how I felt and to explain it to myself. I cried in his presence, and I knew it was all right.

For perhaps twenty minutes we discussed it. David nudged me, and although I knew he was right, it still wasn't easy for me to share my experience.

Finally David said, "I want you to make a covenant with me."

"What kind of covenant?"

"Simple. Pick two people you trust. Just tell them a little of your experience and gauge their response." He went on to explain that if they thought I was crazy or that I had hallucinated, then I would never have to speak about it again.

"But if they rejoice with you," he said, "and if they urge you to tell them more, I want you to take this as a sign—a sign that God wants you to talk about those ninety minutes you spent in heaven."

After considering the matter carefully, I covenanted with him. "I can do that much."

"When?"

"I promise to do it soon."

"Very soon, right?"

"Okay, I promise I won't put it off."

David prayed for me, and as I listened to him speak, the certainty came over me. It was no longer a choice—I had to speak out—but I would do it my way.

First, I decided on those I could trust with my holy secret. Once I had narrowed it down to a handful, I still took a cautious approach. I made sure it was a one-to-one conversation. I'd wait until the matter of my health came up—and it always did—and then I'd say something simple such as, "You know, I died that day. And I woke up in heaven."

The reaction was the same each time: "Tell me more." They didn't always say those words, but that's what they wanted. I could see their eyes widen, and they wanted to know more.

As I shared a little more, no one questioned my sanity. No one told me I had hallucinated.

"You have to tell people about this," one of them said.

"That experience wasn't just for you," another friend said. "It's for us as well. It's for me."

509

As I listened to each one over the next two weeks, I realized I was right back where I had been in the hospital the time Jay had rebuked me. That time I wouldn't let anyone help me, and it was selfish. This time I wouldn't share what had happened to me—and it was also selfish.

"Okay, I'll talk about it," I vowed to myself.

Since virtually everyone already knew about my tragic auto accident, I used the occasion as the natural catalyst to speak about my time in heaven—cautiously at first. As people responded with overwhelming support, I became more open and less careful about the people with whom I shared my story.

I want to make it clear that even though I knew it was what I was supposed to do, it wasn't easy for me. Even now, years later, it's just against my nature to talk deeply and personally about things in my life. Today, I only discuss my glimpse of heaven when someone asks, and then only because I feel that person really wants to know. Otherwise, I still wouldn't talk about it.

That's part of the reason it's taken me so many years to write this book. I didn't want my experience in heaven and my return to earth to be my sole reason for being alive. On the contrary, it was such an extraordinarily personal and intimate experience that going back over it repeatedly isn't something I feel comfortable doing.

I talk about my experience both publicly and to individuals. I'm writing about what happened because my story seems to mean so much to people for many different reasons. For example, when I speak to any large crowd, at least one person will be present who has recently lost a loved one and needs assurance of that person's destination.

When I finish speaking, it still amazes me to see how quickly the line forms of those who want to talk to me. They come with tears in their eyes and grief written all over their faces. I feel so grateful that I can offer them peace and assurance.

I've accepted that my words do bring comfort, but it was never something I thought about doing. If it hadn't been for David Gentiles pushing me, I'm sure that even to this day I wouldn't have told anyone.

I'm also grateful for his urging me, because I've seen the effect not only in worship services but also when I've conducted funerals. In fact, my experience has changed many things about the way I look at life. I've changed the way I do funerals. Now I can speak authoritatively about heaven from firsthand knowledge.

Besides my own miraculous experience, four things stand out from my heavenly journey. First, I'm thoroughly convinced that God answers prayer. Answered prayer is why I'm still alive. Second, I have an unquestionable belief that God still is in the miracle business. Too many people read about the supernatural in the Bible and think, *That's the way it was in biblical times.* I'm convinced that God continues to do the more-than-ordinary. Every day I thank God that I'm a living, walking, talking miracle.

Third, I want as many people as possible to go to heaven. I've always believed Christian theology that declares heaven is real and a place for God's people. Since my own experience of having been there, I've felt a stronger sense of responsibility to make the way absolutely clear. Not only do I want people to go to heaven, I now feel an urgency about helping them open their lives so they can be assured that's where they'll go when they die.

I've actually thought about the people who get killed on the highways. In evangelistic services, some have used such stories as a scare tactic to manipulate people into making commitments to Jesus Christ. But because of my experience, I see such accidents

511

as definite possibilities of death at any moment in our lives. I don't want to see others die without Jesus Christ.

Finally, one time, Dick Onerecker and I talked about this urgency. He understood why I felt that way. Then I told him, "Again, Dick, I want to thank you for saving my life. I obviously can't thank you enough for your faithfulness in obeying God that rainy day."

"It was what anybody would have done," he said, and then he started crying.

"I didn't mean to upset you," I said, feeling bad that I had said something to make him cry like that. "That's the last thing on earth I'd ever want to do."

"That's not what I'm crying about."

Several minutes lapsed before he finally pulled himself back together again.

"What were you crying about?" I asked.

"I was thinking that I came upon the scene of the accident and I asked the officer if I could pray for you—and I thought of it as just something any Christian would do. Although he said you were dead, I knew—I just knew—I had to pray for you. I could only think that you were hurt, and I wanted to make you feel better. I didn't do anything unusual."

"But you did. When the officer told you I was already dead—"

"Listen to me, Don. If you saw a little kid run out in the street, you'd dash out there and try to save the child's life. Human nature is like that. We try to preserve life, and I will do that any time I get the opportunity. So would you."

We were sitting in a restaurant, and he paused to look around. "Yet here we are sitting in this place, surrounded by people, many of whom are probably lost and going to hell, and we won't say a word about how they can have eternal life. Something is wrong with us."

"You're absolutely right," I said. "We're willing to save someone in a visible crisis, but a lot of folks are in spiritual crisis and we don't say a word about how they can get out of it."

"That's why I was crying. I've been convicted about my silence, my fear of speaking to people, my reluctance to speak up."

Dick said then, and again later, that hearing my experience and his role in my coming back to earth had set him free. After that he felt a boldness to talk about Jesus Christ that he hadn't had before.

THE CLASPING HAND

13

He is your God, the one who is worthy of your praise, the one who has done mighty miracles that you yourself have seen.

DEUTERONOMY 10:21

I was privileged to share my story in Dick's church, Klein First Baptist, a little more than a year after the accident. His wife, Anita, was there, and so was my own family. Because I still wore leg braces, two people had to help me walk up on the platform.

I told everyone about the accident and about Dick's part in bringing me back. "I believe I'm alive today because Dick prayed me back to earth," I said. "In my first moments of consciousness, two things stand out. First, I was singing 'What a Friend We Have in Jesus.' The second was that Dick's hand gripped mine and held it tight."

After the morning worship, many of us went out to lunch together at a Chinese restaurant. Anita sat across from me. I remember sipping my wonton soup and having a delightful time with the church members.

When there was a lull in the conversation, Anita leaned across the table and said in a low voice, "I appreciated everything you said this morning."

"Thank you—"

"There's just one thing—one thing I need to correct about what you said in your message."

"Really?" Her words shocked me. "I tried to be as accurate as possible in everything I said. I certainly didn't intend to exaggerate anything. What did I say that was incorrect?"

"You were talking about Dick getting into the car with you. Then you said he prayed for you while he was holding your hand."

"Yes, I remember that part very distinctly. I have a number of memory gaps, and most of the things I don't remember." That morning I had readily admitted that some of the information I gave came secondhand. "The one thing that's totally clear was Dick being in the car and praying with me."

"That's true. He did get in the car and pray with you." She leaned closer. "But, Don, he never held your hand."

"I distinctly remember holding his hand."

"That didn't happen. It was physically impossible."

"But I remember that so clearly. It's one of the most vivid—"

"Think about it. Dick leaned over from the rear of the trunk over the backseat and put his hand on your *shoulder* and touched you. You were facing forward and your left arm was barely hanging together."

"Yes, that's true."

"Dick said you were slumped over on the seat toward the passenger side."

I closed my eyes, visualizing what she had just said. I nodded.

"Your right hand was on the floor of the passenger side of the car. Although the tarp covered the car, there was enough light for him to see your hand down there. There was no way Dick could have reached your right hand."

"But . . . but . . ." I sputtered.

"Someone was holding your hand. But it wasn't Dick."

"If it wasn't Dick's hand, whose was it?"

She smiled and said, "I think you know."

I put down my spoon and stared at her for several seconds. I had no doubt whatsoever that someone had held my hand. Then I understood. "Yes, I think I know too."

Immediately I thought of the verse in Hebrews about entertaining angels unaware. As I pondered for a moment, I also remembered other incidents where there was nothing but a spiritual explanation. For instance, many times in the hospital room in the middle of the night, I would be at my worst. I never saw or heard anyone, but I felt a presence—something—someone—sustaining and encouraging me. That also was something I hadn't talked about. I couldn't explain it, so I assumed others wouldn't understand.

This was another miracle, and I wouldn't have known about it if Anita hadn't corrected me.

Five years after my accident, Dick and I both appeared on Pat Robertson's *700 Club.* A camera crew came to Texas to re-enact the accident and then asked me to talk about my visit to heaven's gates. The *700 Club* aired that segment many times over the next two years.

In one of life's great ironic twists, Dick died of a heart attack in 2001. I confess that I was saddened to hear of his passing, but delighted that he is in glory. Dick saved my life, and God took him to heaven first. I was glad he heard me share about my journey to heaven before he made his own trip.

Since that experience with Anita a little more than a year after my accident, I've been more convinced than ever that God brought me back to this earth for a purpose. The angel gripping my hand was God's way of sustaining me and letting me know that he would not let go of me no matter how hard things became.

I may not feel that hand each day, but I know it's there.

THE NEW NORMAL 14

"I will give you back your health and heal your wounds, says the Lord. Now you are called an outcast—'Jerusalem for whom nobody cares.'"

JEREMIAH 30:17

Some things happen to us from which we never recover, and they disrupt the normalcy of our lives. That's how life is. Human nature has a tendency to try to reconstruct old ways and pick up where we left off. If we're wise, we won't continue to go back to the way things were (we can't anyway). We must instead forget the old standard and accept a "new normal."

I wasted a lot of time thinking about how I used to be healthy and had no physical limitations. In my mind, I'd reconstruct how life *ought* to be, but in reality, I knew my life would never be the same. I had to adjust and accept my physical limits as part of my new normal.

As a child I'd sit on a big brown rug in my great-grandparents' living room and listen to them talk about the good old days. After hearing several stories, I thought, *Those days weren't that good*—at least the recollections they shared didn't seem so great. Maybe for them they truly were the good old days, or perhaps they forgot the negative parts of those days. At some points in our lives, most of us want to go back to a simpler, healthier, or happier time. We can't, but we still keep dreaming about how it once was.

In my twenties, when I was a disc jockey, we used to play oldies, and people who called in to request those songs often commented that music used to be better than it is now. The reality is that in the old days we played good and bad records, but the bad ones faded quickly from memory just like bad ones do now. No one ever asked us to play the music that bombed. The good songs make the former times seem great, as if all the music was outstanding. In reality, there was bad music thirty years ago or fifty years ago—in fact, a lot of bad music. The same is true with experiences. We tend to forget the negative and go back to recapture pleasant events. The reality is, we have selectively remembered—and just as selectively forgotten.

Once that idea got through to me, I decided I couldn't recapture the past. No matter how much I tried to idealize it, that part of my life was over and I would never be healthy or strong again. The only thing for me to do was to discover a new normal.

Yes, I said to myself, *there are things I will never be able to do again. I don't like that and may even hate it, but that doesn't change the way things are. The sooner I make peace with that fact and accept the way things are, the sooner I'll be able to live in peace and enjoy my new normalcy.*

Here's an example of what I mean.

520

In early 2000, I took a group of college kids on a ski trip from Houston to Colorado. Skiing is one of the things I'd always loved doing. Unable to participate, I sat in a clubhouse at the bottom of the hill, gazed out the window, and watched them glide down. Sadness came over me, and I thought, *I made a big mistake. I should never have come here.* As happy as I was for them, I mourned over my inability ever to ski again.

Then I thought for the thousandth time of other things I would never do again. When I was a senior pastor, most of the adults greeted me at the door following each morning service. "Enjoyed your sermon," they'd said. "Great service."

Kids, however, behaved differently. They'd race up with a picture they'd colored for me. Before my accident, I loved the kids flocking around me; I'd kneel down and talk with them. After my recovery, I couldn't squat down and stare at their smiling faces the way I used to before as I said, "Thank you very much. I really like this picture. This is very nice."

After my accident, the best I could do was lean forward and talk to them. Perhaps that doesn't seem like a big thing, but it is for me. I'll never squat again; I'll never be able to kneel so that I can be at a child's level again, because my legs won't give me the ability to do that.

Here's another example: When I go to a drive-through fast-food restaurant, I can't reach for the change with my left arm. The best I can do is reach out across my body with my right arm. It must look strange, and I get a few odd looks, but it's the best I can do.

While neither of these examples is particularly dramatic, they are nonetheless reminders that sometimes things we take for granted every day can be taken from us permanently and suddenly, and we're changed forever.

During my long hospitalization, somebody gave me a magazine article about a young man who lost his sight. He went through an incredibly bitter, depressive time. He wrote that he got so demoralized that a friend who cared enough about him to tell him the truth said, "You just need to get past this."

I paused from reading and thought, *Yes, that sounds like the way I was after my accident.* The article went on, however, to tell the practical instructions the blind man's friend gave him: "I want you to make a list of all the stuff you can still do."

"Now what kind of a list would that be?" the angry blind man asked.

"Just do it for me. You can't write it, obviously, but you can get a tape recorder and dictate it. Just make a list of all the things you can still do. And I'm talking about simple things like 'I can still smell flowers.' Make the list as extensive as you can. When you're finished, I want to hear that list."

The blind man finally agreed and made the list. I don't know how much time passed, but when the friend returned, the blind man was smiling and peaceful.

"You seem like you're in a much better frame of mind than the last time I saw you," the friend said.

"I am. I really am, and that's because I've been working on my list."

"How many things are on your list?"

"About a thousand so far."

"That's fantastic."

"Some of them are very simple. None of them are big, but there are thousands of things I can still do."

The blind man had changed so radically that his friend asked, "Tell me what made you change."

"I've decided to do all the stuff I can. The more I thought about it, the fewer limitations I saw. There are thousands of things I can do—and I'm going to do them for the rest of my life."

After I read that article, I thought, *That's exactly what I need—not mourning, pining, and going back over the way things used to be or what I used to have that I don't have anymore. Instead, I need to discover what I have now, not only to celebrate but also to recognize I'm not helpless.*

As I continued to ponder that idea, I realized I had more going for me than I thought. I had focused so heavily on my losses that I had forgotten what I had left. And I hadn't realized the opportunities I might never have tried otherwise.

In the article, the blind man said something like, "I'm not going to worry about what I can't do. I'm going to do what I can do well." Those words seemed simple.

I read that article at just the right time, and the words seemed incredibly profound. God had sent the message I needed when I needed it. It was one of those powerful moments that caused me to say, "I've got to get on with my life. Whatever I have, I'm going to use it and magnify it to the max."

I'm running out of time, I thought, *but so is everyone else.* I suppose I'm more conscious of time than some people are for two reasons: First, I lost a big chunk of my life because of the accident. Second, I know we don't get to stay long on this earth. As many of the old hymns say, we're really like strangers passing through. It's something we all know from reading the Bible and other books, but those realizations became a wake-up call for me.

I also know that my loved ones are waiting for me at the gate. Some days I can't wait to get back there.

I also realize that I have to wait until God sends me back.

—ᘖᘗ—

Members of South Park Baptist Church moved our family while I was hospitalized. We had been living in a town called Friendswood, about ten miles from the church. We had needed a place nearer the church but hadn't found one. While I was in the hospital, the church leaders found a house, rented it, packed up everything for us, and moved us. When I got out of the hospital, I entered a house I had never seen before. After the ambulance backed up and unloaded me from a gurney to my home hospital bed, I stared at our house for the first time.

I soon adjusted to the new living quarters, because for a long time I could only see the living room, where they set up my hospital bed.

In some ways the move into the rented house was more difficult on the family than on me. I sensed some of the adjustments and difficulties my wife went through with my illness. Eva almost lost her job because she had spent so much time with me that she ran out of conference days, vacation days, and sick days. Other teachers donated their own sick days to her so she could come and be with me in the hospital. Eventually, she ran out of those donated days and had to go back to work. She was our primary source of income.

Eva's colleagues at Robert Louis Stevenson Primary School in Alvin often graded her papers for her, wrote her lesson plans, and covered her classes when she left early to come see me in the hospital. Her fellow teachers even made little gifts to give our kids each day so they would have something to look forward to. They called them "surprise boxes." Fellow teachers also came to our home, along with church members, to clean our house and bring meals. Had it not been for the teachers and the church, Eva would have certainly lost her job and so would I. Yet even with all these incredibly sacrificial gifts and assistance, how she and our children got through that spring semester of 1989 remains a miracle.

One time when Eva inquired about my long-term prognosis, a nurse told her, "Honey, you don't need to know all of that, you're just a wife."

To that nurse, she may have been "just a wife," but Eva took over and functioned for both of us after my accident. I had always taken care of the bills, bank accounts, insurance, and most family matters. She had no choice but to handle them herself, and she did everything well. Eva found strength and a new level of confidence. God provided her with the wisdom to help her take care of family matters. She also learned to remain calm during my complaints and grumbling throughout my lengthy recovery.

The church didn't stop paying me, but we realized that they might, and they were entitled to because I wasn't working. We never talked about the money, but it was always a possibility that hung over our heads.

When the State of Texas was found at fault for the accident, the law limited their liability to $250,000. All the money went to hospital bills, and a quarter of a million dollars didn't make much of a dent.

Ironically, the attorney general of Texas defended the man who drove the truck that hit me, because the defendant was an indigent inmate. Therefore my tax dollars went to defend the state and the man who caused the accident. Isn't life strange sometimes?

—ᴑᴑ—

During the 105 days I spent in the hospital, Eva had the most strain. Not only did she take on the burden of everything in our home, she got up at 6:00 every morning and did everything she had to do around the house and hurried to school. As soon as school was over, she rushed to my bedside, where she stayed until 10:30 every night. Day after day was the same stressful routine.

One of the most challenging experiences for her—by herself—was to buy a van to replace my wrecked car. By then, I was home and able to walk with my Ilizarov still attached. That meant, however, that if I wanted to go anywhere, we had to have a van to transport me. We had no idea how long it would be before I could sit in a normal sedan.

Eva had never bought a vehicle in her life, but she didn't complain. She went to a dealer, test-drove a van, picked out one, and brought it home. "Here's our van," she said.

She made me proud of her—and I felt very grateful.

I learned to drive again in that van. One day as the family was washing it, I walked outside still wearing my Ilizarov. As I lumbered around the van, I noticed that the driver's side door was open. Peering inside, I calculated what it would take for me and my thirty pounds of stainless steel to get behind the wheel. While the family wasn't looking, I maneuvered myself into the seat and started the engine. My family was stunned.

Eva came around to the door and asked, "What are you doing?"

I smiled and said, "I'm going for a drive!"

Incredulous, she stammered, "But you can't."

However, something told me that not having driven for nearly a year, and having had my last drive end in my death, it was now or never for taking the wheel and driving again.

I backed out slowly and drove around the block. It wasn't a long drive, but it was another milestone in my recovery. I'm still not very fond of eighteen-wheelers or long two-lane bridges, but so far I manage to get where I'm going.

Of course, it fell on Eva to make all my appointments and to see that I got to my doctor's office twice a week. And I must add that I wasn't the easiest person to look after. In fact, I was difficult. As my health improved, I became demanding and curt (I wasn't aware of that), and Eva agonized over trying to please me, although she handled it well.

The fact is that I was very unhappy. Many of my problems stemmed from my feeling completely helpless. For a long time I couldn't even get myself a glass of water. Even if I could have poured one for myself, I couldn't have drunk it without help. Even the simplest tasks made me feel useless.

Eva often had to make decisions on the spot without talking to me. She did the best she could. At times, when Eva related what she had done, I was quick to let her know how I would have done it. Almost immediately, I'd realize I hurt her feelings when I did that, but the words had been said. I reminded myself, and her, "I'm sorry. You're doing the best you can." I also reminded myself that regardless of how I would have done things, I wasn't able to do them.

Although she said little during that period, she later allowed me to read what she wrote in her diary. One entry reads: "Don is critical of everything I do. He must be getting better."

That's both sad and funny to me. She knew I was getting better because I started to make decisions again. The desire to get active in doing things was her yardstick for my recovery. I seemed to want to get more involved in life and to question what was going on.

I just wish I had been a better patient and made it easier for her.

The worst part of my convalescence for the family was that we farmed out our three kids. They weren't orphans, but they lived with other people for about six months. Our twin sons stayed with Eva's parents in Louisiana. I know they weren't happy about having to move so far away. The distance made the boys feel detached and separated, but they handled it quite well. They were still in elementary school and, at that age, it probably wasn't too difficult relocating. Nicole, who was five years older and thirteen at the time, moved in with her girlfriend's family and was able to stay in her middle school. It would have been much more traumatic for her to move away.

The accident happened in January, and the kids didn't come home permanently until June. I felt terrible that we couldn't provide for our children.

The kids came to see me on weekends during my hospital stays, which was tough on them. When they made their first visit to the hospital, a staff psychologist did a kind thing for them. He took all three kids into a room and showed them a life-size dummy with devices attached to it, similar to what was on my body. This way he could explain what they would see when they entered my room.

I'm glad he did that for them, because even many adults, not having that kind of preparation, showed obvious shock when they first saw me. In my condition, I interpreted their reactions as horror.

When the children came into my room the first time, all three of them stepped as close as they could to hug me. They loved me and wanted to see for themselves that I was okay. Of course, I was barely alive, but it still did me a lot of good just to see them. The staff didn't let them stay long. As awful as I looked, the children believed me when I said I would get well.

After they left, Eva came back into ICU. I don't remember this—I don't remember much from those days. She said I looked at her through my oxygen mask and said, "We have the best kids in the world."

I've never gotten the impression that our children felt as if they had missed anything, but I sometimes felt they were cheated out of experiences with their father.

When I finally was out and could walk, I remember trying to play pitch with the boys, even though I knew I couldn't take more than a step or two. If one of them hit a ball that went out of my immediate range, I couldn't chase it. They felt terrible about that.

I sensed my limitation kept them from enjoying the game, so we stopped doing it. Although they didn't say so, I knew they didn't want to see me try to run or risk falling down—though many times I did fall.

Also, both boys like to surf, and before the accident, I went surfing with them. After I was able to walk and drive, on several occasions I loaded them and their boards in the van and drove them to the Gulf, but I couldn't do anything with them. I could only watch. They seemed to understand, but it was still hard on me.

I have no doubt that there are things my sons probably wanted to do, but they never mentioned them for fear of putting me in a situation where I'd have to decide whether I might hurt myself. So I do feel that my boys were cheated out of normal boy things in their growing up years.

Nicole, being a girl, had that "Daddy thing." She was our oldest child. She expressed her feelings very differently from Joe, who is a very emotional kid. Chris is the cool one, although deeply sensitive, and doesn't show his feelings as easily as his twin.

While writing this book, I asked my kids to tell me how the accident affected them and our family and how it changed their perception of me. When the accident happened in 1989, Nicole was thirteen years old. Here is her response:

The biggest impact on my life was living away from my parents for several months. I lived with the Mauldin family from our church during that time. The accident taught me to appreciate my own family. I'm very close to all of them, because I realize how fortunate I was to be a part of such a wonderful family. I also feel that I am able to help people in crisis situations because I learned at a young age how to use prayer and friends to help me get through difficult times. It caused me to look at life in a different way. At a young age I was able to realize that life is precious, and that we have to seize every moment.

I feel that our family is very close because of the accident. I also feel we really look after one another, and that we would do anything for our family members. The boys and I have a special bond that we don't always see between brothers and sisters. Daddy's accident and recovery taught us to be there for each other. Mom became a lot stronger and independent, because Dad couldn't take care of the things he always had. I only wish Daddy didn't have to go through this to bring us so close together.

After Dad was hurt so bad, I saw for the first time that he was a vulnerable person. Before the accident, he had seemed indestructible. Over the years since, I have seen that the accident has made him even stronger. He may have been hurt physically, but he is the strongest person I know spiritually and emotionally. To have gone through what he did and still be such a loving and devoted servant of God is amazing to me.

For a long time I was angry about the accident, but I grew up and realized how fortunate we are to still have him and how the accident brought us closer. If he had died in that accident I don't know how I would have made it through some of the toughest times in my life. There is something very special about getting advice from someone who has been to heaven, survived countless surgeries, and lived to tell about it. I tend to listen a little harder to him now.

Joe was eight years old at the time of the accident, and this is how he responded:

My first memory was being picked up by a teacher friend of my mother's. When I saw my mom crying, I knew something was very wrong.

I remember going to the hospital to see Dad. They showed us a doll made up to look like Dad's injuries, so when we went in we would be prepared. It was really hard to see Dad like that. We didn't stay long, which was fine with me because I did not like seeing him that way. Chris and I had to move in with our grandparents in Louisiana. I thought it was cool at first, but then I started to miss my family. I'm really glad I had my twin brother with me. Every weekend we drove from Bossier City to Houston. That got old very fast.

The worst thing about the accident was that while other kids were going camping and fishing with their dads, I never got to experience those things. I still think about that a lot even today. Sometimes I feel kind of angry and cheated or depressed. But in the past few years, I've gotten to go camping and fishing with Dad. I'm not sure that he realizes how happy that makes me. Through this experience I realized how many people loved and cared about our family. If we hadn't had God in our lives, I don't know how we would have gotten through this.

This is Chris's response:

When you're an eight-year-old, your father is a superhero. He's invincible. When I first heard about Dad's accident, I didn't think it was nearly as serious as it turned out to be. Mom was upset when she told me the news and couldn't hide the tears. But Dad was strong, and I'd never seen him cry. Even when I saw him surrounded by monitors in the ICU, hooked up to oxygen, and barely able to speak, I fully expected him to be home in a week.

I wasn't present for most of the major surgeries. I went to live with my grandparents only days after the accident and saw my dad only on weekends. During those brief encounters, I began to understand just how bad he hurt—both his body and his spirit.

I was fascinated by the metal contraptions that surrounded his left arm and leg, but I knew they caused him immense pain. He looked so worn out as if he had just woken up, or maybe could never quite fall asleep. Sometimes I got the impression he didn't want me or anyone else in the room. Even as little as I understood about depression, I knew he was suffering from it.

The first thing I did each time I visited him was to approach slowly and put my arms around him. I hugged him gently. For the first time in my life, he seemed fragile. Even when he returned home from the hospital, I continued the same routine—come home from school and hug Dad. It was as much to reassure me as it was to comfort him. I hope it served both purposes.

As my brother, Joe, and I grew older, and Dad's recovery continued, we became more interested in sports and the outdoors. Dad would do his best to join us. I remember feeling terrible when I threw the football too far for Dad's reach. He'd stumble and sometimes he'd fall. I choked back tears on a number of occasions. I'm sure he did the same. But from an emotional standpoint, Dad was always there for me. He is vitally interested in what his kids do. After all, I suppose we make his return from Paradise worthwhile in some regard.

The family grew closer as a result of Dad's accident. We all took different roles out of sheer necessity. Mom became the decision maker and disciplinarian during Dad's recovery. I tried my best to be the man of the house. Sometimes I was really just a bully, but I grew out of it. I learned to lean on the others as they leaned on me. Nicole mothered Joe and me as best she could.

Dad suffered from depression for years after the accident—still does to some extent. Maybe he struggled with it before the accident, but if he did, I never noticed. Dad is fiercely independent and seldom lets his family into his darkest corners. I guess I'm the same way.

Here is Eva's response to how her perception of me has changed:

I was most surprised by Don's lack of determination during the initial days following the wreck. He had always been a fighter, one who was constantly pushing himself and others to do more. When he wouldn't try to breathe it was almost as if I didn't know him. The depression had also been a new aspect. I learned to recognize the sign of a "bad time" approaching. It is harder when the pain is worse; he doesn't sleep and the stress builds.

Through the years I've learned that if I leave Don alone he eventually returns to a more even keel. When I wanted to tell him something he really needed to hear but didn't want to know, I had to bite my tongue—and on a few occasions I didn't succeed.

Today, I don't think of him as injured, even though I know he is and always will be. Don goes at such a pace that it is easy for me to forget his pain and handicaps. My husband is truly a remarkable person.

_____ ෴ _____

My kids were probably more confident about my recovery than I was. They never saw me receiving therapy, agonizing, or throwing up because I'd gotten so sick, or seen me when I tried to stand up too fast. As much as possible, we tried to insulate them. Eva saw me at my worst, but she protected the children as much as possible.

Although they don't admit it, there probably is a "Dad gap" for my children, especially the twins. Because they were eight years old, they missed my being there for an important developmental time to help them learn to do things such as play team sports and go camping.

Looking back, I think the accident affected my parents more permanently than anybody. In fact, they were devastated. I'm the oldest of three sons, and all of us had been healthy. Then, suddenly, when I reached the age of thirty-eight, they were heartbroken and felt helpless to do anything for me. For a long time, they thought I would probably die.

My dad had been a career military man, and my mother had to learn to handle just about everything. Yet when they came to see me during the first week in the hospital, Mom fainted. Dad grabbed her and helped her out of the room. She wasn't prepared to see me in such bad shape. I'm not sure anyone would have been.

Even now, I'm not sure my mother has fully recovered from my accident. But here are two of many very beautiful memories of my parents' devotion to me.

First, during the summer following the accident, as if Eva didn't have enough to concern herself with, she decided to take the South Park youth to summer camp. That would have been my job had I been physically able. But she tackled it with gusto. That meant someone would have to stay with me while she was away.

My mother cheerfully agreed to do so. The week of the church youth camp came, and Eva left me with Mom. Each day Mother prepared meals for me, and I was so glad to have her there. But I did dread one daily occurrence—my mother would be required to empty my urinals and bedpans. Now, I know she had diapered me when I was a baby, but a lot of time had passed between infant powderings and the present.

I remember the first time I had to go when she was caring for me, and I asked for the bedpan. She acted as if it were the most natural thing ever. After I had finished, I agonized over having to tell her.

She saved me the embarrassment by asking if I was through. I just nodded. She took the bedpan into the bathroom, and then I heard one of the most remarkable sounds I have ever heard in my life. After she entered the bathroom and flushed the commode, I could hear my mother singing. In spite of the most lowly of tasks one human can perform for another, she sang as she washed out the bedpan. It was as if her whole motherhood was wrapped up in that moment. She was again doing something for her son that he could not do for himself, and she was happy and fulfilled. I will cherish that memory, for it defines the devotion that only a mother could have.

Second, I remember one private moment I had with my father, equally poignant and dramatic. One day, following yet another 250-mile trip to see me for an afternoon at St. Luke's, my parents were preparing for the return trip to their home near Bossier City.

For some reason I don't recall, Mom had stepped out of the room. Alone now, my father came close to my bed and took my only unbroken limb, my right hand, in his gnarled hand. He leaned close to me and with great emotion and absolute honesty said, "I would give anything to trade places with you and take this on me."

He's my dad, and more than at any other time, I realized how much he loves me.

—◌◌◌◌—

Repeatedly, my doctor has told me, "Everything we did for you is the best we can do. Don't count on being able to live a long, productive life. Because of arthritis and a lot of other complications that will set in, you're going to have an uphill battle to be even as mobile as you are now."

He knew what he was talking about. It's been fifteen years since my accident. I've already felt the beginning of arthritis. Weather changes affect me; I grow tired faster. Some of it may be age, but I think it's a reflection of the fact that I have to use my legs and knees in ways God didn't design them to be used.

Even today, my left knee hyperextends, so if someone comes from behind and inadvertently slaps me on the back, I have to catch myself or I'll keep going forward. I can't lock my knee into place to keep from losing my balance and pitching forward.

I've tried to make light of this, quipping, "I've fallen in some of the best places in Texas." Or, "I've considered commissioning some little plaques that say, 'Don Piper fell here.'"

One time I led an outdoor conference in the Texas hill country. The ground was uneven and I'd walk along and all of a sudden, I'd fall. I wasn't hurt, but I fell three times the first day.

Despite everything they did for me, one of my legs is an inch and a half shorter than the other. That alone makes my backbone curve. The backbone is beginning to show wear and tear, as are my hip joints. My left elbow is so messed up I can't straighten it out. Doctors did everything they could, including operating on it several times. The elbow was fractured on the inside, and when it knitted back together, it wouldn't allow me to straighten it. To use the doctor's expression, "It's a very gimpy joint."

An injury like that, he pointed out, is not forgiving. Once it gets messed up, it's hard to fix it again.

This is part of my new normal.

Once after a visit to Dr. Tom Greider's office, he asked me back into his private suite. Despite his busy caseload, I felt he was genuinely interested in me, and we talked about a lot of things.

On a whim I asked, "Tom, just how bad was I when they brought me in that night of the accident?"

He didn't flinch. "I've seen worse." He paused for a moment, leaned over his desk, and then continued, "but none of them lived."

I've had to find different ways to do things. I am alive, however, and I intend to serve Jesus Christ as long as I remain alive. But I already know what's ahead, waiting for me.

I'm ready to leave this earth anytime.

TOUCHING LIVES

All praise to the God and Father of our Lord Jesus Christ. He is the source of every mercy and the God who comforts us. He comforts us in all our troubles so that we can comfort others. When others are troubled, we will be able to give them the same comfort God has given us.

2 CORINTHIANS 1:3–4

Sometimes I still ask God why I wasn't allowed to stay in heaven. I have no answer to that question. I have learned, however, that God brings people into my life who need me or need to hear my message, giving me the opportunity to touch their lives.

One of the first times I was able to minister to someone as a result of my accident was when I was the guest preacher in a large church. They invited me specifically to talk about my trip to heaven. A woman who sat near the front and to my left began to weep shortly after I began to speak. I could see the tears sliding down her cheeks. As soon as we closed the meeting, she rushed up to me and clasped my hand.

"My mother died last week."

"I'm so sorry for your loss—"

"No, no, you don't understand. God sent you here tonight. I needed this kind of reassurance. Not that I didn't believe—I did, but my heart has been so heavy because of the loss. I feel so much better. She *is* in a better place. Oh, Reverend Piper, I needed to hear that tonight."

Before I could say anything more, she hugged me and added, "God also sent *me* here tonight because I needed this reassurance. Not that I didn't believe and didn't know—because I'm a believer and so was she—but I needed to hear those words tonight. I needed to know about heaven from someone who had been there."

So far as I recall, she was the first to talk to me that way, but certainly not the last. I've heard this kind of response hundreds of times. It still amazes me that I can be a blessing to so many just by sharing my experience.

For those who already believe, my testimony has been reassuring; for skeptics, it's opened them up to think more seriously about God.

⸺☙❧⸺

Two years after the accident, when I still wore leg braces and walked with crutches, I took a group of our young people to a conference at Houston's First Baptist Church. Dawson McAllister, a great teacher to youth, was the speaker. He's so popular he fills up the place.

As happens when you work with teens, we were late in leaving South Park Church. I didn't say anything, but I felt extremely irritated with the delay. I had wanted to arrive early because I knew the best seats would be taken if we didn't get there at least an hour before starting time.

I tried not to let it show, but I was still upset by the time we reached First Baptist Church in Houston. Once we went inside the huge building, we realized—as I had expected—that all the seats on the lower floor were filled. We'd have to climb the stairs.

I groaned at the thought of having to do more walking. Even though I was mobile, wearing those braces and the pressure of the crutches under my armpits tired me out. To make it worse, the elevator wasn't working. *If that person hadn't been late,* I kept thinking, *I wouldn't have to hobble up all those stairs.*

It wasn't just clumping up the stairs, but the auditorium was so full that the only places left to sit were in the top rows. Our young people, naturally, raced ahead to claim those seats. They promised to save one for me on the end. I counted 150 steps as I painfully made my way up.

By the time I finally reached the top, exhaustion had overcome me. I could hardly walk the last flight and across the back of the auditorium to the seat the kids had saved for me. Before I sat down—which also demanded a lot of effort—I rested by leaning against the wall. As I tried to catch my breath, I asked myself, *What am I doing here?*

I could have gotten other adults to take the kids, but I really wanted to be with them. I wanted to feel useful again. I also knew this would be an exciting event for the youth, and I wanted to be part of it. Boisterous laughter and shouting back and forth filled the place. The youth were ready to be blessed and challenged, but at that moment, I didn't think about the kids or how much they would get out of the meeting. I thought only of being worn out.

At that moment self-pity took over. As I continued to lean against the wall, my gaze swept the auditorium. Two sections over I spotted a teenage boy in a wheelchair. He was sitting with his head in his hands, his back to me. As I stared at him, I *knew* I had to go over and talk to him. Suddenly I didn't question my actions and I forgot about being tired.

I leaned my crutches against the wall and then slowly, painfully made my way across to his section and down the steps. He was a large, good-looking kid, maybe sixteen years old. When I got closer, I realized why I needed to talk to him. He was wearing an Ilizarov frame—which I hadn't been able to see from where I had stood. My tiredness vanished, along with my anger and self-pity. It was as if I saw myself in that wheelchair and reexperienced all the pain of those days.

He was looking away from me when I laid my hand on his shoulder. His head spun around and he glared at me.

"That really hurts doesn't it?" I asked.

He looked at me as if to say, *What kind of fool are you?* Instead he said, "Yeah. It hurts very much."

"I know." I patted his shoulder. "Believe me, I know."

His eyes widened. "You do?"

"I do. I had one too."

"It's horrible."

"I know that. It's just horrible. I wore one on my left leg for eleven months."

"Nobody ever understands," he said plaintively.

"They can't. It's not something you can talk about and have anyone understand your pain."

For the first time I saw something in his eyes. Maybe it was hope, or maybe just a sense of peace because at long last he had found someone who knew what he was going through. We had connected, and I felt privileged to be standing next to him.

"My name is Don," I said, "and you've just met somebody who understands the pain and the discouragement you're going through."

He stared at me, and then his eyes moistened. "I don't know if I'm going to make it."

"You're going to make it. Trust me, you'll make it."

"Maybe," he said.

"What happened?" By then I'd realized it hadn't been a voluntary surgery.

"I had a ski accident."

I noticed that he was wearing a letter jacket. I asked, "You a football player?"

"Yes, sir."

Briefly I told him about my accident, and he told me more about what had happened to him. "I'm going to tell you something," I said. "One day you will walk again."

His face registered skepticism.

"You might not play football again, but you'll walk." I handed him my business card. "My number is on the card, and you can call me anytime, day or night, twenty-four hours a day."

He took the card and stared at it.

"I'm going to walk back up there to my kids." I pointed to where they sat. "I want you to watch me. And as you watch, I want you to know that one day you will walk too." I laughed. "And I'll bet you'll walk better than I do."

He reached up, grabbed me, and hugged me. He held me tight for a long time. I could feel his constricted breathing as he fought back tears. Finally he released me and mumbled his thanks.

"You've found somebody who understands," I said. "Please call me."

That boy needed somebody who understood. I don't know that I had much to offer, but I had my experience and I could talk to him about pain. Had I not gone through it myself, I'd just be telling him, "I hope you feel better. You're going to be okay"—well-meaning words that most people used.

When I reached the top row, perspiration drenched my body from all the effort, but I didn't care. I turned around. He still stared at me. I smiled and waved, and he waved back. The dejection and despair had left his face.

Over the next six months, I received three calls from him, two just to talk and one late at night when he was really discouraged. They were phone calls I will always cherish, one struggling pilgrim to another.

_____ॐॐ_____

One time, a Houston TV station scheduled me to appear on a live talk show. While I was waiting in their greenroom, the producer came in and began to explain how the show worked and some of the questions I could expect to be asked.

"That's fine," I said. "Who else is a guest on the show?"

"You're it."

"Wait a minute. You're going to do an hour-long show and I'm the only guest?"

"That's right."

I wondered what I would talk about for an hour. It was fairly early in my recovery, and at the time I had no idea how interested people were in my story. By then the doctor had removed the Ilizarov frame and I was wearing braces and using crutches. I had brought pictures of me in the hospital, which they televised that day. And I brought the Ilizarov device itself.

Once the TV interview started, I told my story, and then the host asked me questions. The hour passed quickly. While we were still live on the show, a woman called the TV station and insisted, "I need to talk to Reverend Piper immediately."

They wouldn't interrupt the program, but as soon as the program ended, someone handed me a slip of paper with her telephone number. I called her.

"You've got to talk to my brother," she said.

"What's the matter with him?"

"He was involved in a fight in a bar, and another man pulled out a shotgun and blew his leg off. He's wearing one of those things like you used to have on your leg."

"Of course I'll talk to him," I said. "Where is he?"

"He's home in bed."

"Give me the address and I'll go—"

"Oh no, you can't go over there. He's angry and mean. And he's violent. He won't talk to anybody who comes to see him." She gave me his telephone number. "Please call him, but he's so mean right now, I guarantee that he'll cuss you out." Then she added, "And he may just hang up on you, but try him anyway. Please."

As soon as I got home, I called her brother and introduced myself. Before I had spoken more than three sentences, he did just what she had predicted. He yelled at me. He screamed and let me have it with just about every swear word I'd ever heard, and he repeated them several times.

When he paused I said quietly, "I had one of those things on my leg that you have—that fixator."

545

He didn't say anything for a few seconds, so I said, "I wore one of those Ilizarov devices on my left leg. I know what you must be going through."

"Oh, man, this is killing me. It hurts all the time. It's just—" and he went off again as if he hadn't heard me, peppering his anger with a lot of profanity.

When he paused again, I said, "I understand what it feels like to have one of them."

"You don't have it anymore?"

"No, I finally got it off. If you do what you're supposed to do, you can get yours off one day." That didn't sound like much, but it was the only thing I could think to say.

"If I had some wrenches I'd take it off right now."

"If you take it off, you might as well cut your leg off, because it's the only thing that's holding your leg on."

"I know that, but it's just killing me. I can't sleep—" Then he went on again, telling me how miserable he was and how much he hated everything.

Then something occurred to me, and I interrupted him. "What does your leg look like? Does it seem to be hot near the pinholes? Is it the same color up and down your skin? Are there certain holes that hurt more than others?"

"Yeah, that's right. One of them especially—man, it hurts real bad."

"Is your sister there yet?" When he said she was, I ordered him, "Put her on the phone."

He didn't argue and she picked up the phone. "Thank you," she said. "I appreciate so—"

"Listen to me," I said, interrupting her. "I want you to call an ambulance *right now*. Take your brother to the hospital as fast

546

as you can get there. He has a serious infection in that leg. If he doesn't get there soon, he's going to lose his leg."

"You think so?"

"I'm telling you. He has all the symptoms. He's probably got a fever too. Have you checked?"

"Yes, that's right. He's running a fever."

"Get him to the hospital immediately. Call me afterward."

The next day she called. "Oh, you were right! He has an infection, and he was in terrible shape. They gave him all those antibiotics. They said he got there just in time, and he's doing better today."

"I assume he's still in the isolation unit." When she said he was, I added, "I'm going to come and see him."

As a minister I could get in to see him. I went to the hospital, talked to him, and prayed with him. Eventually that young man turned to Jesus Christ.

If I hadn't been on that TV show and his sister hadn't watched it, he might not have only lost a leg; there is a strong possibility that he would have died. Not only had God used me to save the young man's physical life but I had been an instrument in his salvation. That was just one more instance of my beginning to see that God still has things for me to do here on earth.

I had immediately recognized the problem because it had happened to me when I was still in the hospital. I had gotten an infection and began hurting badly. I thought it was just part of the pain I'd have to go through. Then a nurse discovered that I had infection in one of those pinholes.

I remembered then how days before, one of the nurses apparently had cross-contaminated the pinholes. She was a surly type and never showed me compassion like the others. She came in and did her work, but she acted as if she resented having to work with me.

They used Q-tips, and they had been instructed to use a new one to clean each hole. I had noticed that this time, the nurse didn't get a fresh Q-tip each time, probably because it was faster not to reach for a new one. I didn't think anything about that until after the hole became infected. My added pain had come about because of her laziness. Once they discovered the infection and my elevated temperature, they rushed me into the isolation unit, where I stayed for two weeks. While I was there, no one could visit me.

Eva complained and told the doctor what happened. I never saw that nurse again, so I don't know if they fired her or transferred her.

As much as I enjoy public speaking, few opportunities excite me more than speaking at my alma mater, Louisiana State University (LSU). My wife and I met at LSU, and two of our three children also studied there.

One of the on-campus organizations where I have spoken on several occasions is the Baptist Collegiate Ministry (BCM). While Nicole was a student at LSU and served as one of the officers in that group, the BCM invited me to speak. Knowing she would be in the audience made the experience even more delightful.

Among the many campus activities the BCM sponsored was a Thursday night praise and worship service called TNT. The committee asked me to speak to them about my accident.

The students advertised my talk all over campus as "Dead Man Talking." Because so many showed up, they scheduled two back-to-back services. As I spoke, the audience seemed mesmerized by the story of a man who died and came back to life. I spoke of heaven, answered prayer, and miracles. I told them about singing "What a Friend We Have in Jesus" in the car with Dick Onerecker.

As each service ended, the praise band led us in a chorus of that meaningful song. I didn't know they were going to do it. While I have no doubt they were led by the Spirit to do so, "What a Friend We Have in Jesus" remains a difficult song for me to hear or sing.

Afterward a large number of students waited around to ask questions. Among them was an African-American student named Walter Foster. He asked many questions himself and stayed and listened to the other students' questions as well. When I left the auditorium, Walter followed me. Although I didn't mind, I felt as if he pursued me with dogged determination—as if he couldn't get enough details about heaven or hear enough about my experience.

A few months later, Nicole called me. "Do you remember Walter Foster?" Her voice broke and she started to cry. As soon as I said I remembered him, she said, "He . . . he died. He suffered a heart attack! Just like that—and he was gone."

Apparently Walter had known about his serious heart condition and was under medical care; everyone assumed he was doing all right. Obviously his death shocked all the students who knew him.

"Twenty-year-old students aren't supposed to die," one of his friends had said.

After I hung up the phone, I thought back to the day when Walter and I met. I wondered if he had had a premonition about his death. The fact that he followed me the whole time I was at LSU and plied me with endless questions about heaven caused me to wonder. His questions seemed more than just curiosity. *Maybe,* I thought, *even then God was preparing him for his homeward journey.*

His sudden death devastated his friends, especially those involved with the Baptist Collegiate Ministry. They were a close-knit group and mourned the loss of their dear member. The night following his death, they gathered at the BCM building—the place Walter loved most.

During an emotional meeting that night, a number of his friends spoke at length about how much it had meant to Walter that I had shared my experience about heaven. Many mentioned the excitement he expressed to them over what he had heard. He talked about it for days afterward.

"Several times during the day when Reverend Piper was here," one of them said, "Walter told me, 'One day I know I'm going to be in heaven myself.'"

Pressing church business kept me from being at Walter's memorial service at First Baptist Church of Baton Rouge. Nicole represented our family and reported that evening about the celebration of Walter's life. Two special requests from his friends were that the preacher would share the gospel message and that someone would sing one particular song. Of course, it was "What a Friend We Have in Jesus." The audience learned the special significance that hymn held for Walter.

Nicole, a music major at LSU and an excellent soloist, sang the song to the assembled mourners. They responded with both great sadness and glorious hope. Tears flowed and many smiled peacefully.

After the service, many students lingered to talk about how much Walter's unwavering belief in heaven had comforted and encouraged them.

One of the other bright things to emerge from my testimony at the BCM and Walter's later passing was the construction and dedication of a prayer garden at the LSU BCM. That seems appropriate to me, because each time I share my story, I stress the paramount importance of prayer. After all, I'm still alive because of answered prayer.

Like many others whose lives have divinely intersected with mine since my accident and my return from heaven, Walter represents those who will be waiting for me the next time God calls me home.

—◦◦◦—

Sue Fayle's first husband died of cancer. His long torturous passing took a lot out of her. She assumed she would live the rest of her life as a widow. But her neighbor Charles, also without a spouse, changed that. They were not only neighbors, but in their common sense of loss, they became good friends. As time passed, they seemed to fulfill needs for each other in a way that only those who have loved and lost seem to understand. Their friendship evolved into love, and they cautiously considered marriage.

Sue had serious reservations about marrying Charles because he came from what she called a rough-and-tough working-class neighborhood. He had a history of hard drinking, and she said, "I can't live with that."

As their love continued to grow, however, Sue issued one simple condition for marriage: "I won't marry a man who gets drunk."

Charles not only stopped getting drunk, he quit drinking altogether. Now they were ready to talk of marriage.

One day they talked about the death of their spouses—both of whom had died of cancer. "If I'm ever diagnosed with cancer," he said, "I'll kill myself." He knew that not only did the person with the disease suffer but their loved ones went through deep agony as well. "I couldn't put anyone through that ordeal."

They did marry, had a good marriage, and Charles never drank again. Sue had already been active in our church, but after their marriage, Charles also became active.

One day, however, he received the one diagnosis he feared most of all: He had cancer. Now he had to face his deep-seated terror. He was afraid that his diagnosis would put Sue through the same terrible ordeal she had faced before.

He also faced another fear after he received the diagnosis: The news forced him to confront his own mortality. "I'm terrified of dying," he confessed. Although Charles was a church member and said he believed, he was one of those individuals who doubted his salvation. Sue assured him that while she was dedicated to seeing him through this crisis, she was concerned about his lack of assurance of his salvation. She had heard my testimony about heaven on several occasions and had retold my story to others.

"Can you talk to Charles?" she asked me one day. "He needs to hear your testimony from you."

By then I had become the single adult minister of Pasadena's First Baptist Church, where I am today. Sue and I had worked together on projects on many occasions.

"Please talk to him about salvation, but also tell him about what life is like after death. I believe that a man-to-man talk with Charles would do a lot for him."

I knew Charles, of course, and because of his past, I suspected he thought he wasn't good enough for God. I agreed to talk to him.

Charles and I hit it off right away. He was a great guy and easy to relate to. I made it a point to visit him on a regular basis. Whenever I came, Sue excused herself and stayed out of the room until I was ready to leave.

Even as Charles's health deteriorated, he never displayed the least bit of anger or depression. We even talked about how difficult it was to be dependent on others for even the most personal of functions—bedpans, urinals, and bathing.

About the fourth time I visited, Charles finally opened up. "I'm afraid. I want to go to heaven, but I need assurance—I want to be certain that when I die, I'll go to heaven."

As he talked about his life, it was obvious that his experience with God was authentic. As is often the case, for many years before he married Sue, he simply hadn't been a faithful follower of Christ. Several times I reminded him of the verses in the Bible that promise heaven as the ultimate destination for all believers.

"I know, I know," he said. "Before I was saved, I knew I wouldn't go to heaven. I was going to hell. Now I want to be sure about heaven."

My description of heaven encouraged him. "Yes, yes, that's what I want," he said.

On one visit as he talked, he smiled and said, "I'm ready. I'm at peace. I finally know that I'll go to heaven."

On both of the last two visits I made, Charles said, "Tell me again. Tell me once more what heaven is like."

I told him again, even though he had already heard everything I had to say. It was as if his assurance grew each time I talked about heaven.

A short time before he died, Sue put Charles in hospice at the Houston Medical Center, just a few doors away from where I had been hospitalized for such a long time.

On the last day of his life on earth, Charles told Sue, "It's going to be all right. I'm going from pain to peace. Someday we'll be together again."

When Sue called and told me, she added, "He died absolutely without fear."

Charles's calm assurance and acceptance gave Sue peace as she worked through her own grief and loss. She told me that only weeks before his death, he'd said listening to my experience and seeing the positive glow in my life made the difference. "It's settled," he'd said. "I know I'm going to a better place."

As Sue shared her memories of Charles, she laughed and said, "Won't I be the lucky one? I've got two men waiting for me. One day, when my time comes, I'll have one on each arm, former husbands who are also brothers in Christ, and they can escort me down the streets of gold."

—————

When Joe, one of my twins, reached his teens, we decided to look for a used car for him. He wanted a truck, so we searched until we found one he liked, a 1993 Ford Ranger.

The dealer's name was Gary Emmons; he owned a longtime automobile dealership in our area. Once we settled on the truck Joe wanted, we went inside to make the deal. Mr. Emmons gave us an excellent price, and Joe bought the truck.

Because of that experience, a good relationship formed between Gary Emmons and my family. We bought three or four more cars from him after that.

Gary knew a little about what had happened to me, but no details. He was a race-car driver as well as a car dealer. He seemed fascinated with my story. He had said he'd like to hear the whole story one day, but either he was too busy or I had to rush on.

One day Joe went to the dealership to make a payment. Gary waved him over. "You'll never believe this." The man grinned. "An amazing thing happened yesterday."

"What?"

"I went to check out a car that we had just bought. I got inside the car to do the things I usually do—you know, punch all the buttons to see if everything works—things like listen to the engine for any defects, check the air conditioner, and see if the radio works. I noticed a tape inside the cassette deck. I pushed the eject button."

He paused and smiled. "Bet you'll never guess what was on that tape."

"I have no idea," Joe said.

"It was your dad's story. We had bought the car in an auction, so there was no owner to give the tape back to. I took the tape and listened to it. The only thing I could think of when I heard it was one word—*awesome*."

As I look back, it's amazing. Gary had wanted to hear my story, but we just had not gotten together.

"What are the odds of my going to an automobile auction with thousands of cars for sale," Gary asked Joe, "then I sit inside one, push a button, and hear your dad talking?"

For days after that, I think Gary must have told everybody he talked to about my accident.

Of course, that testimony thrilled me. I've also heard many other stories of the way God has used my story.

I had made a tape about my experience while preaching in my church, Pasadena's First Baptist, and had it duplicated. I must have distributed thousands of them. I also know people took the tape and copied it for their friends. I know people who ordered as many as twenty tapes over a period of months.

That testimonial tape just keeps going on and on. Many people who heard my story duplicated it for people going through physical trauma themselves or those who are dealing with the loss of a loved one.

I can only conclude that God had a plan for Gary Emmons to hear that tape and made sure he did.

~~~

One day while I was walking down the hallway of First Baptist Church of Pasadena, a woman stopped me. That's not unusual, of course. In fact, my wife jokes that it takes me thirty minutes to walk twenty feet because everyone has something he or she needs to ask me or tell me. We have over ten thousand members; that's a lot of folks to get around to.

"Oh, Reverend Piper, I came by just to see you. I want to tell you something—something that I think you need to hear."

Usually when someone starts out that way, he usually adds, "It's for your own good," and it's usually not something I want to hear. Several other people were with me, and I wasn't sure how to react. As I stared at her, however, I sensed an urgency in her face and a deep intensity. I turned to the others and asked, "Would you mind?"

They were gracious, of course.

"I'm a registered nurse, and you will never believe what happened."

"I've had a lot of unbelievable things happen. Just try me."

"This happened at the hospital. A woman whose mother was very ill and hospitalized was able to hear your tape, and it changed her life."

I had heard that before, but I never minded hearing new stories, so I said, "Tell me more."

"Somebody brought her this tape and she wasn't a believer. But the person wanted her to listen to the tape anyway. Her friends had tried to talk to her about God. They had given her Bibles, all kinds of books and pamphlets, but nothing affected her. She said, 'I don't want to talk about God, religion, or salvation.' Even though she was terminally ill, she wasn't open to any message about eternity."

She paused to wipe a tear from her eyes before she continued, "Somebody brought her a tape—your tape about your experience in heaven—and asked her if she would listen to it. The friend didn't press it, but said something casual like, 'You might find this helpful. It's about a man who died, went to heaven, and came back to life again.'"

The nurse told me that the woman said that she might listen to it if she thought about it. The friend left. The tape lay on the stand next to her bed, unheard. Her health soon deteriorated so badly that doctors told her daughter that it was only a matter of a week, two at the most.

The daughter, who was a believer, desperately wanted her mother to hear the tape of my testimony. The tape contains two messages. The first side tells of the miracles that had to happen for me to live, and recounts the answered prayer that took place for me to live—as I've written about earlier in this book. The second side of the tape tells about what heaven is like. I called it "The Cure for Heart Trouble." That's the part the daughter wanted her mother to listen to.

But the woman refused. "I don't want to listen to all that stuff," she said.

Days went by, and the older woman's condition grew more desperate. The nurse who was talking to me, and who was a Christian, realized what was going on. After she talked with the daughter, the nurse decided to talk to the patient herself about her soul—something she had not done before. She reasoned that sometimes it's easier for a stranger or someone less known to give a positive witness than it is for a family member.

After working her shift, the nurse walked into the room and asked, "May I sit down and talk to you a few minutes?"

The dying woman nodded.

Gently and discreetly the nurse talked about faith and God's peace and how much of a difference Jesus Christ had made in her own life.

The whole time, the woman said nothing.

The nurse mentioned the tape. "I've heard it, and I think it's something you would like to know. Would you like to listen to the tape?"

The old woman nodded, so the nurse put the tape in the cassette recorder and left.

The next day the dying woman told her daughter and the nurse that she had listened to the tape. "I found it very interesting. I'm seriously thinking about becoming a Christian."

Even though the nurse and the daughter rejoiced, they didn't try to pressure the dying woman. Two days passed before the woman said, "I have become a believer." She told her daughter first and then the nurse. After that, no matter who came into the room to see her, the dying woman would say, "I have become a Christian. I've accepted Jesus Christ as my Savior and I'm going to heaven."

Within hours after her publicly telling others about her conversion, the woman's condition deteriorated. She drifted in and out of consciousness. The next day when the nurse came on duty, she learned that the old woman had died only minutes earlier.

The nurse told me all of that and then said, "You won't believe what was happening during those final moments while she was dying."

Before I could ask, she said, "The tape recorder was on the bed beside her, and her daughter had put in the second side of your tape where you describe heaven. As her life drifted away, she was listening to your account of what heaven is like. The last thing she heard before she left this world to join God in heaven was a description of heaven."

Despite my trying to remain stoic, tears seeped from the corners of my eyes.

"I just thought you'd like to know that."

"Yes," I said. "Thank you for telling me. That's great encouragement for me."

As she retold some of the story to those with me, I thanked God for bringing me back to earth. "Oh, God, I do see some purpose in my staying here. Thank you for allowing me to hear this story."

One time I preached at the Chocolate Bayou Baptist Church, south of Houston. They had asked me to share my death-and-heaven experience.

I was getting my final thoughts together. Typically, in Baptist churches, they have a soloist or some kind of special music just before the guest speaker comes to the pulpit. A woman, who had not been in the service and apparently didn't know what I was going to talk about, came in from a side door to sing.

She had a lovely voice and began to sing a song called "Broken and Spilled Out" about the alabaster jar the woman used when she washed Jesus' feet.

As soon as she sat down, I stood up and began to tell them about my accident. I didn't make any connection between her song and my message, but I noticed that several people kept frowning at the woman.

After the service, I heard someone say to the soloist, "That was an interesting song about being broken and spilled out for you to sing before Don talked." The way he said the word *interesting* really meant *tasteless*.

"Oh!" she said. The shock on her face made me aware that she hadn't known what I was going to speak about. Obviously, she hadn't made the connection either.

Our eyes met and she started to cry. "I'm sorry . . . I'm sorry."

"That's fine," I said. "Really, it's all right." I started to walk on.

"Broken and spilled," someone said. "That's what happened to you, wasn't it?" At least a dozen people made similar comments. A few assumed we had planned for her to sing that particular song.

I stopped and looked back. The soloist stood next to the piano, and she was crying. I excused myself and walked back to her. "That's a beautiful song about a wonderful experience. You didn't know what I was going to talk about, but that's all right, because I can't think of a better song."

She smiled in gratefulness and started to apologize again. "It's fine. Really, it's fine," I assured her.

As I walked away, I thought maybe I had been broken and spilled out. But I smiled at another idea: *I'm also being put back together again.*

FINDING PURPOSE

16

I am convinced of this, so I will continue with you so that you will grow and experience the joy of your faith.

PHILIPPIANS 1:25

B rad Turpin, a motorcycle police officer from the Houston suburb of Pasadena, almost lost a leg. His police motorcycle crashed into the back of a flatbed truck. He would have bled out on the concrete if the EMTs hadn't applied a tourniquet to his leg.

Sonny Steed, the former minister of education at our church, knew Brad personally and asked me to go see him. "Absolutely," I said, especially after I heard that he would be wearing a fixator. I called and made sure he'd let me come. I don't know why, but just before we left, I picked up pictures showing my accident and my recovery.

Sonny drove me to the officer's house. Once we had walked inside, it was almost like seeing the way my living room had looked for months. Brad was lying in a hospital bed with the trapeze bar above him. His device was similar, but not quite the same as mine, because in the dozen years since my accident, technology had improved.

Other people were there, so I sat down and joined in casual conversation. He was nice enough, but I knew he'd seen so many people he was tired of visitors. As soon as the last visitor left, I said, "You really are tired of talking to people aren't you?"

Brad nodded.

"I understand. You almost feel like you're on display here. The phone never stops ringing. Everybody wants to come by to see you."

He nodded again. "I appreciate them coming, but I need some peace and quiet."

"I apologize for interrupting you, but Sonny brought me by to see you because I wanted to talk to you about what to expect. I pointed to the Ilizarov and said, "I had one of these external fixators.""

"Oh, you did?"

I showed him my pictures, beginning with those taken the day after they put on the Ilizarov frame. Each one showed progression to the next step. He stared at each one closely and saw that I had been worse off than he was.

"And you recovered, didn't you?"

"Yes, I did, and so will you."

"That's good that you made it all right, but I don't think I'm going to make it. They can't give me any guarantee that I'm going to keep this leg. The doctors are pessimistic, so that makes it harder for me."

"Well, that's just the way they are," I said, remembering so well my feelings in those early days. "They try to err on the side of being conservative and try not to get your hopes up. Months from now, they know, you could have this fixator and everything could be working fine and then your leg could get infected and you could still lose it."

"That's what I mean. I'm just not sure it's worth all this pain."

"The good news is that the pain will ease up as you get better."

His wife had walked in during the conversation and listened. "I'm just so tired at the lack of progress, and nobody will tell us anything," she said. "We're about ready to change doctors."

"You might find a better doctor," I said, "but wait a bit. Be patient. I'm sure your doctor is doing his best."

Then I told them about the time I reached the end of my patience:

"When my doctor came in to see me I was fuming.

"'Sit down,' I yelled.

"He did, and for maybe five minutes I complained about everything that bothered and upset me. As I watched his face, I realized I had hurt his feelings. I hadn't been thinking about him, of course. I was hurting, never pain free, couldn't sleep, and I wanted answers. 'I get tired of all this not knowing. I ask you how long I have to wear this, and you say, "Maybe another month, maybe two months, maybe three months."' I wasn't through yet, and my anger really burst out with another round of complaints. I ended with, 'Why can't you give me a straight answer?'

"He dropped his head and said softly, 'I'm doing the best I can. I don't know the answers. That's why I can't tell you.'

"'I'm just looking for—'

"'I know you are, but this isn't an exact science. We're re-inventing the wheel. We don't have that much experience in this area, and this is all new technology for us. We're doing the best we can.'"

After I told Brad and his wife about that incident, I added, "Please be patient with your doctor. He can't give you answers he doesn't have. He'll also tell you things to do and load you down with prescriptions. He's going to put you in a lot of therapy, and you're just going to have to learn how to deal with it—with all of it."

"Yeah, I know," he said, "but I just can't control my emotions anymore. I'm a cop. I've seen a lot of hard, bad, difficult stuff. I find myself just breaking down—I mean, real emotional. Know what I mean?"

"Absolutely. Just go ahead and break down. It'll happen again."

"I feel out of control."

"You are out of control!"

Brad stared at me.

"Think about it. What can you control? Nothing."

"I can't even wipe myself."

"That's right. You're totally helpless. There's nothing you can do or control."

"Before this I was a weight lifter and a bodybuilder," he said. "I had a physique you wouldn't believe."

"I have no doubt about that." I could see that he had once been muscular and strong. "But you don't have that now. You may have a great body again someday, but the inability to get up and do the things that you used to do will cause you to change. Be prepared to change. You're going to lose weight; muscles will atrophy. You can't control your body the way you did before."

His wife was obviously feeling all the stress as well, and she was on the verge of tears. "He just feels so bad, even with medication. I just don't know what to do."

"I can suggest a few things. First of all, manage the visits and phone calls. You don't have to let everyone come whenever they want," I said. "Be firm. If you allow everyone to come, you'll wear yourself out trying to be nice. Your friends will understand."

Then I turned to Brad. "Be prepared for all your therapy, because you're going to have to do all kinds of difficult things. Do them if you want to learn to walk again. Be patient, because it will take a long time. Probably one of the best things I can tell you is this: Don't try to act like the Lone Ranger." I paused briefly and almost smiled, because I remembered how I had been. "Let people know where you hurt and how they can help—especially the people you trust. Let them know so they can do things for you. Let them pray for you. You've got a lot of nice folks coming by here, and they want to bring you a cake, cook a meal, or do something for you. Let them express their friendship and love."

After I had talked a few minutes, I got up to leave. I wrote down my phone number. "Call me. If you're struggling to go to sleep at three o'clock in the morning or you're angry, call me. I'll listen. I'll understand because I *can* understand. It's a small fraternity, and none of us joined it by choice."

Before I left, Brad said, "I can't tell you how much I appreciate your coming by. Just visiting with somebody who knows about the pain helps me a lot. You're the first person I've met who understands what it's like to live with pain twenty-four hours a day."

"It's not something I set out to do—visiting people who are where I was," I said, "but I'm willing to do it. I want to help, but you're going to have to make the effort to call me. Remember—don't try to tough it out alone."

Brad's wife followed me out to the car and said, "He needed this. In public he tries to be the source of strength and sound positive. In quiet moments he's frustrated and emotional, and he falls apart. I've been really worried about him. Never in our lives together have I seen him this way."

"I remember my wife working hard all day teaching school and then coming to spend the evening with me," I said. "Just hang in with him. He will get better."

I told her that one time when I was at my worst, Eva had tried to encourage me and had said something like, "Just give it time. You're going to be fine."

I had exploded with frustration and rage—"What makes you think I'm going to be fine? What are the odds of my ever being fine? Nobody can ever tell me that. Nobody can promise me that."

To her credit, Eva hadn't argued. She'd wrapped her arms around me. I had wept. I had never done that before in her presence.

After I told that story to Brad's wife, I said, "Be prepared for changes in your life and his. He can't control his emotions, but don't take it as a personal attack when he yells or screams. It's the pain and the frustration, not you." I shook her hand and said, "And for goodness' sake, call me if you need me. Push Brad to call me."

After that, I saw Brad four or five times. Weeks later when he was able to get out of the house with his walker, I spotted him in a restaurant. I went over to his table and sat down. "How are you doing?" I asked.

"I'm doing okay. Really okay." He thanked me again for coming at one of his lowest moments. He still wasn't in top shape, but he was getting healthy again. When he clasped my hand and held it a long time, I knew it was his way of expressing his appreciation in ways he couldn't put into words.

I felt grateful to God for being able to help Brad in his dark time.

_____ᏩᏊ_____

About two years after my accident, I heard that Chad Vowell had been in a serious car accident. He had been a member of our youth ministry at South Park, and his parents were among the most supportive parents I had at the church. His mother, Carol, was on the committee that came to my hospital room with others to plan youth retreats. I hadn't been very helpful, but it had been their way of making me feel useful and needed.

Chad had been an outstanding soccer player and was with our youth group about a year before he went to college.

When I called his mother, she told me they had helicoptered Chad to John Sealy Hospital in Galveston. I had no idea just how serious he was until she added, "The report is that he has mangled his lower leg and is in a fixator."

When I heard the word *fixator*, I knew I had to see him. I would have gone anyway, because he was a member of South Park. But the word *fixator* gave extra urgency.

When I walked into his room, Chad lay there depressed, and he obviously didn't want to talk. This wasn't the Chad I knew. Before that, he'd always been glad to see me, and his face would light up in recognition. This time he acknowledged my presence but made no effort to engage in conversation.

"Are you okay? Are you going to be all right?" I asked and then looked at his leg. "I see they gave you a fixator."

"Yeah, they did," he said.

"Chad, you remember when I had my accident? That's the same thing they put on me."

"Really?" he asked. For the first time he looked at me with interest. I don't know if he'd never seen me with mine or if he just didn't remember. I leaned closer and said, "Just remember this: I know what it feels like to have one of them."

His injury was on the lower leg. Because there are two bones in the lower leg it's less difficult to heal. As I learned before I left, his prognosis was very good.

I was able to talk to that boy, hold his hand, and pray with him in a way that made him realize I identified with his plight. For the first time, he had a sense of what he had to look forward to in his treatment. Until then, like me after my accident, no one would give Chad any specific information. Like me, he felt angry and depressed.

"The pain will last a long time, and the recovery will seem to last forever, but you'll get better. Just remember that: You will get better."

And he did.

Cancer claimed Joyce Pentecost one week before her thirty-ninth birthday. I loved her very much. She was married to Eva's brother Eddie and left behind two beautiful redheaded kids, Jordan and Colton.

Not only was Joyce one of the liveliest people I've ever met, and a fireball of a singer, but she could also light up a room by merely entering it. She rarely just sang a song; she belted it in the great tradition of Ethel Merman.

I felt honored to speak at her memorial service at First Baptist Church of Forrest City, Arkansas. More than six hundred people packed the auditorium. Because Joyce had recorded several CDs of Christian music, she left a legacy for the rest of us. On that sunny afternoon, we heard Joyce sing her own benediction.

Following her recorded music, her father, Reverend Charles Bradley, delivered a message of hope and salvation. He told the crowd, "Years ago Joyce and I made a covenant. If I went first, she would sing at my funeral. And if she went first, I would speak at hers. Today I am fulfilling that promise to my baby girl."

That moment still stays with me. Melancholy smiles broke out, tears flowed, but I don't think anyone felt anger or hopelessness.

After Joyce's father concluded his message, it was my turn to speak.

"Some may ask today, 'How could Joyce die?'" I said. "But I would say to you the better question is, how did she live? She lived well, beloved. She lived very well."

I told the hurting throng that Joyce was a redheaded comet streaking across the stage of life, that she lived and loved to make people happy, that she was a devoted friend, an ideal daughter, a doting aunt, a sweet sister, a loving mother, and a wonderful wife. I admitted freely that I didn't have the answer to the question that must have penetrated many hearts in the room: Why?

"There is comfort when there are no answers," I said. "Joyce firmly believed that if she died, she would instantly be with God. She believed that if she lived, God would be with her. That was her reason for living. That can be our reason for carrying on."

I concluded by sharing one personal moment. The last extended conversation I had with Joyce before she returned home from the hospital was about heaven. She never tired of hearing me describe my trip to heaven, so we "visited" there one final time. We talked of the angels, the gate, and our loved ones. (Joyce's own mother had died of cancer.) Joyce always wanted me to describe the music, and our final conversation together was no different.

"Just a few days ago," I said to the congregation, "I believe God was sitting behind those gates, and he told the angels, 'What we need around here is a good redheaded soprano.'

"'That would be Joyce Pentecost!' the angels said.

"God sent for Joyce, and she answered the call. She is singing now with the angelic hosts. Joyce Pentecost is absent from the body but present with the Lord."

My final words at the service were a question: "Can you lose someone if you know where she is?"

I was thirty-eight years old when I was killed in that car wreck. Joyce was the same age when she was diagnosed with cancer. I survived the ordeal; Joyce did not. But I know this: Because I was able to experience heaven, I was able to prepare her and her loved ones for it. And now I am preparing you.

—✂—

Many times since my accident I have wished someone who had already gone through the ordeal of wearing a fixator for months had visited me in the hospital. I know it would have relieved a lot of my anxiety.

Whenever I hear about people having a fixator, I try to contact them. When I talk to those facing long-term illness, I try to be totally honest. There is no easy way through that recovery process, and they need to know that. Because I have been there, I can tell them (and they listen) that although it will take a long time, eventually they will get better. I also talk to them about some of the short-term problems they'll face.

572

My visits with Chad and Brad and others also remind me that God still has a purpose for me on earth. During that long recovery period, I sometimes longed for heaven. Looking back, however, I can see how the personal experiences I have shared with others provided a gentle pull earthward when I was in heaven. "When God is ready to take me," I was finally able to say, "he'll release me." In the meantime, I try to offer as much comfort as possible to others.

Like me, when other victims first see the fixator attached to their leg, and especially when they begin to experience the pain and their inability to move, depression flows through them. They have no idea what's going to happen next. Even though doctors try to reassure them of recovery, they hurt too much to receive comfort from the doctors' words.

Sometimes, however, the patients may be inadvertently misled into saying to me, "I'll get over this soon."

"You may get over it, but it won't be soon," I say. "This is a long-term commitment, and there's no way to speed up the process. When you face injuries of this magnitude, there is no easy way out. You have to live with it for now."

—⟨⟩⟨⟩—

I could share other stories, but these are the experiences that kept me going through some of my own dark periods. I found purpose again in being alive. I still long to return to heaven, but for now, this is where I belong. I am serving my purpose here on earth.

17
LONGING
FOR HOME

You do this because you are looking forward to the joys of heaven—as you have been ever since you first heard the truth of the Good News.

COLOSSIANS 1:5

One of my favorite stories is about a little girl who left her house and her mother didn't know where she had gone. Once the mother missed her, she worried that something might have happened to her child. She stood on the front porch and yelled her daughter's name several times.

Almost immediately the little girl ran from the house next door. The mother hugged her, said she was worried, and finally asked, "Where have you been?"

"I went next door to be with Mr. Smith."

"Why were you over there?"

"His wife died and he is very sad."

"Oh, I'm so sorry, I didn't know that," the mother said. "What did you do?"

"I just helped him cry."

In a way, that's what I do. Sharing my experiences is my way of crying with others in pain.

I've discovered one reason I can bring comfort to people who are facing death themselves or have suffered the loss of a loved one: I've been there. I can give them every assurance that heaven is a place of unparalleled and indescribable joy.

Without the slightest doubt, I know heaven *is* real. It's more real than anything I've ever experienced in my life. I sometimes say, "Think of the worst thing that's ever happened to you, the best thing that's ever happened to you, and everything in between; heaven is more real than any of those things."

Since my return to earth, I've been acutely aware that all of us are on a pilgrimage. At the end of this life, wherever we go—heaven or hell—life will be more real than this one we're now living.

I never thought of that before my accident, of course. Heaven was a concept, something I believed in, but I didn't think about it often.

In the years since my accident, I've repeatedly thought of the last night Jesus was with his disciples before his betrayal and crucifixion. Only hours before he began that journey to heaven, he sat with his disciples in the upper room. He begged them not to be troubled and to trust in him. Then he told them he was going away and added, "In my Father's house are many rooms; if it were not so, I would have told you. I am going there to prepare a place for you. And if I go and prepare a place for you,

I will come back and take you to be with me that you also may be where I am" (John 14:2–3 NIV '84).

I had never really noticed it before, but twice Jesus used the word *place*—a location. Perhaps that may not stir most people, but I think about it often. It is a literal place, and I can testify that I know that place. I've been there. I know heaven is real.

Since my accident, I've felt more intensely and deeply than ever before. A year in a hospital bed can do that for anyone, but it was more than just that. Those ninety minutes in heaven left such an impression on me that I can never be the same person I was. I can never again be totally content here, because I live in anticipation.

I experienced more pain than I thought a human could endure and still live to tell about it. In spite of all that happened to me during those months of unrelenting pain, I still feel the reality of heaven far, far more than the suffering I endured.

Because I am such a driven person and hardly ever slow down, I have often felt I needed to explain why I can't do certain things. When I'm fully dressed, most folks would never realize I have such debilitating injuries. However, when I face an activity that this reconstructed body just can't do (and people are sometimes surprised how simple some of those acts are), I often get strange responses.

"You look healthy," more than one person has said. "What's the matter with you?"

Occasionally, when I follow someone down a flight of stairs—a difficult experience for me—they hear my knees grinding and turn around. "Is that awful noise coming from you?" they ask.

"Yes." I smile and add, "Isn't it ridiculous!"

My relative mobility is quite deceptive. I get around better than anyone imagined I would. But I know—even if it doesn't show—that I'm quite limited in what I can do. I work hard to walk properly, because I don't want to attract attention to myself. I had enough stares and gawks when I wore my fixator.

Trying to act and look normal and to keep pushing myself is my way of dealing with my infirmities. I've learned that if I stay busy, especially by helping others, I don't think about my pain. In an odd way, my pain is its own therapy. I intend to go on until I can't go anymore.

We're such victims of our human invention of time that we have to think in temporal concepts—it's the way we're wired. That's an important point for me to make. My human inclination is to wonder what my welcoming committee is doing during these years while I'm back on earth.

As I ponder this, I don't believe my greeting committee said, "Oh no, he doesn't get to stay." They're still there at the gate. They're waiting. For them, time is not passing. Everything is in the eternal now—even if I can't put that into words. Even if ten more years pass, or thirty, in heaven it will be only an instant before I'm back there again.

Going to heaven that January morning wasn't my choice. The only choice in all of this is that one day I turned to Jesus Christ and accepted him as my Savior. Unworthy as I am, he allowed me to go to heaven, and I know the next time I go there, I'll stay.

I don't have a death wish. I'm not suicidal, but every day I think about going back. I long to return. In God's timing, I know with utter certainty that I will. Now I look forward to that time and eagerly await the moment. I have absolutely no fear of death. Why would I? There's nothing to fear—only joy to experience.

As I've pointed out before, when I became conscious again on earth, a bitter disappointment raged through me. I didn't want to return, but it wasn't my choice.

For a long time, I didn't accept that God had sent me back. But even in my disappointment, I knew that God had a purpose in everything that happened. There was a reason I went to heaven and a purpose in my returning. Eventually, I grasped that God had given me a special experience and a glimpse of what eternity will be.

Although I long for my heavenly home, I'm prepared to wait until the final summons comes for me.

—❦❦—

Going through thirty-four surgeries and many years of pain has also helped me realize the truth of Paul's words to the Corinthians: "Praise be to the God and Father of our Lord Jesus Christ, the Father of compassion and the God of all comfort, who comforts us in all our troubles, so that we can comfort those in any trouble with the comfort we ourselves have received from God" (2 Cor. 1:3–4 NIV '84).

As long as I'm here on earth, God still has a purpose for me. Knowing that fact enables me to endure the pain and cope with my physical disabilities.

In my darkest moments, I remember a line from an old song: "It will be worth it all when we see Jesus."

I know it will.

18
THE *WHY* QUESTIONS

Now we see things imperfectly as in a poor mirror, but then we will see everything with perfect clarity. All that I know now is partial and incomplete, but then I will know everything completely, just as God knows me now.

1 CORINTHIANS 13:12

M any times I've watched people on TV who say they've had near-death experiences (NDE). I confess to being fascinated, but I also admit to being skeptical. In fact, I'm highly skeptical. Before and after those people spoke, I thought, *They've probably had some kind of brain lapse. Or maybe there was already something in their memory bank and they just re-experienced it.* I didn't doubt their sincerity; they wanted to believe what they talked about.

I've watched many talk shows and read about victims who had died and been heroically resuscitated. Descriptions of their ordeals often seemed too rehearsed and disturbingly similar, as if one person copied the story of the last. One person who claimed to have been dead for more than twenty-four hours wrote a book and said he had talked to Adam and Eve. Some of the things the first earthly couple purportedly told him don't measure up with the Bible.

Despite my skepticism—even today—of many of their testimonies, I have never questioned my own death. In fact, it was so powerful, so life-changing, that I couldn't talk about it to anyone until David Gentiles pried out the information almost two years after the accident.

I have looked at the research on NDE and thought about it often during the years.

In December 2001, *Lancet,* the journal of the British Medical Society, reported research on NDE. Most scientific and medical experts had previously dismissed these dramatic occurrences as wishful thinking or the misguided musings of oxygen-starved brains.

The study, conducted in the Netherlands, is one of the first scientific studies. Instead of interviewing those who reported they had once had a NDE, they followed hundreds of patients who had been resuscitated after suffering clinical death—that is, after their hearts stopped. They hoped that approach would provide more accurate accounts by documenting the experiences as they happened, rather than basing them on recollections long after the event of resuscitation.

Their results: About 18 percent of the patients in the study spoke of recollection of the time in which they had been clinically dead. Between 8 and 12 percent reported the commonly accepted NDE experiences, such as seeing bright lights, going through a tunnel, or even crossing over into heaven and speaking with dead relatives and friends. The researchers concluded that afterlife experiences or NDE are merely "something we would all desperately like to believe is true."[1]

Conversely, other scholars made conclusions based on their study of 344 people (ages twenty-six to ninety-two) who had been resuscitated. Most of them were interviewed within five days of the experience. The researchers contacted those same people two years later and then eight years after the event.

Researchers discovered that the experiences didn't correlate with any of the measured psychological, physiological, or medical parameters—that is, the experiences were unrelated to processes in the dying brain. Most patients had excellent recall of the events, which, the researchers said, undermined the idea that the memories were false.

The most important thing to me is that those who had such experiences reported marked changes in their personalities. They lost their fear of death. They became more compassionate, giving, and loving.

The study really proved nothing about the reality of NDE. As had been the case before the studies, one group believed NDE were merely the psychological states of those dying; the other group maintained that hard evidence supported the validity of near-death occurrences, suggesting that scientists rethink theories that dismiss out-of-body experiences.

I have no intention of trying to solve this debate. I can only relate what happened to me. No matter what researchers may or may not try to tell me, I *know* I went to heaven.

I've devoted an immense amount of time to considering *why* it happened rather than *what* happened. I have reached only one solid conclusion: Before being killed in a car accident, I remained skeptical of near-death experiences. I simply didn't see how a person could die, go to heaven, and return to tell about it. I never doubted dying, the reality of heaven, or life after death. I doubted descriptions of near-death stories. These stories all seemed too rehearsed and sounded alike. Then I died, went to heaven, and returned. I can only tell what happened to me. Not for an instant have I ever thought it was merely a vision, some case of mental wires crossing, or the result of stories I'd heard. I *know* heaven is real. I have been there and come back.

It comes down to this: Until some mere mortal is dead for a lengthy period and subsequently returns to life with irrefutable evidence of an afterlife, near-death experiences will continue to be a matter of faith, or at the very least, conjecture. But then, as one of my friends would say, "What else is new?"

One time I shared my experiences with a large congregation that included my wife's parents, Eldon and Ethel Pentecost. They've been consistently supportive and made great sacrifices during my accident and lengthy recovery.

After the service, we went to their home. At one point, Eldon and I were alone, and he told me, "I was angry the first time you shared your story of your trip to heaven."

I had no idea he felt that way.

"You finished by saying you never wanted to come back to earth."

I just nodded in affirmation, not knowing where this was going.

"I didn't understand it then, but I've changed. Now when I hear you talk about heaven's beauty, I understand a little better why you'd willingly be separated from my daughter and grandkids for a while. You know—you really do know, don't you—that they'll join you someday?"

"Without a doubt," I said.

Eldon's revelation caught me off guard. He was right, of course. I had the distinct privilege of baptizing my own children and seeing my wife baptized as well. I knew that their professions of faith were authentic. By faith, I knew that they would be residents of heaven someday. Being separated from them had never crossed my mind while I was in heaven. People in heaven simply don't have an awareness of who is *not* there. They do know who is coming.

Even today, I can say honestly that I wish I could have stayed in heaven, but my ultimate time had not yet come. After leaving heaven, if I had known that I would face two weeks in ICU, a year in a hospital bed, and thirty-four operations, I surely would have been even more disheartened from the outset. However, this was not my choice, and I returned to the sounds of one voice praying, boots crunching glass underfoot, and the Jaws of Life ripping through my shattered auto.

One question keeps troubling me: *Why?* It takes many forms.

Why did I die in that car wreck?

Why did I have the unique privilege of going to heaven?

Why did I glimpse heaven, only to be sent back?

Why did I nearly die in the hospital?

Why has God let me live in constant pain since January 18, 1989?

The short answer: I don't know. And yet that single word, *why*, remains the consummate human query. By nature, we're curious. We want to know.

All these years later, it's still not easy for me to relate what happened. Several times I tried to write this myself but couldn't. That's why I asked my friend Cec Murphey to help me with this book—if it were up to me, this book would never have been written. The emotional trauma of reliving all the events is too difficult. Only with someone else actually writing it has it finally been possible to go through this ordeal.

I still don't know why such things happen.

I do know God is with me in the darkest moments of life.

Besides asking why, there are other questions. I think they're even more important for me to ponder.

Did God want me to know how real pain could feel so that I could understand the pain of others?

Did God want me to know how real heaven is?

What did God want me to learn from all my experiences, my death, and the long period of recovery?

How can my experiences be of the most benefit to others?

After all these years, I don't have the answers to most of those questions either. I have learned a few things and realize that God still has reasons for keeping me alive on earth. I may never know his reasons, and God has no obligation to explain them to me.

Even though I don't have full answers to many of my questions, I do have peace. I know I am where God wants me to be. I know I'm doing the work God has given me.

I find comfort in a story recorded in John's Gospel. A man born blind meets Jesus and is healed. After that, he runs around praising God, but his healing is an embarrassment to the religious leaders who have been trying to turn the people against Jesus.

They interrogate the formerly blind man, trying to force him to admit that Jesus is a sinner (that is, a fraud).

The man wisely says, "Whether he is a sinner or not, I don't know. One thing I do know. I was blind but now I see!" (John 9:25 NIV '84). In the same way, some may not believe my account; they may think it was some kind of wish fulfillment during a point of severe trauma. I don't have to defend my experience.

I know what happened to me. For those of us whose faith is in the reality of heaven, no amount of evidence is necessary. *I know what I experienced.*

I believe God gave me a hint of what eternity in heaven will be like.

I also believe that part of the reason I am still alive, as I've already pointed out, is that people prayed. Dick Onerecker prayed me back to life—to live without brain damage. David Gentiles and others prayed so that God wouldn't take me back to heaven just yet.

I am here, I am alive, and it's because God's purposes have not yet been fulfilled in my life. When God is finished with me, I'll return to the place I yearn to be. I have made my final reservations for heaven and I'm going back someday—permanently.

Prayerfully, I'll see you there too.

NOTES

Chapter 4

1. Commonly called "Jaws of Life," this is a brand of tools trademarked by the Hurst Jaws of Life Company. The term refers to several types of piston-rod hydraulic tools known as cutters, spreaders, and rams that are used to pry trapped victims from crashed vehicles.

2. "What a Friend We Have in Jesus," words by Joseph Scriven, 1855.

Chapter 18

1. Pim van Lommel, Ruud van Wees, Vincent Meyers, Ingrid Elffench, "Near-death Experience in Survivors of Cardiac Arrest: A Prospective Study in the Netherlands," *Lancet* 358, no. 9298 (December 15, 2001): 2039–45.

Don Piper has been an ordained minister since 1985 and has served in several capacities on church staffs, including six years as a senior pastor. He and his wife, Eva, are residents of Pasadena, Texas, and are the parents of three grown children. Don has appeared on numerous Christian and secular television and radio programs and has been the subject of countless newspaper and magazine features. He writes a weekly newspaper column, and every week you will find him preaching and leading conferences and retreats all over the United States and abroad. Don can be contacted at donpiperministries@yahoo.com.

Cecil Murphey has written or coauthored more than one hundred books, including his work on the autobiography of Franklin Graham, *Rebel with a Cause*. Cecil can be contacted at www. cecilmurphey.com.

TRUE STORIES OF HOPE AND PEACE
AT THE END OF LIFE'S JOURNEY

Through the eyes of a child, we see glimpses of heaven

"These stories will rock your world. I know I will never be the same again after reading *Touching Heaven*."

—LEONARD SWEET, bestselling author, professor at Drew University and George Fox University, and chief contributor to Sermons.com

"Rewarding, comforting, and reassuring."

—Christian Review

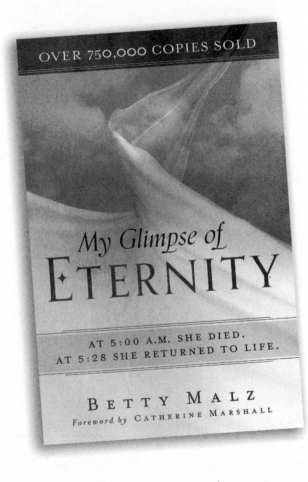